G000166966

1 MONTH OF
FREE
READING

at

www.ForgottenBooks.com

By purchasing this book you are eligible for one month membership to ForgottenBooks.com, giving you unlimited access to our entire collection of over 1,000,000 titles via our web site and mobile apps.

To claim your free month visit:
www.forgottenbooks.com/free170162

* Offer is valid for 45 days from date of purchase. Terms and conditions apply.

ISBN 978-0-266-17611-4
PIBN 10170162

This book is a reproduction of an important historical work. Forgotten Books uses
state-of-the-art technology to digitally reconstruct the work, preserving the original format
whilst repairing imperfections present in the aged copy. In rare cases, an imperfection in
the original, such as a blemish or missing page, may be replicated in our edition. We do,
however, repair the vast majority of imperfections successfully; any imperfections that
remain are intentionally left to preserve the state of such historical works.

Forgotten Books is a registered trademark of FB &c Ltd.
Copyright © 2018 FB &c Ltd.
FB &c Ltd, Dalton House, 60 Windsor Avenue, London, SW19 2RR.
Company number 08720141. Registered in England and Wales.

For support please visit www.forgottenbooks.com

SEVENTEEN
DISCOURSES

ON SEVERAL

TEXTS OF SCRIPTURE;

ADDRESSED TO

CHRISTIAN ASSEMBLIES,

IN VILLAGES

NEAR CAMBRIDGE.

TO WHICH ARE ADDED

SIX MORNING EXERCISES.

———

BY ROBERT ROBINSON.

———

ALL NATIONS OF ·MEN....SHOULD SEEK THE LORD, IF HAPLY THEY
MIGHT FEEL AFTER HIM, AND FIND HIM.   Acts, xvii. 26, 27.

═══

FIRST AMERICAN EDITION.

WITH A

LIFE OF THE AUTHOR.

═══

NEW Y
PUBL
LIBRA

BOSTON:
PUBLISHED BY CUMMINGS, HILLIARD, & CO.
HILLIARD AND METCALF, PRINTERS.
1824.

THE NEW YORK
PUBLIC LIBRARY
828542
ASTOR, LENOX AND
TILDEN FOUNDATIONS
R   1919   L

LIFE

OF

ROBERT ROBINSON.

———

Robert Robinson was born at Swaffham, county of Norfolk, on the eighth of October, 1735. His father was a native of Scotland, and an exciseman, of whom little needs be said, except that his humble sphere in life received no dignity from his understanding, and no brightness from his virtues. Mary Wilkin, the mother of Robert Robertson, was descended from a respectable family, and to the advantages of a good education she added the charms of a beautiful person, an amiable temper, and gentleness of manners. She was the daughter of a second marriage, and, as unnatural as it may seem, the affections of her father were centered in the children of his wife by a former husband. Mary was doomed to experience from him less of the tenderness of a parent, than of the austerity and unfeelingness of a severe master. He delighted to thwart her purposes ; and on several occasions, through mere caprice, he rejected the overtures of worthy and respectable persons, who solicited his daughter's hand.

Disheartened by the severity of her father's treatment, and impatient to escape from it, she imprudently resolved on marrying without his consent. This step was a prelude to untried evils. She united herself to a man in all respects unworthy of her, possessing neither the qualifications for making her happy, nor the disposition to soften and conciliate her father.

They had three children, of whom Robert was the youngest. The elder son was apprenticed to a painter, and the daughter to a mantuamaker. Robert was put to school when six years old, and soon drew the attention of his teacher, as exhibiting more than usual promise. In the mean time, his father removed from Swaffham, and settled at Scaring. He soon after died, and left the destitute mother to provide for herself, and three children. At Scaring was a grammar school, where Lord Thurlow, and some other distinguished persons, received the rudiments of their education. Desirous of encouraging her son's predilection for learning, Mrs. Robinson made an effort to maintain him at this school, but her resources proved inadequate to the expense. So favourable an impression had he made, however, on his teacher, the Rev. Joseph Brett, and so much did this gentleman respect the motives and virtues of the mother, that he kindly offered to instruct his pupil without compensation.

On these terms he continued at school till he was fourteen years old, studied the French and Latin, and made rapid proficiency in most of the branches commonly pursued at such institutions. The time had now come when it was necessary to decide on his future destination. So many discouragements were in the way of his being a scholar, and so many difficulties to be encountered, that his mother resigned this hope, which she had suffered to rise and brighten for a time, and was only concerned to place him beyond the reach of want by providing for him an honest calling. His benevolent instructer, Mr. Brett, made interest to procure a situation suited to his capacity and inclination, but without success. He was finally bound an apprentice to a hairdresser in London.

To this new employment he at first devoted himself with commendable industry, received the approbation of his master, and was able to boast of a due proficiency in the mysteries of his trade. But his thoughts were not to be chained, nor could nature be forced. His mind was too active to rest in vacuity, and his love of books too strong to be conquered by the routine of a barber's shop. It was his custom to rise at four in the morning, and from that hour till called to his master's service, he was busy in reading such books as he could collect from the cheap stalls or borrow from his friends.

His thoughts early took a religious bias, and after going to London a constant attendance on public worship was among his greatest pleasures. Gill, Guise, Romaine, and Whitefield were his favourite preachers. His diary at this time indicates no small degree of religious enthusiasm, and proves him to have gradually attached himself to the Methodists. Whitefield, in short, was his adviser and friend, to whom he applied in all cases of spiritual difficulty, and with whom he familiarly corresponded. On one occasion Whitefield read to his congregation at the Tabernacle two of Robinson's letters, while the writer was present. Encouraged by the favourable opinion of so distinguished a man, and moved by the advice of his friends, it is not a matter of surprise that he should begin to think himself destined to walk in a broader sphere, than the one on which he had entered.

So great, indeed, were the esteem and respect which he gained by his genius and good character, that his master was not reluctant to comply with the general voice, and give up his indentures. At the age of nineteen he commenced preaching among the Methodists. His youth, his amiable manners, his vivacity and native eloquence drew around him many hearers, and gave a charm to his preaching, which could not fail to please. His voice was clear and melodious, his elocution easy and distinct, his language flowing, and all his external accomplishments engaging. These advantages, heightened by a liberal degree of youthful enthusiasm, crowned his first efforts with success, and animated his future exertions. He spared no pains to cultivate the powers which nature had bestowed on him, and frequently declaimed by the hour in private, that he might acquire the habit of a ready delivery, and a free use of language. In this practice the foundation was laid of his subsequent eminence as a public speaker. He thought no time misspent, which prepared him for winning the

a*

ear and gaining the hearts of his audience, and thus more effectually discharging the duties of his sacred office.

Among the Methodists Mr. Robinson preached chiefly in Norwich, and different parts of Norfolk and Cambridgeshire. While thus employed he resisted a temptation, which deserves to be recorded as a proof of his early integrity and strength of principle. He had been educated in the established church, and had not joined himself to the dissenters without examining the causes and nature of their dissent. When his talents and virtues had gained him a name in the world, some of his relations, who seem to have forgotten him before, made an attempt to bring him back to the episcopal church. The following incident is mentioned by Dr. Rees, the learned editor of the Cyclopædia, in his Sermon preached on the occasion of Mr. Robinson's death. "A rich relation, who had promised to provide liberally for him, and who had bequeathed him a considerable sum in his will, threatened to deprive him of every advantage which he had been encouraged to expect, unless he quitted his connexion with the dissenters; but the rights of conscience, and the approbation of God, were superior, in his regard, to every worldly consideration; he preserved his integrity, steadily maintained his principles, and persevered in his connexion with the dissenters, but forfeited the favour of his relation, and every advantage, which, living or dying, he had in his power to bestow."* This conduct was consistent with his character through life. A high-minded independence, conscientious regard for truth and liberty, and unyielding adherence to his religious impressions, were among the shining virtues, which never forsook him.

The causes leading to his separation from the methodists are not distinctly known, but he had not preached with them more than two years, when, at the head of a few persons associated for the purpose, he formed an independent society in Norwich. At this time he was a Calvinist, and constructed the confession of faith

* Dr. Rees's Sermon on the Death of Mr. Robert Robinson, p. 59.

for his new society on Calvinistic principles. He adopted the rules and discipline common to other independent churches, and administered the ordinances after the same manner.

In the year 1759, not long after this society was organized, Mr. Robinson was invited to take charge of a Baptist congregation at Cambridge. He was already convinced, that adults only were the proper subjects of baptism, and he had himself been baptized by immersion. The Cambridge society was small, and the pecuniary circumstances of its members such, as to afford him no more than a very scanty support. When he commenced preaching in Cambridge he was twenty-three years of age, and two years afterwards he was ordained according to the usual mode of the dissenters. He had been married a little before to a young lady of Norwich.

Mr. Robinson's own account of his settlement, written at a later period of his life, will show his prospects to have been not the most flattering. In reference to this subject he observes; "The settlement of Robinson seems rather a romantic, than rational undertaking, for this pastor was to be maintained. He had not received above ten guineas from his own family for some years; he had no future prospect of receiving any; his grandfather had cut him off with a legacy of half a guinea. He had received only a hundred pounds with his wife, and this he had diminished among the Methodists. He had never inquired what his congregation would allow him, nor had any body proposed any thing. They had paid him for the first half-year, three pounds twelve shillings and five pence; they had increased since, but not enough to maintain him frugally; there was no prospect of so poor a people supplying him long, especially should his family increase, which it was likely to do. Besides, the congregation, through the libertinism of many of its former members, had acquired a bad character. These would have been insurmountable difficulties to an older and wiser man; but he was a boy, and the love of his flock was a million to him. His settlement, therefore, on this article, should be no precedent for future settlements."

The situation here described could have few charms for a man who had set his heart on the things of this world, or whose fancy was quickened by the kindling visions of power and fame. But Robinson was not such a man. He loved his profession, and every motive of self-aggrandizement was absorbed in the deeper and purer desire of witnessing the growth of piety, good order, and happiness among his people. His congregation grew larger, and the time came when his annual income was increased to more than ninety pounds. At first he lived at Fulbourn, five miles from the place of his sabbath duties, where he contracted an acquaintance with Mr. Graves, a gentleman of property and benevolence, from whom he received many substantial tokens of friendship.

He next removed to Hauxton, about the same distance from Cambridge, where he resided for several years, the tenant of an humble cottage, devoted assiduously to his professional labours, and providing for the support of a numerous family, and an aged mother. His disinterested ardour, his kindness to the poor, his love of doing good, and his unwearied activity in making himself useful, attracted to him the notice of all the respectable part of the community, and quickened the generosity of some worthy and opulent persons. On the sabbath he often preached three times, and during the week several times in the neighbouring villages. He was intimate with all the surrounding clergy among the dissenters, and had for his early companions Roland Hill and Charles de Coetlogon. His congregation increased so much, that a more commodious place of worship was found necessary, and the pastor was highly gratified with the promptness and unanimity with which it was erected.

In the midst of his professional labours he was a diligent student in theology and literature. Free access to the libraries of the University of Cambridge, and conversation with the learned men residing there, enabled him to pursue his studies with advantage. He was an admirer of Saurin, and in 1770 translated and published two of his sermons. These were sent out as specimens,

which, if approved, he promised should be the forerun-
ners of others. The success of his project was quite
equal to his expectation, and he afterwards translated
at different times five volumes of sermons selected from
Saurin. These have gone through several editions, and
together with a sixth volume by Hunter, and a seventh
by Sutcliffe, they constitute the works of Saurin, as they
now appear in the English dress.

While residing in the cottage at Hauxton he also published his *Arcana, or the Principles of the late Petitioners to Parliament for Relief in Matter of Subscription,
in eight Letters to a Friend.* These letters were adapted to the times, and attracted a lively attention. The
dissenters were making all possible exertions to have
the law repealed, which required from them subscription to the articles. Presbyterians and Baptists, ortho-
dox and heterodox, united their forces to abolish a law,
which operated with equal severity on them all, and
which was in itself so flagrant an encroachment on justice, liberty, the rights of conscience, and the claims of
humanity. All rallied under the same banner, and cried out with one voice against the oppression which
weighed them down, till, after many unsuccessful strug-
gles, their voice was heard, their petitions heeded, and
dissenting ministers and schoolmasters were allowed the
privilege of prosecuting their peaceful avocations with
out violating their conscience by subscribing the Thir-
ty-nine Articles, or subjecting themselves to a civil pen-
alty by resisting so unholy a requisition. During this
struggle for Christian freedom the above letters were
written. Clothed in a language always sprightly, sometimes adorned with glowing imagery, sometimes rising
with the majesty of argument, and at others pungent
with satire, they were well calculated for popular effect. They enter largely into the chief points of the
controversy, and bating some defects of style, and perhaps occasional faults of sentiment, it will be rare to
find a more ingenious vindication of the rights and privileges of Christian liberty.

Robinson left Hauxton in 1773, and settled at Ches-
terton within two miles of Cambridge. This brought

him nearer to the centre of his parochial charge, and
the facilities for his literary pursuits were multiplied
by his proximity to the University.   But his income was
not yet adequate to support a family of nine children,
and he was compelled to look around him for other
sources of emolument.   He turned his attention to ag-
riculture. By rigid economy, personal inspection of
his affairs, judicious investments, and a spirit of enterprise that never slumbered, he found himself in a few
years a thriving farmer, and had the joy to feel, that by
the blessing of Providence his numerous family was beyond the grasp of want, and the caprice of fortune.   Mr.
Dyer thus speaks of his character as a farmer and econ-
omist. "It would be no less agreeable than instructive
to survey his rural economy, and domestic arrangements
in his new situation ; the versatility of his genius was
uncommon ; and whether he was making a bargain, repairing a house, stocking a farm, giving directions to
workmen, or assisting their labours, he was the same
invariable man, displaying no less vigour in the execution of his plans, than ingenuity in their contrivance.
The readiness with which he passed from literary pursuits to rural occupations, from rural occupations to domestic engagements, from domestic engagements to the
forming of plans for dissenting ministers, to the settling
of churches, to the solving of cases of conscience, to
the removing of the difficulties of ignorant, or softening
the asperities of quarrelsome brethren, was surprising."*
This is the language of one who lived near him, for
many years, and saw him often.
   His professional duties were numerous.   Those per-
taining to his own parish made but a part.   He was invited to attend ordinations in all the counties around
him ; his judgment was respected and his advice sought
in cases of differences between churches ; he was the
counsellor of his parishioners in their temporal as well
as spiritual concerns ; the watchful guardian of the un-
protected and distressed ; the patron and benevolent
friend of the poor.   These calls of duty did not relax
his literary ardour.   He went on with his translations
of Saurin, printed now and then an occasional sermon

* Dyer's Life of Robinson, p. 98.

of his own, and, at the request of two or three eminent gentlemen, wrote a treatise on Affinities in Marriage, which was highly commended by jurists, as marked by an acute discrimination and force of argument.

About the year 1776, Robinson published his *Plea for the Divinity of Christ.* This topic was now much agitated by reason of the late resignation of Lindsey and Jebb for scruples of conscience concerning the trinity. Robinson's Plea is drawn up with ingenuity, in a popular style, and winning manner. But even this popular treatise did not please all parties. None withheld from the author the merit of ingenuity; some professed to admire the force and accuracy of his reasoning; while others were troubled with a kind of indefinable suspicion, that he had stopped short of the desired object. These latter seem to have been alarmed, that the author was so sparing of the fire and the rage of controversy. Robinson observes, in writing to a friend, "The temper of the Plea has procured me a deal of blame from the good folks, who inhabit the torrid zone." These zealous partizans were not satisfied, that he should win the day, unless he carried war with flames and sword into the conquered enemy's camp.

Others, however, were of a different mind, and the author received a profusion of complementary letters from dignitaries in the established church. It was whispered, and more than once proclaimed aloud, as a thing to be lamented, that such a man should be a dissenter, and waste his days in strolling with a bewildered flock beyond the enclosures of the true faith. Gilded offers were made to him, if he would have the conscience to slide out of his errors, go up from the unseemly vale of poverty, and take his rest on the commanding eminence of church preferment. To these overtures he was deaf; from his principles he could not be moved. When Dr. Ogden said to him, in trying to unsettle his purpose, "Do the dissenters know the worth of the man?" he replied, "The man knows the worth of the dissenters." This reply he verified by his warm devotedness to their interests through life. He received many letters approving his work from persons not belonging to the episcopal church, especially his Baptist associates in the ministry.

The year after the Plea, Robinson published a curious tract, entitled the *The History and Mystery of Good Friday.* In this pamphlet he traces back the church holydays to their origin, and proves them for the most part to have arisen out of heathen, or Jewish practices, and to derive no authority from the Christian religion. It contains a severe, and somewhat rough philippic against the church of England, which boasts of being reformed, and having cast off the abuses of the Romish church, while yet many are cherished, as unwarrantable and pernicious as those severed from the old stock. This tract was exceedingly popular, and ran speedily through several editions.

But the work, which produced greater excitement than any of our author's writings, was a *Plan of Lectures on the Principles of Nonconformity,* published in 1778. Within a moderate compass, it embraces all the points of controversy between the established church and the dissenters. Its manner is original and striking. The time of its appearance was favourable to its currency and interest, for the dissenters' bill was then pending in parliament. In the House of Lords this Plan of Lectures was honourably mentioned by Lord Shelburne, and in the House of Commons, Burke read passages from it, which he attempted to turn to the advantage of the petitioners. Fox repelled his attack, and foiled his attempt. Many articles were written against it, and, among others, strictures by Mr. Burgess, prebendary of Winchester. Robinson replied to none, except the latter, on which he bestowed a few remarks in his preface to the fifth edition.

The next literary enterprise of Robinson was his translation of *Claude's Essay on the Composition of a Sermon.* To this essay the translator added a life of the author, remarks on the history of preaching, and a vast body of notes, making together two thick volumes. The notes are written in the author's peculiar manner, full of spirit and vivacity, and discover a prodigious extent of reading. Some of them are valuable, and many are highly entertaining, but they seem to have been hastily thrown together, and collected with too little discrimination. They occasionally descend to trifling incidents, anecdotes, and inapposite reflections, equally offensive to good taste, and barren of instruction. But with all these defects, Robinson's original edition is vastly preferable to those coming after, in which the editors took the liberty to abridge the notes, and add others of their own. In the Rev. Charles Simeon's edition, the notes are chiefly omitted, and their place supplied by skeletons of his own sermons.

Mr. Robinson's celebrated volume of *Village Discourses* was published in 1786. We have already observed, that it was his custom to preach in the neighbouring villages, and frequently he tarried at a place over night, and held religious service early in the morning, before the labourers were gone to their work. In summer these exercises were conducted in the open air, and fully attended. The abovementioned volume is composed of discourses delivered on these occasions, and written out afterwards as dictated by the author to an amanuensis. They had evidently been prepared with care in his own mind, and they contain a copiousness of language, a felicity of illustration, and a readiness in quoting and applying appropriate passages of Scripture, rarely to be witnessed. They were framed for a particular purpose, that of enlightening and improving the less informed classes of society ; and whoever reads them will not wonder, that this purpose was attained, and that even those for whom the things of the world had attractions should resign for an hour the labour of gain, and listen with delight to the persuasive accents of the preacher. They may be read with profit by all, who love to contemplate the workings of a powerful mind in recommending and enforcing the principles of a holy religion, who are captivated with the inventions of genius, the current of a natural eloquence, sound words uttered in the spirit of Christian philanthropy, and sentiments breathing the influence of a rational, fervent piety.

The last works in which our author was engaged were the *History of Baptism*, and his *Ecclesiastical Re-*

searches. These were also his largest works, each making a closely printed quarto volume. It had long been
a source of regret among the Baptists, that no full and
authentic history of their brethren existed, and that
their opinions, character, and progress had never
been represented to the world in the light they deserved. It was at length resolved by some of the leading
members of this denomination to supply the deficiency,
and appoint a suitable person to write a copious and
accurate history. The general voice fixed on Robinson,
and in 1781 he was invited by an authorized committee
to undertake the task. He complied with the request,
and immediately set himself about the gigantic labour of
wading through the ecclesiastical records of ancient and
modern times, appalled neither by the lumber of anti-
quity, nor the mountains of volumes, which have been
raised by the prolific industry of later ages.

That he might have a more ready access to scarce
books, it was a part of his plan to reside a few days in
every month in London. This design, however, was
soon given up as impracticable, for so much was he
sought after as a preacher, that he found his attention
perpetually diverted from his studies. Appointments
were made by his friends for preaching every day in
the week, and so slowly did his history advance in the
midst of these interruptions that he was glad to escape
from them to his farm, his family, and his people, in
the country. Here he was kindly favoured with books
from the University, and occasionally from London, and
here he completed the History of Baptism.

This volume was chiefly printed before the author's
death, but not published till after that event. It contains a vast fund of historical knowledge on the subject
which he professes to treat, and indicates an uncommon-
ly deep and patient examination. The " Ecclesiastical
Researches" was a posthumous work, and having been
left in an unfinished state, is in many respects imperfect. It contains some curious facts relating to the history of the existence and progress of the principles of
religious liberty and a rational faith during the early
periods of Christianity, and throughout the dark ages.

It proves, that these principles were never extinct in the gloomiest times, but that they were cherished in the hearts of a few sincere, secluded worshippers, who were either too remote from the public eye to be observed, or too insignificant to draw down upon themselves the wrath of bigotry, or the rod of persecution. In this respect the Ecclesiastical Researches supplies a valuable link in the history of the church. But on the whole, neither this nor the History of Baptism, is equal to the author's other performances. While preparing them, it is evident his mind had lost much of its former vigour, and was approaching that state of inefficiency, which it was the melancholy lot of his friends to contemplate in the latter days of his life. However much the cause of truth may have gained by these works, they have added little to the author's fame.

During the last year of Robinson's life, his health and his intellect gave symptoms of a rapid decline. Of this he appeared to be fully aware, for to a friend, who visited him not long before his death, he said, " You are come to see only the shadow of Robert Robinson." In the spring of 1790 he engaged to preach the charity sermons for the benefit of the dissenting schools at Birmingham. He left home on the second day of June in a languid frame of body and mind, but so well did he bear the fatigue of the journey, that he preached twice on the following sabbath. On monday evening he was taken ill, and his friends were alarmed; but he gained strength the next day. He retired to rest late in the evening, after eating his supper with a good appetite, and by the ease and cheerfulness of his conversatiou relieving those around him from all apprehensions of immediate danger. But how frail are the foundations of human confidence, how deceitful the visions of human hope! When the morning came he was found lifeless in his bed. His features were tranquil, and his spirit seemed to have deserted without a struggle its mortal tenement. His body was interred at Birmingham, and on the sabbath following a discourse adapted to the occasion was preached by Dr. Priestley.

In the year 1807, Mr. Flower published the *Miscellaneous*

Works of Robert Robinson, in four volumes, to which he
prefixed a brief memoir of the author's life and writings. This edition comprises all his works, except the
History of Baptism, Ecclesiastical Researches, Village
Discourses, and Notes to Claude. Among his best writings are the prefaces to the several volumes of Saurin,
especially the one on Christian Liberty. The Life of
Claude is well written, but a dissertation on Public
Preaching, prefixed to the second volume of Claude's
Essay, although it contains some novel thoughts, and
valuable facts, is imperfect, and obviously put together
from ill digested materials. This remark, indeed, applies to several of his minor pieces, where a broader
plan seems to have been laid, than his leisure and opportunities allowed him to fill up.

Among the numerous excellencies of Robinson's style,
there are some glaring faults. His imagination is bril-
liant and active, but it rambles without license, and lux-
uriates without moderation. He never wants an appo-
site figure to illustrate any position, but his choice is
frequently ill-judged, and rests on low images unworthy
of his subject. This may be accounted for, perhaps,
from the circumstances of his education, and from his
invariable habit of bringing down his language to the
plain country people to whom he preached. Another
fault is want of method, and looseness of reasoning.
This fault is not perpetual, but it occurs too often.
Logic was not his strongest point; he loved not that his
fancy should be clogged and hampered by the trammels
of the schools; he chose a path of his own, and in his
passion for freedom was impatient of the restraints
which others have thought so wholesome a branch of
discipline, and so useful in checking the exuberance of
a prurient imagination, and maturing the decisions of a
wayward judgment. It hardly needs to be added, that his
taste partook of these defects; it is sometimes bad, and
often not to be commended.

But these are small imperfections compared with the
predominant features of Robinson's mind. The comprehensive views which he took of every subject, the
richness and abundance of his thoughts, the power of

intellect which weighs in his sentences, the point of his expressions, the varied and playful, although erratic excursions of his imagination; and, above all, his sincerity and ardour, the justness of his sentiments, his undisguised manner, his benevolence, charity, and Christian temper, his independence and love of freedom, his unconquerable hostility to all religious domination under whatever name or character, his aversion to bigotry and narrowness, his adherence to the simple truths of the Gospel; these give a charm and value to his writings, by which none can fail to be instructed and improved. Whoever would look for pleasure or benefit from the productions of a writer with traits like these, will find his labour well rewarded in perusing the works of Robert Robinson.

b*

ADVERTISEMENT,

PREFIXED TO THE ENGLISH EDITION, PRINTED AT HARLOW, 1805.

Sixteen of the following Discourses were published by the Author. The seventeenth was printed in the *Second edition,* from a Manuscript copy prepared by him for the press, but not published during his life.

PREFACE.

THE Protestant dissenting congregations at Cambridge, from the first forming of them, have always consisted, besides inhabitants of the town, of a great number of families, resident in the adjacent villages. In these last families there always have been children and servants, aged and infirm persons, who could attend the public worship in town only occasionally, some once a month on the Lord's Supper day, others once a quarter, and the very aged only once or twice in the summer. It hath therefore been the constant practice of their teachers, in compliance with their own desire, to instruct them at their own towns about once a month. In some there are houses fitted up on purpose ; and in others, barns in summer when they are empty, and in winter dwelling-houses, answer the same end. When either have been too small to accommodate the auditors, as they often have been on fine evenings, sometimes they, and sometimes the teachers have stood abroad in an orchard, or a paddock, or any convenient place. The following discourses are a few of many which have been delivered in such places. They are printed, as nearly as can be recollected, as they were spoken.

In some places, and in some seasons the teacher hath tarried all night, and half an hour early in the morning hath been employed in devotion and giving instruction. The short discourses, called for distinction sake Exercises, were delivered at such times. It was usual too, before sermon in the evening, to catechise the children, by hearing them read a short scripture history, and questioning them about the sense of it.

The propriety of every action depends on circumstances; and nobody can judge of the fitness or unfitfitness of a *subject*, or a *part* of a subject, or a *manner* of treating of it, except they who know all the circumstances; for the same method in different circumstances would be unedifying, if not impertinent and rude. This publication therefore, is not intended either to blame or to direct any other teacher; but merely to gratify the long and importunate requests of some in the congregations who heard the discourses, and beyond whom we have neither inclination nor ambition to publish them. However, it will be necessary to apprize an occasional reader of *three* things; for we do not love, and we think we do not deserve contempt.

The first regards the *subjects* themselves. The author of these discourses is of opinion that the Christian religion ought to be distinguished from the philosophy of it. On this ground he studies to establish facts; and he hath no idea of guilt in regard to different reasonings on the nature of those facts, or the persons concerned in them. He hath his own opinions of the nature of God, and Christ, and man, and the decrees, and so on: but he doth not think that the opinion of Athanasius, or Arius, or Sabellius, or Socinus, or Augustine, or Pelagius, or Whitby, or Gill, on the subjects in dispute between them, ought to be considered of such importance as to divide Christians, by being made standards to judge of the truth of any man's Christianity. He thinks virtue and not faith the bond of union, though he supposes the subject ought to be properly explained. His design therefore in these discourses was to possess people of a full conviction of the truth of a few facts, the belief of which he thought would produce virtue, and along with that, personal and social happiness. His ideas of this subject do not meet the views of some of his brethren : but while he wishes they may enjoy their own sentiments, he hopes they will not deny him their friendship, because he hath it not in his power to think as they do. It is on supposition of the harmlessness of philosophy, or rather of the benefit of getting into a sound philosophy, which is nothing but right reason, that he inculcates with all his might a spirit of universal liberty ; for he never saw any danger in a difference of opinion, till some unruly passion, by disturbing the disputants, and souring their tempers, brought the subject into disgrace.

It is necessary also to observe in regard to a *part* of some subjects, that as there are various difficulties in the minds of different Christians arising from their different prejudices, it is but just in an assembly greatly diversified to give each one a solution of his own difficulty ; for otherwise the zest of the sermon is lost in regard to him, and that it ought not to be.

In an assembly of learned youths, whose faith in Christianity had been shaken by polished and bewitching recommendations of infidelity, it would be proper to take off the varnish, and discover the futility and inconclusiveness of such essays; and this ought to be done with wit, vivacity, ingenuity, address, and point, superior if it were possible in salt and savour to the style of unbelievers. On the contrary, in an assembly all made up of rustics, who never saw any charms in schools, whose ears are not accustomed to honeyed accents, and who have only vulgar prejudices against Christianity, the method of recommending it should be quite different. The objections of the learned lie against the supposed philosophy of Christianity, and point at what are called the *doctrines* of it; but the objections of the uneducated are vulgar prejudices, which rise out of the love and the practice of sin. These people do not object against the doctrines; indeed they are apt to err on the other side, and to believe too much, sinking into a torpid state through credulousness as their opposites do through unbelief. They have no objection against any thing in the Gospel, except the virtue of it. To remove their prejudices against evangelical virtue is the peculiar work of their teachers. It is easy to see that either of these assemblies, taken separately, may be addressed with great propriety in their own way; but should a few of the one sort mingle themselves in the assemblies of the other, it would become necessary to treat them all with justice and respect, and consequently to direct a *part*, a line or two, a sentence, a hint, a word, or an argument to the edification of each. Should it even not answer the end, the good intention of the teacher ought to be allowed.

As to the *manner* of treating of the subjects of religion, that ought to be formed as nearly as possible on the manners of the hearers. Indeed, what does it signify by what sounds, or by what sentences, or by what similitudes we set men a thinking, and convey information to their understandings ? From the melody of a nightingale to the croaking of a frog, from the eloquence of Cicero to the vulgar gabble of Mrs. Quickly, the renowned hostess of the knight of inexhaustible humour, from the manly reasoning in Butler's Analogy, to the doleful dialogues between Epenetus, the devil, and Mr. Hobbes, all are, in some sense, indifferent. Many great masters have given rules, which have their use to teach boys at school, how to practise a pace, which it may be proper for them to go in some even paths in future life : but there are some rugged roads in which rules would be an hindrance, and it may become necessary for travellers to scramble along as well as they can. The great end of teaching is to enable men to get above the want of teaching ; and if that end be answered, the manner, it should seem, is an article of no very great consequence.

Petilian had an only son, who disgraced his family, wasted his property, half broke his father's heart, and fled, all profligacy and diseases as he was, abroad. Petilian never forgot he had a son, often wept at recollecting it, and grew grey with hoping against hope that he should live to clasp his penitent son in his arms. After twenty-five years, in which he had often been informed that his son was alive but become worse and worse, Rufus, a rough but honest and benevolent captain of a ship came to pay Petilian a visit . . . "Pardon me, Petilian, if I ask, when you heard of your son" . . . The old gentleman took out his handkerchief and wiped his eyes . . . "I can give you some intelligence of him," added Rufus, "and on the whole not unpleasant" . . . Petilian looked hard at him, his jaw quivered, he drew himself forward, and sat on the edge of the front of his chair . . . Rufus added, "He is become a Quaker" . . . Petilian lifted up one hand, the tears ran down from both his eyes, and he exclaimed, "Is he alive!" . . . "He is alive and well" . . . "My son !" . . . "Yes, your son. I have seen him and conversed with him, and what I tell you is true" . . . Petilian fainted. Rufus recovered him, and when he was cool told him : "I have been abroad. One day a shipwright, a rough blunt man, came on board, and told me that he had reproached your son with his conduct, in a manner so forcibly that he could not resist it, and that in consequence of the remonstrances of his own conscience, excited by his conversation, he had laid aside the practice, and quenched the love of vice, and that he now for four years past had lived a life of devotion, temperance, and justice. After his reformation he had gone to work with this shipwright, and had married his daughter, and was led by that family into that mode of Christianity, which we here call Quakerism, for the shipwright himself was a Friend, and held forth on the nature and practice of virtue in a little assembly of his own people. I was curious to see him, and went with my informer on shore. There I found him, with his broad brim, eating his morsel with his Abigail, one of the neatest of women, and two children, the eldest of whom is the picture of yourself, and called friend Petilian, after thee. I proposed an interview with you, which he refused with tears of the most unaffected re= pentance for his sins, and expressions of esteem for your virtue. He said, " I ought to ask pardon of my father, and I would, but, recollect, Captain, my father is a man of birth, fortune, and fashion, and of the Roman catholic religion. Thou wilt forgive me if I say, I fear the pre= judices of that very virtuous man will not allow him to take pleasure in me now that a change, so barbarous in his eye hath taken place in me ; for virtue, unaccompan= ied with the gaiety of the world and the ceremonies of the church, hath no being, much less beauty, in the eyes of such men. I think, therefore, on the whole, that it would be an act of cruelty to disturb the peace of my father ; perhaps he hath long ago buried me in imagination, and it would revive his grief to raise me from the dead. I trust, at the resurrection of the last day the infinite mercy of God will make the sight of me an addition to his joy"... Rufus paused... Petilian wept, and exclaimed, " O that I could see him ; proba= bly I might engage him to lay aside his garb of virtue without endangering his virtue itself" ... " O no," said Rufus, " it would be dangerous to make the attempt ; beside, I can tell you he is an inconvertible man. You must either see him as he is, or never see him at all" ...

c

"Is it possible to see him?" . . . "It is. I have prevailed with him, and brought him and his family over" . . .
"Holy virgin!" exclaimed Petilian. "Where is he?
I must see him. I have forgiven him. I feel I love
him. I long to embrace him. I have already forgotten,
and I will never recollect the impropriety of any means
made use of to recover a sinner from the error of his
way, and to fill a father with a joy like that of God, when
he embraces a long lost, once prodigal, but now penitent son." "Come then," said Rufus, "give passage to
the finest emotions of the human heart. Your son saith,
in language canonized by both your churches, *Father, I
have sinned against heaven, and before thee, and am no
more worthy to be called thy son: make me as one of thy
hired servants:* and he is now saying this, all heretic
as he is, in a room in this house where I have desired
him to wait. You *have compassion*, Petilian. Go, *run
fall on his neck and kiss him*, and then *let us* all, in spite
of forms, *eat and be merry, for*

> "Pleasure and praise run through God's host
>   To see a sinner turn;
> Then Satan hath a captive lost,
>   And Christ a subject born."

To people who have any interest in the knowledge
and virtue of their fellow-creatures, though it be not so
great as that of a parent, yet we cannot but think that
all modes of communicating virtue are comparatively
indifferent. Let the reader think of this, and forgive
whatever may have the air, and in some cases the nature, of impropriety, in these discourses, which were
intended to edify many, and to give offence to none.

CONTENTS.

MORNING EXERCISES.

DISCOURSE I.

THE CHRISTIAN RELIGION EASY TO BE UNDERSTOOD.

[*AT DRY-DRAYTON.*]

EPHESIANS iii. 4.

When ye read, ye may understand my knowledge in the mystery of Christ.

BRETHREN,

SUPPOSE the apostle Paul, when he first stood up in the synagogue at Ephesus to teach Christianity to the Jews, or in the school of Tyrannus to a mixed assembly, had begun his discourse by saying, " Men of Ephesus, I am going to teach a religion which none of you can understand;" I say, suppose this; put yourselves in the place of the Ephesians, and you must allow, that he would have insulted his hearers, disgraced himself, and misrepresented the religion of Jesus Christ.

He would have *insulted the assembly;* and they would have thought, This man either doth understand the subject of which he is going to speak, or he doth not. If he doth not understand it himself, he hath gathered us together only to hear him confess his ignorance; and what have we to do with that? If he be ignorant, let him sit silent as we do, and give place to such as do know what they talk of. If he does understand it himself, why should he affirm we cannot? Are we assembled to hear him boast? Does he take us for idiots, who have no reason, or for libertines, who make no use of what they have?

He would have *disgraced himself;* for what can render a man more ridiculous than his pretending to instruct others in what he doth not understand himself? Paul would have appeared in the pulpit just as one of you taskers, would appear in the chair of a professor of Hebrew at a university. What character more disgraceful can a man assume, than that of the leader of a credulous party, whose religion doth not lie in understanding and practising what is taught, but in believing that the teacher understands it! A provision indeed for the glorious consequence of a blind guide; but not for the freedom, and piety, and happiness of the people!

I said, he would have *misrepresented the christian religion;* and I am going to prove this, by showing you, that Christianity is not a secret but a revealed religion—that you are all of you able to understand it—and that there is every reason in the world - why you should apply yourselves to the thorough knowledge of it.

By Christianity, I mean that religion which Jesus Christ taught his disciples, and which is all contained in the New Testament. Retain this observation, for it frees the subject from many difficulties. Some misguided Christians propose a great number of mysteries, that is, secrets to us; such as that the bread and wine in the Lord's supper cease to be bread and wine, and become the flesh, and bones, and blood of Christ; such as that a wicked man is inspired by the Holy Ghost to lead us to heaven without our knowing the way; and that these wonders are performed by the uttering of certain words by a certain set of men; and these secrets, which nobody so much as pretends to understand, we are required to believe. However, we have one short answer for all mysteries of this kind; that is, they are *not* taught in the New Testament, and therefore they are no parts of the Christian religion.

When I affirm the Christian religion is not a secret, observe, I speak of Christianity *now*, and not formerly. Thus we free the subject from all the objections which are made against it from many passages in the New Testament. Christianity, say some, is often called a mystery, or a secret; even the text calls it so. True; but the same text says, Paul *knew* this secret, and the Ephesians might *understand* what he knew of it, if they would *read* what he wrote to them. " When ye read, ye may understand my knowledge in the mystery of Christ."

Strictly speaking, the text intends only *one part* of Christianity, that is, the uniting of heathens and Jews in one religious community; but what. is affirmed of this one part is equally true of the whole. True religion had always been hid from the wisest of the heathens; and the Christian religion, which was then the only true religion, had not been made known in other ages to the Jews, as it was then to the Apostles; but Paul knew it, and he proposed to make all men see it. "I preach to make all men see." We allow, the wisest man could never have known (for his life would have been too short, and his faculties too much confined) the true character of God; but we affirm, God revealed, that is, made it known unto the prophets and apostles by his Spirit; and these prophets and apostles have made it known to us by their writings.

When I affirm, the christian religion hath no mysteries now, I do not mean to say that the truths and the duties of Christianity are not *connected* with other truths and other exercises, which surpass all our comprehension; but I affirm, that the knowledge of the incomprehensible parts, and the belief of what people please to conjecture about them, though they may be parts of our amusement, and perhaps improvement, are yet no parts of that religion which God requires of us under pain of his displeasure. Suppose I were to affirm, there is no secret in mowing grass, and in making, stacking, and using hay; all this would be very true; and should any one deny this, and question me about the manner in which one little seed produces clover, another trefoil, a third rye-grass, and concerning the manner how all these convey strength and spirit to horses, and milk to cows, and fat to oxen in the winter; I would reply, All this is philosophy; nothing of this is necessary to mowing, and making, and using hay. I sanctify this thought by applying it to religion. Every good work produces present pleasure and future reward; to perform the work, and to hope for the reward from the known character of the great Master we serve, is religion, and all before and after is only connected with it.

What part of the christian religion is a mystery? Divide the whole into the three natural parts, of *plan, progress*, and *execution;* the first was before this world be-

gan ; the last will be after this world shall end ; the mid
dle part is before us now.   There is no secret in either o
these parts ; but there are incomprehensible mysterie
connected with each of them.   In regard to the first, it i
impossible to be supposed, by a man who knows any thin
of God, that the christian religion came into the worl
without the Creator's knowing that such an event woul
take place ; and it is impossible for such a man to imagin
that, after the present life, there will be no distinctio
made between the righteous and the wicked.   There i
no mystery in these general principles ; but we may ren
der them extremely perplexed by rashly agitating questions connected with them.

In regard to Christianity in this present life, every thin
in it is exceeding plain.   Is the character of Jesus Chris
a secret ?   Did ever any body take him for an idle gen
tleman, a cruel tyrant, a deceitful tradesman, a man o
gross ignorance and turbulent passions ?   On the contrary
is it not perfectly clear that he was the person foretold b
the prophets of his country, who should come, himsel
perfectly wise and good, to instruct mankind in the know
ledge and worship of God ?   Is the character of Scripture
a secret ?   Is it not perfectly clear, that it is a wise an
good book, full of information on all the subjects that con
cern religion and morality ?   Is it a secret that we are
mortal and must die ; or that we are depraved, and apt t
live in the omission of duty and the practice of sin ; o
that a life of sin is connected with a course of misery, fo
pursuing which we deserve blame ?   Is it a secret wheth
er God takes notice of the actions of men, or whether he
will forgive a penitent, and punish the impenitent ?   In
word, is the character of God a secret in the christian re
ligion ; and is it a mystery whether he be an object wor
thy of our adoration and imitation ?   Were I obliged t
give a short account of the Christian Religion, I would no
say it is a revelation of the decrees of God, or a revela
tion of the resurrection of the dead, or a revelation of the
mercy of God to a repenting sinner through the merit o
Jesus Christ ; for though each of these be true, yet al
these are only *parts of his ways ;* but I would call Chris
tianity a revelation, or a making known of the true anc

real character of God ; and I would affirm of the whole, and of each component part, that it was so made known as to be free from all mystery in regard to the truth of the facts, and yet so connected as to contain mysteries beyond the comprehension of finite minds. I would affirm further, that our religion is confined to the belief and practice of only what is revealed, and that every thing untold is a matter of conjecture, and no part of piety towards God, and benevolence to mankind.

Take heart, then, my good brethren ; you may understand, practise, and enjoy all this rich gift of God to man, just as you enjoy the light of the day, and refreshment by rest at night. Let no one say, I was born in poverty, I have had no learning, I have no friends, my days are spent in labour, and I have no prospect except that of drawing my last breath where I drew my first. All this may be true ; but all this will not prevent your knowing, and practising, and enjoying the Christian Religion, the founder of which had not, what the birds of the air have, " where to lay his head."

When I say all may understand it, I mean, if their own depravity does not prevent it. Plainly, you cannot know it if you do not attend to it ; nor can you know it though you do attend, if you do not attend to Christianity itself, and not to something else put instead of it. Let me explain myself.

One says, I cannot understand the nature and force of religion ; and pray, is there any thing wonderful in your ignorance ? Consider, you never read the Scriptures ; you never ask any body to read them to you ; you hate and persecute good men ; you seldom enter a place of worship ; you keep wicked company like yourself ; you are often seen in the practice of enormous crimes. Are you the man to complain, " I cannot understand religion ?" It would be a mystery indeed, if a man who never turned his attention to a subject, should know any thing certain about it. We have no such mystery in all the christian religion. Christians do not live like you.

Another says, I am a very sober man, I go constantly to a place of worship, and I cannot comprehend the christian religion. All this is very true ; you are a sober, decent

1*

character, and regular in your attendance on public wor
ship; but recollect, I am speaking not of your body, bu
of your mind.   Now, it is a fact, abroad or at home, in th
church or in the barn, your attention is always taken u
with other things, and so taken up as to leave no roo
for " the things which belong unto your *everlasting* peace."
Sometimes your corn, sometimes your cattle, sometime
taxes and rates, and sometimes your rent and your ser
vants' wages; but, at all times, to live in the presen
world, engrosses all your attention.   You, you resembl
yon child fast asleep, without knowing it, in the arms of
parent. " God besets you behind and before, and lays his han
upon you. It is he that watereth the ridges of your corn, an
settleth the furrows thereof; he maketh the earth soft wit
showers; he clothes thy pastures with flocks, and crowns the
year with his goodness. It is he that giveth thee power to ge
wealth, and multiplieth thy herds and thy flocks, and thy sil
ver and thy gold, and all that thou hast." And you, inatten
tive man! you cannot comprehend that you are under a
obligation to know and do the will of this generous bene
factor.   What does Christianity require of you but to love
and serve this God? If you do not serve him, it is be
cause you do not love him; if you do not love him, it i
because you do not know him; and if you do not know
him, it is not for want of evidence, but attention.
    It is not only to you that I affirm this connexion betwee
attention and knowledge; for if this barn were filled with
statesmen and scholars, generals and kings, I should be al
lowed to say to one, Sir, you understand intrigue; t
another, Sir, you understand war, to besiege a town, an
rout an army; to a third, Sir, you understand law, an
every branch of the office of a conservator of the peace
to another, Sir, you understand languages and arts anc
sciences; and you all understand all these, because you
have studied them; but here are two things which you
have not studied, and which therefore you do not know
the one, how to plough, and sow, and reap, and thresh a
acre of wheat; and the other how to live holily in thi
world, so as to live happily in the world to come. Ar
you not convinced, my good brethren, that the same cir
cumstance, which prevents those gentlemen from knowin
how to perform the work that you perform every day

with pleasure, prevents you from knowing the practice and the pleasure of true Christianity? In both cases the subject hath not been attended to.

I go further, and venture to affirm, if religion could be understood without attention, it would be a misfortune; a misfortune depriving us of many advantages and leading us to commit many crimes. The ease with which we acquired knowledge would sink the value of it, and "darkness would have communion with light."

As attention is absolutely necessary, so it is equally necessary that attention should be fixed upon the christian religion itself, and nothing else. We hear often of the mysteries of religion; let us not forget that there are *mysteries of iniquity*. Ignorance, covetousness, tyranny, especially tyranny over *conscience*, all wrap themselves in mystery; but if we incorporate any of these mysteries with the christian religion, and attend to them, instead of distinguishing and attending to pure Christianity, we may attend and study, but we shall never know; we shall be ever learning, and never able to come to the knowledge of the truth. The doctrine, manner of life, purpose, faith, longsuffering, charity, patience, persecutions, afflictions, and deliverances of the apostle Paul, were *fully known*, and diligently followed by common Christians; but who ever knew the *doctrine* of transubstantiation, or that of the infallibility of a frail, sinful man? Who of us, uninspired men, knows the feelings of a person under the immediate influence of the Holy Ghost? In vain we pursue such mysteries as these; the stronger the attention, the greater the mortification of not being able to succeed. If one place religion in impulses, another in new revelations, a third in a state of perfection, a fourth in discoveries and enjoyments inconsistent with our present state, and not set before us in the christian religion, they may well be filled with doubts and fears, and spend life in complaining of the crooked and dreary paths of religion. If, on the contrary, we attend only to what is revealed, to believe only what is reported with sufficient evidence, to practise only what is commanded by the undoubted voice of God; if we seek only such pleasures and distinctions as we are taught in scripture to expect; in a word, if we would acquaint ourselves only with God, and be at peace one with another, thereby good should come unto us.

When I said, all of you might understand Christianity, I meant, there was nothing in Christianity but what might be understood if it were properly attended to, and nothing in the natural condition of any individual (I do not say his moral state), to prevent his attending to it. There is no capacity so mean, no creature so forlorn, as to be beyond the reach of the benefits conferred upon men by Jesus Christ. You are a babe; in his gospel there is " milk for babes ;" truths adapted to nourish and cherish a little, feeble mind. You are poor; " the poor have the gospel preached to them ;" the glad tidings of a Redeemer, and all his benefits. You are unlearned; but the " highway of holiness" is so plain, that the " way-faring man, though a fool, shall not err therein." You are so bashful, and so unused to company, that you are necessarily deprived of the pleasure of the company and conversation of good men ; but you have better company than that of good men ; and you, you poor shepherd, you will behold the heavens, the work of the fingers of your God; you will consider the moon and the stars, and the Saviour and the heaven which he hath ordained, till you cry out, " What is man that thou art mindful of him, and the son of man that thou visitest him ?" And upon these subjects " the tongue of the stammerer shall be ready to speak eloquently!" The Christian religion enlarges and ennobles the mind, purifies and refines the heart, and adorns the life ; and a Christian labourer, exercising his own understanding, is a more beautiful sight than an unjust judge in all the pomp of his office.

Let us finish, by remarking the reasons that should induce you to apply to religious knowledge. There are reasons in God—reasons in the christian religion—reasons in the world—and reasons in yourselves ; and if all these reasons be not sufficient to prevail with you to love and serve God, reason will require but one thing more, that is, " your everlasting destruction from the presence of the Lord, and from the glory of his power, when he shall be revealed from heaven, with his mighty angels, in flaming fire, to punish them that know not God, and that obey not the gospel of our Lord Jesus Christ."

Do not think I mean to frighten you. Fear is one of the lowest passions; and though "the fear of the Lord is" in some men "the beginning of wisdom," yet it is not the whole of it. Consider God. Is there nothing in him to engage you to esteem him? Can your mind be so drenched in sin as to dislike a being of perfect wisdom, justice, goodness, and power? Hath he no right over you by creating and preserving you? Is there nothing in all the tender compassion of the Gospel worth your regard? His promises, are they not worthy of your desires? His threatenings, is there nothing in them that you ought to fear? God is the chief example, and the first reason of holiness. If we wish to please him, it must be by making him, the sovereign beauty, the first cause of all things, the chief object of our esteem; and if we esteem him, we must take pleasure in every thing that represents him. If the glorious perfections of God shine in the face of Jesus Christ, we shall reverence Jesus Christ. If the Scriptures be a picture, so to speak, of this parent, whose face none of his children can see in this life, we shall study the Holy Scriptures. If "the heavens declare his glory," if "the earth be full of his praise," we shall see God in every thing, and in every thing shall discover a reason for obeying him. Oh how full of preachers is this well adjusted world! Had we attention equal to our means of instruction, how wise and good should we become! The twittering of a sparrow, the chirping of a grasshopper, the music of a May morning, and the whistling of winter winds, speech that showeth knowledge to the end of the world, would sound in the ears of man, make the simple wise, and compel him to say, "The statutes of the Lord are right," and "more to be desired than much fine gold; sweeter also than honey, or the honey-comb."

When this "God so loved the world as to give his only begotten Son, that whosoever believed in him should not perish, but have everlasting life," he commanded the "angels of God to worship him:" he said, by a voice from heaven, both to the apostles alone, and to the whole multitude of the Jews with them, "This is my beloved son, hear ye him." He declared by the mouth of an inspired man, "This is the Prophet whom the Lord your God hath raised up unto you; him shall ye hear in all things whatsoever

hé shall say unto you.   And it shall come to pass, that eve
ry soul which will not hear this Prophet, shall be destroye
from among the people."   Remark this expression, "ever
soul—every soul that will not hear this Prophet, shall b
destroyed from among the people."

Why ? Is this an arbitrary command ; as much as to say
you shall be Christians ; and I your God will have it so
No such thing ; but because the christian religion is the per
fection of reason, and intended to explain and establish the
three branches of the eternal and unchangeable law of nature

The first of these is *piety* towards God.   Doth God re
quire us to fear, to love, to trust, to obey, to worship him
He hath displayed himself in the christian religion as mos
worthy of all this worship.   He hath removed all the sus
picions of heathens, by express declarations of his min
and will.   He hath taken away all the horrors excited b
apprehensions of danger, from the guilty bosoms of men
by suitable promises, and by signal proofs of his kind at
tachment to their being and happiness.   Doth he require
us to believe ? It is upon evidence.   Doth he require us
to obey ? He condescends to set us an example, by a
thousand acts of justice and generosity.

A second branch of righteousness is, *love to our neighbours*.
The christian religion is the highest reason for this jus
esteem; for thus it argues, "If God so loved us, we ought al
so to love one another."   If any of our fellow-creatures ren
der themselves so odious by sin, that they cease to be objects of esteem, the Gospel teaches us to consider them as
objects of pity, and sums up all morality in one word, " All
things whatsoever ye would that men should do to you, do
ye even so to them ; for this is the law and the prophets."

The third part of righteousness is *to love ourselves ;* and
the christian religion, by declaring the immortality of the
soul, the resurrection of the body, and the whole appointment of man to be a " temple of the Holy Ghost," an " hab
itation of God through the spirit," lays us under the strongest
obligations to " live soberly in this present world."   The
christian religion, too, gives us the irresistible motives of the
love of God, the example of the death of Christ, the last
judgment, hell with all its horrors, and heaven with all its
pleasures, as reasons why we should " work out our own

salvation with fear and trembling." There is, therefore, in the christian religion itself the highest reason for our acceptance of it.

There are reasons in the *world* that surrounds you, for your attending to the christian religion. Consider four sorts of men, in a manner four worlds, more strictly four different views of the same world, and from each derive instruction. Observe, first, that great multitude of men, who live in the constant practice of sin, drunkards, liars, thieves, extortioners, and all the rest of that black list, who are expressly, by name, as it were, doomed not to inherit the kingdom of God. Is there any thing to tempt a man of sense and reason to live as they do? Is it a desirable thing to die as they die? And would you wish to be a companion of such odious monsters in a future state of punishment? The christian religion calls you out of this company, and finds you other work and different wages.

Look next at the prosperous part of the world. See with what hazard they get, with what anguish they keep, and with what agony they part with the good things of this life; the reason is, they have mistaken the nature of these things, they take them for their chief good, and part with them as if they were torn from Almighty God. Even innocent prosperity is a temptation to guilt, and the down bed of success is apt to make men sleep when they should wake, and waste that life in idleness, which was intended for action. That religion which teaches us how to use the world without abusing it, and how to "lay up treasures in heaven;" that religion which preserves the heart from taking damage by a plentiful harvest, a prosperous trade, and such other little advantages of life; that is the religion, which, if we were sure of prospering in all our undertakings, we ought first of all to embrace, lest the end of a prosperous life should be a miserable death, as that of all, who are wicked in prosperity, must necessarily be.

Remark the afflicted part of the world. The poor, the lame, the blind, the deaf, the dumb, the man in prison for his debts, and the man in an hospital with his sores, the poor father reduced to live upon charity through the extravagance of his son, the grey-headed, lame, and shrivelled mother, left and forgotten, neglected and insulted by her proud children, who have prospered in the world; look at the man afflicted with the gravel, and dying by inches, and ask what can support the spirits of all this company, except religion? What but the prospect of a future state of happiness can administer a sufficient relief to them? The christian religion is a general balm to heal all their wounds. It teaches the doctrine of Providence, that God brings good out of evil, and communicates the greatest blessings to mankind, under appearances the most mortifying to our senses. Observe, finally, the religions world, the good people gone before, and the rest now on the road. That religion, which supported Job under all his adversity; that religion which kept Joseph from losing his soul in prosperity; that religion, which held the arm of David from making an unjust use of the sword of the magistrate, and kept the fine abilities of Paul from serving the interests of sin; that religion, which saved Peter from distraction and despair; that religion, which every day suppresses so much sin, binds up so many broken hearts, produces so many just and generous actions, communicates so much pleasure through life, and " a joy unspeakable and full of glory" at the hour of death;—that is the religion, which my own reason commands me to receive. There are reasons in yourselves, in your nature—in your depravity—in your condition—and in your prospects. Your *nature* is capable of high improvement. By becoming a good christian, you will improve your body, even here; for temperence, sobriety, chastity, industry, and, above all, the government of the temper, that calmness, which religion produces, is " the health of the countenance;" and at the resurrection of the dead, religion will change the natural into a spiritual body; " corruptible shall put on incorruption, mortal immortality, and then shall be brought to pass the saying that is written, Death is swallowed up in victory." Your souls also are capable of great advancement. Have you no ambition to know more than how to manage a few acres of land, how to dispose of a little corn, or a little money? Rise, men! rise into an apprehension of your dignity. You were made in the image of God; and though the picture is dirtied and defaced, yet Christianity calls you to aspire to such noble sentiments and worthy actions, such high enjoyments, and such duration, as become the majesty of your nature. Hear the great master: When good men " rise from the dead, they neither marry, nor are given in marriage ;" and we may venture to add, they neither sow nor reap, buy nor sell, build nor adorn ; but, far, far above all these little things, " are as the angels which are in heaven."

Think of your *depravity*. Are you perfectly reconciled to your own sins, to wilful ignorance ; would you always be a fool? To discontent ; would you always be gloomy and apt to despair? Are you quite easy with anger and malice, and are you never afraid that the violence of your passions may bring you to shame here, and to hell hereafter? But without religion, they will bring you to " shame and everlasting contempt."

Attend a moment to your *condition ;* every thing in that is a reason for religion. You are a father: would you go, at the head of a family of eight or ten children, a guide to hell? You are poor: and is not a poor man without religion comfortless in himself, and offensive to others? Is there any encouragement to the rich to find you work, or to give you charity, if you consume all in the service of sin?

Such of you as are young should remember, that a youth without religion is a dangerous person : and such of you as are old should remember, that sober people always consider an old man teaching others, by his example, to sin, as a public nuisance. Such as are in health should not abuse those precious days: such as are sick should improve every moment in " preparing to meet their God," the judge that standeth before their door.

This brings us to the last article, your *prospects.* It was a very alarming question, which the prophet Jeremiah put to his countrymen, after he had described the wicked state in which they lived. " The prophets prophesy falsely, the priests bear rule by their means, and my people love to have it so." There can be no worse state of a people than this. The prophets might say any thing, true or false; so that these wretched people might be released from the trouble of examining, and be left to pursue every one his own sinful pleasure. The priests might do any thing, introduce idolatry instead of the worship of the true God, practise every crime instead of exemplifying every virtue, on condition they would let this base people share their guilty enjoyments. Miserable people! you *love to have it so*, in the time of a Jeremiah too, and when the enemy is just at your gates, and the judgments of God, hanging like a thick cloud, just ready to overwhelm you with misery! You *love to have it so ;* so did not Abraham your father : but you keep bad company, and place a superstitious confidence in your profligate guides! "If a man say, I will prophesy unto you of wine and of strong drink, even he shall be the prophet of this people !" But what says your compassionate friend Jeremiah? He asks this alarming question, " What will you do in the end thereof?" Suppose this prophet to return to the world again, pity you as he did the people of his own times, meet you in some of your walks, look steadfastly at you, and with tears running down his cheeks, gently ask you, " What will you do in the end thereof?" Are you wiser than the old world, who lived as you do, while Noah was building and entering the ark, and knew not till " the flood came and swept them all away?" Will you provoke the Lord to jealousy? are you stronger than he ? What will you do in the end? I defy you to give an answer that will not be a reason for your immediate attention to Christianity. If that punishment, which is at the end of your path, and is in full prospect all the way, be before your eyes, you will instantly " make supplication to your judge," that you " come not into that place of torment :" if, on the contrary, you have repentance, forgiveness, and heaven in prospect, you will be confounded for your ingratitude to that benefactor, from whom you live in hopes of receiving such undeserved favours.

Brethren, if there be in you the least degree of self-love, or the fear of God ; if you have not lived in sin till your understandings are blasted and perished, I conjure you, respect the Apostle of us Gentiles, who now says to us, " If you read, you may understand my knowledge in the mystery of Christ." Tell him, if you have the heart, We will not read, nor will we hear any body else read the book that contains the christian religion. Religion is the last thing we desire to understand, and we prefer a newspaper

and a ballad, before all your histories and prophecies, and
epistles and gospels.   If this be your case, when heathens
are pitied, some of whom went half over the then known
world in pursuit of wisdom, but never saw the wisdom of
God in the Christian religion ; I say, when you and they
stand at the judgment-seat of Christ, to receive for the
deeds done in the body, their condition will be more tolerable than yours.

Oh ! may that God " whose tender mercies are over all his
works, who desireth not the death of a sinner, but that he
should return and live," inform your minds, by means of
our instructions, and so " may he enlighten the eyes of
your understanding, and give you the spirit of wisdom and
revelation, that you may know what is the hope of his calling, and what the riches of the glory of his inheritance in
the saints !"   When you come to die, may he " show you
the path of life ;" and in the world to come may you " see
him face to face, and know even as also you are known !"

DISCOURSE II.

LUKE xi. 2.

When ye pray, say, Our Father.

LUTHER, that great reformer of religion in Germany, about two hundred and fifty years ago; Luther was one day catechising some country people in a village in Saxony. When one of the men had repeated these words, " I believe in God the Father Almighty," Luther asked him what was the signification of *Almighty?* The countryman honestly replied, " I do not know." " Nor do I know," said Luther, " nor do all the learned men in the world know : however, you may safely believe that God is your Father, and that he is both able and willing to protect and save yourself, and all your neighbours." The reformer might have added, that " no man had seen God at any time ;" that no man had " either heard his voice, or seen his shape ;" that, when Moses said to God, ".I beseech thee show me thy glory," the answer was, " thou canst not see my face, for there shall no man see me and live ;" and that all the displays of God, by his works, in the eyes of men, were rather a " hiding of his power," than a discovery of it. Yes, my brethren, " the blessed and only Potentate, the King of kings, and Lord of lords, who alone hath immortality, dwelleth in the light which no man can approach unto ; and him no man hath seen nor can see." It was wise, therefore, in Luther not to pretend to teach what neither the countryman, nor himself, nor all the men in the world understood ; and he had the advantage of the best examples to justify the method he took ; that is, to allow what all mankind are obliged to allow, that there is a God ; that God hath all possible perr.

fections, is perfectly wise, perfectly just, perfectly good, too wise to do any thing wrong, too good to do any thing unkind; and that all these perfections are the guardians, protectors, and friends of every good man.

Moses began to write the Holy Scriptures, but he did not begin by attempting to prove there was a God; but, taking this for granted, the first line he wrote was this, "In the beginning God created the heaven and the earth." When the same Moses besought God to show him his *glory*, meaning by that *himself*, God said, " I will make all my *goodness* pass before thee :" and, on the same principles, when one of the disciples of Jesus Christ said unto him, *Lord, teach us to pray,* Jesus, who was *with God,* and *knew* God, and *came from God,* said unto them, *When ye pray, say,* What ? Jehovah, First Cause, Supreme Being, co-equal, co-essential ? No : but, when ye pray, say, *Our Father.*

In order to enter into the spirit of our subject; that is, so to know God as to love and obey him, we will endeavour . . . to take off some of the veils which conceal our heavenly Father . . . to examine the representations which he hath given us of himself . . . and to apply the whole to the improvement of our hearts, and the amendment of our lives. " Our Father, who art in heaven, hallowed be thy name ; thy kingdom come ; thy will be done, as in heaven, so in earth ; forgive us our sins ; and lead us not into the temptation" of thinking meanly and wickedly of thee ; but deliver us from all the *evil* notions of God which ignorant and vicious men entertain, and to this end condescend to bless the good word which we are now going to hear.

My brethren, if you desire to form just notions of Almighty God, *lay aside all creatures.* Your Father, who is in heaven, is not earth, water, air, light ; he is not gold, silver, precious stones ; he is not fire, a star, a sun ; he is not a man ; he is not any of these apart ; he is not all these put together; he is not great or little, tall or low, round or square ; he is not white or red, or of any colour ; he is not to be smelled, tasted, felt, weighed, or measured. All these are his works ; but none of these is himself. Your forefathers, like all other uninstructed people in the world, made images to represent God ; and, as they could not think of any one thing sufficient to describe even what lit-

2*

tle they knew of God, they endeavoured to represent one of his excellencies by one image, and another by another, till they were multiplied beyond reckoning ; and, as they paid that respect to such images, which was due to none but Almighty God, the images were called *idols*, and the people *idolaters*, who amidst all their gods and lords, were " without God in the world."

Suppose an old Briton, one of your fathers, about two thousand years ago, to have fallen blind, and to have lost the use of his limbs, so that he could neither see nor feel the parish idol ; yet if he, lying in his bed, or sitting over his fire, remembered the form of the idol, and felt respect for it in his heart, should we not have reason to say he was an idolater ? Now this may be your case ; for if you think of God under any form, and respect that form as God, though you cannot produce any likeness of the form in your mind, yet this idea of God will become a veil thrown over your understanding, and will prevent your entertaining just notions of Almighty God. This you must lay aside, if you desire to know God.

In like manner, if you would form just notions of Almighty God, you must *lay aside all the similitudes of Scripture*, under which the inspired writers speak of God. I exact nothing of you in this respect, but what you yourselves perform every day in other respects. You say, A sharp man, with a sharp scythe, on a sharp morning, with a sharp appetite, mowed an acre of grass before breakfast, which was sharp work : but you mean, an ingenious man, whose scythe had a keen edge, early in the morning, while it was yet cold, and though he was all the while very hungry, cut an acre of grass before breakfast, which was hard work. Now why do you use the same word to express wit, cold, hunger, hardship, which properly signifies only the fine edge or point of a tool ? You do so, because you have more thoughts than words to express them, and because there is some one general likeness in which all these things agree ; and as you understand one another, there is no danger ; for you lay aside, when you hear of a sharp appetite, the ideas of edge, wit, cold, hardship, and understand hunger.

If words be too few and too poor to express other sub-.

jects, they must, for a much stronger reason, be fewer and poorer to describe Almighty God.   The Scriptures, there-fore, are to be read with this caution.   They speak of the eyes, and hands, and feet of God ; they speak of the heart, and the anger, and the love of God ; they speak of God's waking, and watching, and going, and coming ; and yet there is in God no parts of head or hands, no passions of hatred or anger, no motion from a place where he was, to a place where he was not before.   Take our text for an example.   God is called a *father*, not because he is in the form, or shape, or any thing like the person you call fa-ther ; so that when you pray to God, you must not think of him as one in the form of your father.   In like man-ner, God hath not such passions as your father hath ; no-thing like his anger, nor any feelings like what you call love in your father : he is not, like him, sometimes full of affection, at other times displeased and angry, sometimes more kind, and sometimes more angry than at other times. What is called *love* in God doth not make him go and come, and so on ; for none of these things agree with the spiritual, independent, and unchangeable perfection of God. If therefore we would entertain just notions of God, we must lay aside all similitudes, even those which the pov-erty of language made it necessary for inspired men to use.

Further, having rent the veil of gross matter, and that of resemblance or similitude, you must, in order to form right notions of God, *lay aside a partial-view of him.*   I will explain myself (and let it not surprise you, if I be at a loss for words plain enough to bring down this subject to the size of our understandings).   A partial view of any thing is such a view as a man takes of an object too big for his eyes to take in at once.   For example ; if a man goes up a hill to see the town of Cambridge, he will indeed see the town ; that is to say, one side of the town ; and if he would see the whole town, he must go from place to place all round it, from street to street all through it ; and every step would bring him to see some part of the town which he had not seen before.   Thus every one of us hath seen Cambridge, and no one of us hath seen Cambridge ; we have all seen it partially.   In like manner, if a man would see how wheat grows, it would not be enough to see it in January; for this would be a partial sight; but he must watch it from seed-time till harvest. Apply this to our subject. We speak of God. God is a great Being, and this world is a very little part of his empire; and the whole of God is from everlasting to everlasting. When therefore we speak of the justice of God, the goodness of God, the power of God, we speak partially, according to the little views we have of acts that appear just, and good, and powerful; but we should not be such children as to think that God lays aside what we call one perfection, when he exercises another; that he is more kind in harvest than he is in December; that he is more powerful in a tempest than he is in a calm day; that he is merciful when we recover from a sickness, and cruel when we die of it. Strictly speaking, there are not more perfections in God than one, that is a general excellence, a love of order: in this he agrees with our idea of a father, who nourishes, cherishes, feeds, clothes, instructs, corrects, and protects his child, intending by all to make him happy by making him holy.

I wish I knew how to make this subject so plain, particularly the last article mentioned, that you might not mistake it. The excellence of instruction is not that it may be understood, but that it cannot be misunderstood. There was lately a man executed at Cambridge, for robbing and murdering one of your neighbours. Was the execution of this man a judgment or a mercy, an act of justice or an act of kindness? We call it the just judgment of the law upon this criminal. It was so: but was it not also an administration of kindness and mercy? Perhaps to the man; for it might save him from a hotter place in hell, which he might have deserved, had he gone unpunished here, by robbing and murdering twenty more of you. Perhaps, too, the process of justice, from his apprehension to his death, might bring him to repentance; and certainly it was an act of mercy to us, as well as to other people disposed to rob and murder us, but who may be deterred by this example. An unthinking man at this execution, especially if he had, like too many, been drinking to cheer his spirits before he saw the dismal sight, would have wondered, had any one on the spot exclaimed, Oh the goodness and mercy! Oh the excellent compassion of the laws of England! Apply this to our subject, and always remember, that the most terrible dispensations of Almighty God are as kind in one view as they are dreadful in another: that the greatest profusions of his goodness are as just in one view as they are kind in another; and that when we speak of one perfection of God, we always mean all the rest, and speak thus only to adapt this great subject to the littleness of our minds.

It is to this littleness of mind that God condescends to adapt himself. We are taught in the text to consider God as *our Father.* As a wise and good father he instructs his children, and, strictly speaking, every benefit which God bestows on us is intended to give us an education. If we be nourished by our food, warmed by our clothes, corrected by our afflictions, and protected from our enemies, all these are for the sake of instructing us, that so by knowledge and virtue we may be trained up, and fitted and prepared to live in heaven. For this purpose God hath laid open before us, so to speak, four books, in each of which he is represented as the Father and Friend of man.

The first is the book of *Creation!* "Heavens that declare the glory of God; a firmament that sheweth his handy work; days and nights teaching knowledge;" a whole world to make us understand "his eternal power and Godhead," and to inform us that the Father of spirits is the Father of the rain, and the Father of all our mercies, and all our comforts of every kind. Read the two first chapters of Genesis, the book of Job, the hundred and fourth Psalm, the fortieth chapter of Isaiah, and other passages of scripture, which describe the world in which we live; and expounding what you read by what you see in the world, acknowledge that the wisdom and goodness of God to man are laid open in a manner so clear, as to fill us with a conviction that he is, and that he is the object of our chief confidence and esteem, "a rewarder of them that diligently seek him." It is he that "giveth to all nations of men life, and breath, and all things." It is he that "determined our times, and appointed the bounds of our habitation." It is he "in whom we live, and move, and have our being;"

and we " are his offspring," the offspring of God. It is he
who is " not far from every one of us." To use the language of an Apostle, let us " feel after him, if haply we
may find him."

See here, I hold a Bible in my hand, and you see the
cover, the leaves, the letters, and the words; but you do
not see the writers or the printers, the letter-founder, the
ink-maker, the paper-maker, or the binder. You never
did see them, you never will see them, and yet there is not
one of you who will think of disputing or denying the being
of these men. · I go further: I affirm that you see the very
souls of these men in seeing this book; and you feel yourselves obliged to allow that they had skill, contrivance,
design, memory, fancy, reason, and so on. ' In the same
manner, if you see a picture, you judge there was a painter; if you see a house, you judge there was a builder of
it; and if you see one room contrived for this purpose,
and another for that; a door to enter, a window to admit
light, a chimney to hold fire, you conclude that the builder
was a person of skill and forecast, who formed the house
with a view to the accommodation of its inhabitants. In
this manner examine the world, and pity the man who,
when he sees the sign of the wheat-sheaf, has sense enough
to know that there is somewhere a joiner, and somewhere
a painter; but who, when he sees the wheat-sheaf itself,
is so stupid as not to say to himself,—This creature had
a wise and good Creator.

It is impossible for me, in this place, to pursue this part
of our subject fully, and therefore I shall conclude it with
two words of advice, and I give you these on this principle, that a little thought of your own, on any subject, is of
more worth to you than all the thoughts of other men
sounding in your ears, or clattering through your lips. I
have that confidence in your memories, that I do think I
could soon teach you to utter these words—causes—effects—combinations—proportions—circulations--equipoise
—uniformity—variety—series of events—gravitation—and
so on: and I would do so, if you would give me leave, did
I not know that, after all my teaching, and your repeat-
ing what I taught you, you would know just as much of
the subject as a musical instrument does of the tune play-

ed upon it.   Would-you not rather be the herdman's poor-
boy, than the finest instrument of music ?   Think for
yourselves, if you think ever so little.

My first word of advice is, Read the account of the six
days-works of creation, contained in the first chapter of
Genesis, and read it over and over again; let your chil-.
dren get it by heart, so that they may all understand what
Moses intended to teach; that is, that God made the heavens and the earth, and all that is therein.

My second word of advice is,—Attend diligently to the
properties, qualities, characters, laws (what shall I call
them) of creation.   Observe one word of Moses; he says,
" the heavens and the earth were finished, and all the
host of them."   Observe the word *host ;* it signifies army :
and Moses resembled the collection of creatures, which
we call *the world*, to such a collection of men as we call
an *army*, for the sake of putting people upon thinking of
several articles not mentioned in the history.   For example : when you see an army, you think of a commanding
officer, whose order the army obeys, and which, properly
speaking, is his power, the general's power to protect or
to destroy.   An army makes us think of wisdom that disposed the men in order, and put them in various ranks, and
disciplined them with one design, to perform various exercises, to produce one great end.   Hence you will trace
the laws, orders, and rules of moving and acting, which
prevail through the whole creation, up to " the king,
whose name is the Lord of Hosts ; who measured the waters in the hollow of his hand, who meted out heaven with
a span, who weighed the mountains in scales, and the hills
in a balance ; who hangeth the earth upon nothing ; who
bindeth up waters in thick clouds, and the cloud is not
rent under them ; who made a weight for the winds, a
decree for the rain, a way for the lightning and the thunder ;   who gave goodly wings unto the peacock, and
sent out the wild ass free ; who deprived the ostrich of
the wisdom of preserving her eggs and her young ; who
taught the hawk to fly toward the south, and the eagle
to make her nest upon the crag of the rock ; who feeds
man as a shepherd feeds his flock, and carries him in his
bosom ;" who doth all this without direction or control;

and who, though " all nations before him are as nothing, less than nothing, and vanity ;" and though all the whole world is not sufficient for one offering to him, yet condescends, kind Father that he is, to instruct man, and to " say unto him, Behold, the fear of the Lord, that is wisdom, and to depart from evil is understanding."

The second book for us to read is that of *Providence.* The doctrine of providence, like that of creation, is abundantly taught in the Holy Scriptures ; and our Saviour represents God in Providence, under what I will venture to call his favourite notion of God, the idea of a Father. " One sparrow shall not fall on the ground, without your Father : your Father knoweth that ye have need of meat, and drink, and clothing." Let it not seem strange to you, that God is considered as the friend of a sparrow ; for it is no more beneath the majesty of God to provide for a mean animal, than it is for him to create it.

If you would attend to this subject properly, you must distinguish two sorts of providence ; the one I call natural, the other moral : but I will explain myself. By *natural providence*, I mean that wise care which God hath taken so to dispose all his works, as to make them produce the end for which they were created, which respects all things that do not come under the description of good and bad, righteous and wicked. There is a dependence of one thing upon another, like links in a chain, among all the creatures in the world. These words of Hosea will explain my meaning : " The Lord saith, I will hear the heavens, and they shall hear the earth, and the earth shall hear the corn, and the wine, and the oil ; and they shall hear Jezreel." Jezreel is either the son of the prophet, or the inhabitants of a place called Jezreel. The health and strength, the rest and the lives of these people depended on corn, and wine, and oil. Corn and wine and oil depended on the earth ; the earth depended on the heavens, that is, the dew, the air, the sun ; and all these depended upon God ; and on this account the Lord calls all the productions of the earth his own. " She did not know that I gave her corn, and wine, and oil, and multiplied her silver and gold"—she said, " my lovers give me my bread and my water, my wool and my flax"—but I the Lord will

" return, and take away my corn and my wine, and will recover my wool and my flax ;" and by so doing, I will instruct these ignorant and forgetful children, that I " cause
the bud of the tender herb to spring" forth ; that I am the
" Father of the rain," the Author of " the drops of the
dew," the Creator of ice, the Parent of the "hoary frost
of heaven," and of all the powers and productions of the
world. This is the wisdom which Solomon sent the sluggard to an ant-hill to learn ; and it is on supposition that
we observe these things, that the Scriptures direct us to
consider how lilies grow, how ravens live, and what attention oxen and asses pay to their owners. This should
teach us to be humane and kind to animals, because animals have no depravity, the peacock no pride, the
horse no malice, the bee no anger ; the fowls that take
your seed do not steal it ; the cattle that break your
fences have no guilt for doing so ; for they have a charter, which says, " I, God, have given every herb, and
every tree to you for meat ; and to every beast of the
earth, and to every fowl of the air, and to every thing
that creepeth upon the earth wherein there is life, I have
given every green herb for meat :" but " let man have
dominion over them" all. You, little boys, while I think
of it, let me give you a lesson. Do not make yourselves
sport with what gives other creatures pain. Do not torment and kill frogs, birds, and flies. You would not, I am
sure, hack, and chop, and torture my horse, or my cow, or
my milch-ass, or my chickens, because they are mine ;
and though you may not love them, yet you would not
hurt them for love of me. Remember, my good boys, all
live creatures belong to Almighty God, and he will be displeased with you if you hurt them. When you become
men, you will know that some animals, like some men,
must be put to death for the safety of the rest ; but none
are put to death, except such as do mischief to others ;
and the way for you to come to that end is to learn, by
tormenting and killing animals, how in time to pluck up
your hearts, and murder men.

By *moral Providence*, I mean that connexion which God
hath established between virtue and happiness, vice and
misery ; and by which he discovers himself the just pro-

3

tector of goodness, and the punisher of wickedness. Glut.
tony, drunkenness, and debauchery, are attended with diseases, and often death itself. Envy, malice, and revenge,
are productive of uneasiness, guilt, and shame. Conscience makes man happy when he does right, and miserable when he does wrong; and it is here, in the heart,
that you are to look for this kind of government of God,
and not in the outward circumstances of your neighbours.
In some cases, it is not in the power of outward calamities
to make a man unhappy! in other cases, the stings of conscience are so piercing and keen, that it is not in the power of all the wealth and splendor in the world to make a
man happy. Do not judge of this moral order by the
stroke of a thunderbolt, the falling of the tower in Siloam,
the cruelty of Pilate to the Galileans: but look at the king
of an hundred and twenty-seven provinces, who could not
command one night's rest. Look at the king walking in
his palace, and saying, " is not this great Babylon, that I
have built for the honour of my majesty?" See his pride
distracts him; he is " driven from men, and eats grass like
an ox." Observe the restlessness of cruel Pharaoh, the
convulsions of carousing Belshazzar, the distress of treacherous Saul, and the despair of covetous Judah. So true is
that saying, whether we see it or not; " The wicked man
travelleth with pain all his days; a dreadful sound is in
his ears; trouble and anguish prevail against him, as a
king ready to the battle; and he knoweth that the day of
darkness is ready at his hand." All these discover God
as the Father and Friend of piety, justice, and benevolence; and so a " Father of the fatherless," and the husband of the desolate widow. So the " poor hath hope,
and iniquity stoppeth her mouth."

The third book is literally that of *Scripture*. My brethren, know the worth of this book; it may serve to you for
a life of uncommon length, a genius of uncommon pene-
tration, and an experience of uncommon exertion. The
Bible, as a history, makes you acquainted with the substance of all that passed in the world worth remembering,
for the space of four thousand years, and upwards. By acquainting yourselves with this history, you will seem to be
alive with Adam, to outlive the flood, to travel with Abra-

ham, Isaac, and Jacob; to go down into Egypt, to come
out through the wilderness and Red Sea with Moses, to
sit with the Judges, to reign with Solomon, to weep in
captivity with Ezekiel, to return to Judea with Nehemiah, to see John the Baptist, to hear Jesus Christ, and to
go with his apostles over various countries. By acquainting yourselves with this book, you will understand a thousand subjects, which otherwise you could never know.
You will sit in the councils of princes, dive into the designs of armies, see through the temples of idols, behold the
various modes of worshipping the true God; yea, you will
be admitted into the councils of God, and " know the
thoughts of peace he thinks towards you."

By acquainting yourselves with this, you will have
all the benefit, without the pain of experiment. All the
trials of Solomon to make himself happy in creatures; all
the trial of Jonah to protect himself in disobedience to
God; all the exercises of Job under affliction, and of David in raptures of devotion; all the pain of Peter when
he fell; and all the pleasure of Paul under persecution;
all these will be yours: advantages which a long life, a
fine genius, and a thousand trials could not have procured
you. If you attend properly to this book, I am confident
you will say, " these things were our examples, to the intent we should not lust after evil things, as they lusted."
One will say, " I will not be an idolater, as were some of
them; as it is written,—The people sat down to eat and
drink, and rose up to play :" another will say, I will " not
commit fornication, as some of them committed, and fell
in one day three and twenty thousand :" a third will say,
I will " not tempt Christ, as some of them tempted, and
were destroyed of serpents :" a fourth will say, I will " not
murmur, as some of them also murmured and were destroyed of the destroyer." In every period of this history,
God seems to say of each of us, " wilt thou not, from this
time, cry unto me, My Father, thou art the guide of my
youth? Thou shalt call me, My Father, and shalt not turn
away from me.

The last book, in which you may read the favour and
friendship of God, is *Jesus Christ*, whose person indeed is
in heaven; but who, by his history, contained in the four

Gospels, may be said, in some sense, to be living, and walking, and preaching among us. I am sorry to say, the coming of such a person, on such an errand, into this world, supposes that we were ignorant, wicked, and idle children. Such children might well be afraid to go home at night to a father, whom they could not but know they had grievously offended. Our heavenly Father knew this, and " so loved the world, that he sent his only begotten Son, the brightness of his glory," to calm our fears; his own exact likeness, as far as man could represent God, to publish his eternal love to his abandoned family, and to declare, that whosoever believed in Jesus Christ, how poor, how wicked, how wretched soever he had been, need not be afraid of the gloom of death, and the midnight of eternity, but " should have everlasting life." Such good news, so undeserved, and so far beyond the manner of man, demanded proof of an extraordinary kind; and this proof Jesus Christ gave by fulfilling prophecy, and working miracles; which he wrought not for the sake of ostentation, but to fix beyond a doubt, in this forlorn world, full and everlasting proof of the truth of his doctrine. Draw near to this *express image* of God, ye ignorant and disobedient children! See, in his eyes, how the God of thunder, and lightning, and terror, will look at you. Behold, you are the prodigal son, and he is the Father, who sees you, and " has compassion, and runs and falls on your neck, and kisses you, and says, Bring forth the best robe, and put it on him, and put a ring on his hand, and shoes on his feet; and bring hither the fatted calf, and kill it, and let us eat and be merry; for this my son was dead, and is alive again; he was lost, and is found." Do not say, this is an old history of what was done eighteen hundred years ago: no such thing, it is a history of all ages, and hath been doing every day, from the time in which " the voice of the Lord God walked in the garden of Eden in the cool of the day, and said unto Adam, where art thou? Hast thou eaten of the tree whereof I commanded thee that thou shouldest not eat?" Did the serpent beguile thee? " Cursed be the serpent above all cattle: but the seed of the woman shall bruise the serpent's head." Every penitent, convicted in his own conscience, and returning to

God, through Jesus Christ, meets with a like treatment, and " receiveth the spirit of adoption, whereby he cries, Abba, Father. Wherefore he is no more a servant, but a son ; and if a son, then an heir of God through Christ."

If you would learn more of this subject, inquire of " the woman taken in adultery," condemned to be stoned by Moses in the law, exposed by her fellow sinners, and referred to Jesus Christ. Ask her how he looked, and in what tone he spoke, when he said, " Woman, where are thine accusers? Hath no man condemned thee? Neither do I condemn thee ; go, and sin no more." Ask that other woman, " who was a sinner," who durst not look him in the face, but " stood at his feet, behind him, weeping ;" ask her to describe the melody of that voice that said, " There was a certain creditor which had two debtors, the one owed five hundred pence, and the other fifty, and when they had nothing to pay, he frankly forgave them both." I venture to affirm, that the great apostle Peter never had ability enough fully to express the wisdom, the tender compassion, and the irresistible power of that one act, contained in one line of an evangelist, " the Lord turned, and looked upon Peter :" and that Paul never was able fully to express the tone of that voice, which said unto him, " Saul, Saul, why persecutest thou me ?" For " the love of Chris passeth knowledge," and is " able to do exceeding abundantly, above all that we ask or think." To use the language of the last mentioned apostle, " Jesus Christ shewed forth exceeding abundant grace, and love, and longsuffering" in these cases, " for a pattern to them which should hereafter believe on him to life everlasting."

In these four ways our heavenly Father makes known his esteem for us ; and wilfully blind is that worthless child who doth not perceive it. I quit the subject with reluctance ; but as it is nearly time to conclude, I will close with one remark, which, I earnestly pray God, may improve our hearts, and amend our lives.

There are four sorts of people, each differently affected towards " our Father, who is in heaven." The first are *without* him . . . the second are *against* him . . . the third *dread* him . . . and the last, of which sort may you all be,— the last *love* and adore him.

4*

Some men are " without God in the world ;" and to such a degree of inattention hath a habit of sin brought them, that they are blind amidst all the light of proofs that there is a God, and dead to all the feelings that his fatherly goodness ought to excite in their hearts. Do not deceive yourselves : it is impossible to know God, and not love and obey him ; and you yourselves prove this. Did you ever spend one half hour in your life to inquire into this question, " Where is God, my maker, who teacheth me more than the beasts of the earth, and maketh me wiser than the fowls of heaven ?" On the contrary, do not all your actions " say unto God, Depart from me, for I desire not the knowledge of thy ways ? What is the Almighty, that I should serve him ? What can the Almighty do for me ? and what profit should I have if I pray unto him ?" Do you not " go in company with workers of iniquity," like yourself, and " walk with wicked men," who say, " It profiteth a man nothing that he should delight himself with God ?" Poor child ! The Scripture pronounceth thee *a fool.* Well, go on ; follow that great ideot Pharaoh, and continue to say, " Who is the Lord, that I should obey his voice ? I know not the Lord, neither will I obey his voice :" but settle as you go toward the gulf, where, like Pharaoh, you will " sink into the bottom as a stone ;" I say, think of this dreadful question, and come to some conclusion about it :—" Who *ever* hardened himself against God, and prospered ?"

Stupid as this first class of men is, the second is more so ; those men I mean, who set themselves *against* God. These are said, in Scripture, to hate God, and to resist him. What a character, what a monstrous character, my brethren, is this, *haters of God !* I know no men who so justly deserve this character, as they who hate and persecute good men for being religious ; yet, in general, all who oppose the great design of God, our heavenly Father, in creating the world and redeeming the church, may very properly be said to be at enmity with God. God intends to make his children happy, by giving them life, liberty, property, reason, religion, and so on. A murderer, by taking away the life of another, expresses his hatred of God's design of making the other happy by life. A tyrant, who deprives a person of liberty, resists the design of God in making his children happy, by making them free. A miser who hoards wealth, and a thief who steals it, both resist the design of God, which was to make men happy by giving them property. A persecutor, who will not allow people to be governed in the choice of a religion by their own convictions, but requires all to act according to his wisdom, or perhaps his folly and worldly interest, he also withstands the design of God, which was to make all his children happy, each by the exercise of his own reason. A bigot, who will suffer no sense of Scripture but his own, and that perhaps doubtful or false, and taxes the Gospel itself with being of his spirit, he also is a reviler of the Gospel, an enemy to the religion of his neighbours, and an antagonist, contending against God. Let us lay aside all these wicked dispositions, and remember that great lesson given from heaven to a man of this sort, " It is hard to kick against the pricks ;" which either means, that it is impossible to succeed in attempting to oppose God ; or that all such attempts come from the hardness or insensibility of our own hearts. Had we such feelings for mankind, as children of the same parent ought to have for one another ; or had we such emotions towards God as children ought to have for such a Father, we should not make these rash attempts.

Our third class are objects of pity ; they are not without God ; they do not set themselves against him ; but they *dread* him ; that is, their fear of God is excessive. The cause of this dread is a partial knowledge of God. Recollect what I said to you sometime ago, concerning knowing only part of a subject. This is your case : you have attended to the judgments of God ; to his threatenings against the wicked, and to that punishment which awaits them in another state ; but you have not turned your attention to the mercy of God, expressed in his promises, and in his dispensations of goodness to other sinners in your condition. Suppose I could take a person out of this assembly, one who had never seen the sea, and carry him in an instant to the seaside, and set him down there ; and suppose the sea at that instant to be in a storm ; the great, black, and dismal clouds rolling, thunders bellowing, lightnings flashing, the winds roaring, the sea dashing ten thousand watery mountains one against another, the beach covered with shattered timber and cordage, mer- chandise and corpses; this man would instantly conceive a dreadful idea of the sea, and would shudder, and shriek, and flee for his life. It would be hard to give this man a pleasant notion of the sea, especially if he had been well informed that several of his relations and friends had per- ished in the tempest; yet this man would have but half a right notion of the sea; for could he be prevailed on to go down to the beach a few days after, the heavens would smile, the air be serene, the water smooth, the seamen whistling and singing, here a vessel of trade sailing before the wind, there a fleet of men of war coming into har- bour, yonder pleasure-boats basking in the sun, the flute making melody of the breeze, the company, even the soft- er sex, enjoying themselves without fear; this man would form the other half-notion of the sea; and the two put to- gether would be the just and true idea of it. Apply this to our subject. You have seen your heavenly Father re- prove Adam, chide Moses, drown the old world, burn the cities of the plain, cause the earth to open and swallow up Dathan and his company, send a Joseph to prison, put a Jeremiah into a dungeon, and a Daniel into a den of lions; you have seen him fell a Paul down to the earth; not on- ly kill an Ananias and Sapphira upon the spot, but strike a Zechariah dumb, and cleave the heart of even a Peter asunder with recollection and repentance; but go back to these persons, and see a Paul " preaching the faith which he once destroyed;" a Peter " begotten again unto a live- ly hope by the resurrection of Jesus Christ from the dead;" a Zechariah filled with the Holy Ghost, and singing, " Blessed be the Lord God of Israel, through whose ten- der mercy the dayspring from on high hath visited us, and hath delivered us out of the hands of our enemies, that we might serve him without fear, in holiness, all the days of our life." I might go further, and affirm, that your confidence in God ought to be as much greater than your dread, as his mercies are greater than his punishments. True, five wicked cities are burned; but how many fives are preserved! one Zechariah is struck dumb for unbelief; but how many unbelievers have the gift of speech! And you, yourself, how many comforts to set against one twig of his rod! Do not add ingratitude to fear; but listen to these words, sweeter than honey and the honeycomb; "Who is among you that feareth the Lord, that obeyeth the voice of his servant, that walketh in darkness, and hath no light? let him trust in the name of the Lord, and stay upon his God."

The last class *love* God and adore him. They have studied his excellent nature, and are fully persuaded, there is nothing in him to inspire his children with horror, but every thing to animate them with esteem. They have examined his works, and they exclaim concerning the whole world, "Behold, it is very good." The good man every day considers his dispensations of Providence; how "he leads men forth by the right way, to a city of habitation;" how "he filleth the hungry soul with goodness;" how he "sends his word, and heals" the sick; how he makes the storm a calm, and brings men who have been at their wits end unto their desired haven; how he makes the fields and vineyards yield fruits of increase; how he poureth contempt upon princes, and yet setteth the poor on high from affliction. The good man is "wise, and observes these things, and so understands the loving kindness of the Lord;" he searches the holy Scriptures, and beholds in all a God of inexpressible goodness and love, "pitying them that fear him, like as a father pitieth his children. Mercy great, above the heavens; truth, reaching unto the clouds; compassion, from everlasting to everlasting; goodness, kept for thousands;" an eminence of perfections "exalted above all blessing and praise." The good man is captivated with the character of God, as it is displayed in Jesus Christ: him he accounts fairer than the children of men. Grace, he thinks, is poured into his lips; and to him he saith, "Thy throne, O God, is forever and ever: the sceptre of thy kingdom is a right sceptre. Thou lovest righteousness, and hatest wickedness" more than all mankind; "therefore God, thy God, hath anointed thee with the oil of gladness above thy fellows." Full of these ideas, and full of blessings and good wishes toward all mankind, the good man waits for his dissolution ; hoping he shall go down by soft and easy steps, fast hold of that friend who was born to serve him in adversity, into the grave, and thence rise into the temple of that God, in whose presence is fulness of joy, and at whose " right hand there are pleasures for evermore."

DISCOURSE III.

———

[AT HAUXTON.]

PSALM xvi. 6.

The lines are fallen unto me in pleasant places ; yea, I have
a goodly heritage.

" True," says one of my hearers, " you had a goodly heritage, David; and I would say of my lot, as you did of yours,
had I a Jesse for my father, a Solomon for my son, a palace for my habitation, gold and silver in abundance, ability to write scripture, and hope in a joyful resurrection :"
but, recollect, if David had a Jesse for his own father, he
had a Saul for his father-in-law ; if he had one son a Solomon, he had others who were disobedient, rebellious, and
wicked; if he had a palace, he could not sometimes get an
hour's rest in it; he was " weary with groaning, made his
bed every night to swim, and watered his couch with his
tears ;" if he had riches, and abilities, and religion, he had
also a lady for his wife who ridiculed religion, and despised him for employing his wealth and abilities in the
service of it. In a word, happiness is distributed among
mankind much more equally than most men imagine. My
design, this evening, is to convince you of this, to persuade
you to apply the language of the text to your own lot,
and so to engage you to offer to Almighty God that noble
evening sacrifice of content, gratitude, and praise.

Do not suppose, I am insensible of your afflictions. How
is it possible, that a man, like yourselves, subject to the
same sickness and pain, and calamities, and death, should
be blind to such events ? Even self-love obliges us to feel
for others what we fear ourselves. I say more, I affirm
that God himself " sees the affliction of his people, hears

their cry, knows their sorrows, considers all the oppress
ions that are done under the sun, beholds the tears of th
oppressed who have no comforter," and with a sympathy
beyond all conception, delicate and tender, reaches out i
religion his own soft hand to " wipe away tears from al
faces."

This sixteenth psalm is quoted by the apostle Peter, i
his first sermon after the pouring out of the Holy Ghost
and applied to Jesus Christ: but the reason given by th
apostle, why the latter part of the psalm was not fulfille
in David, furnisheth us with a reason why the former par
of the psalm was fully accomplished in him. The latte
part of the psalm speaks of rising from the dead befor
the body of the deceased person began to decay. Thi
was not true of David; but it was true of one of his fami
ly, Jesus Christ, and of him David spoke in the characte
of a prophet: but the former part of the psalm speaks o
living contented, and holy, and happy under the protectio
of God in this world; and all this David experienced i
his own person. He was willing to profit us, by telling
his own experience, and therefore " said unto the Lord
My goodness extendeth not to thee, but to the saints tha
are in the earth, and to the excellent in whom is all m
delight." With this view he describes, in the fourtl
verse, the misery of such as live in idolatrous countries
" their sorrows shall be multiplied, that hasten after anoth
er God;" and the happy situation of himself and others,
who had an inheritance in a land where the true God was
known and worshipped. He calls his family estate a *lot*,
because, when Joshua divided the land of Canaan among
the tribes of Israel, to prevent all disputes, and in obedience to the express command of God by Moses, they drew
lots for their parcels of land; and as some families, in all
the tribes, were fewer than other families, these lots were
subdivided, and measured out by a *line*. " Many had the
more inheritance, and few the less inheritance, to every family according to the number of names." Thus God " casi
out the heathen, and divided his people an inheritance by
line, and made the tribes of Israel to dwell in their tents."
The lot of the tribe of Judah is exactly described in the
fifteenth chapter of Joshua; and the book of Ruth is a

pleasant history of the manner in which Boaz, the great grandfather of David, lived on the family estate.

My brethren, of such importance to the present and everlasting happiness of man is the knowledge of the true God, that we ought to prefer the condition of a beggar in the streets of a christian country, or that of a patient in a hospital, yea more, that of an unfortunate debtor in a county jail, in such a country, before that of the most rich and prosperous emperor in heathen ignorance and wickedness. Heathen countries are "dark places of the earth, full of habitations of cruelty," and "the curse of the Lord is in every house of the wicked!" "O!" said the holy Psalmist, "deliver not the soul of thy turtle-dove unto the multitude of the wicked!" If, therefore, I were only able to convince you, that in this valley of trouble there was a door of hope, that your dreary path led to your Father's house in heaven, I should have a right to require you to say, "The lines are fallen unto me in pleasant places; yea, I have a goodly heritage:" but though I am going to endeavour to convince you of this, yet I shall not content myself with this, but shall prove that you have so many accommodations on the road, that nothing but ignorance and ingratitude can make you discontented.

I will not conceal from you the principle on which I go in this discourse. I deny myself the pleasure of examining the general laws of Providence, by which the whole world is governed, from the smallest particle of dust to the noblest creature in it. It would be delightful, delightful beyond expression, to trace the wisdom and goodness, the power and the justice of God, through every part of his dominion: but it is with the mind as it is with the hand; if we would grasp too much, we lose all. Instead, then, of attempting to refresh you with the smell of all the flowers in the world put together, I pluck one, and bring you to night the Providence of God as it regards yourselves, the inhabitants of this little village, this very little spot of the boundless territory of God. Let us go to the subject.

Consider first *the age* of the world in which you live. Carry back your attention to the state of the world nearly six thousand years ago, and consider what a dreary desert the earth was before any of the works of art had been employed to render it an agreeable habitation. There was the same sun, the same rains, the same winds, the same tempests, the same long cold winters, in which Providence "gave snow like wool, scattered hoar frost like ashes, cast forth ice like morsels," and made men cry, "Who can stand before the cold?" I say, there were the same inclemencies of seasons as now: but where were the carpenters, bricklayers, thatchers, colliers, clothiers, and all that multitude of benefactors, who contribute to the pleasure and safety of life? Even within the memory of some present, instruments of husbandry, and common conveniencies of life, have been rendered far more handy and commodious than they were formerly. In those ages, one part of the world produced one kind of fruits, and animals, and foods, and another part of the world produced different sorts; and hence, in those times, little variety, great scarcity, and frequent famine, in which men, like vultures, tore one another in pieces for the necessaries of life. We need not go so far back; we will just glance at our own country a few hundred years ago. There were no printed books, no paper, no spectacles, no glass, no clocks, no candles, no fireplaces, no linen, no silver or gold for common uses; the women rode astride through the streets of the best cities, in the mud; and wine was sold only by apothecaries, as a cordial, and hence came the word *dram*, which signified the eighth part of an ounce, the quantity then taken by our ancestors at a time. It would be endless, and almost incredible, to relate the abject condition of all nations, in the first periods of their history. They always appear one degree above a herd of cattle, and no more.

Let no one think we are trifling, and got out of the bounds of scriptural instruction. It is lamented in sacred history, that at a certain time there was "no smith found throughout all the land of Israel; but all the Israelites went down to the Philistines, to sharpen every man his share and his coulter, and his axe and his mattock; so that in the day of battle there was neither sword nor spear found in the hand of any of the people that were with Saul and Jonathan." It was very proper, therefore, for an inspired writer to make honourable mention of one, who taught men to dwell in tents, and of another, who instructed artificers how to work in brass and iron. How think you, my brethren, when God shall judge the world, and the two men shall stand before him, one the Tubal Cain, who taught men to work iron, and the other, king Jeroboam, who taught Israel to sin; which of these two men will appear most respectable in the eyes of the Judge, and of all mankind? For my part, I look upon the smith in a parish, as a disciple of Tubal Cain, and I respect him, because he contributes to your ease in the field; to your pleasure, when you travel; to your safety by locks and bolts at home; and to your defence in case of danger; and what I say of him, I affirm of every one, who hath contributed in former times, or who doth contribute now, to render life easy and agreeable: and when I observe, that *others* have been *labouring* for almost six thousand years, in their several occupations, for us, and that we are entered into their labours, that one soweth and another reapeth, and that we reap that whereon we bestowed no labour; I cannot help exclaiming with the text, " The lines are fallen unto me in pleasant places; yea, I have a goodly heritage!" Our condition resembles that of the Israelites, and God hath placed us in a land, " to give us great and goodly cities, which we builded not; houses full of all good things, which we filled not; wells, which we digged not; and gardens, and orchards, and trees, which we planted not." Observe, my brethren, what the man of God added to all this,—" Then beware lest thou forget the Lord;" beware, lest you be ignorant of your first benefactor, the instructer of all artists among mankind, and ungrateful to him, who " created the smith that bloweth the coals in the fire, and that bringeth forth an instrument for his work;" who " instructed the plowman to open and break the clods of his ground," to harrow and roll, and make smooth the face thereof, to cast wheat in the principal place, or in the strongest soil, and rye and barley in

soils appointed for them; who gave man discretion to
beat out vetches with a staff, and to thresh cummin
with a rod, to bruise bread-corn, and so to prepare
nourishment for himself, and his family, and his neighbours. All these " come from the Lord of Hosts, who
is wonderful in counsel, and excellent in working ;" and
all these demand of us a tribute of gratitude and praise.
Every time, therefore, that you take a receipt, or write
a date, or hear the sound of One thousand seven hundred and sixty, or eighty, remember the text, and think,
".The lines are fallen unto me in pleasant times, yea, I
have a goodly heritage."

Consider next *the country* which you inhabit. Could
you rise so high as to see all the kingdoms of the earth
roll under your eye ; could you survey them all as easily as you can a terrier of your lands, you would
feel a disposition to prefer this in which you dwell, and
of your being born in which you may truly say, " Not
unto us, O Lord, not unto us ; but unto thy name we
give glory." I say nothing of those burning countries,
where the heaven over head is brass, and the earth
under the feet iron ; where the sun rises more like a
strong man to destroy, than like a " bridegroom coming
out of his chamber" to make men rejoice : nothing of
those frozen countries, where God " sealeth up the hand
of every man," and where he " reserves treasures of
snow and hail against the day of battle :" nothing of
those dreadful countries, where whirlwinds and earth-
quakes, and thunder, and lightning, and hurricanes, destroy all the hope of man ; where the God of glory
thundereth so as to break the cedars, to shake the wilderness, to make huge mountains skip like calves, to
force the hinds to calve, and to strip whole districts bare
of every green thing : nothing of those countries, where
fevers, inflammations, extreme burning, and diseases
peculiar to the situation, kill the wretched inhabitants :
so we read of " the botch of Egypt." I say nothing of these ;
for which of these do we desire ? Nor will I detain
you to observe the natural advantages of our country,
which is the first in the world : an island guarded by
the ocean, and open to all its treasures, with docks and

harbours to our utmost wishes : a land productive of corn, herbs, grass, timber, and fruits : a country water- ed with the dews and the rains of heaven, feeding in- numerable springs and wells, and navigable rivers : a land, out of whose hills you may dig brass, iron, stone, marble, coals, clay, marles, and innumerable articles of daily use : a land that maintains cattle, fowls, flocks, dairies, hives, and a thousand other classes, labouring for the inhabitants. I will not enlarge on these advan- tages, nor will I at present speak of the improved state of husbandry, building, trade, learning, and the other ornaments of our country.

Let me, however, be allowed to observe what more immediately concerns you all ; that is, the civil liberty we enjoy. The life of the meanest of you all is so guarded by the law, that in the heat of the day, after you have mowed half an acre of grass, you may lie down and refresh yourself by sleep at the end of the swathes ; and should any daring hand take away your life, your blood would be required of the murderer by the hand of the magistrate. What God formerly said of the patriarchs, the law of England saith of every one of you ; yea more, of every limb of every one of you : " Touch not mine anointed, and do my prophets no harm." Your property, little or much, is equally guarded by law. No master can " keep back the hire of the la- bourers, who have reaped down his fields ;" nor can any man deprive you of what you have, without your consent. You may lay it up, or lay it out ; you may give it to others, or spend it on yourself ; you are the absolute lord of your little all. I love to see the plow- man leave his coat at the land's end, and the gleaner trust her gleans, her bread, and her bottle, on a balk ; and I always conceive of the law, as a wall of fire round about them. The law saith, in effect, he that toucheth you ; he that toucheth your garden-stuff, your fruit, your cattle, your poultry, your linen on the hedge, any thing that is yours, " toucheth the apple of mine eye." Your freedom, too, is fully established, except in one single case, which regards the settlements of the poor ; and that case hath been taken up by a humane gentleman

4*

in this country, and I hope in due time will be attended
to. Except that, your freedom is fully established. You
may live where you please, go and come when you
please, and do what you please, provided you injure no
other person. You need never want a day's work if
you be well, nor the necessaries of life if you be sick.
In other countries the life of a subject is at the will of
his lord: property in some countries they have none,
the poor are property themselves, the slaves and beasts
of the gentry, who buy and sell them with their estates.
There are subjects on which no conversation may be
allowed, and there is nothing but one general slavery;
like Egypt, the whole country is resembled to a large
jail, a house of bondage, in which the chains of some are
of iron, and those of others are of gold; but all are in
slavery, and have no deliverer to set them free. Oh
happy people of this country! your " garners afford all
manner of store; your sheep" (they are your own, remember) " bring forth thousands, and may bring forth
ten thousands in your streets; your oxen may be stronger to labour" than those of others: you may be, on account of your advantages, an object of envy, but you
cannot be subject to plunder; for there is no violent
" breaking in, no complaining in your streets! Happy
is that people that is in such a case! The lines are
fallen unto them in pleasant places; yea, they have a
goodly heritage." Whenever you hear the sound of
these words, parish-rates . . . constable . . . justice of
peace . . . assizes . . . law . . . liberty . . . property . . .
life . . . recollect the text, and remember your happiness;
for " touching the bone and the flesh" often makes a
man " curse God to his face. Skin for skin, yea, all that
a man hath, will he give for his life."

If this article ought to affect other men, it ought
much more to stir up thankfulness in husbandmen. Almost all the property of a farmer lies abroad: your cattle are abroad night and day; the corn of last harvest
lies abroad in stacks; the hay and fodder for the winter
lie abroad; your firing lies abroad; the wheat of next
year is abroad, and the tender blade is exposed to danger; yet all these in this country lie safely. It is not

so in some other countries now; it was not so with Job formerly.   Job was at home sacrificing to God, his ten children were feasting at their eldest brother's house, when, lo, a messenger came, and said " the Sabeans fell upon the oxen and asses, and took them away; and they have slain the servants with the edge of the sword:" another came and said, " the Chaldeans made out three bands, and fell upon the camels, and have carried them away."   And thus the greatest of all the men of the East was in one day reduced to a state of extreme poverty; and all that his friends could do was to try to comfort him under his losses.   It is more desirable not to be exposed to such sufferings, than to have friends to comfort us under them.

Consider further the *religion* of this country.   Though we are not all christians, yet there are many societies of true Christians among us; and we are in a country where nothing but our own obstinacy can prevent our being Christians ourselves.   To be a Christian, it is necessary there should be a Christ, a person appointed to redeem us from ignorance, guilt, and inaction.   There is such a person; we know where he was born, how he lived, what he taught, how he was put to death, whither he is gone, what is to be done in his absence, when he will come again, how he will reckon with all mankind, and give up the kingdom to his Father.   It is necessary we should have full proof of the truth of all this; and such is the connexion which the wisdom of God hath established between prophecy and promise, that every travelling Jew is himself a living witness to establish the truth of our holy religion.

To be a Christian, it is necessary to have the holy Scriptures: you have them in you own mother tongue, so cheap that any body may buy the book, and so plain that the meanest creature may understand it.   If any one be so extremely poor, that he cannot purchase a bible, the charity of other Christians will bestow it for nothing: and if any one cannot read it himself, other Christians will read it to him.   How often have I had the honor of doing this for some of you!   We had in our congregation a poor, aged widow, who could neither read the Scriptures, nor live without hearing them read; so much instruction and pleasure did she derive from the oracles of God. She lived in a lone place, and the family where she lodged could not read; but .there was one more cottage near, and in it a little boy, a shepherd's son, who could read; but he, full of play, was not fond of reading the Bible. Necessity is the mother of invention. The old widow determined to rise one hour sooner in a morning, to spin one haif-penny more, to be expended in hiring the shepherd's boy to read to her every evening a chapter; to which he readily agreed. This little advantage made her content in her cottage, and even say, " The lines are fallen to me in pleasant places." You, little boys, learn to read, and read the Scriptures, to comfort the old people about you. Perhaps you may make lame and blind people say, for your sakes, " The lines are fallen unto us in pleasant places ; yea, we have a goodly heritage."

To be a Christian, it is necessary to judge of what we read, or hear read, and to form sentiments of our own concerning it. You have judgment and full liberty to make use of it. You may, if you think it necessary to salvation, enter into all the questions debated among Christians, and, take what side you will, you risk nothing. You may worship God in what form your conscience approves; and " who is he that will harm you, if ye be followers of that which is good?" In some countries there is, established by law, what is called a public faith; and in such countries people are treated as if they were destitute of reason, as they are supposed to be, if they doubt the truth of any part of the established faith. They are treated as if they either had no conscience, or as much command over it as the steersman hath over a ship, who, " with a very small helm, turneth it about whithersoever he listeth." Oh happy people! could you consult the dead, " the souls of them that were slain for the word of God, and for the testimony which they held ;" some " who were tortured, others who had trial of cruel mockings and scourgings, yea of bonds and imprisonment ;" some who were stoned; others, who were sawn asunder; and others, who

" wandered about in sheep skins and goat skins, destitute in deserts, afflicted among mountains, tormented in
dens and caves of the earth," and whose cries never yet
pierced the ears of men, so artfully have their murderers managed their cruelties ; I say, consult this " great
multitude, which no man can number, of all nations, and
kindreds, and people," who came out of such great tribulation, and they, with one voice, will inform you, that
while they are ascribing salvation to God in heaven,
you ought to be exclaiming on earth, " The lines are
fallen unto us in pleasant places ; yea, we have a goodly heritage !"

My brethren, it is glorious to be a martyr ; and the
public worship of God is worth all the blood that hath
been shed in the world to support it ; but have we all
the courage necessary to martyrdom ? Let us be thankful that we are not led into this temptation. This re-
minds me of another consideration, which ought to engage us to be content with our condition : let us consider our *afflictions.* Discontent is not always the child
of affliction, for some people are determined at all adventures to be unhappy, and to disturb the quiet of all
about them. Sometimes imaginations of distant ills
which may never come, and at other times trifling accidents of no signification at all, agitate the bosoms of unhappy mortals, who think it worth while to raise a tempest to kill a fly. No *place,* however *pleasant,* no *inheritance,* however beautiful, can make such people happy : but the fault does not lie in the *lot,* but in the owner of it.

To people under affliction, I would give four words
of advice ; do you consider the fitness of them. First,
observe the *false principle* on which you have founded
your discontent. You have laid it down as a principle,
that you ought to be free from all trouble in this present life. This is a bold step. It seems, Almighty God
does not think so, for who among all his millions of
creatures is not subject like you to pain, sickness, sorrow, and death ? Beside, this is an unjust principle.
You have laid it down as a principle, that you ought
to be perfectly happy here. But who are you ? Have

you never tasted the forbidden fruit? Does it become you, a sinner, who have given yourself so many stabs, to complain of smart? If it be true, as we are taught, that " the soul that sinneth, it shall die," and if you be that soul, all places short of the place of execution ought to make you cry with the Psalmist, Considering what I deserve, " the lines are fallen unto me in pleasant places :" this is not " the valley of the shadow of death," this is not the bottomless pit, my affliction is not the angel with the great chain in his hand. If I be not obstinate, my house may be a house of prayer, and my old pillow a gate of heaven. Moreover, this principle is selfish. The holy men, who are proposed to you for examples, rejoiced in tribulation, because the patience, content, and prudence, which they exercised under their afflictions, instructed and edified others. They considered themselves as parts of a whole, and submitted to sufferings not necessary to themselves for the sake of their brethren. Thus the death of Christ is the life of the religion of his afflicted followers.

Let afflicted people observe, in the next place, the sufferings of others, and *compare conditions*. It is not wise to compare ourselves with ourselves, ourselves in sickness with ourselves in health, ourselves in old age with ourselves in youth, ourselves in disgrace with ourselves in reputation. Let sick people compare themselves with other sick people, the old man on his crutches with the old man confined to his bed, the man neglected by his children, with the man under the frown of his Almighty Judge. Such a comparison always tends to content, and always must do so as long as we can conceive any thing capable of increasing the load we carry. " Oh thou afflicted! tossed with tempest and not comforted? Come now and let us reason together." Hath " God from above sent fire into your bones?" Hath he " caused Sabbaths to be forgotten in Zion? Is the law no more?" Do your children say to you, where is corn and wine? do your sucklings swoon in the streets for hunger, and pour out their soul into their mother's bosom? Are you driven to eat your children of a span long? Have you, tender woman, full of pity,

sodden your own children for meat? Is your skin
black like an oven? Is your affliction like a great sea-
breach, that none can heal? Ah! nothing of all this:
but something which, compared with all this, hardly deserves the name of affliction. Oh, look short of these,
look only into hospitals, mad-houses, and jails, and, comparing your situation with theirs, adopt the text, "The
lines are fallen unto me in pleasant places; yea, I have
a goodly heritage."

Still, say you, we have our afflictions, and we do and
must feel them. I believe so; consider therefore a
third article, the *benefits* you derive from affliction. Do
you know what we most admire in you? It is not your
dress; we could make a beast fine with trappings. It
is not your abilities; it would not be your abilities, if
you had such powers as angels have, for indeed what
but a fine creature is Gabriel to us? A fine speculation,
more beautiful than the rainbow to look at: but what is
it to us? What we admire, and what we ought to admire in man is that collection of fine feelings which
make him a human creature, social and useful. Sympathy and fellow-feeling, tenderness of heart and pity
for the wretched, compassion for your neighbours and
reverence for your God, the melting eye, the soothing
tone, the silver feature, the ingenious devices, the rapid actions of a soul all penetrated with reason and religion, these are the qualities we admire in you, and all
these you learned in the school of affliction. Oh, I love
the soul that must and will do good, the kind creature,
that runs to the sick bed, I might rather say bedstead,
of a poor neighbour, wipes away the moisture of a fe-
ver, smooths the clothes, beats up the pillow, fills the
pitcher, sets it within reach, administers only a cup of
cold water; but, in the true spirit of a disciple of Christ,
becomes a fellow-worker with Christ in the administration of happiness to mankind. Peace be with that good
soul! She also must come in due time into the condition of her neighbour, and then may "the Lord
strengthen her upon the bed of languishing, and," by
some kind hand like her own, "make all her bed in her
sickness."

Is it a benefit to understand the spirit, and see the beauty of the Holy Scriptures? Afflictions teach Christians the worth of their Bibles, and so wrap up their hearts in the oracles of God. The Bible is but an insipid book to us before afflictions bring us to feel the want of it, and then how many comfortable passages do we find, which lay neglected and unknown before! I recollect an instance in a history of some, who fled from persecution in this country to that then wild desert, America. Among many other hardships, they were sometimes in such straits for bread, that the very crusts of their former tables in England would have been a dainty to them. Necessity drove the women and children to the seaside to look for a ship expected to bring them provision; but no ship for many weeks appeared; however they saw in the sand vast quantities of shellfish, since called clams, a sort of muscles. Hunger impelled them to taste, and at length they fed almost wholly on them, and to their own astonishment were as cheerful, fat, and lusty, as they had been in England with their fill of the best provisions. A worthy man, one day after they had all dined on clams without bread, returned God thanks for causing them to "suck of the abundance of the seas, and of treasures hid in the sand;" a passage in Deuteronomy, a part of the blessing, with which Moses blessed the tribe of Zebulun before his death, a passage till then unobserved by the company, but which ever after endeared the writings of Moses to them.

Finally: Consider afflictions in the light of *preparations for glory.* Eternal duration, everlasting employment, and a perfection of happiness, are lofty objects for us frail men to aspire at; and when we consider our extreme littleness, it seems presumptuous for such worms to expect such exaltation. I doubt whether we might presume to expect it without the express declaration of God; however, I venture to affirm that afflictions have been the occasions of throwing great light upon this subject. Man is a creature of astonishing powers; but these powers lie hid in the breasts of all, like diamonds in a rock, till the convulsions of nature bring them to light. Hunger makes the infant cry, crying is exercise and makes him struggle and grow. When he grows up to play, the sting of a nettle or a bee gives him pain, and makes him fear ; fear teaches him caution, an hour's sickness gives him a lesson on the worth of health, and leads him to plan and to execute means to preserve it. As dangers multiply, his powers of preventing, resisting, and subduing them break forth. Not content with remedying past ills, he foresees future ; there is no end of his invention, and there would be, if his life were not cut short, no end of the execution of his designs. All the great, all the useful, and all the ornamental works of art in the world were once nothing but ideas without substance in the minds of men, and who would have thought that the soul of one single Adam, our first father, could have contained the seeds of such an amazing quantity of fruit ! What a soul must that man have who formed, perhaps lying in pain on his pillow, the collecting of materials, adjusting apartments, and providing funds for the support of a spacious hospital ! How many fine operations must his mind perform ! Fancy, pity, judgment cool and sedate, love to his fellow creatures quick and alive, and many more such efforts must go to make up the generous present to his country. The same may be said of all the works of mankind, and probably, could we trace them, we should find them the offspring of pain and sorrow. Man considered in this light seems a noble creature ; it is a pity he should die to rise no more. But, passing this, we know God intends us to live in a future world, and we know that the school of affliction in this life is a necessary preparation for that, and hence it is that Scripture considers the man, who hath well understood the exercise of religious tempers, as a man *ready* to die. " Be ye ready ; they that were ready went in with the bridegroom."

Let us finish. Christians, of all men, should be the least prone to discontent. A Christian, who hath God for his portion, and who, dissatisfied with that, renders himself unhappy about the little things of this life, behaves as if he could not enjoy the day for want of a

5

glowworm, or the ocean for want of one little drop
more. How old are you, and how many years more
have you to live, that you should be so anxious about
this little remaining time? What could prosperity do
for some of you? Behold, the day cometh, in which
you must die, and then every thing will be indifferent
to you except the favour and friendship of your God.
" Behold, happy is the man whom God correcteth,
therefore despise not thou the chastening of the Almighty." If he maketh sore, yet he bindeth up, though he
woundeth, yet his hands make whole. " He shall deliver thee in six troubles, yea, in seven there shall no
evil touch thee. Thou shalt come to thy grave in a
full age, like as a shock of corn cometh in, in his season. Lo this, we have searched it, so it is; hear it, and
know thou it for thy good."

'Thank God, says one (and let me not forget you),
thank God, " the lines are fallen unto me in pleasant
places;" I am very content, and very happy; I thrive
and prosper in the world, and I live cheerfully on what
Providence hath bestowed. But doth your pleasure
proceed from your prosperity only, or doth it proceed
from a conviction of that goodness of heart, which prosperity produces in you? Examine: doth not your prosperity and pleasure resemble that of a fat ox in pasture?
and is there much more difference between you and
him, than that of shape and make? You eat and drink,
and sleep in the lap of plenty; but do you feel like a
man and a Christian for the lean people over the hedge?
Alas! without virtues that do good to your fellow-creatures, you are only fatting for slaughter, and your hungry relations will be glad when you die, that they may
step into your lot, and cry, " The lines are fallen unto us
in pleasant places, and we now have the goodly heritage." Where do you stand, when you make use of the
text; amidst your corn, your flock of sheep, or your
bountiful feasts at home? Alas! poor man, what a child
art thou in understanding! You resemble a lord of a
great estate got down into a gloomy hole, where some
of his tenants' cattle drink, enchanted with a few white
thorns and willows growing on the ragged edges of the

pit, having forgotten all the other parts of his estate, and shouting about this one pit, " The lines are fallen unto me in pleasant places ; yea, I have a goodly heritage." What would you think of such a man ? You would think him distracted, and seeing his distraction endanger his health and life, your humanity would forget his rank, and you would hazard yourself to get him out. This nobleman is your picture. You are of high birth, you were made in the image of God. You rank with men, above all other animals, and only a *little* lower than the angels. You have a large inheritance, an " inheritance incorruptible and undefiled, and that fadeth not away, reserved in heaven for you." How is it, that you have so forgot yourself as to sink your soul into a little earthly good, and, so to speak, to incorporate yourself with your flock of sheep, as silly and senseless as they ? You, lost sheep ! Do you mean to bury yourself alive in such a dirty pen ? What if your justly offended Creator should say, " Your fathers tempted, proved me, and saw my work." Forty years long have I been grieved with you, and said, He is a man, who errs in his heart, he hath not known my ways. " I swear, he shall never enter into my rest !" Would to God, you might recover yourself before this decree goes forth ! Would to God, you might say, " The Lord shall be the portion of mine inheritance, I will bless him for giving me counsel. I will set him always before me. I will kneel down before the Lord, my maker, for he is my God, and I am one of the people of his pasture and the sheep of his hand. To day I will hear his voice. He will show me the path of life ; in his presence is fullness of joy, and at his right hand there are pleasures for evermore." Then I may say without hesitation what I could never utter before without exposing my folly, " The lines are fallen unto me in pleasant places ; yea, I have a goodly heritage." God grant you this grace ! To him be honour and glory forever. Amen.

DISCOURSE IV.

[*AT SAWSTON*]

———

LUKE xxi. 14, 15.

Settle it therefore in your hearts, not to meditate before what ye shall answer ; for I will give you a mouth and wisdom, which all your adversaries shall not be able to gainsay nor resist.

WISDOM is something to say, and *mouth* is ability to speak it; *wisdom* is the testimony or evidence to be given by the apostles, when they should be brought before kings and rulers for Christ's name sake, and *mouth* is courage to deliver this testimony ; *wisdom* is the Gospel to be taught in synagogues, and confessed in prisons, and *mouth* is the gift of tongues, and all other means necessary to publish it through the whole world. This was the wise and generous intention of Christ, and into his views his apostles most heartily entered, and, immediately after Pentecost, when "Jesus was received up into heaven, and sat down on the right hand of God," they went forth, and preached every where.

Here is an ugly word in the text, *adversaries*, enemies, and it is not in my power to conceal what I blush to declare, that is, that there always have been, and yet are a great number of foolish and wicked people, who are enemies to the redemption of mankind. Had you never seen one of these enemies, one ignorant man who hated instruction, one wicked woman who hated reformation, one disobedient child who hated religion ; had you never seen a despiser of those that are good ; yet it would not be in my power to conceal what the text says, and what follows ; " Ye shall be betrayed both by parents, and brethren, and kinsfolks, and friends ; and some of you shall they cause to be put to death. And ye shall be hated of all men for my name's sake.". The Gospel, however, suffers nothing by the enmity of such men ; for the bare sight of the characters of those, who crucified Christ, persecuted his apostles, and opposed the kind intentions of our heavenly Father to us in giving us the Gospel, is a recommendation of the Gospel. The Jews killed the Lord Jesus ; but they had long before habituated themselves to shed the blood of their own prophets ; they persecuted the apostles ; but they were " contrary to all men :" they forbade the salvation of the Gentiles ; but they " displeased God," and " wrath came upon them to the uttermost." And now-a-days, what kind of men are they, who " resist the truth ?" Are they not " men of corrupt minds, covetous, boasters, proud, blasphemers, fierce, lovers of pleasure more than lovers of God, laden with sins, led away with divers lusts, whose folly is manifest unto all men ?" What sort of a gospel must come from heaven to please men of this kind ? One must have a gospel according to cruelty, another a gospel according to pride, a third a gospel according to divers lusts ; but a gospel according to truth and holiness must be disagreeable to them, for the same reason that a bill for the payment of his debts is disagreeable to a dishonest man.

The Lord Jesus promises in the text to make the mouth and wisdom of his apostles irresistible, and I have the proof of the accomplishment of his promise here in my hand. You know this little book. It contains the four Gospels, or rather one Gospel related by four credible witnesses, the wisdom of God imparted by his Spirit to the apostles of our Lord Jesus Christ ; and in spite of all the interest the wicked have had to destroy this book, and all the power they have employed to rob the world of this treasure of wisdom and knowledge, here it is, undamaged at the distance of seventeen hundred years after it was written. Kings may set themselves up for gods upon earth, " rulers may take counsel together

5*

against the Lord and against his anointed," heathens may rage, and common people may "imagine a vain thing;" but "he that sitteth in the heavens shall have them in derision." His "decree hath set his king upon his holy hill of Zion," and shall give him the "heathen for his inheritance, and the uttermost parts of the earth for his possession."

The doctrine of our text is taught by our Saviour, I think, three times in the course of his ministry in almost the same words; the first in the ordination sermon, which he delivered to his twelve apostles, when he first appointed them to teach; this you may read in the tenth chapter of Matthew. The second time was in a discourse addressed to an innumerable multitude of people, or, to speak more accurately, in a discourse in the hearing of an innumerable multitude, the first part of which was addressed to his disciples, and the rest to all the company; you may read this in the twelfth chapter of Luke, and remark particularly the first, and the forty-first verses. The doctrine of our text is in the first part of that sermon. The third time was when he was with his disciples coming from the temple on the mount of Olives. Some of them were speaking of the beauty of the building, and our Lord took occasion to speak of the destruction of it, and of the city in which it stood, and foretold the persecutions and afflictions of his disciples; and in order to prevent their fears, and even their prudence in giving evidence of his Gospel, he strictly charged them to "settle it in their hearts not to premeditate what they should speak;" but, saith he, "speak ye whatsoever shall be given you in that hour, for it is not ye that speak, but the Holy Ghost." Remark two words. Observe the word *hour*. Our Lord fixes the time for this inspiration; it was "when they should be brought before kings and rulers, councils and synagogues, and while they should be in any manner bearing their testimony. There is therefore no reason, as there is no necessity for Christians to suppose, that this promise is made to all good men to the end of the world. Observe further, it is said: (this is the account given in Mark), "It is not ye that speak, but the Holy Ghost," or, as Matthew expresses it, " It is not ye that speak, but the Spirit of your Father that speaketh in you." From these passages, as well as from many more like them, we conclude that the Holy Spirit extended his inspiration both to the matter taught by the apostles, and to the words in which they taught it. " We speak," said the apostle of the Gentiles, " in the words, which the Holy Ghost teacheth." The conclusion is equally strong for the words in which they wrote their testimony.

Let us attend to the subject. I am going this evening to try to engage you to love the Bible, both on account of the wisdom contained it, and the good which you derive from it ; and in order to this I shall endeavour to convince you . . . that the holy Scriptures were inspired by the only wise God . . . and that the truths contained in them, have an irresistible power to answer the end for which they were given. O Almighty God, our heavenly Father ! " who at sundry times, and in divers manners, didst speak in time past unto the fathers by the prophets, and hast in these last days spoken unto us by thy Son," grant we may " give the most earnest heed to that great salvation, which at the first began to be spoken by the Lord, and was confirmed unto us by them that heard him ;" thou, irresistible God ! " bearing them witness with signs and wonders, and divers miracles and gifts of the Holy Ghost, according to thine own will !"

My brethren, signs and miracles, and gifts of the Holy Ghost there are without number, to prove the truth of our holy religion in general, and of the inspiration of the holy Scriptures in particular. There are learned proofs to satisfy the doubts of learned men, and there are plain proofs to satisfy plain men ; there were prophecies fulfilled in the person of Christ to satisfy his countrymen in his own time, and there are prophecies concerning Christ and his church, the Jews and other nations, to satisfy people of all nations and in all ages ; there were miracles wrought by Jesus Christ to satisfy those who inquired at his mouth, " who gave him authority," and which were so satisfactory to the inquirers, that they could not help exclaiming, " This is, of a truth, that prophet that should come into the world;" and 'though there are no miracles now, yet there are irresistible motives to engage us to say to him, " Lord, to whom shall we go? thou hast the words of eternal life, and we believe and are sure, that thou art the Christ, the son of the living God." All these I lay aside, for the same reason that you have left your money at home, you have no occasion for it in this barn. I choose one proof of the inspiration of the Holy Scripture, and that is, that it is a *good* book, and therefore the gift of a good God. I do not mean a good book in common with other good books ; but a book so true as to have no falsehood in it, so wise as to recommend nothing foolish, and containing a religion so good as to have nothing weak or wicked in it. A common good book, like a good man, is not without its defects, but good upon the whole ; but this good Gospel resembles a good angel, perfect without a mixture of imperfection. I confirm this notion of Scripture by the words of the apostle Paul ; " All Scripture given by inspiration of God is profitable for doctrine, for reproof, for correction, for instruction in righteousness, able to make the man of God perfect, thoroughly furnished unto all good works, wise unto salvation through faith in Jesus Christ." Further, I lay aside all the books of Scripture except the four Gospels, because if the four Gospels be true, the Old Testament, and the remainder of the New must be true also ; and as is the complexion of the one, so is the colour of the other.

Are you aware what a dangerous task the man would undertake, who should presume to deny either that the Gospel is good, or that, though it be good, yet it was not inspired by God? If it be not good, it must be wicked ; but what order of bad men could write such a book? Do you know any ignorant people who could do so ? Is it conceivable that misers, or drunkards, or swearers, or liars, or any other sort of profligate people, could or would compose such a book as this? It is both above their virtue, and above their invention. No, the Gospel is not the production of such men. Matthew was not a blasphemer of God, Mark was not a slanderer of man·

kind, Luke was not a stupid ignorant man, John was not an artful propagator of false and idle tales. Would the profligate forsake father and mother, houses and lands; would the wicked expose themselves to poverty, and ridicule, and imprisonment, and death, to give credit to a lie? If the book were written by good men, then it was inspired, for the writers expressly declare that it was *not they* who spoke, but the Holy Ghost who taught them what to say. A man who invents and spreads a false report is wicked; but his wickedness becomes ten-fold more, if he affirms the God of truth spoke in him, it was not he himself that spoke, but the Spirit of the Father of all mankind. In one word, the apostles were good men, and their testimony ought to have been cred-ited even before the contents of their message had been examined by such as had personal knowledge of them. For our parts, we ask no favour for men, who are above the want of any; and we are going to examine the Gos-pel without regard to the characters of the writers, as if the book had been brought to us in the bill of a bird flying with it into this assembly.

- Though we do not avail ourselves of the characters of the writers, yet this article must have great weight with every reasonable inquirer.. There were at the time great numbers of witnesses, and Christ was seen after his resurrection from the dead, " of above five hundred brethren at once." Now here are four credi-ble witnesses, though in general it is allowed that " the testimony of two men is true," and the law of Moses allows the sufficiency of *two* witnesses, and requires no more than three in capital cases. Our four evangelists are men of good character, virtuous and good men, whose testimony would obtain credit in any court in the world. There is also an exact harmony among the evangelists; there are differences, but no contradictions; though it is very clear, that the four had not consulted together, that one had not read the Gospel written by another, and that John, the last writer, who had probably read the other three Gospels, took no pains to agree in every circumstance with the other three. Suppose yourselves sitting as jurymen in a court; suppose four witnesses to

come in and relate the same fact with the same circumstances in the very same words, and you would instantly
perceive that they had consulted together, and that their
testimony had the air of a forgery. Suppose, on the
contrary, four witnesses relating a history in the manner
of the evangelists, and their very differences are arguments in favour of the truth of their testimony. The
differences are only small circumstances of time or
place ; but their agreement in persons and facts is exact
and convincing. Our evangelists persisted to their death
in attesting the same facts, and there is no instance of
any one having ever denied them. Observe further,
they bore witness not in a cause of their own, but in
that of Jesus Christ, who had he been an impostor could
never reward them for their fidelity. They had no interest in reporting falsehood ; on the contrary, all their
worldly interest lay on the other side. Nor were our
evangelists credulous men, easily imposed upon ; they
discovered a backwardness to believe Christ himself.
They were eye-witnesses, and sensible men. Collect
these *nine* characters of the witnesses of the life and
doctrine, death and resurrection of Jesus Christ, and you
will perceive an irresistible argument for the truth of
the Christian religion. I repeat these characters again.
Observe the number . . the virtue . . the harmony . . the
constancy of the evangelists . . not in their own cause . .
having no interest in falsehood . . far from prejudice
and credulity . . being eye-witnesses . . and men full of
prudence and good sense. In pleading for the truth of
Christianity we are in the condition of men of immense
riches, who lay aside the far greater part for the sake
of tasting and enjoying a little. We lay aside, for the
present, the characters of the evangelists, and attend to
that single proof of their inspiration, which rises out of
the goodness of the Gospel itself. We contend, the
evangelists wrote by inspiration of God, and the goodness of what they wrote proves their inspiration.

It is an undeniable fact, that Jesus Christ promised
extraordinary assistance to his apostles. " Settle it
therefore in your hearts, not to meditate before what ye
shall answer ; for I will give you a mouth and wisdom,

which all your adversaries shall not be able to gainsay nor resist. Take no thought how or what ye shall speak, for what ye shall speak shall be given you; for it is not ye that speak, but the Spirit of your Father which speaketh in you." Nothing can be more plain and express, and less liable to mistake than this promise; and the subject is explained at large in the last discourse of our Lord to his disciples, which is recorded in the fourteenth, fifteenth, and sixteenth chapters of John, where Christ promises the Comforter under the description of the " Spirit of Truth, to testify of him." This was a great promise, and the character of Christ depended on the accomplishment of it.

Observe again, that we have a clear history of the accomplishment of this promise in the second chapter of Acts, six weeks after the resurrection of Christ, in the same city in which he was put to death, in the presence of " devout men of every nation under heaven," and which was accompanied with so much conviction, that the very crucifiers of Christ " gladly received the word," and the " same day there were added" to the Christian faith " about three thousand souls." This was not a sudden start, but a cool deliberate act, for " they continued steadfastly in the apostles' doctrine and fellowship, and in breaking of bread, and in prayers."

Moreover, the apostles expressly pretended to a divine inspiration. Thus Paul: " I certify you, brethren, that the gospel which was preached of me, is not after man, for I neither received it of man, neither was I taught it, but by the revelation of Jesus Christ." They not only pretended to be inspired to preach, but also to write; not only to be inspired with ideas, but to be directed in the choice of words proper to express them; " God hath revealed things unto us by his Spirit; which things also we speak, not in the words which man's wisdom teacheth, but which the Holy Ghost teacheth." Divine inspiration, extending both to matter and words, was of much more importance to their writings than to their sermons, because their writings were to serve for a perfect rule of faith and practice to all Christians to the end of the world. On these accounts they preferred themselves before the prophets, and said, " God hath set in the church, first apostles, secondly prophets, third-ly teachers," agreeably to the instruction of their divine Master, who had taught them, that the *least* apostle (for so we understand the words) was greater than John the Baptist, though " among them that were born of women, there had not risen a greater man than John." God hath set in the church, primarily, apostles, secondarily (in the second order), prophets, and so on. Had the apostles been only inspired to preach, and not to write, they would have been inferior to the prophets ; but having the same assistance, and more miraculous pow-ers, and being employed to propagate a more noble and more durable religion than that of the Jews, they as-sumed the rank due to their condition. Of the four evangelists, two of them, Matthew and John, were com-panions of Christ, and John was related to him, and be-fore he became acquainted with him was a disciple of John the Baptist ; then very young, and when he wrote his Gospel, very much in years. Our Lord loved him beyond his other disciples, placed an entire confidence in him, and not only admitted him, with only two more, to see the resurrection of the daughter of Jairus, the transfiguration on the mount, the agony in the garden, but also committed his mother to his care while he hung on the cross. Mark, or John Mark, as he is called, was the son of a Mary, who dwelt at Jerusalem, and at whose house the christians held their assemblies. He was cousin to Barnabas, and Peter was familiarly acquainted with him and his family ; for when he came from prison, and knocked at the door, Rhoda, a damsel in the house, *knew his voice.* Mark was a son or disciple of Peter, and travelled sometimes with Paul, and sometimes with Barnabas. This evangelist wrote his Gospel from Peter and Barnabas, and he was the same to them as Timothy was to Paul. He wrote his Gospel for the use of the Romans, as Matthew did his for the use of the Jews. Luke was by birth a heathen, and by profession a phy-sician, a constant traveller with Paul, and his Gospel was delivered unto him by those, " who from the beginning were eye-witnesses and ministers of the word," and he himself " had a perfect understanding of all things from the very first." When we affirm that these four men wrote by inspiration, we mean that the Spirit of God preserved them from all error, infused into their minds some ideas, enabled them to retain and recollect others, to understand the whole, and to express all in a just and proper manner, exactly as Moses wrote what he had seen, what he had heard, what he had read, and what God imparted to him, making in the whole a body of information, far above the invention of any one man, and truly and properly ascribed to inspiration of God.

Many are the characters of inspiration, and the four Gospels have them all. A book pretending to come from God must be wise, true, powerful to answer its end, and so on; because God is a wise, a just, a faithful, a powerful Being, and it would be a gross insult upon such a being to attribute folly and injustice to him. For this reason the Psalmist saith, " All thy works shall praise thee, O Lord;" for every work of God is known to be his by certain characters which resemble his perfections. If therefore the Lord be " righteous in all his ways, and holy in all his works," we must examine whether the Gospel bears this character. Is it a righteous, a holy, a just, a good book? Doth it teach us a just and good religion? This is a question, which the feelings of all mankind put, and to which the Gospel is able to give a most satisfactory answer. I am going to show you that the Gospel teaches us a good morality . . . and good motives to practise it. Hence we shall infer, that none but bad men can refuse to embrace the gospel of our Lord Jesus Christ.

By *morality* I mean the doctrine of the duties of life, and by calling this morality good, I mean to affirm that it is just, virtuous, proper, and the cause of happiness. As this is too general, we will examine particulars. For example, morality being a rule of practice must be *clear.* It is a great fault in masters giving orders, to be obscure. Even a willing servant may err through the doubtful meaning of a direction, and in such a case we ought not to tax him with carelessness, but ourselves for not speaking clearly and plainly. This is one proof of the good-

6

ness of the morality of the Gospel, that it neither is, nor
can be misunderstood.   A man desires to be informed
what God expects him to do towards himself.   The Gospel tells him, God requires him to fear him, to love
him, to confide in him, to imitate him, to pray to him,
to treat him as the first cause, and the chief good.   A
man desires to know what Jesus Christ expects of him.
The Gospel informs him, that he expects to be heard, to
have his doctrine examined and believed, his life imitated, and himself " honoured by all men as they honour
the Father," to be treated as the Teacher, the Saviour,
the Judge, and the Friend of mankind.   One wishes to
know how he ought to conduct himself to his neighbours.   The Gospel tells him, " All things whatsoever
you would that men should do to you, do ye even so to
them, for this is the law and the prophets."   Another
wishes to know what conduct he ought to observe to his
enemies.   The Gospel says, " Love your enemies, bless
them that curse you, do good to them that hate you, and
pray for them which despitefully use you and persecute
you."   Another asks, How ought I to manage myself?
The Gospel answers, " If thy right eye cause thee to
offend, pluck it out, and cast it from thee ; if thy right
hand cause thee to offend, cut it off, and cast it from
thee ; it is better for thee to enter into life with one
eye, than having two eyes to be cast into hell-fire."
These duties are so clear that all the world understand
them ; therefore Christians love the morality of the Gospel, and therefore the wicked hate it.   Clearness is one
character of goodness, and the morality of the Gospel
hath it.

Morality being a rule of action for imperfect men,
must be *practicable*.   Nothing shows the weakness of a
lawgiver more than prescribing impossible duties, duties
beyond the power of those to perform, on whom they
are enjoined.   This is always the case when too many
in number are required to be done in a time not sufficient for the performance of them, and when services
too hard and difficult in their nature are required of
those, who have not powers equal to the task.   If the
Gospel required as many duties to be done in ten years

as would take twelve ; or if it exacted as great a perfection of man as an angel is capable of rendering ;
in either of these cases it would be unfit for us, and consequently he, who should require us to practise it, would
discover his folly. Christian morality is a perfect rule
of action ; it is not accommodated to the imperfections
of any man, but,it requires us to take the perfect God
for our example ; " Be ye perfect, even as your Father
which is in heaven is perfect." At the same time it
encourageth the most feeble and faltering soul ; " For if
there be first a willing mind, it is accepted according to
that a man bath, and not according to that he hath not."
In perfect agreement with this, it is said of our Lord,
" A bruised reed shall he not break, and smoking flax
shall he not quench, till he send forth judgment unto
victory." This is a second character of Christian morality, it is performable, such duty as may be done, and
on this account we pronounce it good, just, and right,
and tending to happiness.

A good morality is *universal*, and binds all alike, without partiality and preference. The Gospel requires us
to be just and good ; but it informs us, God is just and
good. It teacheth us to be mild and humble ; but it as-
sures us Jesus Christ himself was "meek and lowly in
heart." It requires us to be inoffensive and useful, but
it informs us that " the apostles of Christ were gentle,
even as a nurse cherishing her children ; behaving themselves holily, and justly, and unblamably, willing to have
imparted not the Gospel of God only, but also their own
souls." It requires not only children to obey their parents, but " fathers not to provoke their children to
wrath, but to bring them up in the nurture and admonition of the Lord." It not only requires servants to obey
their masters, but " masters to forbear threatening,
knowing that their master also is in heaven," and that
" there is no respect of persons with him." To use the
language of our Lord, he hath " left his house,
and given to every man his work, and commanded the
porter to watch. What I say unto you, I say unto all,
Watch." The morality of Christ is addressed to all,
and this is the excellence of it. It is as free from par-

tiality as it is from obscurity. In the world, great men have one law for themselves, and another for their dependents: servants have a law of negligence for themselves, and another law, a law of fidelity, for their masters. All bad men live by one rule, and exact another of the rest of their fellow-creatures, and therein they discover their injustice. The duties of religion are not so : no man is so great as to be above law, no man is so mean as to render his service officious and unacceptable. In this manner pursue the subject of Christian morality, and you will find that strictly true of the Gospel, which an apostle said of the Law, which is incorporated into the Gospel : it is holy, just, and good : it is spiritual ; it is *I* who am carnal, sold under sin : yet my hatred of what I do, is equal to " consenting unto the law that it is good."

The chief excellence of divine morality is, that it supports itself without any foreign aid. It is not a good practice upheld by bad or doubtful motives ; but it is religion grounded on religion, and always able to maintain itself without any assistance from accidents, and remote and precarious causes. For this reason we call Christian morality good, because it is enforced by good motives. It may happen, it often hath happened, that the duties of Christianity have fallen in with the interests of mankind, and it hath suited their convenience more to perform than to neglect them. In this case base motives have given birth to laudable actions, and men have done right for the sake of what was wrong. This is not Christianity, this is an abuse of Christianity ; and on what an uncertain ground would the duties of the Christian religion rest, were they left to such shifts as these ! Alas ! how often doth it happen to be more convenient to neglect our duty than to do it ; to say of Christ, " Crucify him, crucify him ; not this man, but Barabbas," rather than to render such homage as is due to him ! It may happen, it doth daily happen, that the morality of the Gospel cannot be practised without exposing ourselves to difficulty, danger, and distress. What is to support the christian character then ? The smiles of the world ? Alas, they frown and threaten ! The hope of gain ? No, here is nothing to be gained, but every thing at stake, and all likely to be lost. Will our own passions and senses, right eyes, right hands, right feet, favourite sen-, sations, will they support the practice of Christianity? Quite the contrary: the heart will join with the world, conspire against God, dethrone the Saviour, and trample upon his law; "without will be fightings, within fears." The primitive Christians experienced many hardships, and surmounted many difficulties, in order to practise the duties of their religion: yet they "took joyfully the spoiling of their goods;" because they were supported, by motives good and religious like the practice itself: "Ye took joyfully the spoiling of your goods, knowing in yourselves that ye have in heaven a better and an enduring substance."

A motive is that which hath power to move, and a religious motive is that in religion which causeth a man to practise the duties of religion. What a powerful motive to practise is the doctrine of *future punishment!* Jesus Christ taught a state of future punishments. A Christian examines this doctrine, considers it in the light in which Jesus Christ has placed it, not as an arbitrary exercise of power by a being above control, but as a sanction necessary to a law, and thus views hell as a great prison,, or rather a scaffold for the execution of incorrigible criminals. Being persuaded that such a state is just and proper, his fear is excited, and as he believes he fears, as he fears he flees: his flight is in proportion to his fear, and his fear is of the same strength as his faith. Our Lord often applies this truth of religion to practice, and uses it as a motive to duty. "Whosoever shall say to his brother, Thou fool, shall be in danger of hell-fire." "If thy right hand offend thee, cut it off and cast it from thee." Why? "Because it is profitable for thee that one of thy members should perish, and not that thy whole body should be cast into hell." "Fear God rather than man." Why? What should move me to do so? Because man can only kill the body, but God "is able to destroy both soul and body in hell." Let every man exercise his several ability. Why? Because an "unprofitable servant shall be cast into outer

6*

darkness, where shall be weeping and gnashing of teeth."
Feed the hungry, clothe the naked, do unto one of the
least of my brethren as you would do unto me.   Why?
What should engage me to do so?   Because "the King
shall say unto them, who did not minister unto him" in
his members, "Inasmuch as ye did it not unto one of the
least of these, ye did it not unto me."   Depart, cursed
man! depart from me, cursed woman!   "Go away into
everlasting punishment!"   Thus Christ taught, and this
word, *Depart!* hath been in all ages since a thunderclap in the ears of Christians; and though we acknowledge it is one of the lowest motives, yet we affirm it is
far more powerful and effectual than all the boasted motives of heathen moralists.   My brethren, heathens have
taught duties of life, but heathens could never set their
rules a-going; they had not a power to give their
good advice effect; and when we compare the least motive of Christianity with the greatest powers of heathenism, we triumph over them in the language of a Jewish
proverb, "Is not the gleaning of the grapes of Ephraim
better than the vintage of Abiezer?"

Another motive is the doctrine of *future rewards.*   A
view of this supported Moses, who "had respect unto
the recompense of reward."   A prospect of this supported Christ, "who, for the joy that was set before
him, endured the cross, despising the shame."   Our
Lord often urged this motive to his disciples, sometimes
this alone, but more frequently this in contrast with future punishments, and both heightened with many circumstances of time, as "at the end of the world;" place,
as "before my Father which is in heaven;" company,
as before "all the holy angels, and all nations."   The
rewards are exactly such as a virtuous and good man
would wish to receive, and such as he ought in justice
to receive: the approbation of God, the best Judge of
worth; the calm pleasure of reflection, the constant enjoyment of knowledge and virtue in perfection; behold-
ing universal justice administered by the Governor of
the world to all his creatures; "tribulation and anguish
upon every soul of man that doeth evil; but glory, honour, and peace to every man that worketh good; for

there is no respect of persons with God." Heaven excites hope, as hell stirs up fear, and both, considered in firm persuasion of the day of judgment, are powerful motives to Christian obedience. Faith realizes these truths, and brings these distant objects near, so that a Christian seems to himself sometimes to hear the trumpet, to see the heavens pass away, and the dead rise, to rise from the dead himself, and to " sit in heavenly places with Christ Jesus;" to be dead, and to have a " life hid with Christ in God."

Sometimes our Lord binds his morality on his disciples by the soft and silken bands of *love*, touches their tender feelings, and says, " Love me, and love one another, as I have loved you," making his love to us a motive to engage us to love him, and to perform all the duties of life. What a motive, what an irresistible motive to this! The love of Christ to us is pure in its principle, for it rises out of wisdom ; rich in its effects, for all the benefits conferred on us by him are effects of his esteem ; it is uniform and invariable, not eager to-day and indifferent to-morrow, but " the same yesterday, and to-day, and forever ;" it is peculiar to himself, above the tenderness of a parent to a child, beyond the esteem of the husband to the wife of his bosom, or his friend which is as his own soul ; a love above what mortals know, peculiar to himself, suited to the dignity of his nature, having breadth, and length, and depth, and height ; a love which passeth knowledge, an esteem longer in duration, stronger in production, extending to all our interests and beyond all our conceptions. There are two things remarkable in the manner of our Lord's treating this subject. The first is the determinate manner in which he speaks of its effects. His love produces ours, and our love to him produces infallible effects. " If a man love me, he will keep my words. He that hath my commandments and keepeth them, he it is that loveth me." The other is the affecting manner in which he connects together love and obedience : " If ye love me, keep my commandments." At the sound of this word *if*, the Christian starts ; all the tenderness and gratitude of his soul move to meet his duty ; he conceives a horror for disobedience, because it make his love suspected; he turns all his attention to render his christian duties just, complete, beautiful, and strongly expressive of the inward esteem from which they flow; and he endeavours to give his morality a refinement and delicacy suited to the nature of that grand and noble virtue, from which it proceeds. Doth he fall into sin? No motive like this to make him rise; "If a man love me, he will keep my words?" Doth he feel himself indifferent to duty? No motive like this; "If ye love me, keep my commandments." How can I forgive myself for not loving Christ? But I cannot prove I do love Christ any other way than by keeping his commandments. I will therefore keep his commandments both in gratitude to him, and in mercy to myself. For what is disobedience but the parent of a thousand cruel doubts and uncertainties in my soul?

In this manner we might go through many other motives, and all would tend to establish the truth we have laid down, that is, that the gospel was written by Divine inspiration, and that, among a thousand other evidences, the goodness of the book puts the matter out of all doubt. It lays down good rules of living, and it gives the rules the force of law by motives good like themselves. The rules live in the life, because the affections of the heart compel the obedience of the life; and the affections of the heart proceed from a persuasion in the mind, which persuasion is produced by the truth of the doctrine, the author of all which is the blessed Spirit of God, to whom Christians attribute, as to the first cause of their religion, the honour and glory of the whole.

To bring the matter to a conclusion, I affirm, and I flatter myself you will not contradict it, that this book is good for other men, and good for you in every possible condition of life. Bad as the world is, and wickedly as most men live, few, perhaps none, are so far gone as not to wish other men virtuous. The prince requires virtue of the people, and never engages them in any service, no not in the most bloody undertakings, without some plausible pretences of justice in the name of God,

The people expect, at least they recommend virtue to their magistrates, and execrate injustice and impiety in their superiors ; robes of office, say they, should never conceal wickedness ; they do not adorn, but expose a man in power, who should be a guardian of virtue and not an example of vice. Parents recommend virtue to their children, and children expect their parents to be virtuous. " If the buyer saith, it is naught, it is naught," yet when he hath bought, and is become a seller, " he boasteth :" that is to say, he expects a commodity truly and honestly when he buys, and would reproach the seller for attempting to defraud him, though when he becomes a seller himself, he changes his language with his condition. Even the most dull and stupid of mankind dictate laws of virtue to others, and the poor master of only one poor boy advises the boy to be a good boy, and do his duty. It should seem then, I am not alone in recommending religion to you, for you all recommend it to one another, and to the whole world except yourselves. I will suppose a case. Imagine yourselves assembled to-day, by desire of all your countrymen of every rank, to determine a question of consequence, whether they should all live by the rules of the Gospel, or by the maxims of the world. Suppose some child of the devil, some " enemy of all righteousness, full of all subtilty and all mischief," should stand up, and " seek to turn us away from the faith," by recommending murder, adultery, theft, lying, impiety, and all kinds of debauchery and wickedness, and should say, " All the glory of the world, riches, honours, pleasures, will you obtain by practising these profitable exercises." Would not every one of you say, " Get thee hence, Satan : away with such a fellow from the earth, for it is not fit that he should live." The father would say, " Away with such a fellow," he would introduce discord into my family, and teach one of my sons to become a Cain, and to kill his brother. The mother would cry, " Away with such a fellow," he would rob my daughter of her innocence and her character, and bring down my grey hairs and her father's grey hairs " with sorrow to the grave, seeing that his life is bound up in her life."

Each child would say, " Away with such a fellow," what good would riches and honours do me, and what pleasure could I take in them, if I were so unhappy as to see " evil come upon my father." You would have no patience to see this bad man decoy one little boy out of the church into the world; you would say, " Away with such a fellow, we have a father, an old man, and this is a child of his old age, a little one, and his brother is dead, and he alone is left of his mother, and his father loveth him, and it shall come to pass, that when he seeth that the lad is not with us, that he will die." All these are only the inconveniences of a moment, and there are yet stronger reasons for resisting such a tempter as this : there are all the agonies of guilt in the article of death, and throughout a boundless eternity. I am certain, you would all advise one another to pass a vote for all ranks and degrees of men to make this good book the rule of their action. You need not be ashamed to present it on your knees to a prince : you might safely recommend it to a judge : one verse of it would turn your country into a paradise, a verse which it is a shame not to know by heart : " All things whatsoever you would that men should do to you, do ye even so to them, for this is the law and the prophets." It is not this rule of action, it is the want of it that fills every parish, and every house, with so many complaints of injustice. It was the want of this, that made the wise man say, and hath made many a man since his time say, " I considered all the oppressions that are done under the sun, and beheld the tears of such as were oppressed, and they had no comforter, and on the side of their oppressors there was power to relieve their miseries, but they had no comforter. I saw the place of judgment that wickedness was there, and the place of righteousness that iniquity was there." Man, what hath man done by violating the law of his Creator? This was the question put by God to the first sinner :—" What is this that thou hast done ?" The history of all the crimes committed in the world is the long but proper answer to this question. What hath man obtained by sin ? An ability to " cause his heart to despair, for all his days are sorrows, and his travel grief, yea, his heart taketh not rest in the night." Let any man show such effects caused by a close attachment to the morality of the Gospel of Christ.

Is there any person in this assembly, who hath the face to recommend justice to others, and the heart to practise injustice himself? I hope not. This book is good for each of you in every possible condition of life. It is good by its laws of temperance and chastity, for the health of the body : it is " health to the countenance, and marrow to the bones." It is good by its laws of industry, frugality, and abstinence for lengthening out life, and procuring and blessing the enjoyments of it : " length of days is in the right hand of this wisdom, and in the left hand riches and honour. The ways are ways of pleasantness, and all the paths are peace." It is, by its laws of fidelity, gentleness, and goodness, the highest ornament of character : it is " life unto the soul, and grace to the neck, an ornament of grace, and a crown of glory to the head." The wisest and best advice therefore that can be given, is " Take fast hold of instruction, let her not go, keep her, for she is thy life."

To be more particular. There are four conditions of life, in which nothing but the good morality of the Gospel can give us satisfaction. Consider *prosperity*. May the God of providence make you all as prosperous as you wish to be, as far as is consistent with his noble design in creating you ! May you thrive, and succeed, and attain all your just wishes, and long may you live in the enjoyment of them ! But what is prosperity without morality? It is a most deplorable sight to see an immoral man prosper : not that we envy his prosperity, but that it is shocking to see his wickedness increase as his reasons for being righteous multiply. Such a man only steps forward out of his cottage into a good house, to be pointed at as a wretch ungrateful to his Benefactor, unjust to his fellow-creatures, unmerciful to his family, and cruel to himself. The more he prospers, the more cups of deadly poison does he drink, and at length dies, in the opinion of all good men, " a vessel of wrath fitted to destruction." At his funeral no widow weeps, no orphan sheds a tear; the poor have got rid of a tyrant, and the parish of a scourge, and his little history, told by many a tongue round many a fire, amounts to this; " I have seen the wicked in great power, and spreading himself like a green bay tree, yet he passed away, and lo, he was not. I have seen the foolish taking root; but suddenly I cursed his habitation. Even as I have seen, they that plough iniquity, and sow wickedness, reap the same." This is the certain condition of every wicked prosperous man : but it is not so with a good man, when he prospers. The language of his good heart is, What shall I do to glorify God ? How shall I best express my gratitude to my benefactor ? He goes with all advantages into his closet, consults the Prophets and Apostles, and asks each, What would you do in my condition ? He does more, he kneels before the throne of God, and saith, " Lord, what wilt thou have me to do?" What wilt thou have me to do with my wealth ? What with my reputation and credit in the world ? How beautiful is such a man ! Remember it is not his prospesity, but the noble use he makes of it, that constitutes his beauty. It is that, which wins the hearts of all around him while he lives, and bedews his name with tears of affection as long after his death as his name is remembered. When we pray for your prosperity, then, we do so with this caution, that you may have grace to make a religious use of it : otherwise it would be equal to praying God to bestow on you a sword to stab yourself, and perhaps your wife, and your children, and your dearest friends.

What can men do in adversity without morality ? Adversity alone is pitiable : adversity in company with virtue is respectable : but when adversity and wickedness unite, they make a man resemble a lion in chains, miserable himself, and a terror to others. A good man under afflictions retains the affections of his fellow Christians, and excites the compassion of his fellow-creatures ; and on this account David said, " I have been young, and now am old, yet have I not seen the righteous forsaken, nor his seed begging bread." No, the righteous rich will relieve the righteous poor : the rich who have business will employ the good man's poor children, who have nothing to do. No, they shall not be forsaken, but found out and comforted: they shall not beg their bread, but their petitions shall be prevented. The church always had, and always will have liberal men devising liberal things: not vile persons called liberal, nor churls said to be bountiful; but men, who like their great Master, will be in their little sphere "an hiding-place from the wind, a covert from the tempest, as rivers of waters in a dry place, as a shadow of a great rock in a weary land." Poor afflicted people, who are wicked, are miserable indeed, despised by others, and distressed in themselves; in this world poverty and pain, in the world to come punishment everlasting; to use the language of a prophet, they are "destroyed with double destruction."

Consider yourselves in a state of guilt, arising from reflection, sharpened by the Scripture, and meeting you like a "flaming sword turning every way" when you would approach the throne of God. It is very true, that the relief of a sinner comes by believing the record which God hath given of his Son, by apprehending and laying hold of the mercy set before him in the Gospel; but it is equally true that this faith cannot maintain its character, and prevent suspicion, unless it be accompanied with fruits. The heart doth not, cannot hope without holiness. Watch the frames of Christians, and you will find doubts are nothing but effects, and every doubt hath a sin for its cause. Adam in innocence was free from suspicion; it was after he had sinned that he said, "I heard thy voice and I was afraid, because I was naked, and I hid myself." Every attempt to procure peace of conscience without holiness is a mad and wicked project: mad, because it cannot succeed, and wicked, because it is in direct opposition to the law of nature, and the language of Scripture. Would you avoid the smart? Avoid the wound. Would you enjoy peace? Seek it in conformity to God, who is therefore a happy God, because he is a holy God. One of the greatest misfortunes, that can befall a man in this world, is to bring himself to be content and easy without religion;

7

a fatal art, which some men have found out, and daily practise by strength of liquor, a round of company, a hurry of business, and so on. When Cain, the first murderer, was first called to account for his brother's blood, and told, " Thou art cursed from the earth, a fugitive and a vagabond shalt thou be," he said, " My punishment is greater than I can bear :" it should seem, his sense of guilt must shorten his life. No, he went out, took a wife, builded a city, called it after the name of his son, Enoch, and in these employments got rid of a horror which otherwise must have shortened his days. It is at the peril of bad men to be idle, it is the high road to melancholy or madness. There are, however, times in which guilt will rise like a ghost, and haunt every sinner ; and there is no real relief except in the path struck out in the Gospel. Though comfort may come slowly, it is sure to come that road according to the express appointment of the God of the spirits of all flesh, who hath said, " Though the vision tarry, wait for it, because it will surely come, at the end it shall speak and not lie ;" it saith, " The just shall live by faith, but if any man draw back, my soul shall have no pleasure in him."

Consider *death*. How different is the dying of a good man from the dying of the wicked ! The latter is against his will " driven away in his wickedness :" the former placid and happy, at peace with God and with all mankind, " hath hope in his death." What makes the difference ? It is not the room in which or the bed on which he dies. It is not the property he hath acquired, or the rank he hath occupied among his fellow-creatures. It is his character, his true and real character, his moral or immoral state, which now is just finished, and therefore may now be judged. This makes all the difference, and it is impossible to make any thing supply the place of goodness. Now the understanding recovers its discernment of right and wrong : now the memory faithfully records the whole history of life : now the conscience rises from the meanness of a slave to the majesty of a judge : now the heart meditates terror, and feels the approach of an Almighty Judge : now the whole world retires, and something within saith, " One thing thou lackest," while every thing without, saith, " Behold, the Judge standeth before the door." A man must be wilfully blind, not to foresee this ; and desperately wicked, if he doth foresee it, not to provide for it, especially as the provision is set before him as a present from his God. One may very well say in this case what was said in another, " My father, if the prophet had bid thee do some great thing, wouldst thou not have done it? How much rather then, when he saith to thee, Wash and be clean ?"

Can any man say, I hope to prosper, I expect also to suffer, I sometimes blame my conduct, and have a sense of guilt, and as surely as I stand here to day, so surely must I die, and pass from death to judgment, and from thence to a state either happy or miserable forever : but I will venture all these, and run all hazards rather than receive the Gospel for a rule of my faith and practice. It may be good for others for any thing I know : but it is not, it never can be good for me. I ask, can any man say this, and be reckoned a reasonable creature ? Methinks I hear you say, God forbid we should " refuse him that speaketh ! for if they escape not who refused Moses that spake on earth, much more shall not we escape if we turn away from him that speaketh from heaven. Let us have grace whereby we may serve God acceptably with reverence and godly fear. For our God is a consuming fire." May the Lord cherish these good resolutions in your hearts ! My prayer for you shall be, " Oh Lord God, who triest the heart and hast pleasure in uprightness, keep this for ever in the imagination of the thoughts of the heart of thy people. and prepare their hearts unto thee !" Amen.

DISCOURSE V.

———

[AT FULBOURNE.]

BEFORE I read my text, give me leave, brethren, to open my heart to you. As I was coming hither this evening, and meditating on my text, I thought, Suppose, instead of going alone into the assembly this evening, as I shall, suppose it were possible for me to have the honour of leading by the hand through this numerous congregation up to the frame on which I shall stand, the Lord Jesus Christ in his own person, " the first-born of every creature, the image of the invisible God." Suppose I should then open the twenty-second chapter of the Gospel according to Matthew, and with a clear, distinct voice summon each of my hearers to give me an answer to the questions contained in the forty-second verse, which are these :

What think ye of Christ ? Whose son is he?

Affection for you set me a thinking further on such answers as the most strict attention to truth would compel you to give. I thought, Suppose one should say, I never thought about Christ, and I never intend to think about him ; suppose a second should say, I have thought of him, and I despise him, because he is not " a minister of sin ;" and suppose a third should say, I hate him, and, as it is not in my power to persecute him, I express my hatred of him by ridiculing and tormenting all who respect and resemble him. My brethren, it is not for me to pretend to know your hearts, or to pronounce any thing certain; but the bare apprehension of such dispositions excited in me, as it must in every one who loves his neighbour as himself, a thousand suspicions and fears.

Dreading such answers as these, I thought again, What if I should bend my knee to the insulted friend of sinners, and humbly ask, O Son of David! what think you of these people? Whose children are they? Alas! I thought I saw him looking round about on you with anger, being grieved for the hardness of your hearts; then turning about, melting with compassion, going down the steps, walking slowly out of the assembly, and all the way weeping, and saying, "O that thou hadst known, even thou, the most inveterate of the congregation, at least in this thy day, the things which belong unto thy peace; but *now*, but now they are hid from thine eyes."

Alas! thought I, suppose this inveterate enemy of Christ should recover his reason after he is in bed tonight, what sort of a night's rest would he have? Ah! miserable man! I see you start out of your sleep, as if a thunderclap woke you, with the last words of Jesus sounding in your ears, " But now they are hid from thine eyes!" and " This night thy soul shall be required of thee." Alas! disobedient Jonah! where are you now? " Waves and billows pass over you, and the earth with her bars is about you forever." Is this unjust? Why should you have any more opportunities of rejecting mercy, and insulting your only friend? What hath all your life been but ruin to yourself, and a cruel snare to others? No, you " would none of my counsel, and despised all my reproof;" now, you may " call, but I will not answer;" you may " seek me, but you shall not find me; yea I will laugh at your calamity, and mock when the whirlwind of distress and anguish cometh upon you."

Jesus Christ could have done all this, this day month, when you set at nought all his counsel before, for all power is given unto him in heaven and in earth; but see what a merciful use he makes of his dominion over you! He pities your condition, loves you better than you love yourself, and proposes the questions in the text, with a design to prepare you to meet his messenger, Death, " the king of terrors."

Christians, hear this, and know it for your good. " The king of terrors," Death, large as the space which he occupies in Scripture is, Death is not the principal king mentioned in Scripture ; there is a king mightier than he, a " King of kings, and Lord of lords," who " must reign till he hath put all enemies under his feet," the last enemy, death, not excepted, and so bring to pass the saying of a prophet, " Death is swallowed up in victory." This is the delightful subject which I am going this evening to teach, for to this end come proper answers to the questions proposed by our Saviour in the text, " What think ye of Christ? Whose son is he?"

You know, we hold it a just and sacred law of preaching from Scripture, from which we never allow ourselves on any consideration to depart, to give the literal and true sense of the writer, and never to warp the word of God from its own meaning. However, when the sense and scope of a passage is easy, and not perplexed by popular errors, we do not think it always necessary to speak of the context, that is, the words before and after a text. Sometimes we take the general truth, on which a particular text is founded, and at other times one out of many truths contained in it, and provided we establish the literal and true sense of Scripture, nothing of this kind is improper, and the public edification must be our guide. The text before us is a particular question leading to a general truth ; for by inquiring what family Christ was of, we shall find he was a descendant of David, and that his ancestor David, though himself a king, and an inspired prophet, thought his son Christ a greater person than himself, and " called him Lord." If we pursue the subject further, and examine the reasons which induced David to give him the preference, we shall be convinced that the same reasons, which prove him a person of more dignity and worth than David, prove him also superior to all the first characters among mankind. This was the declaration of an apostle, " The

Son of the love of God is the image of the invisible God,
the first-born of every creature," who ranks before all
persons, and in all things must have the pre-eminence.

Justice to Scripture, however, requires us to detain
you a moment on the particular sense of the text. You
know those Jews who are called *Pharisees* in the verse
before the text. Every body knows, and every body
abhors these hypocrites, whose ignorance and hypocrisy
were always in opposition to the wisdom and sincerity
of Jesus' Christ. Who can help detesting a false and
hungry hireling, who makes a long prayer, uttered with
a sad face in long robes, "a pretence for devouring
widows' houses?" Jesus Christ wept over other sinners,
but he denounced judgments against these, because though
they were wilfully ignorant, yet they pretended to teach,
and though they were extremely wicked, yet they set
themselves up for examples of piety to others. "Wo
unto you, blind guides! How can ye escape the damnation of hell?" It was to a company of these men that
Jesus Christ addressed the text, "What think ye of
Christ? Whose son is he?" Their prophets had taught
them to expect a Christ, that is, one appointed of God
to officiate among them in his stead, to administer justice, to bestow mercy, and to make them great, and
good, and happy. They had even named the tribe and
family of which he should be born, and for this purpose
had preserved histories of the succession of families,
which histories are called in Scripture *genealogies*.
The Jews had always been very careful of these histories, for all Israel were reckoned by genealogies, and
those of the reigning family were kept by prophets and
seers. You have one of these in the first of Matthew,
and another in the third of Luke. It was extremely
proper in our Saviour to put this question, "Whose son
is Christ?" to his company, both as Jews who understood
genealogies, and as Pharisees who pretended to more
understanding than other men, and who were also keepers of those useful records, so proper to make out a title,
or to detect an impostor. There, in a list of men, beginning with Adam and ending with himself, stood "the
name of Jesus, the name above every name, at which

every knee should bow." "Call his name JESUS," said an angel from heaven, "for he shall save his people from their sins."

To be first in some catalogues is a disgrace; to be first in some others is no honour; but to be the chief where all are excellent is a high degree of merit. What a dreadful thing it is for a man to be chief in the profession and practice of any sin; how shameful to be the chief of drunkards, the chief swearer, the chief liar in a parish! A sort of schoolmaster of vice, to ruin all the young people in a parish by teaching them the maxims of a drinking-house, and by showing them how to put the rules in practice. Brutal pride! Infernal ambition! The pride of "Beelzebub the chief of devils!" Even where it is no shame to be chief, yet it may be no honour. It is a very silly vanity that bewitches some men; they must be first, first of any thing, but they must be first! Would to God, my brethren, we had a sound understanding to direct our ambition! The ambition of a man directed by the understanding of a child, always forms a very ridiculous character, and makes the man of six foot high, at forty years of age, glory in being the mighty monarch of sixteen little boys at school.

A sound understanding would direct us to excel, and to know, allow, and admire the excellencies of others. It was the wish of the apostle Paul, that Christians of his time might not come behind in any gift. He wished they might excel in such honest trades as they professed, for so we are to understand the fourteenth verse of the last chapter of Titus. To be the chief singer in a christian society, to be the chief speaker, to sit chief among our neighbours in wisdom, integrity, courage, and tenderness of heart for the afflicted, are honours to which you should all aspire. To this thousands have aspired, and if Jesus Christ occupy the first seat among the excellent of the earth, it is because that seat is due to his merit. "He, being in the form of God, thought it not robbery to be equal with God; but made himself of no reputation, and took upon him the form of a servant, and was made in the likeness of men; and being found in fashion as a man, he humbled himself, and became obedient unto death, even the death of the cross. Wherefore God also hath highly exalted him, and given him a name above every name ; that at the name of Jesus every knee should bow, of things in heaven, and things in earth ; and that every tongue should confess that Jesus Christ is Lord to the glory of God the Father."

Would you know what the writers of Scripture " think of Christ, whose son he is ?" They all wait to answer your reasonable inquiry. They describe him as chief in dignity of nature . . . first among the prophets . . . principal in sacred history . . . higher in power, perfection, and honour, than the highest of mankind ; " fairer than the children of men, the head of all principality and power."

When we speak of the nature of Jesus Christ, and ascribe dignity to it, we do not mean to intrude into those things which we have not seen, vainly puffed up by a fleshly mind. The Scripture is not a book of philosophy, intended to instruct us in the specific nature, construction, and properties of persons and things. The doctrines of the Gospel are reports to be believed on the credit of the speaker ; and in all cases where the report includes any thing beyond our comprehension, it is our wisdom to be modest in regard to that particular article. The Scripture calls Jesus Christ God and man, and we believe him to be God and man in one person. " The word, which was made flesh and dwelt among us, was with God, and was God. Had more been necessary, more would have been added. This is enough to justify all the homage, which men and angels pay to Jesus Christ ; for to which of the angels said God at any time what our Lord told the Pharisees, a little after our text, God had said to him, " Sit thou on my right hand, till I make thine enemies thy footstool." To angels he saith, " Let all the angels of God worship him ; but unto the Son he saith, Thy throne, O God, is forever and ever, a sceptre of righteousness is the sceptre of thy kingdom." On this account " David in spirit called his Son Lord ;" and, on this account, " the redeemed of every kindred, and tongue, and people, and nation, with ten thousand times ten thousand, and thousands of thousands of angels,

and every creature, which is in heaven, and on the
earth, and under the earth, and in the sea, say with a loud
voice, Worthy is the Lamb that was slain to receive
power and riches, wisdom and strength, and honour and
blessing : glory be unto him that sitteth upon the throne,
and to the Lamb forever and ever." This is the person, who asks you in the text, " What think ye of Christ?"
The proper answer is, we form no rash conjectures concerning questions of the schools, which perhaps we have
no capacity, and certainly no information from Scripture to enable us to determine; but we think, agreeably to the declarations of him who thoroughly knew the
nature of Jesus Christ, that he is " Lord of all, far above
all principality and power, and might and dominion, and
every name that is named, not only in this world, but
also in that which is to come." We think " that all
men should honour the Son, even as they honour the
Father."

When I am given to understand that this eminent person, who was in " glory with the Father before the world
was," intended to quit " the bosom of the Father," to
honour this world with a visit, and to execute a public
office in it, I cast about in my mind to find out what
charge is proper to employ a mind so exalted. Where
will he reside, or what will he do? Will he dwell in
the country, and instruct mankind in the art of husbandry? Will he honour artists and manufacturers with his
advice and improvements? Will he teach the sailor
how to pass and re-pass with safety the boisterous waves
of the sea? Will he head an army, and perfect mankind in the dreadful art of slaughter? Will he improve
commerce, or will he exemplify in his own person the
character of a king? Childish as all this may appear,
this was the employment which the sensual Jews expected their Christ to perform, and such performances
would have gratified their senseless love of dominion
and wealth. Jesus Christ had nobler views, and better
works than these to perform in this world. His wise
mind penetrated into the nature and duration of man,
and his generous heart undertook an office, which was
to end in the highest glory to God, and the best estab-

lished peace among men. He was to rise like the
"sun with healing in his wings," lest the just judgments
of God should come and smite the earth, all stained with
crimes and human blood, with a curse.

To this most important service the love of God appointed this Son of David; and as men were set apart to
officiate among the Jews by the ceremony of anointing
with oil, God was pleased to describe Jesus by the name
of *Christ*, or *Messiah*, that is the anointed, the person
set apart and appointed to be the Saviour of the world.
So the Samaritans, under the instruction of Jesus, understood the word. He said to the woman of Samaria,
" I am the Messias," and the Samaritans " said unto the
same woman, now we believe, not because of thy saying, for we have heard him ourselves, and know that
this is indeed the Christ, the Saviour of the world." To
save the world was a fine thought, and will always do
its author honour : but, my God ! what an undertaking !
An undertaking, however, to which Jesus Christ was
every way equal. It was no rash enterprize, taken up
without much thought, and ending in the disgrace of the
manager. Cool, mature deliberation, a prudent comparison of difficulties with abilities to surmount them,
patience to endure much contradiction, compassion to
pity and goodness to pardon the most cruel affronts, justice to claim and dignity to support rights and privileges due to the office, perfect purity towards God, and
general good will towards all mankind, these, and whatever else were necessary to the execution of this grand design, were all found in the Son of David. " What think
ye of Christ ? Whose son is he ?" The proper answer
is, He is the Christ, exclusive of every other, " the son
of the living God, full of grace and truth."

The world had lost its understanding, and lost it so
completely as not to know its Creator. The salvation
of the world from such gross ignorance, therefore, required the revelation of a body of sound religious information, and this the prophets gave. Jesus Christ was
the chief subject of prophecy, and himself the greatest
of all prophets. A prophet is one who foretells future
events, and various are the events both of nations and

individuals foretold by the Jewish prophets : but there
is one person, of whom " all the prophets witness," that
is Jesus Christ, and of him they speak in raptures, attributing to him the most noble of all qualities, the most
difficulties and the greatest success and honour. Time
would fail me, should I tell of all the prophecies concerning Christ uttered by these inspired men. In general, we may observe, that the path of these exact men
was " as the shining light, that shineth more and more
unto the perfect day." Christ was in the prophecies
like one sun in the world ; and every age, like every
hour, brought new light, till he made his personal appearance ; and then he as far outshone all description,
as the sun outgoes in a morning, when it rises to sight,
all the images that twilight teaches us to form of it.
From Adam to Noah mankind were taught, that " the
seed of the woman should bruise the serpent's head."
From Noah to Abraham they understood, that God would
dwell in the person of his Son " in the tents of Shem."
From Abraham to Jacob they believed that in a son of
this patriarch " all the families of the earth should be
blessed." Many years after, when Jacob was dying,
the spirit of prophecy informed them that the people
should be gathered unto a descendant of Judah, and that
he should make his appearance in the world before that
tribe should cease to be a distinct tribe of itself. When
Moses was about to quit the world, he informed the
Jews that the promised Christ would be a " prophet
like unto himself," perhaps like him in person, but certainly like him endowed with singular powers to discharge the high trust of delivering mankind from slavery, and teaching them a perfect religion. In process
of time more particulars were added concerning the person, the work, the place, the time, the treatment, the
life, death, resurrection, and ascension of Jesus Christ ;
and so well was this understood, that the chief priests
and scribes, even they at Herod's court, the most ignorant and wicked of all, could tell that tyrant the village
where Christ should be born. When there is but one
person of a kind, and he of the utmost importance to
the world, it is absolutely necessary to be punctual in

describing him, that if God intends a blessing to mankind they may know where to find it. Such punctuality the prophets use concerning Christ, and I would desire no plainer direction to find the best beloved friend in the world. " What think ye of Christ? Whose son is he ?" The proper answer is, The Son of God, the son of Adam, the son of Noah, the son of Abraham, the son of Jacob, the son of Judah, the son of David, the son of a virgin, born at Bethlehem in the days of Herod the king, and named Emanuel, that is, God with us. Thus " we have found the Messias, which is, being interpreted, the Christ, of whom Moses in the law, and the prophets did write, Jesus of Nazareth."

Jesus of Nazareth perfectly understood all the Scripture, how it was written, and how it " behoved Christ to suffer, and to enter into his glory." When he read the Scriptures in the synagogues, as his custom was, and found the place in Isaiah " where it was written, The spirit of the Lord hath anointed me to preach the Gospel," he said, " This day is this Scripture fulfilled in your ears." When he conversed with his disciples, he said, " Think not that I am come to destroy the prophets; I am not come to destroy but to fulfil. Verily, I say unto you, many prophets have desired to see those things which ye see, and have not seen them, and to hear those things which ye hear, and have not heard them." After his resurrection, he gave two of his disciples the very idea we are now trying to give you; for " beginning at Moses, and all the prophets," he omitted the fate of kings and kingdoms, and " expounded unto them in all the Scriptures the things concerning himself." What think ye of Christ as an expositor of Scripture ? His two hearers " said one to another, Did not our hearts burn within us," did we not feel the fire that animated the prophets, did we not enter into both their sentiments and emotions, " while he talked with us by the way, and while he opened to us the Scriptures ?"

Himself was the greatest of all prophets. He not only foretold the actions and sufferings of his apostles, but the fate of all Christians to the end of time. He not

8

only foretold the destruction of his country, but that of the whole world, laying open the rising of the dead, the last judgment, the joy of heaven, and the horror of hell. He was not only a prophet himself, but he communicated a spirit of prophecy to his Apostles, and taught them to speak " all mysteries, and all knowledge, with the tongues of men and of angels," and, what was more, he communicated to them a charity that will never fail, though prophecies, and tongues, and knowledge, shall all fail and vanish away. " He set in the church apostles, prophets, teachers, miracles, gifts of healings, helps, governments, diversities of tongues," and all to show unto us, blind gentiles, the more excellent way of love to God and all mankind. And now, my brethren, what ought we, forlorn gentiles, to think of Jesus Christ? Shall we, too, " crucify the Lord of glory ?" shall we, by imitating the wicked Jews in their vices, call him, " the master of the house, Beelzebub ?" Merciful God ! To what a degree of wickedness must a man go, before he can bring himself to utter such a cruel outrage !

The history of the Jews is a history of guilt, and the Saviour, who undertakes to redeem them, must exemplify a new history, the history of one, who could so remove guilt as to render the guilty proper objects of mercy. The Redeemer did this. He wept, he prayed, he died to effect this, and his history is at once the scandal and glory of his country. The history of the Jews sets before us many eminent characters, and no nation but they can show such men as Abraham, Moses, Daniel, and John the Baptist ; but take away the life of Christ from the history of the Jews, and you strip it of its chief ornament. Jesus of Nazareth was the most considerable person of that nation, and he is emphatically styled, not only " the desire of all nations," that is, such a person as all nations looked for among themselves in vain, but " the glory of the people of Israel :" the glory of that people, who of all the world had produced the most exalted characters. In this view the Jews are objects of envy, and when all the world was sunk into idolatry, " God was known in Judah, and his name was great in Israel :" but never was God so well known in

Judah as in the days of Jesus Christ. To consider the Jews, as they appear in the history of this ornament of their country, they become objects of pity, and seem the most execrable of all nations in the world; and the crucifixion of Christ hath made a blot in their history, which time can never wipe out. Jesus knew all this; he knew Herod was a crafty fox, the scribes and pharisees, and principal churchmen, ignorant hypocrites, dangerous to society as whited sepulchres to unwary travellers; he knew the common people had given up their understandings, and consciences, and feelings to their blind guides; he knew they all despised his ministry, slandered his character, derided his warnings, attributed his miracles to the devil, and thirsted for his blood; he knew, for he felt, they set him at nought, insulted his sufferings, made game of his person, and numbered him with transgressors; nailed him to a cross, and not satisfied with all the cruelties they exercised upon him, glutted their rage also on all his family, friends, and followers. Brethren, " What think ye of Christ? Whose son is he ?" Is he a descendant of the favourite king David, and is it possible a people should be so ungrateful to a family, that deserved so well of their country? Barbarous Jews! What blame, what enormous guilt does your conduct bring upon yourselves? The history of Christ is the scandal of your records.

Amidst all this treatment, you see nothing in Jesus but a firm perseverance in doing good, a mind uninterrupted in its deliberations, a heart unruffled with passion, a conduct inoffensive to all, a doctrine serene and placid, and a life all filled up with good and useful actions; where ordinary means were not sufficient fully to answer the just wishes of all about him, he was ready to exercise extraordinary powers, to feed the hungry, to heal their sick, and to raise their dead. Sometimes he wept over his country; often, very often he taught in all their cities and villages, and when he was dying, he prayed God to forgive them. After his resurrection, he did some of their nation the honour of appointing them to teach all other nations; perfectly free•from all resentment, he directed them to begin to preach repent-

ance and remission of sins at Jerusalem ; forty days after he poured out his spirit upon them, and added unto
his followers " three thousand souls" of this untoward
generation ; a few days after he made the number "five
thousand ;" and, that nothing might be wanting to display the abundance of his mercy, he made " a great
company of the priests," his old inveterate foes, " obedient to the faith." Long after this, he inspired an
apostle to say to them, " I could wish that myself were
accursed from Christ, for my brethren, my kinsmen according to the flesh ; my heart's desire and prayer to
God for Israel is, that they might be saved:" he left it
upon record for all succeeding Jews, that they also, " if
they abode not still in unbelief, should be grafted into
the church," and that, after all the punishments that
should befall them, and all the crimes they should commit, they should " be saved, when the fulness of the
Gentiles came in." " What think ye of Christ ?" Did
ever, could ever any other person of his own, or of any
other country show such a history of unwearied goodness as he ? " Whose son is he ?" Of what father is
he the " express image ?"

Greatly as this history is to the honour of Jesus
Christ, all this is little in comparison with the rest. Jesus sent his apostles " into all the world, to preach the
gospel to every creature," and they were empowered as
well as commissioned to go into the " uttermost parts of
the earth," to bring " all nations under obedience to the
faith," yea to " bring into captivity every thought to
the obedience of Christ." The history of Christ is connected with that of all nations that have received his
Gospel, and it is the history of the best benefactor of
every kingdom ; for the Gospel is a greater blessing to
any country than trade and wealth, and even civil government itself. A pardon for all the sins of Jews and
Romans, English, French, and all other nations ; a pardon for sins of ignorance, and sins against light and
knowledge ; a pardon coming to us through the bloody
death of this illustrious Jew ; benefits in consequence
flowing down from father to son, from family to family,
magnifying and multiplying for " a thousand genera-

tions" in this life, and after this life in a future state:
what a history, what an astonishing history is this!
" What think ye of Christ?" What think you of a mind
that could plan, a power that could execute, and a heart
that could bestow such a present as this? " Who hath
ascended up into heaven? Who hath established all
the ends of the earth? What is his name, and what is
his Son's name; canst thou tell?"

It was prophesied of Christ, that " a seed should serve
him," which should " be accounted to the Lord for a
generation;" that " his kingdom should be exalted higher than that of Agag;" that he should be " higher than
the kings of the earth;" that " all kings should serve
him, and all nations call him blessed, as long as the sun
and the moon endure." As a proper foundation for all
this power and honour, an absolute perfection is ascribed
to him, and the homage paid to him is both for his own
personal excellence, and for the benefits which we derive from it. Do all nations call him blessed? It is
because " in his days the righteous flourish in abundance of peace;" because " he redeems the souls of the
poor and needy from deceit and violence;" and esteems
their " blood precious in his sight."

The perfection, which we ascribe to Jesus Christ, is
not like that which is attributed to men or angels;
but is to be understood both absolutely and relatively.
I will explain myself. Jesus was absolutely perfect and
complete in all the senses of his body and in all the faculties of his mind, so that without any relation to us he
would have been the most complete person in the universe: this I call absolute perfection. This perfect
person, by undertaking a public trust, and by executing the office of a Mediator between God and men, became related to mankind, and to all the events that happen in this world; and by relative perfection, I mean all
the powers, privileges, and qualities necessary to the
regulation of all affairs in discharge of the high trust
committed to him by the Father. " What think ye of
Christ?" Is any other person possessed of such a perfect " spirit of wisdom and understanding," such a " spirit
of counsel and might," such a " spirit of knowledge and of
8*

the fear of the Lord?" Can any compare with him for "judging with righteousness, arguing with equity, and slaying the wicked with the breath of his lips?" "Whose son is he," that tames the tempers of wolves, lions, and leopards, so that lambs and kids may lie down with them, and a "little child lead them?" These are the perfections of " a branch out of the stem of Jesse," a son of the decayed family of David, a root out of that dry ground, Judea.

And now, my brethren, what honour shall be conferred on this son of David? God, the just rewarder of merit, hath conferred the highest honours upon him. A long train of prophets came first in the procession of our King, and foretold his approach. The ceremonies of the Jewish religion were drafts and pattern of him. At his coming, a new star appeared to wise men, angels came down to join with shepherds in singing his praise ; his mother and his family, and even the hoary Simeon and Anna, were inspired to compose hymns in his praise. During his life, the whole world felt his presence, winds and waves, the stubborn ass, the wary fish, the diseases and vices of men obeyed his word, and Death yielded up his prey. When he quitted the world an eclipse, an earthquake, and a resurrection of the dead published the news. Him God raised from the dead, and him he shewed openly, having spoiled principalities and powers, and publicly triumphing over them. Now that he is ascended to heaven, and set down at the right hand of God, he receives all possible honour, and will come again to raise the dead, to judge the world in the glory of his Father and of his holy angels. " What think ye of Christ?" Doth he not deserve all these honours? Was ever power more nobly employed than in raising him to all this dignity, a dignity never abused by him, never perverted to an unjust or an unkind purpose, but always employed for the benefit of the wretched? " What think ye of Christ?" Do you consent to his ascending the throne, and being " crowned with glory and honour?" The day is fixed for his coronation, and then on his head will be many crowns. Even the most glorious creatures, who have deserved best of their fellow-creatures, will "cast their crowns before his throne, saying, Thou art worthy, O Lord, to receive glory and honour!" There will be no apostle weeping, because no man of merit can be found, but all will exclaim, "Behold the man! Behold the Lamb of God, that taketh away the sin of the world! Lo, this is our God, we have waited for him!"

For my part, when I consider the little projects of the proudest of mankind, and the tawdry pomp of the most elevated mortal, I see nothing, but a tiny scheme of glossy wretchedness; and when I compare this with the wisdom and power of God manifested in Christ at the last day, I pity and weep over the folly of my little fellow-creatures. Poor Haman! Is this honour, to ride on the horse of a king in royal apparel through the streets of a little city. Simple Ahasuerus! What are "white, and green, and blue hangings," what are "silver rings, and pillars of marble;" what are "beds of gold and silver;" what are "pavements of red and black" polish; what are your "hundred and twenty-seven provinces," and your "feasts of a hundred and four-score days," compared with the everlasting happiness of the court of the Son of David! With what unspeakable pleasure will Christ survey the innumerable multitude, which he shall have plucked from the jaws of destruction! With what eyes will all his followers behold such a benefactor! How sincerely will many a soul exclaim, "I had not thought to see thy face; and lo, God hath shewed me thy family also." Then should any disciple of Christ summon the company to answer the questions in the text, "What think ye of Christ? Whose son is he?" then you would hear an answer in "unspeakable words, which it is not possible for a man in this life to utter."

Brethren, send me away to-night with a blessing. Let me return with that high reward of my labour, the joy of hoping that I have not been speaking to the deaf and the dead. There is a set of men, who "are like the deaf adder that stoppeth her ear," and would "not hearken to the voice of charmers, charming ever so wisely." Such as they, are of no party; they hate the very forms of religion, and would not give even an apostle a hearing. You are not of this sort, you are willing to hear even me lisp on the subject of religion. I love you, it is all the qualification I have to preach to you: but this love, like that of the mother for her child, wakes my grief, and rouses up ten thousand fears. I fear, you should not be found when "the Lord shall count, and write up his people." I can with pleasure "make mention of Rahab and Babylon;" I can say with a heart full of satisfaction, "Behold, this and that man was born in Zion;" but you, what can I say of you? Alas! "Joseph is not, and Simeon is not; all these things are against me."

True, you are not of those serpents that refuse to hear; but yet "the poison of adders is under your lips," and "with your tongues you use deceit." True, your mouth is not "full of cursing and bitterness;" but yet "there is no fear of God before your eyes." Your feet are not swift to shed blood;" but yet "destruction and misery are in your idle ways." Your "throat is not an open sepulchre;" but yet you are "gone out of the way, and become unprofitable." Let us put the matter to proof. "What think ye of Christ?" What do you think of the doctrine he taught? Have you examined, and do you believe it? What do you think of the blood he shed? Have you examined sin, your own sin, which caused the shedding of that precious blood? What think you of the laws he gave his disciples to "love their enemies," to "shine as lights in the world," to "pluck out a right eye," to be "perfect as their Father which is in heaven is perfect?" Do you approve of these laws, and make them the standing rules of your actions? What think you of the Jews insulting Christ? Are you a Jew, do you justify them by imitating their example? What think you of the honour done to Christ by his Father, and by all good men? Are you an enemy to good men of every nation, and to a good God, who giveth you "life, and breath, and all things?" Search and see. Recollect, there is a glory of Christ, which I have not yet mentioned, that is, the glory of his justice in punishing the wicked at the last day. For the present you may go on; you need not take thought, say-

ing, What ought I to think of Christ: you may lay
this aside, and spend all your life in putting and an-
swering other questions, as, " What shall I eat? What
shall I drink? or wherewithal shall I be clothed?" and
you need not blush for being singular, for " after all
these things did the Gentiles seek," who like you were
" without Christ, having no hope, and being without
God in the world :" but, recollect, after you have set all
these things in your hearts instead of God, the slighted
Saviour will " come with clouds, and every eye shall
see him ;" the Jews " who pierced him, and all kindreds
of the earth," who rejected him, shall " wail because of
him." And in that sad day, when trouble and anguish
shall come upon you, what will all the friends of Christ
say of your case? They will say, " Even so, Amen !"
Miserable man! See the " great white throne and him
that sits on it, from whose face the earth and the heaven flee away." See " the dead, small and great, stand
before God, the books opened, and the dead judged according to their works." Behold " the sea giving up
the dead which were in it, and death and hell delivering
up the dead which were in them." See, " whosoever
is not found written in the book of life, is cast into the
lake of fire, cast alive into a lake of fire burning with
brimstone." I do not ask what the condemned will
think of Christ then, for love of self will triumph over
love of justice ; but I ask the " people in heaven," and
they reply, " True and righteous are his judgments."
Now I ask you, what think you of that Christ, who is
both able and willing to deliver you from all this punishment, and from all fear of suffering it? O sweet and
comfortable declaration! " This man, because he con-
tinueth ever, is able to save them to the uttermost, that
come unto God by him, seeing he ever liveth to make
intercession for them !" How well doth " such an high
priest become us!" How much doth he deserve the
first and finest emotions of my soul! Not " think of
Christ!" That would be wretchedness complete! What
have I to think of beside? Pain in my body, guilt in
my mind, the malice of my enemies, the treachery of
my friends, disappointment of my hopes, vanity and vex-

ation of business, old age and sickness, death, the grave, and the fear of the " damnation of hell," these are black and gloomy things, and a perpetual attention to these, through all which I have to travel in the night without a guide, would drive me to distraction. Monster that I should be, if I could find in my heart to reject Jesus Christ as my guide! Not think of him! I will think of nothing else; he shall be to me instead of every other subject, the food and fire of my soul. If I pray, he will become my advocate too. If I repent, he will forgive me. When I wander, he will restore me. When I tremble at the dreary path through " the valley of the shadow of death," he will say to me, " Fear not, thou worm Jacob, for I am with thee; when thou passest through the waters, I will be with thee, and through the rivers, they shall not overflow thee; when thou walkest through the fire thou shalt not be burnt; neither shall the flame kindle upon thee." Not think of Christ! "If I forget thee," O Saviour of my soul! "let my right hand forget her cunning! If I do not remember thee,.let my tongue cleave to the roof of my mouth!" May God inspire us all with such sentiments! To him be honour and glory for ever. Amen.

DISCOURSE VI.

[*AT ICKLETON.*]

MARK vii. 24.

And Jesus entered into an house, and would have no man know it : but he could not be hid.

THERE are two sorts of persons who cannot be hid; the first are men of remarkable qualities, and the other are men in public offices. It is impossible to both these classes to escape the public eye, and, whoever enjoys the pleasure of privacy, they must not expect it. It is a wise management of Providence, a perpetual restraint upon sin, and a constant motive to virtue.

Men of remarkable qualities of vice are necessarily exposed to contempt, and the higher the rank, the more horrible their crimes appear. Belshazzar was a king of this sort, Caiaphas was a priest, Pilate a judge, and Judas a friend of this class, whose unworthy names are so well known as to stand for the foul and filthy crimes, for which they rendered themselves remarkable. Such may well desire to retreat from the eyes of men, and, if it were possible, from the censure of Almighty God. Thus the prophet Micaiah reproached Zedekiah, a false, and cruel prophet of Ahab, " Behold, thou shalt go from chamber to chamber to hide thyself." Thus also, the apostle John represents the wicked at the last day as " saying to mountains and rocks, Fall on us, and hide us from the face of him that sitteth on the throne." I call this shame a restraint upon vice; and low as this passion is, even this shadow of virtue is necessary to the good of society; for the monstrous crimes now committed by great men are nothing to what they have an inclination to commit, durst they, when they had done, look either God or man in the face. No, singular abilities for the commission of sin cannot be exercised in secret, the owners of them want room; they are not, like some little insects, hardly known to be in the world; but they resemble the "lion coming up from his thicket," his "voice publishing affliction," and his fellow-creatures crying, "Destruction upon destruction, woe unto us, for we are spoiled." Happy for us, mighty powers for mischief can neither be concealed nor approved!

Men of remarkable good qualities of either body or mind cannot be hid. "Saul was the desire of all Israel, for he was a choice young man, and there was not a goodlier person than he; from his shoulders and upward he was higher than any of the people." His size showed itself. It is the same with remarkable genius, and endowments of mind; for skill will break out, and show itself; it "cannot be hid." It was the art of David in "playing on an harp," that first recommended him to king Saul; and it was the singular sweetness of his manner, as well as the "comeliness of his person," that obtained him the friendship of Jonathan, who "loved him as his own soul;" and it was his remarkable courage and address, that gained him the esteem of "all Israel and Judah," as well as the dread of Saul, who envied and feared his abilities. It was skill "to work in gold and silver and brass, to cut stones, and to carve timber," that distinguished Bezaleel and Aholiab from the rest of their brethren in the wilderness; as genius for all works of art hath always distinguished one man from another in all countries. God himself hath been pleased to point out to us the remarkable faith of Abraham, the eminent meekness of Moses, and the singular patience of Job, admirable qualities which "cannot be hid!"

As qualities distinguish men, so do public offices.

Thus Daniel was distinguished in the court of Darius, and thus Joseph was noted in that of Pharaoh; for public offices are instituted for the convenience of many, and they who hold them are bound to execute them faithfully; and envy as well as respect keeps a watchful eye on the conduct of such men. You may see what passes in the whole world by the tranactions of a little parish. The integrity and humanity of a good man in a parish-office may expose him to the censure of a few; but it will always secure him the esteem of all such as know how to value uprightness and sympathy. Happy the man who always acts with a view to examination and account, who, in private, places himself before both the judgment of his fellow-creatures, and the tribunal of a righteous God!

Where a man holds a public office of great importance, when he hath all the great abilities and virtues necessary to the discharge of the trust, and when he actually so discharges it as to render remarkable services to society, all the reasons for being every where known will unite in this one man, and he " cannot be hid." He is a man, and fatigue of business will make nourishment and refreshment necessary; but on pressing occasions such a man will deny himself for the public good, and, to use a scriptural expression, he will remember, the saying that is written, " The zeal of thine house hath eaten me up."

Such was the condition of Jesus Christ, when he went into the borders of Tyre and Sidon, " and entered into an house, and would have no man know it: but he could not be hid." I think, I see three principal reasons, beside that just now mentioned, for the conduct of our Saviour. "He would have no man know it." Why? Because he would fulfil prophecy . . . explain his own character . . . and leave us an example of virtue. Once, "when great multitudes followed him, and he healed them all, he charged them that they should not make him known; that it might be fulfilled which was spoken by Esaias the prophet, saying, Behold, my servant shall not cause his voice to be heard in the streets;" that is, he shall not affect popularity, nor stoop to use any arti-

fice to make proselytes.   Most likely this was one reason
of our Lord's desiring to be concealed on the occasion
mentioned in the text._ Probably, he intended also to
explain his own character to the family where he was.
Jesus was a person of singular modesty, and a high degree of every virtue, that can adorn a man, was a character of the promised Messiah.   It was necessary to
give frequent proofs by his actions of the frame and
temper of his heart, and he discovered the tenderness
of a friend to the family where he was, and to his disciples, who were along with him, just as he had done before, when there were so " many coming and going,
that they had no leisure so much as to eat."   Then,
" he said unto his apostles, Come ye yourselves apart
into a desert place, and rest awhile.   And they departed into a desert place by ship privately."   Further, in
the case before us 'we have a fine example of the conduct proper for men exalted above their fellows.   They
ought not to make a public show of themselves, nor to
display their abilities in vain ostentation. . All their
abilities should scent of piety and the fear of God.   The
apostle Paul reproved the Corinthians for abusing extraordinary gifts to make the people think them prophets and spiritual persons, while they ought to have applied them " to the edifying of the church."   " God,"
adds this apostle, " is not the author of confusion ; but of
peace."   For such reasons, we suppose, our blessed Saviour desired concealment in this house ; and so much
right had he to rest after a journey, to refresh himself
with food and sleep, to retire from the malice of his enemies, and to enjoy all the uninterrupted sweets of privacy, that had not his presence been indispensably necessary to the relief and happiness of mankind, one
would have wished to have hushed every breath, and
to have banished every foot, lest he should have been
disturbed : " but he could not be hid.   His fame had
gone abroad into all the land, and throughout all Syria ;"
and his wisdom exceeded his fame, " the one half of the
greatness of it was not told."   Enough, however, had
been said to engage a woman in distress for a young
daughter, to come and solicit relief.   A woman in like

distress once went to the prophet Elisha, and when his
officious servant Gehazi came near to thrust her away,
the man of God said, " Let her alone, for her soul is vexed
within her." In both instances, it was a case of deep
distress. Who but God can tell the pangs of a mother's
heart! In both cases it was an appeal to compassion,
and in both cases wisdom administered instant relief.
Should such a person "be hid?" Thanks be to God, it
is impossible! This woman forbids silence ; her daughter, her family, her neighbours, all others, who had
been relieved by Jesus Christ, prophets, apostles, christians of all ages, and of all countries forbid a concealment of him : he himself will justify the conduct, and to
every Pharisee, who saith, " Master, rebuke thy disciples," he will reply, " I tell you, that if these should
hold their peace, the stones would immediately cry
out."

Christians, let us feast our souls this afternoon with
this heavenly manna ; and, in order to give our meditation a kind of form, let us remark . . . that Jesus Christ
is not hid . . . that Jesus Christ ought not to be hid . . .
and that Jesus Christ cannot be hid. O may that God,
" whom we serve with our spirits in the Gospel of his
son," preserve us from being " ashamed of the Gospel
of Christ !"

I say, Jesus Christ is not hid. Have you observed,
my brethren, one word of the apostle Paul in his speech
to king Agrippa? " The king, before whom I speak
freely, knoweth of these things; for I am persuaded that
none of these things are hidden from him, because this
thing," the resurrection of Christ from the dead, " was
not done in a corner." This is one argument for the
truth of the resurrection of Christ, and so of the whole
of revelation, which we are taught by our apostle to
use. This is a " tried stone," upon which we may build
our faith with all possible safety, and in defiance of
every attack. When " the hail shall sweep away the
refuge of lies, and the waters shall overflow the hiding-
place," this " precious corner-stone" shall support the
whole Christian Religion.

The prophet Isaiah defended the Jewish religion on

this principle, and reproached false prophets, who pretended to call up and consult the souls of departed men, in this descriptive manner: " Seek not unto them that peep and mutter. Should a people seek for the living among the dead? Should not a people seek unto their God?" How much like a servant of the God of the whole earth doth he look, when he steps forward and saith, "I have not spoken in secret, in a dark place of the earth;" I say " Look unto me, and be ye saved, all the ends of the earth!" The prophet saith more; In the name of God, " hear ye this, I have not spoken in secret from the beginning." This was very true, for Moses published his commission in the court of Pharaoh, and confirmed it by miracles in the land of Ham. Hence he informed the Jews in the wilderness, that the " commandment, which he commanded" them, was " not hidden from them, neither was it far off. It is not," said he, " in heaven, that thou shouldest say, Who shall go up for us to heaven, and bring it unto us, that we may hear it, and do it? Neither is it beyond the sea, that thou shouldest say, Who shall go over the sea for us, and bring it unto us, that we may hear it, and do it? But the word is very nigh unto thee, in thy mouth, and in thy heart, that thou mayest do it." A passage quoted by the apostle Paul, and applied by him with equal force to the Christian religion, and from which he made this just inference, " Whosoever believeth on the Lord Jesus, shall not be ashamed."

There is not in the Christian Religion a single article of faith or practice unpublished to the world. The Jews knew, the Greeks knew, and we know, the time and the place, the family and the circumstances of the birth of Christ. His doctrine spoken at first " in the ear in closets," hath been, according to his express order, " proclaimed upon the house-tops." This remarkable charge he gave to his friends, " Be not afraid of them that kill the body. He that denieth me before men, shall be denied before the angels of God. What I tell you in darkness, that speak ye in light; for there is nothing hid that shall not be known." Herod saw him, the multitude heard him, Nicodemus consulted him, the doctors in the temple conversed with him, the Scribes and Pharisees and Sadducees questioned him, Pilate and Caiaphas tried him, the Roman soldiers saw him die, and beheld him also rise from the dead; "Jerusalem was filled with his doctrine," his fame was known at Rome, and the faith of that church was "spoken of throughout the whole world;" and one single messenger preached his Gospel fully from Jerusalem unto Illyricum, that is, through a compass of two thousand miles. Jesus himself "spake openly to the world; he ever taught in the synagogue, and in the temple, whither the Jews always resorted, and in secret he said nothing." Observe the remarkable words of our Lord, "Behold! they know what I said." Yes, they understood him, the devils knew he came to destroy their empire, and they hated him for it; and the wicked Jews knew he meant to subdue their passions, and they crucified him for the attempt. So true is this expression of Paul, "This thing was not done in a corner!"

Hence we reason thus: if Jesus Christ was thus publicly known; if he was put to death, and rose from the dead in a great and populous city; if his iniquitous judges with all the power of government in their hands, with the most violent inclination to make use of it, and with actual repeated trials in open courts, could not discover any fraud; and if, on the contrary, his judges were compelled against their will to pronounce him innocent; and if forty days after his death his crucifiers were "pricked in their heart" with shame and remorse for what they had done, and became his disciples and followers; then ."Christ is risen from the dead," our faith is firm, not vain, and "he must reign till he hath put all things under his feet." Jesus Christ "is not hid," he is ascended to God, and at his right hand he will sit, till he "shall appear the second time without sin unto salvation."

Brethren, Jesus Christ ought not to be hid; for if ever any person had no reason to blush, if ever any one had reason to look the world in the face, our Divine Saviour is that person. I am always moved with pity and astonishment when I see a sneaking Christian, afraid if

9*

not ashamed to own his Lord. We forgive Peter, for his master was then on trial, and he himself was fiercely attacked by desperate Jews : but what excuse can be made, timorous Christian ! for you, who, now that Christ hath risen from the dead, and is " declared to be the Son of God with power," blush among Christians to be accounted " one of them ?" What are you afraid of ? Make full proof of the character you assume. Follow your guide. " Curse and swear," and say, " I know not the man."

There is more truth in the profession of such a Christian than he is aware of. He saith, "I know not the man." True, you do not know him as he is to be known, and your ignorance occasions your fear. O ! did you know the dignity of his person and the eminence of his love ; did you know the worth of his doctrine and the excellence of his example ; did you know your obligations to him and his intentions of goodness to you ; you would say to him, " O Lord, I have gone astray like a lost sheep ; seek thy servant ! Let me not be ashamed of my hope ! How sweet are thy words unto my taste ! I will speak of thy testimonies before kings, and will not be ashamed."

Such a Christian affects honour. I commend him. Such a Christian would have nothing in his religion to be ashamed of. I admire his disposition. There are assemblies, and even assemblies called religious, of which sense of honour ought to make each of us say, " O my soul, come not thou into their secret : unto their assembly, mine honour ! be not thou united : instruments of cruelty are in their habitations." There is many a pilgrimage, and many a path travelled by men under pretence of religion, to each of whom it may be truly said, " The journey that thou takest is not for thine honour ;" it neither does honour to thine understanding, nor to thine heart. I repeat it again, all men, even the meanest of mankind, ought to regard their reputation, and, especially in an affair so public as that of the profession of a religion, should believe nothing, and do nothing to be ashamed of. Let " walking in craftiness, handling the word of God deceitfully," and all other " things of dis-

honesty be hidden :" let Achan say of his Babylonish
garment, his two hundred shekels of silver, and his
wedge of gold, " Behold I coveted them, and took them,
and they are hid in the earth in the midst of my tent :"
let the deceitful tradesman, who "goes beyond and de-
frauds his brother in any matter," let him conceal the
art by which he gets, the book in which he sets down,
the place in which he hides, and the use to which he
applies his " wages of unrighteousness :" let the " eye
of the adulterer wait for the twilight, saying, No one
shall see me," and let him " disguise his face :" all
these men " are of those that rebel against the light,
for the morning is to them even as the shadow of death,"
and they are always, if one know them, as they ought
to be, " in the the terrors of the shadow of death."   But
is Jesus Christ one of this midnight band ? Is his Gospel a
talent for a " wicked and slothful servant to hide in the
earth ?"   Let us understand our religion better.   Let us
paint, if we can, the fire and the force of that angel of a
man, who in open court, in the place of hearing, before the principal man of a large city, in the presence
of chief captains, governors, and gods upon earth, cried,
" At mid-day, O king ! I saw a light at mid-day, O king !"

Consider, bashful christians ! consider the dignity of
the person of your Divine Master. Strictly speaking,
Christ hath a dignity of person, and a dignity of office ;
he is the wisest and the best of persons in the highest
of all possible preferment. He is not merely what Job
wished for, a days-man betwixt God and man, that is, an
umpire for a day to settle one difference : but he is a
" priest forever, the Son," who is " consecrated for
evermore to make intercession for us." Is there any
thing in this noble office, so worthy of the justice and
goodness of God to institute, so honourable in Jesus
Christ to execute, so necessary to the religion of mankind to receive, to be ashamed of ? Let those, who
have " lords many and gods many," be ashamed and
confounded ; but, let us, who have " but one God the
Father, of whom are all things, and we in him ; and one
Lord Jesus Christ, by whom are all things, and we by
him ;" let us glory in our God and Saviour. Christians

should be, I had almost said, proud of this golden sentence, " There is one God, and one Mediator between
God and men, the man Christ Jesus." Conceal what,
the perfections of God? Hide what, the life of the
world, " the light of men," Christ Jesus? Blush at
what, that " God is not ashamed to be called our God ;"
that Christ is not " ashamed to call us brethren ?" This
is not the pride of a beggar; this is the rage and madness of a devil : a sullenness that should have no quarter in the bosom of a Christian.

Consider the eminence of the love of Christ. It
would be saying little to affirm that he gave us his time,
his advice, his apostles, his friendship and good wishes ;
he did more ; he gave us " himself : his own body on
the tree to heal our stripes ;" his character to be disgraced with that of transgressors ; his liberty as that of
a sheep under the hands of her shearers ; and his soul
to be " poured out unto death," an " offering for sin"
to justify many. Brethren, we celebrate the praise of
such men as love their country so as to " expose their
lives unto death in the field," especially if they " take
no gain of money ;" we call such men " stars in their
courses," fighting against Sisera ; we say of such men,
they " came to the help of the Lord against the mighty"
robbers and murderers of his creatures ; in such cases
of extreme danger, we forgive a woman forgetting for
a moment her sex, and shedding a tyrant's blood, and
we praise the soft hand for taking for once " the nail
and the workman's hammer," and " piercing through the
temples" of the chief of plunderers ; we say of her,
" Blessed above women shall she be !" If the saviour of
our liberties and properties and natural lives be so worthy of publication and praise, what must we think of
him, who without fee or reward, from principles of the
strictest justice and the greatest love, redeemed us from
sin, and all its fatal consequences? Conceal what, perfect justice and disinterested love? Hide what, that
" Christ, when we were without strength, died for the
ungodly?" Blush at what, that " when we were enemies, we were reconciled to God by the death of his
Son, and that as sin hath reigned unto death, even so

shall grace reign through righteousness, unto eternal
life by Jesus Christ our Lord? Ungrateful shame! do
we " thus requite the Lord that bought us ?"

Fearful soul! observe the worth of the doctrine of
Christ. David thought the law " better than thousands
of gold and silver." What would he have said, if he
had received along with the law all the Prophecies, and
all the New Testament ? The man, who had these, called them " treasures of wisdom and knowledge, unsearchable riches" of Christianity. Every part of the doctrine of Christ is wise and good, and there is not a line
of his Gospel that needs concealment. His doctrines
are not a troop of robbers lurking in darkness to work
mischief, but they are an army to defend in broad daylight the worship of God, and all the just rights of mankind. I lay aside the whole, though each part would
bear the most strict scrutiny in this view; and I confine
myself to one character of the whole Christian religion
stated and explained by the apostle Paul. He says, that
there were in his doctrine " all riches of the full assurance of understanding to the acknowledgment of the
mystery of God, and of the Father, and of Christ, wherein" (see the margin of your Bibles), wherein " are hid
all the treasures of wisdom and knowledge." By the
mystery of God, and so on, the Apostle means the
Christian religion, which had been formerly a mystery,
or a secret, but which was then " made known unto the
sons of men." In this religion, he says, all treasures of
wisdom and knowledge are hid, that is, every article of
information necessary to our salvation is contained. One
chief excellence of the wisdom contained in the Gospel
is, that it hath a character of evidence ; it is rich in
proof of its truth and goodness, so rich as to produce the
" full assurance of the understanding." The Christian
religion doth not direct its professors to say, Perhaps
there is a God, possibly he might create the world, may
be he sent his Son to instruct and bless mankind, peradventure we may be good and happy by believing and
practising this religion: language fit enough for a drowsy Rabbi uttering traditions of men ; but a language not
proper to a wise God, and his inspired messengers.

" Thus saith the Lord," said the prophets; " This commandment have I received of my Father," said Jesus
Christ; " We preach not ourselves," said an apostle;
" God hath shined in our hearts, and the excellency of
the power is of God and not of us." This is the Gospel, of which you, feeble and timorous souls, are ashamed! There is one point, which I ought not to conceal
from you, for p erhaps you may err more through ignorance than malice. Perhaps, you " know not the man."

Have you attended to one word of the apostle Paul
concerning the subject, of which we are speaking, which
we just now called proof, or evidence of the truth of the
Christian religion, and which the apostle calls " manifestation of the truth?" That word is *conscience*. Hear
our apostle. " By manifestation of the truth we commend ourselves to every man's conscience in the sight
of God." Now, if you mistake conscience for convenience, and address the Gospel not to the natural justice, but to the pride and prejudices of mankind, you
may very well tremble for the fate of the Gospel, and
be ashamed of professing such an inconvenient religion.
If, on the contrary, you appeal to the consciences of
men, the very worst will be obliged to own, that the
morality of the Gospel is *holy*, and every part of it just
and good; and that if that which is good, works dislike
in any, it is because they are carnal, and sold under sin.
What we affirm of the morality of the Gospel, we affirm
of the just principles on which it is founded, and the
just motives by which it is enforced. Now we affirm,
with the Apostle, that the truth hath not only a character of evidence to the conscience, but that the proofs
are innumerable, and beyond all valuation. They are
riches, riches of assurance, riches of full assurance, producing " steadfastness of faith in Christ."

If you think fit to pursue this subject further, you
may inquire after the worth of the doctrine of Christ
among poor, sick, afflicted, persecuted, and dying Christians; they will tell you, it is their only support, and
their all-sufficient consolation: or you may ask the
young, the rich and prosperous disciples of Christ, and
they will tell you, it " puts more gladness into their

hearts than all the times in which their corn and their wine increased :" in short, in the " temple of God every one speaks of his glory," and every one saith to the bashful Christian, "Worship the Lord in the beauty of holiness by giving unto him the glory due unto his name." There is nothing to be ashamed of in the doctrine of Christ, nor need any man blush for believing what all the reasonable part of the world allow to be true. Let us not creep slily to worship God, and render by our meanness " the table of the Lord contemptible." Let us listen to him, who saith, " A son honoureth his father, and a servant his master: if then I be a Father, where is mine honour?" Let us reply to this gentle reproof, " The Lord is my light, whom shall I fear? The Lord is the strength of my life, of whom shall I be afraid? Though an host should encamp against me, my heart shall not fear ; though war should rise against me, in this will I be confident."

Should I proceed to examine the excellence of the example of Christ, our obligations to him, and his kind intentions towards us, it would appear, that Jesus Christ *ought not to be hid*, and that those servants who thought his livery fit only to be worn within doors, and that of the world most proper to appear in abroad, have not well understood the Christian religion. Their conduct implies an abominable error, a cruel slander upon the best of masters, that is, that there is some error, some injustice, or some impropriety in the Christian religion. Such people look less like the disciples of Christ, " whom God hath exalted to be a Prince and a Saviour," than the followers of " Theudas, who boasted of himself to be somebody, and to whom a number of men joined themselves, but who was slain, and all his followers scattered and brought to nought."

Let us remark, finally, that Jesus Christ *cannot be hid*. Long before we were born " the Lord multiplied visions, and used similitudes, and spoke of him by the ministry of the prophets." When he made his public appearance, " innumerable multitudes trod one upon another" to hear him. When he died, he was lifted up from the earth, and drew the attention of " all men unto him." The Pharisees could prevail nothing; but exclaimed, " Behold, the word is gone after him." Ma-·ny nations have said, " How beautiful are the feet of them, that preach the Gospel of peace ! Have they not heard ? yes, verily, the sound went into all the earth, and the words unto the ends of the world. Did not Israel know ?" Did not Ephesus and Antioch know ? Did not Rome know ? Did not Spain, Britain, and all the provinces of the empire know ? These " foolish nations ask-·ed not after him," but he was found of them though they sought him not. It is now too late to think of concealing a person so well known, and whom every eye shall see in the day of judgment.

As the person of Christ cannot be hid, so neither can his doctrine. There is, my brethren, a beautiful connexion established in the world between the condition of man and the compassion of God. Blessings are prepared for our necessities, and our necessities prepare us to receive these blessings. Doth God intend to incline the Egyptians to support the children of Jacob ? A long train of events, with a dreadful famine in the land shall endear a son of Jacob both to the prince and the people. The wise frugality of Joseph is a preparation for famine, and famine is a dicipline to bring the Egyptians acquainted with Joseph, and perhaps with Joseph's God. It was God, who both " called for a famine and sent a man before" to provide for it. Did the Egyptians, when the famine was very sore in the land " cry unto Pharaoh for bread ? Pharaoh said, Go unto Joseph." The necessity of the Egyptians, and the office of Joseph rendered it impossible for him to be hid. He was known, Pharaoh called him a " revealer of secrets," and the Egyptians honoured him with the name of " tender father." Thus the necessities of mankind oblige them to look out for a bosom of pity and love. And such an one is that of Jesus Christ. " He could not be hid," saith my text, " because a certain woman, whose young daughter had an unclean spirit, heard of him, and came and fell at his feet, saying, Lord, help me ; the dogs under the table eat of the children's crumbs." Numbers in the time of Christ were in conditions as bad or worse than that of this woman, and they must see him or die.

What can ignorant, guilty, or afflicted people do without this friend " born for adversity ?"   What can a man do, in whom all these disasters meet ?   Suppose any one of you should get a mischief in harvest-time, and should be obliged " to say unto the driver, Turn thine hand and carry me home, for I am wounded."   Suppose as you are carrying home, and your " blood running out of the wound into the midst" of the carriage, you should find yourself oppressed with a remembrance of all your sins, and guilt lie hard and heavy on your conscience ; then you would feel your mind overwhelmed with a thick midnight ignorance, and something in your soul foreboding danger.   Suppose, when your neighbours come round, one should shake her head, another wipe her eyes with her apron, and a third wring her hands, and say, " Prepare to meet thy God ; behold the Judge of all the earth standeth before the door ;" I ask, in such a case, would you, could you help asking, " Is there no balm in Gilead, no physician there ?   Is the harvest of life past, the summer ended, and I not saved ?"   You would ask such questions, the necessity of your case would compel you to ask such questions, and perhaps there would be no person about you that knew what to say ; perhaps some more intent upon your money than your soul, would thrust these questions aside to make room for a lawyer to make your will ; and perhaps some as ignorant as yourself would quiet you with superstition instead of the religion of faith and repentance, saying, " Peace, peace, when there is no peace ; for there is no peace," with the sacrament or without it, " there is no peace, saith my God, to the wicked."

Brethren, are there no death wounds but such as we receive in the manner just now mentioned?   Fevers, consumptions, and old age, do they never kill ; and if accidents slay thousands in a hundred years, do not diseases slay ten thousand every day ?   Let us foresee our end, and, if nothing else prevail with us, let the necessity of dying engage us to inquire, " If a man die, shall he live again ?   If man wasteth away, and give up the ghost, where is he ?"   Yes, he shall live again, he must live again, " the trumpet shall sound and the dead shall

be raised;" " the heavens shall pass away with a great
noise, the elements shall melt with fervent heat, the
earth also and the works that are therein shall be burnt
up ;" " the Lord Jesus shall be revealed from heaven,
with his mighty angels in flaming fire, taking vengeance
on them that know not God, and that obey not the Gospel
of our Lord Jesus Christ; who shall be punished with
everlasting destruction from the presence of the Lord,
and from the glory of his power." Are we under a necessity of passing through all these events, and will not
a conviction of this establish the text in regard to us ?
Jesus Christ " cannot be hid ;" our necessities oblige
us to inquire after him. We are under a necessity of
dying, and the power that brings us to the grave will
not consult us about the time or the means. We are
under a necessity of rising from the dead, and we shall
have no choice to rise, or to " sleep in the dust of the
earth." We are under a necessity of meeting the Judge,
and standing trial before God : we shall have no choice
to be tried, or not to be tried. We must of necessity
live in a future state, either in happiness or misery.
All these events are fixed, and the whole world can alter nothing. And do not all these become preachers to
us ? Doth not conscience within join with events without, and doth not each say, " I would make supplication
to my judge ?" " Seek the Lord while he may be found,
call upon him while he is near." " Surely the floods of
great waters shall not come nigh unto him, who pray-
eth unto God in a time when he may be found."

How many Christians can look back, and bless the
hand that compelled them to inquire after a Saviour !
They were once " at ease in Zion." Affliction joined
with a prophet, and poured into their ears, " Wo be to
them that are at ease. Wo to the drunkard. Wo to him
that striveth with his Maker. Wo to him that buildeth
his house in unrighteousness, and that useth his neighbour's service without wages. Wo to him that putteth
his bottle to his neighbour, and maketh him drunk. Wo
unto you, Scribes and Pharisees, hypocrites." Surrounded with warnings and proofs of danger, and being
like Noah " moved with fear," lest the flood coming up-

on ungodly men should carry him away, each entered into an examination of himself, and full of a conviction of the injustice of his life, the enmity of his heart, and the danger of his condition, fell down on his knees, all contrite and broken, and said, " Wo is me, I am undone, because I am a man of unclean lips!" The more he thought thereon, the more he wept. He seemed to himself like a man woke out of a dream, the day almost gone, the night near at hand. He said, " I perish with hunger." I hunger and thirst, not for the perishing things of this world, not for my own innocence, which is irrecoverably lost, not merely for repentance, for what can repentance do, unless God will accept it; "I will arise and go to my father," and ask him to feed my soul with forgiveness : but the nearer I approach him, the more fully I perceive he is of "purer eyes than to behold iniquity." What shall I do ? Or whither shall I flee ? Full of these just reflections he became grave, serious, and thoughtful, left off his former course of life, and forsook his old companions in sin. In vain they endeavoured to administer relief by telling him, God was merciful, he was no worse than his neighbours, repentance would make him melancholy, and raptures in religion raving mad. To all these he replied, " Miserable comforters are ye all. If your soul were in my soul's stead, I also could speak as ye do." Christians came round him ; he read the book, and heard the Gospel, from which they assured him they had derived instruction, that had relieved them in the same condition. He thought within himself, I am in the condition of the four lepers, who sat between the walls of a city perishing with famine, and the army of an enemy full of riches and plenty of provisions, and who reasoned thus : " If we say we will enter into the city, then the famine is in the city, and we shall die there ; and if we sit still here, we die also." We will repair unto the army, " if they save us alive, we shall live, and if they kill us, we shall but die." He applied this to himself, and said, if I return to the practice of sin, I shall be inevitably lost ; if I continue as I am, reflection and remorse will make me die with despair : I have been an enemy to good men, and even fighting against God ; " my soul hath

loathed them, and their soul also hath abhorred" such
characters as mine ; however, I will repair to Christian
assemblies ; the church is Bethesda, a house of mercy,
" it may be that the Lord of hosts will be gracious :"
yet God is a just and holy being, and his law saith, " The
soul that sinneth, it shall die ;" at all events, I must go,
and " I will go in unto the king, which is not according
to the law, and if I perish, I perish." To how many
trembling souls hath God, who " delighteth in mercy,"
held out the golden sceptre of grace, and said, What wilt
thou ? it shall be given thee ! Hence that joy unspeakable and full of glory, that " health of the countenance,"
that " strength of the heart," and all the holy exercises
of a pious, just, and benevolent life, " full of mercy and
good fruits."

Whither hath this subject carried me ! I have followed it, and I am got beyond what I proposed to treat
of. I was to show you, that the person of Christ, and
the Gospel of Christ " could not be hid :" but it seems,
the Gospel not only cannot be concealed in the bosom
of the Saviour, where there is nothing to resist its effu-
sion toward us ; but it cannot be hid even in the heart
of a wretched sinful man, whose dispositions are strongly bent to confine it. No, religion is of divine origin,
noble by nature, and disdains confinement. Repentance
in the heart will get into the eye, and come out into ·
company trickling down the cheek in silver drops like
dew. Meekness in the heart will make its way to the
countenance, and sit there smiling like a morning in
spring ; pity will slide the hand into the purse, and by
procuring relief for the wretched, publish the inexpressible feelings of the heart. Justice will be at every bargain, along with every contract, sometimes in the hand
holding the pen, and at other times in the tongue, saying both at the manor court and in the field, " Cursed
be he that removeth his neighbour's landmark, cursed
be he that confirmeth not all the words of the law to do
them." Christianity " cannot be hid." I might go further, and show you, that it will break out, even where
frail men, under the power of violent temptation, take
the utmost pains to suppress it. Whence that half-en-

joyment of sin, which men of little religion, eager to
glut themselves with it, so often discover? Observe
Peter. He sat among the enemies of Christ. Said one,
" Thou wast with Jesus :" No, said he, " woman, I know
him not." Said another, presently, " Thou art one of
them :" No, said he, " man, I am not." About an hour
after, a third said, " Surely thou art one of them, for
thy speech betrayeth thee." Was it only the Galilean
broad country way of speaking that betrayed him ?
Were there no looks of anxiety toward his master ? No
indignation in his countenance against the cruel talk of
the company? Was there never a sigh stole out un-
perceived by him, but observed by the company ? Did
he utter, " I know not the man," without blushing and
hesitating ? When he began to curse and to swear, did
he go about his work like a workman, a master blasphemer ? I think not. I think a good man swears, as
a blasphemer prays, that is, with an ill grace; the very
tone and air of the speech betray the temper of the
heart.

To conclude. If we love concealment, let us observe
the kingdom of sin ; it is a kingdom of darkness. Remember what the Scripture calls the place of him that
knoweth not God. " The light is dark in his tabernacle. The snare is hidden for him in the ground, and a
trap is set for him in the way. He walketh upon a
snare, and his own counsel shall cast him down. Destruction shall be ready at his side, and the first born of
death shall devour his strength. He shall be chased
out of the world, and be brought to the king of terrors.
He shall flee from the iron weapon, and the bow of steel
shall strike him through. The heaven shall reveal his
iniquity, the earth shall rise up against him, and he
shall drink of the wrath of the Almighty. This is the
portion of a wicked man, the heritage appointed unto
him by God." God grant us grace " to flee from the
wrath to come." To him be honour and glory for ever.
Amen.

10*

DISCOURSE VII.

JOHN vii. 46.

Never man spake like this man.

So said the officers, whom the Pharisees and chief priests had sent to take Jesus Christ into custody, assigning this as a reason why they had not executed their commission: but before we attend to what they say, we will make two observations on the officers themselves, and the offices they held.

Observe, first, how dangerous it is to a man's virtue to hold places in some times, under some governments. It is impossible to be truly happy without being truly good and virtuous; it is impossible to be good without being free; and it is impossible to be free without being independent; for he, who depends on a master for his whole support, and who hath the misfortune to serve an unjust master, cannot obey some orders without giving up either his integrity or his livelihood, and few men have goodness enough to give up the last for the sake of the first. These officers of the board of priests were in this dangerous condition. They were kept for the sake of executing such orders as their unjust masters thought fit to issue. It was on the day of a great religious festival, when the inhabitants of Jerusalem were performing their devotions, that these priests held a council, and, having determined to seize the person of Christ, sent these officers to take him. When they returned without him, their masters reproved them, and gave them a very just notion of their condition, by saying, " Have any of the rulers believed on him ?" To which the officers made no reply, for they thoroughly understood that underlings in office are not supposed to have any sentiments of their own, but receive their salaries for doing only what they are bid.

These men might have known this by reading their own Bible. There the punishment denounced against the family of Eli is described. " Every one shall come and crouch to the high priest for a piece of silver, and a morsel of bread, and shall say, Put me, I pray thee, into one of the priest's offices, that I may eat a piece of bread." ' It was not the poverty, but the cringing slavishness of the family, that was intended in the threatening, a part of which was, " they that despise me shall be lightly esteemed." There also, in the tenth Psalm, are fully described the practices of those who make slaves, and the misery of those poor people, who submit to slavery for the sake of worldly advantages. The first are said to be men of " strong parts," whose " mouths are full of deceit," who " sit in the lurking places of the villages," and who " crouch like lions in their dens to catch the poor in a net." The last are said to be " poor, fatherless, and oppressed, taken in times of trouble, in the devices imagined" by their betrayers. O the ingenious devices ! O the goodly pretences, which both sides use to carry on this " merchandise of slaves and souls of men." Let us learn to live by our own industry, then we shall be independent: let us live within our income, then we shall be virtuous: let us never fix our attention on public money, then we shall be free, at least we shall never be obliged by a pretended duty of office to violate an actual duty of religion. Some miserable parents train up their children at a great expense, and with great guilt ; and having at length taught them to be very expensive themselves, and not having a fortune to support luxury, they are obliged to sell them to the highest bidder, and expect to be repaid by turning these hungry wolves out upon the public. What a beggarly ambition, to be a Pharisee's man! How much better, because how much more innocent, is it to be an honest day-labourer! Little do labouring men think what Pharisees and task-masters and Pharoahs say to their officers in private, and how well the officers of such men are trained up to understand looks; and hints, and half-words, where no express orders are given! Some officers of these priests, perhaps the same men who uttered the text, " took Jesus and bound him ;" and one of them, perhaps to make peace with his masters for not having done his duty before, " struck him with the palm of his hand" in open court, and said, " Answerest thou the high priest so ?" For Jesus Christ had just said to the high priest, " Ask them which heard me what I said; behold they know what I said ;" referring very likely to this very saying in the text, " Never man spake like this man."

However, let charity expound this history; and let us observe in the next place, and let us hope for the honour of human nature it is true, that there are upright men, who dare not execute some unjust commissions, though they seem bound by office to do so. Such instances are rare ; but there have been instances of men, who have quitted offices, and all the wealth and honours annexed to them, rather than do an unjust thing. It is said to the honour of two women, who held a useful office in Egypt, that they did not commit murder " as the king commanded them ;" and to their integrity we owe that eminent servant of God, Moses. How many such as Moses we have been deprived of by such orders, " the day shall declare."

When these officers went to take Jesus Christ, he was " standing in the temple and speaking boldly of the spirit, which they that believe on him should receive, when the Holy Ghost should be given, after he was glorified." Very likely our Lord was expounding some of the prophecies, for he said, " If any man thirst, let him come unto me, and drink. He that believeth on me, as the Scripture hath said, out of his heart shall flow rivers of living water." It must have been very delightful to hear Jesus Christ explain the prophecies, and particularly such as are contained in the thirty-fifth and forty-fourth of Isaiah, the second chapter of Joel, and other places, where the Holy Spirit is spoken of under the similitude of a well, or a spring in the minds and hearts of inspired men. " The mouth of a righteous man is a well of life," and Christian knowledge is a " well of water springing up into everlasting life."

· " Many of the people, when they heard this" discourse, were persuaded that the speaker was an extraordinary person, and others thought, he was the promised Messiah. " Many said, of a truth this is the Prophet," that is, the Prophet spoken of by Moses; others said, " This is the Christ." The officers ventured to say in general, " Never man spake like this man." We unite these opinions, and affirm, Jesus is the Prophet like Moses, he is the Christ, he is the man who spoke as no man but himself ever did speak; and we are going to show you this evening that Jesus Christ is the most excellent of all teachers. They who were so happy as to attend his ministry, as it is written in the Prophets, were " all taught of God;" and they who are so happy as to hear his doctrine now, though not honoured to hear it from his own lips, may truly say, " Master, we know that thou teachest the way of God in truth." " Blessed is the man, O Lord, whom, thou teachest out of thy law," though not out of thine own mouth.

Our Divine Instructer excelled all others in that eminent qualification of a public teacher, a " perfect knowledge of what he taught." Jesus Christ understood the subject of religion: Jesus Christ understood the whole of religion : and Jesus Christ understood the whole perfectly. I say our instructer understood religion, and herein he differed from many who have pretended to instruct mankind; but who, to use the language of an apostle, have taught " fables and questions, which have turned men aside unto vain jangling, understanding neither what they said, nor whereof they affirmed." The heathens pretended to teach religion; but what they taught for religion was superstition founded upon fable, and their instructions concerning worship and devotion, all led an ignorant multitude after their ignorant teachers up to " an altar with this inscription, ' To the un--, known God.' " None of these men ever saw God at any time ; but it was the only-begotten Son, who was " in the bosom of the Father," who declared him to us. To be in the bosom of any one, signifies to know that person thoroughly : in this sense Jesus Christ was in the bosom of the Father, and hence this expression, " No man knoweth the Father save the Son, and he to whomsoever the Son will reveal him." And again, " No man hath seen the Father, save he, which is of God, he hath seen the Father." I said, Jesus Christ understood the whole of religion : and herein he differed from all the Prophets, who searched " what the spirit of Christ which was in them did signify," and from all the apostles, who " knew only in part, and prophesied only in part." The understanding of Jesus Christ comprehended the past, the present, and the future ; and this is one reason for his saying to his servant John, " I am Alpha and Omega, the first and the last ; what thou seest, write in a book, and send unto the seven churches." Further, I said Jesus Christ understood the whole of religion perfectly. His understanding of religion was clear, complete, full, without any defect, and there is not in all the instructions given us by him a single line of guess work. He hath built the whole of the Christian religion on certain principles, beyond all conjecture and peradventure. On this account the Scriptures are called the " lively oracles of God," the first principles of which were committed to the Jews, carried to perfection by the apostles, and given to us with this express charge, " Minister one to another as good stewards ; if any man speak, let him speak as the oracles of God." " Never man spake like this man" in regard to a perfect knowledge of the subject.

He knew the perfections of God, the nature of man, the laws of Providence, which govern this world, and all the distributions of happiness and misery, which will take place in the next. Wisdom in him was natural, perfect, and eternal, and " of his fulness have all inspired writers received, and grace for grace." What a mind, what an astonishing mind was that of Jesus Christ ! If all inspired men were only distributors of his wisdom ; if they knew nothing of themselves, and received all their just sentiments out of his fulness, how far beyond all our conceptions of a wise man must Jesus Christ be ! What a character of majesty is there in these words, " I am the vine, ye are the branches,—without me ye can do nothing,—the branch cannot bear fruit of itself!" Christians ! follow this heavenly idea of husbandry. Take up the fourteen epistles of Paul, and consider them as a rich cluster of grapes, like that which " two men bore upon a staff between them," when they returned from searching the promised land, and examine what a number of just and excellent notions on a multitude of subjects are contained in them. To these add the writings of all the other inspired men, which, like the mantling branches of a luxuriant vine, have been shooting out their soft tendrils for almost eighteen hundred years over all countries, and " bringing forth fruit in all the world ;" and ask, Whence had these men this knowledge ? And the Jews, even priests, captains, and Sadducees will tell you, they " had been with Jesus," and they themselves will confirm it by saying, " Of his fulness have all we received a spirit of prophecy" to enable us to prophesy, " divers kinds of tongues, gifts of healing, words of wisdom and knowledge," dispositions of piety and justice, and every thing else that made us what we are ;" " we are the branches, Christ is the vine," without him we should have known and done nothing. Hence these expressions, " I laboured, yet not I, but the grace of God which was with me ; I live, yet not I, but Christ liveth in me. I am not in any thing behind the very chiefest apostles, though I be nothing." It would become the wisest of mankind in the presence of these inspired men to say, " We are in our own sight, as we were in their sight, as grasshoppers :" but even these angels of mankind, in the presence of Jesus Christ, are not as grasshoppers, but as nothing.

Our heavenly Teacher, out of the rich abundance of his knowledge, made a judicious choice of the subjects of his ministry. This is a second excellence, and it is edifying to see what directed his prudent mind in mak-

ing the choice. He was governed by the condition of
his disciples. When he was taking his leave of them,
he said, " I have many things to say unto you, but ye
cannot bear them now :" as if he had said, I perfectly
understand every thing, and did I consult my fame more
than your good, I would tell you every thing ; but I love
you, I know the infancy of your faith, and the strength of
your temptations to be vain in yourselves, forgetful of
me, undutiful to God, and unprofitable to society; and
therefore I will adapt my instructions to your present
condition, and reserve full information till you arrive at
a perfect state. On this principle all revelation is built,
and such subjects are taught as are necessary to make
us good men. So much of history, so much of prophecy, so much of doctrine, and so much of motives to obedience are told us as our present condition in this life
requires. The Christian religion is addressed to a sober conscience, not to a vain curiosity : it is intended to
make us righteous, not cunning.

Our Saviour hath discovered his eminent prudence in
the choice of his subjects, by selecting what is true,
important, and proper. The subjects taught by Jesus
Christ are all strictly and wholly true. The prophets
speak of two sorts of teachers, whom they plainly call
teachers of lies. The first were such as taught idolatry : " what profiteth a graven image, and a teacher of
lies ?" What is an idol, or what is a teacher of idolatry good for? The whole is falsehood. The second
were leaders of the people of God, who caused them to
err by mixing folly and falsehood with divine truth : " the
prophet that teacheth lies, he is the tail." Jesus Christ
was a teacher of truth in opposition to both these. He
taught the perfections, goverment, and worship of the
true God, and he mixed no traditions of men with his
instructions. When truth comes to us through uninspired men, it comes to us like light through a dusty or
discoloured window, so treacherous are the memories,
and so imperfect are the minds of the best of men : but
truth coming immediately from Jesus Christ resembles
the light abroad, all unpolluted and pure. As all his
doctrines were true, so he chose to make those truths

.the subjects of his ministry, which were important; and there is not in all the information given us by him a single trifle. · Every thing is of the utmost consequence for somebody to know, and most articles are of great moment- to all his disciples. How important to devotion is it to know the God we adore! How important ·to the exercise of repentance is the knowledge of ourselves! How important to our faith is the knowledge of the true and real character of Jesus Christ! How important to our safety is the knowledge-of this world, and how necessary to the regulation of our lives is the knowledge of the world to come! In all these articles Jesus Christ hath fully instructed us. There are truths, from the knowledge of which we should derive no more benefit than we should by knowing that a crow dropped a feather as she flew over a mountain in Ireland. Our Lord knew the little time and the little capacity of his disciples too well, to waste his breath, and their attention, about articles of no consequence to them. "Lord," said Peter " what shall this man do?" To which our Lord replied, "What is that to thee?" How many questions, and even questions concerning religion, deserve the same answer, " What is that to thee?" Whether it be friendship or curiosity, that makes thee inquisitive about the duty and the fate of John, it is indifferent; for either would serve, through thy depravity, to divert thine attention from thyself. I have been telling thee, thou shalt live to old age, and then be girded and carried to die whither thou wouldest not, and I have been ordering thee to spend the remainder of thy life in feeding my sheep and lambs : study thy duty, prepare for thy death; what is the fate of John, to thee but a dangerous speculation ? " Follow thou me."

There was in the choice of subjects by Jesus Christ, not only truth and importance, but propriety. Every thing he taught was proper for him to teach, and suited to his disciples to learn. There was a justness in both these respects in all his instructions. He never forgot his own dignity, so as to utter any thing unsuitable to the eminent character he assumed ; and he always at-

11

tended to the imperfections and infirmities, the real conditions and the best interests of his disciples.   Were
they in danger ? He gave them friendly warnings.   Did
they sin ?   He gave them gentle, and sometimes sharp
reproofs.   When they were inquisitive on proper subjects he poured forth instruction ; and when an idle curiosity put them on asking questions, he restrained their
folly, and turned their attention to what was substantial,
and fit for men in their condition to know.   When they
were in trouble, he supported them with the comforts of
religion ; and when they were attacked by their enemies, he showed them how to defend themselves with
the weapons of it.   It would be easy to exemplify the
justness and propriety of all the ministry of Jesus Christ
by comparing each of his discourses with the persons to
whom, and the times and circumstances in which it was
spoken ; but we will leave this for you to examine at
your leisure.   You will find, that though he was always,
humble, yet he was never mean ; you will find him always zealous, never frantic ; always kind, never fond ;
always firm, never sour ; always various, yet always the
same ; his wisdom manifold, but all tending to "the two
commandments, on which hang all the law and the prophets : the first, Thou shalt love thy God with all thy soul ;
and the second, Thou shalt love thy neighbour as thyself."   For choice of subjects true, important, and proper, " never man spake like this man."

One chief excellence of our heavenly teacher is the
plainness of his instructions.   All his discourses have
a singular artlessness and simplicity ; they not only may
be understood, but they cannot be misunderstood.
There are none of what an apostle calls " great swelling
words of vanity," such as an extravagant genius invents
to give himself consequence.   There are no new fine
terms taken from the court of Herod after the fashionable polish of the court of Herod's master the Roman
Emperor, the language usually of a man, who affects
not to think and speak like the vulgar.   Even the style
of the prophets was simplified by him, and *Jehovah* softened into *Father*.   What he affirms of every person and

every thing is expressed so clearly, that whoever attends to his descriptions must take in his meaning, and
no other. The connection, which he establisheth, be--
tween one part of religion and another part, is equally
clear; as for example, between sin and punishment,
faith and holiness, repentance and forgiveness, christianity and persecution, holiness and happiness, his own
glory and that of all his followers. If a person cannot at
first enter into all these particulars, yet it is impossible he should not see the general sense of the Christian
religion : as, that it is from heaven, that it is an enemy
to error and sin, that it directs men to be holy, and rewards them for being so, that Christ is a Redeemer, and
all his people free. When John the Baptist sent two of
his disciples to inquire of Jesus, whether he were the
expected Messiah, Jesus answered, " Go, and shew John
the things which ye do hear and see," one of which
was, " the poor have the gospel preached to them," that
is to say, the glad tidings of salvation are so preached
by me that the uneducated poor understand them as
the prophets foretold. " The king's son shall save
the children of the needy. He shall come down like
rain upon" . . . . . what, think ye, my brethren ? Like
rain upon the tall cedars, and the lofty mountains, the
painted tulip, and the snow-white lily ? No, upon the
" mown grass, and the bare earth ;" " he shall come down
like rain upon the mown grass, as showers that water
the earth." This is a constant character of the Messiah
in the prophecies, and if you doubt whether I have
given you the true sense of the passage just now mentioned, consult the thirty-fifth chapter of Isaiah, in
which the prophet considers *fools*, that is the poor, neglected, untaught part of mankind, who are generally reputed fools, as finding, and walking in " the way of holiness" made " an highway" by the teacher sent from God :
and he resembles these people to a " wilderness, a lone
place, a desert, a parched and thirsty piece of ground,"
on account of their being neglected and uncultivated, and
even despised and cursed by the proud Rabbies. The
language of a Rabbi to these people was, You were " al-

together born in sin, you know not the law, and are cursed;" but the language of Jesus Christ was, "Go tell John, the poor have the Gospel preached to them. Go tell that fox, Herod, I must walk to-day, and to-morrow, and the day following, for it cannot be that a prophet perish out of Jerusalem." Go, christians, tell the whole world that Jesus Christ preached the Gospel to the poor in a wicked city, when he knew it would cost him his life.

For artlessness and simplicity, for a plainness that could not but be understood by people the most likely to misunderstand it, "never man spake like this man."

There is one circumstance mentioned by the prophets, and accomplished in the life of Christ, which does great honour to his ministry, and which is a full proof of the simplicity and plainness of his doctrine; that is, the part which the little folks in Jerusalem, the children of the poor inhabitants, took in the ministry of Jesus Christ. When Jesus made his public entry into Jerusalem riding on a colt, the foal of an ass, "the multitude, the blind, the lame," and even the "children," told the daughter of Zion, Behold thy mild and lowly King cometh; and the children sung part of a psalm in honour of the son of David, and blessed him that came in the name of the Lord. The citizens said, "Who is this?" The chief priests and scribes pretended not to know; but the multitude knew, and said, This is Jesus the prophet; and the children knew, and Jesus Christ declared that God had "perfected praise out of the mouths of babes and sucklings." "Have ye never read this?" said he to the priests and scribes. We have many instances in the Gospel of the sound knowledge, which some of the lowest of the people had of the true character of Jesus Christ, and we have both a satisfactory account given of him, and a fine train of substantial reasoning to support that account, by a blind beggar before a council of Rabbies holding a court session. For using great plainness of speech "never man spake like this man."

By what unheard of method did Jesus Christ teach poor children and blind beggars to understand the holy Scriptures? By what means did he convey this kind of knowledge to whole multitudes? By what art did he carry such full conviction into the minds of his hearers as to force them publicly to express their approbation on the spot, and even women, contrary to their usual bashfulness, to exclaim, " Blessed is the womb that bare thee, and the paps which thou hast sucked ?"　By what method did he take twelve " unlearned and ignorant men," and enable them so to teach, that the heathens took them for the chief of their gods, and would have sacrificed oxen adorned with garlands unto them, and that the wisest of the Rabbies were " not able to resist the wisdom and the spirit by which they spoke ?　It was by his skill in bringing down the great truths of religion to the size of the understandings of his hearers, and by doing this without sinking the dignity and importance of the truths, and without racking and torturing the minds of his disciples.　Two things are necessary to this plainness of speech ; the one, that the subjects themselves be stated simply without being mixed with other subjects, without being rendered abstruse by needless arguments and ornaments ; and thus Jesus Christ proposed his doctrine : and the other, that the persons to whom the doctrine is addressed be taught to make use of their own understandings ; for it is with the mind as it is with the body, a man does not know what he can do, till he tries.　Both these are included in these words of the wise man, " All the words of my mouth are in righteousness," or right, " there is nothing froward or perverse in them; they are all plain to him that understandeth," that is, to him who dare make use of his own understanding.　When the officers listened to Christ, and judged for themselves, they thought " Never man spake like him ;" but when they returned, and began to inquire whether any of the rulers believed on him, the subject became perplexed, and this unparalleled teacher seemed a cheat.　All the words of the law were written very plainly ; the prophecies were " written plain upon tables, that he might run that read them ;" the apostles " used great plainness of speech ;" but for this excellence Jesus Christ exceeded them all, and " never man spake so plainly as this man."

Another excellence of our heavenly teacher is the
11*

affecting manner, in which he proposes all his instructions to us. He was himself a person of the finest feelings. He had fears and hopes, joys and sorrows, anger
and love, and all the passions of a perfect man. He
thoroughly knew by his own experience what was in
man, and was " touched with a feeling of our infirmities." His doctrine therefore was taught with emotions
of pleasure and pain in himself; sometimes he rejoiced
with his disciples, and sometimes he wept; and it was
accompanied with emotions of pleasure and pain in his
hearers. The subjects of religion are chiefly invisible.
Who ever saw, or can see God? Who can see the soul
of man, or heaven or hell? What living man can see
sin in all its effects in regard to God, himself, and other
creatures? Who hath seen the resurrection of the
dead, the day of judgment, the spirits of the just, and
" the devil and his angels?" " Where wast thou when I
laid the foundations of the earth? Have the gates of
death been opened unto thee? Shall it be told God
that we speak of these subjects? If a man speak, surely he shall be swallowed up." Yes, my brethren, these
subjects would have swallowed up the capacities of all
mankind, and there is but one way of making men so
understand them as to be properly affected with them;
so as to have fear enough to make them humble, but
not enough to drive them mad; so as to have love
enough to make them holy, but not enough to make
them neglect their families, and their employments in
life; this way is to use similitudes, and to liken the objects which we cannot see, to other objects which we
do see, and with which we are well acquainted. The
prophets used this method much, and therefore were
understood; the apostle Paul used it least, and therefore
in all his epistles are some things hard to be understood;
but the instructions given us by Jesus Christ are chiefly
similitudes, and for properly moving the heart, " never
man spake like this man."

For example, what a picture of four of these articles
doth Jesus Christ give us in the parable of the Prodigal
Son! The principal figure is Almighty God, the God of
the " whirlwind and the storm, whose way is in the sea,

whose path is in the great waters, and whose footsteps are not known; whose voice thunders in the heaven, and whose lightnings make the earth tremble and shake; whose fury is poured out like the fire, which throws down rocks, yea, burns the world, and all that dwell therein." In what light doth the parable present this God, so terrible to the wicked, to the eyes of a repenting sinner! It is but one word; but, my God! what a whole Gospel doth that one word, " Father," contain! A Father patient and silent during all the provocations of his son; a " Father seeing him, when he was a great way off, melting with compassion for him, running, falling on his neck, and kissing him." A Father cutting short the confession of his son, preventing him with his goodness, receiving him liberally, and upbraiding him not. A Father ordering, " Bring forth the best robe, and bring hither the fatted calf, and let us eat and be merry:" a Father filling his house with " music and dancing," overflowing with happiness in himself, and telling his other son and all his servants, I have " received my son safe and sound; this my son was dead, and is alive again, he was lost and is found!" O lovely picture of the best of beings, my Father and my God, always be before my eyes, when I presume to approach the " throne of grace to obtain mercy, and to find grace to help in time of need!"

What a picture of sin and wretchedness doth the life of the prodigal afford! A son, a son of such a Father, a younger son dead to the edifying example of his elder brother, going from home, with all his fortune, into a far country, and wasting all his substance in riotous living: a son of such a family disgracing himself in the service of a swine-herd, a keeper of cattle expressly forbidden to be eaten by man, or offered in sacrifice to God: a wretch perishing with hunger, and wishing himself one of these execrated animals, that he might eat and fatten and die like them: a son who had behaved in his prosperity so brutally to others, that in his extremity no man would give him even the privilege of a beggar, a morsel of bread to save him from starving to death: a son trembling at the thought of seeing such a

Father, and hardly daring to ask the favour of being admitted among the lowest of his servants ! What a number of just and affecting ideas of sin are contained in this live picture of profligate men ! Every sinner in the whole world is in some stage of this wretchedness. Some are now receiving, others are now spending, and others are half distracted for the waste of their "portion of goods." In what stage, my hearers, are you ?

There is a third subject, that is, repentance, described in a very pathetic manner, in this parable. The son "came to himself," that is, recovered his lost senses, his memory, his reason, his duty, his sense of honour, respect for his Father, disdain for his condition, and a modest ambition to aspire at something like his former happy state. Hear him: "How many hired servants of my Father have bread enough and to spare, and I perish with hunger ! I will arise, and go to my Father." Go, young man, it is the best thing you can do ; "the Father of whom you speak is yet alive," and yet a Father; he "knows your sorrows ; behold, he cometh forth to meet thee, and when he seeth thee, he will be glad in his heart."

A fourth picture is contained in this parable ; and the joy of good men at the repentance of a sinner is set forth by the pleasure of the servants, and the censure, which the proud and unfeeling part of the Jews passed, undutifully on the goodness of God, and cruelly on the condition of such penitents as the Gentiles, is held forth in the conduct of the elder brother, who yet at last recovers by the reasoning of his Father from the sullen temper, into which he had fallen at the first admission of such great sinners into the church of God. This short parable is so constructed as to contain a history of all times from Adam to the end of the world ; and the few characters exhibited in it are almost all, that are worth knowing in the universe. The subjects go home to the business and bosoms of all mankind, and probably his one parable hath "brought many sons to glory."

It would be easy to show, were it necessary, that the same ease, convenience, and address to the passions for the best and noblest purposes run through the whole doctrine of our teacher. Ask an exact philosopher, What is conscience? He will tell you; It is a man's opinion of his own actions. Ask him, What is hell? He will tell you; It is a state of future punishment. Ask him, what repentance is. He will tell you: It is a sorrow for sin. All true; all just; all exact; but all as cold as clear, like a sharp frosty night. Jesus Christ will inform you, that repentance is the return of an undutiful profligate, home to his kind, though insulted Father. Conscience is " the worm that never dieth ;" hell is " the fire that never shall be quenched." " The words that I speak unto you," said he, " they are spirit, and they are life." Hence thousands join with the officers in the text, and say, " Never man spake like this man."

Finally, consider one excellence more in the instructions given us by our Saviour; they were all *confirmed by his own example.* Many teachers of mankind have been mere teachers of words, and their lives have falsified all they said. What a sad course of life : to render truth probable by our preaching, and doubtful by our practice : to describe the path to heaven on the Lord's day, and to tread out the road to hell all the week! Even the best of men have exemplified only a part of their doctrine : such are the imperfections of the most wise and willing! But Jesus Christ exemplified every part of religion. Did he teach piety? He was pious himself, and paid his heavenly Father the first and highest adoration. Did he teach us to love our neighbours? And who ever carried his love to others so far as our Divine Instructer? Did he teach us to love ourselves? He showed us in his own person what a wise and well directed self-love is. In short, he never did any thing to render his religion suspected; and every action of his life tended to establish it. His vile disciple, Judas, who betrayed him, and whom he kept in his family perhaps for the sake of submitting his most private actions to examination, Judas, I say, hanged himself for betraying innocent blood. It is the privilege of Jesus Christ alone to stand up, and say " Which of you," friends or enemies, you strangers, or you of my own family,—" which of you convinceth me of sin?"

Blessed Lord! Far be it from us to blame any one action of thy life! We admire the whole, we subscribe to the description of one, who thoroughly knew thee, and say with him, Thou art " the only-begotten of the Father, full of grace and truth:" full of truth, and endowed with the most graceful manner of uttering it. No, " never man spake like this man."

Sum up all these excellences; a perfect knowledge of all truth in every part; a wise choice of such truths, and such parts of truths as were proper to constitute a religion fit for this world; a clear manner of stating them so as to carry conviction to the understanding, and to obtain assent and belief; an affecting colouring, natural, beautiful, and pathetic, engaging all the emotions of the heart in the service of truth; an example showing religion alive in real actions of every kind of holiness, of piety towards God, purity in self, and love to all mankind,—and allow Jesus Christ the honour due to his merit, that he was the first and most excellent of all teachers, and that " never man spake like this man."

Consider the dignity and duration of his doctrine. Spoken only in the little kingdom of Judea, it hath sounded through all parts of the world; and thousands living and dying have reported it, and set their seal to the truth and goodness of it. It hath not been supported in the world by arms or artifice, learning or wealth: but it hath stood where a religion ought to stand, in the convictions and consciences of mankind; and so forcible hath it been, that it hath withstood all the attacks of learning and ignorance, riches and cruelty, the malice of its enemies, and the unguarded injuries of its friends. How many ignorant minds hath it enlightened! How many hard hearts hath it softened! How many daring rebels hath it subdued! How many wicked thoughts hath it prevented from growing into actions! How many tears of repentance, how many holy resolutions, how many just and charitable actions, how many exercises of piety, how many holy lives, and happy deaths hath it produced! Were the effects of his doctrine suspended only for one day, how many would spend that one day in crying, " Return, O Lord, unto the many thousands of Israel ?" What am I saying, one day ? I venture to affirm that of the doctrine of Christ, which the Scripture says of the air, " If he gather unto himself his spirit and his breath, in a moment shall they die, all flesh shall perish together, and man shall turn again unto dust."

My brethren, the day will come, in which Jesus Christ will, so to speak, "gather up his breath and his spirit," call again for the Bible he lent you, and inquire what use you made of it. I hope you will not say as the unjust Jews did, " God forbid." Our Lord was one day teaching the people in the temple ; and the chief priests, and the scribes, and the elders were present. He told them in a parable, which they well understood, that they were tenants to God for a well planted vineyard, and that justice required they should pay their rent : but that, instead of doing this, they wounded and shamefully treated the servants of their Lord, who were sent to demand it ; and when he sent his son on the same errand they murdered him. To which he added this question, " What therefore shall the Lord of the vineyard do unto them?" And as they made no answer, he assured them, " the Lord of the vineyard shall come and destroy these husbandmen, and shall give the vineyard to others." When they heard this they cried, " God forbid !" Forbid what? Would you, priests, murder the son of God, and not be tried for the crime ? Would you, scribes, read and write over the contract between the Lord and his tenants, and know the profits of the vineyard to be immense, and the rent to be small and easy,—would you abuse the produce and pay no rent, and insult your Lord, and after all not be called to an account? And you, grey-headed elders, where is your gravity, and wisdom, and justice, where are all the laws and rules of court, by which you judge your fellow-creatures? would you be above law, and set the law-giver of the world at defiance ? God forbid justice should not be done ! God forbid there should be no difference between " him that sweareth, and him that feareth an oath !" " If the foundations," the first principles

of all order and government, "be destroyed, what can the
righteous do?" No, do not say, "God forbid;" but rather say, "Thy kingdom come! Come, Lord Jesus, come
quickly!" Weigh this well, before you put up a prayer
so dangerous to some people. Do you know what answer Jesus Christ makes to this prayer? He confirms
what was just now said to you, that when he comes he
will call for an account of the book he lent you. Hear
him. "Behold, I come quickly; blessed is he that
keepeth the sayings of this book. For I testify unto
every man that heareth the words of the prophecy of
this book, if any man shall add unto these things, God
shall add unto him the plagues that are written in this
book: and if any man shall take away from the words
of this book, God shall take away his part out of the
book of life, and out of the holy city and from the things
which are written in this book."

Let us conclude by establishing the wisdom and goodness of this last declaration, in substance an answer of
the prayers of good men, and as applicable to all other
inspired books as to that of the Revelation of John, to
which it is affixed. In order to this we will apply the
subject to two characters.

Can any thing sufficiently expose the folly of such
as would either increase, or diminish the Gospel of Jesus Christ? Suppose I should say to you, Good people, in the course of my ministry, I perceive I give you
offence; I am determined to do so no more; and in order to give you a full proof of my sincerity, I will in
future sit one hour before preaching in the cottage just
by the barn, and receive your instructions in writing.
If you would have me not preach any part of the Gospel, signify that part, and if you would have me mix
with the Gospel any thing to suit your disposition,
only speak the word, and it shall done. If a people
could be found so silly, and so wicked, what a collection of notes should I have! One would be, Sir,
I beg you would not speak against covetousness: it
will offend me. Another would be, You are desired to
say nothing against slander: it is the pleasure of my
life. A third would be, Pray, preach nothing but the

terrors of the law ; and a fourth, Please to dwell wholly
on the promises of grace, and say nothing about duty.
One would say, Mix a little personal abuse with the
Gospel, and rage and rail at my enemy ; my pleasure rises with his pain.   Although nobody is so lost to shame as
to speak thus, and to say to a teacher of religion, Pray
flatter my sins, and make me " twofold more a child of
hell than before," yet almost all love to have it so : but at
this rate what of the Gospel should we have left ?   As it
is, it is the wisdom of God, and the power of God ; and
though it be a " stumbling block to the Jews, and fool-
ishness to the Greeks," yet it is that by which " it
pleaseth God to save them that believe."   Let us renounce such idle dreams and let us " search the Scriptures, for in them we have eternal life, and they are
are they which testify of Jesus Christ."   Let it never
be said of any of us, " Ye have not his word abiding
in you."   Bold undertaking !   Burn the old Gospel of
Jesus Christ, it is too hard or too easy, too holy or
too patient, too zealous or too cool, or too something, that does not suit the taste of the world ; and let
me compose and publish a new Gospel, with a God but
without a law, with a Saviour but without a cross, with
a heaven but without a narrow way to it !   Bold and
daring rebel !   Who are you ?   The whole world shall
rise up against you ; you shall not leave out such essential parts, you shall not add, or diminish one word, one
jot, or one tittle, till all be fulfilled :   and " whosoever shall break one of the least commandments, and
shall teach men so, he shall be called the least in the
kingdom of heaven."

Christians, I address myself to you, to you who " esteemed the word of God more than your necessary food."
Enjoy this evening the pleasure, that this rich subject
affords.   You love your Divine Master, you think, for
you know by experience, " never man spake like this
man."   You wish others knew the wisdom and goodness of his doctrine, and especially your near relations.
You envy Martha, and could you have the honour she
had of entertaining Jesus Christ in person, you would
ask him to use his influence with your friends to direct

12

them to their duty : you would say, Lord, "bid my sister help me ; dost thou not care that she hath left me to serve alone ? " Peace ! careful Martha ! Do not tax thy Divine Master with taking less care of thy sister than thou dost. "He careth for thee," he careth for her ; he is not "an hireling, who careth not for the sheep," he is "the good shepherd, he knoweth his sheep," and all his "sheep hear his voice," and follow him. Yes, all his sheep hear his voice, and by the wise management of teaching a Gospel, and causing it to be written, he hath established an universal conversation, and though dead, and gone far, far from us, "yet speaketh" by his word in all our religious assemblies, in all our houses, and in every place where the heavenly instruction comes. See, he is this moment speaking terror and reproof to that man, in whose ears, by his own fireside, one of his children is now reading this passage, "How often would I have gathered thy children together, even as a hen gathereth her chickens under her, wings, and you would not." Observe that other wandering sheep looking once more toward the fold, from which his rov- ing disposition made him stray ; see, he is sitting under a tree, and now reading this passage, "Simon, son of Jonas, lovest thou me ? Simon, son of Jonas, lovest thou me more than thy sins ? " See, his countenance changes, he is grieved that his conduct should make his love to Christ suspected, he bursts into tears, and saith, "Lord, thou knowest all things, thou knowest I love thee !" Behold yon distressed family, the man and his wife, and two sons, and three daughters, just returning from burying Isaac, the eldest son, the support and de- light of the family. Listen ; the youngest son is now reading to the rest, the eleventh chapter of John ; Jesus saith, "Thy brother shall rise again. I am the resur- rection and the life, he that believeth in me, though he were dead, yet shall he live ; and whosoever liveth, and believeth in me, shall never die. Believest thou this ?" Observe in another house that old disciple just at the brink of the grave, now lying in his last illness. Mark, his aged companion through life, sitting by his bed-side, and with his spectacles reading to him these words, "Let not your heart be troubled: you believe in God, believe also in me. In my Father's house are many mansions; if it were not so, I would have told you: I go to prepare a place for you. And if I go and prepare a place for you, I will come again, and receive you unto myself, that where I am, there ye may be also." O wise and judicious management! O incomparable gift of tongues, lent and distributed awhile at Pentecost, but resting now forever on the head of the church, speaking to the dwellers in Asia, Egypt, Rome, and all other places, and obliging all to say, "Never man spake like this man."

Before we part, let us see whether a Christian be able to answer the objections made by the Pharisees against our most excellent instructer. Say they, "Have any of of the rulers believed on him?" We reply, Yes, Nicodemus hath, and so hath Joseph of Arimathea: but what if they had not? Are rulers always the wisest and the best of men? Do they of all men spend most time in examining religion? Are they infallible guides in religion, and do truth and virtue stand in absolute need of their approbation to be or not to be? Have they the Scriptures of the Prophets? So have we. Have they understanding? So have we. Have we a Master in heaven? So have they. Dare they impartially examine every part of religion? We dare do more: we dare follow our convictions to prison, and to death. But the Pharisees do not believe on him! O! the Pharisees of all men! "Blind hypocrites, full of all uncleanness and iniquity," shedders of the blood, and builders of the tombs of the prophets! The object of a Pharisee's hatred stands on that account recommended to good men. But the common people, who follow Christ, "know not the law, and are cursed!" No, they are not cursed for their poverty. Is the God of the whole earth the God of the rich only? Why should they not know the law? The laws of religion are plain and easy, and the poor do know the law, and make it the rule of all their actions. You, poor people! Go home, and by a holy life wipe off this cruel slander cast upon you. No, you are not cursed, and doomed to be igno-

rant. If the disciples of Moses could understand and
practise the religion he taught them, how much more
reason have we to expect that you should understand
and practise the religion of Jesus Christ; for "never
man spake like this man," whose disciples you profess
yourselves to be. May God grant you this grace! To
him be honour and glory forever. Amen.

DISCOURSE VIII.

THE DEATH OF JESUS CHRIST OBTAINED THE REMISSION
OF SINS.

[AT HARSTON.]

———

HEBREWS ix. 22.

Without shedding of blood is no remission.

BLOOD! . . . shedding of blood! . . . my soul recoils at
the thought, and the feelings of a man, the reason of
the whole world, and the dictates of religion justify me
for shrinking, and " stopping my ears from hearing of
blood." Peace be with the worst enemy I have in the
world! Precious may his blood be in the sight of all
mankind! A tender heart feels pain at the shedding
of the blood of animals, and it was to nourish this tenderness, that one of the earliest commandments given
to the world from heaven was, " You shall not eat
blood," that is, the blood of animals; and " whoso shed-
deth man's blood, by man shall his blood be shed." So
sacred was the blood of man held, that God would not
forgive a beast for shedding it; but required it to be
slain; " I will require your blood at the hand of every
man, and at the hand of every beast." These laws
given to Noah were incorporated by Moses into his
laws, and speak nothing but the sense of all mankind.
Many, very many laws have been made to guard the
lives of mankind, and some few to take away the lives
12*

of such bloody men as would not suffer others to live in
quiet; and there have been too many instances in this
wretched world of shedding innocent blood: but if reason and Scripture unite to inspire us with pain at the
shedding of man's blood, what horror doth it not excite
in us at the shedding of the blood of an innocent man!
When Jonah was thrown overboard, at his own request,
to perish in a great tempest raised for his sake, even
the sailors, who are not the most religious of mankind,
prayed and said, We beseech thee, O Lord, " lay not
upon us innocent blood!" Even Judas, that shame to
human nature, could not bear the thought of his having
betrayed innocent blood: but cast down the price, " and
departed, and went and hanged himself."

Where then are we to-day? Here is Moses with the
blood of calves and goats sprinkling "the tabernacle,
the vessels, the book of the law, and all the people, and
saying, This is the blood of the covenant which God
hath made with you." If Moses uses blood, in religion,
surely there must be a necessity for it; for Moses was
a great character, and respect for the man obliges us
at least to examine what reason he assigns for a practice, which must give pain to a man of his mild temper.
" The man Moses was very meek, above all the men
which were upon the face of the earth," and on this account we admire the prudence of his father-in-law for
setting him to " keep his flock." Moses does not pretend to institute shedding of blood to gratify his own
temper; he does not even pretend to do it, either to offend the Egyptians, or to please the Jews: but he pretends to have the express command of God, and to kill
by authority from heaven.

What the inspired writers of the New Testament tell
us of this subject, is more astonishing still. They not
only commend the fidelity of Moses, but they inform us
that the blood-shedding instituted by him was a " necessary pattern," and that the pattern was copied exactly
by a better person, who shed " his own blood," and
that by so doing he " obtained eternal redemption for
us," freeing us by his death, not only from an obligation
to offer sacrifices, but also from sin and punishment due

to it. Hence they attribute many benefits to the death
of Christ, and, to use an expression of Jesus Christ,
" eat the flesh and drink the blood" of this innocent sufferer. One saith, " The blood of Christ cleanseth us
from all sin." Another saith, " He made peace through
the blood of his cross." All the saints in heaven sing,
" Thou hast redeemed us to God by thy blood; glory be
unto thee forever and ever."

A subject, that comes so recommended to us, demands
the most reverent and modest examination. I tremble
at opening a book first given to the world besprinkled
with blood, and I think I hear over again the voice
calling out of the midst of the bush, and saying, " Moses,
Moses, draw not too nigh, put off thy shoes from off thy
feet: I am God." Let us draw nigh enough to God to
hear what he says: but let us not draw nigh enough to
be burnt alive. Let us lay aside the extravagant folly
of supposing that even God can say nothing of himself
beyond what we understand; and that nothing ought to
be done in approaching him but what is fit to be done
by one mortal when he solicits the friendship of another
worm like himself. " O God of peace! who didst bring
again from the dead our Lord Jesus, that great shepherd of the sheep, through the blood of the everlasting
covenant, make us perfect in every good work to do
thy will, working in us that which is well-pleasing in
thy sight, through Jesus Christ; to whom be glory forever and ever. Amen."

Without shedding of blood there was no abatement
according to the law; and without shedding of blood
there is no forgiveness according to the Gospel. Let
us enter on this subject with two cautions. First, let
us observe, that this subject is one of pure revelation,
and all we know of it is what we are told by men appointed by God to inform us. This is not, like some
other subjects, a doctrine, the first principles of which
may be discovered by the mere exercise of sense and
reason, and which Scripture allows, amends, and improves: but the whole of it is revealed, and to examine this revelation, and reason from it as well as we can,
is all our duty.

Secondly, let us take care not to forestall the Inspired Writers, by seizing their general notion of the death of Christ, and supposing several absurd things about it, which they never thought of. It would be easy at this rate to make a monstrous errour of a scripture truth; as for example, were we to suppose that God was out of temper with mankind, and that Jesus Christ brought him to good humour by offering to shed his blood; or that God was a cruel being, who delighted in human blood; or that Jesus Christ died to save his disciples the trouble of being holy. Such notions some unthinking people have entertained, perhaps from their own negligence, and perhaps too from the wild way in which some rash teachers, more zealous than wise, have treated of this awful subject: a subject which demands, both in speakers and hearers, the utmost caution, gravity, and seriousness. Were I to give you one general rule for expounding subjects of pure revelation, I would say, explain the doctrine by itself, the principle by the practice, the practice by the principle, the cause by its effects, the effects by their cause; and never expound an article of pure revelation by your own tempers, good or bad. A very good tempered man is apt to think God must be like him, and therefore must forgive offences without requiring any sacrifice to the honour of his justice. An ill-tempered man is apt to think, Jesus Christ suffered in consequence of a barbarousness in God, something like what he feels when his temper is roused and savage. Let us be sober, my brethren; let us not expound the wisdom of God by our own folly, and say, I would have done so and so, and therefore God should have done so and so, and if he hath not done so, then I doubt whether he hath done right.

I am going to explain this doctrine, that the death of Jesus Christ obtained the remission of sin, a doctrine of pure revelation, and expressly contained in the text; and I am going to endeavour to teach you how to expound this doctrine by its own principles. If we allow the foundation truths, we cannot deny this doctrine, which is built on them, and which is so full of practical goodness. Lend me your attention, exercise your own understand-

ings, and I will not despair of making this subject sufficiently clear to answer the end, for which it is taught.
That end is expressed in these words, " Ye were not
redeemed from your vain conversation with corruptible
things, as silver and gold : but with the precious blood
of Christ, as of a lamb without blemish and without spot :
who verily was raised up from the dead, that your faith
and hope might be in God."

  It is a first scripture truth, that there is a natural and
necessary *difference between just and unjust*, right and
wrong, good and evil. I call this a truth of Scripture, not because the declaration of God creates this difference, making by his command an action just or unjust,
which without that command would have had no qualities of right or wrong, but because the Scripture allows, amends, and improves that sense of right and
wrong, which all mankind without Scripture are forced
by their own feelings to avow. The apostle Paul speaks
of this subject in the second chapter of Romans, and
says, " The Gentiles who have not the written law, do
by nature the things contained in the law ; these, having
not the law, are a law unto themselves : which shew
the work of the law written in their hearts, their conscience also bearing witness, and their thoughts the
mean while accusing, or else excusing one another."
This is one of the finest passages of Scripture on this
subject : let us not pass it over lightly. The apostle
speaks of a law of *nature*, that is a rule of action rising
out of the very being of man, so that because he is what
he is, and as long as he is what he is, a man, he must
necessarily have in himself, go where he will, do what
he will, this rule of acting. The apostle tells us further, where this law is ; it is in the heart ; that is, in our
secret thoughts : and moreover, he informs us how our
thoughts move in regard to our actions. One thought
excuses another thought, and a second thought accuses
a first thought, contending together, as if ten just men
were disputing with ten unjust men ; ten patient men
against ten passionate men ; ten wise and honest men
setting ten foolish men right. The heart is in this case
like a court ; if ignorance or presumption sit to judge,

the law will be for sin; but if reason and religion judge,
the law of righteousness will sway the heart and guide
the life : but take which we will, our actions do not alter the nature of things, right is right, and wrong is
wrong, let what will come of us. Which of you does
not know the truth of all this without my giving you
any examples to explain it! Remember then there
is a difference between just and unjust, right and wrong;
and that when one of the speakers in that dialogue in
Scripture, which we call the book of Ecclesiastes, says,
" As is the good, so is the sinner, and he that sweareth
as he that feareth an oath; no man knoweth either love
or hatred by all that is before him;" it is a profane
wretch disputing against Solomon, who says so.

Another principle, or foundation truth, like the former is, *that all men have sinned,* and that there is
none righteous, no not one. There are as many degrees of sin as there are of size and sense : but in some
degree all have sinned ; to use the language of David,
"All have gone aside ;" or that of the apostle Paul,
" All have sinned, and come short of the glory of God."
By the glory of God he means the rule of right, for holiness, or always doing what is just and right, is the glory of God, as doing what is right is the glory of man,
and doing wrong, his shame. Where is the happy man,
who can stand up and say, I never did, in all the course
of my life, any one action, which I ought not to have
done. I have been as good in every instance as I think
I ought to have been. I have discharged every exercise of piety towards God, every duty towards my fellow-creatures, and myself, in every instance, with so
much integrity and cheerfulness, that I have nothing,
no, nothing to repent of. I have been humble in prosperity, patient in adversity, diligent in business, fervent
in spirit, serving the Lord. I am every moment, and
always have been, ready to die. I ask no favour, I approach my Judge without any misgiving or fear, and
while others say, " God be merciful to us sinners," I
shall say, " God, I thank thee that I am not as other
men are." No, my brethren, you are not of this number, and you know, were you to pretend to this, you

would find some of your friends, as well as your enemies, contradict you.   One would say, " I have surely
heard Ephraim bemoaning himself thus, I was a bullock
unaccustomed to the yoke."   Another would cry, " How
canst thou say, I am not polluted ; see thy way in the
valley !"   In the absence of these, thine own conscience
would make thee acknowledge, " I have sinned against
the Lord, and thus and thus have l done."   Yea, were
thy conscience asleep, the voice that raises the dead
would cry, " When thou wast under the fig-tree, I saw
thee ! "
    This leads us to a third principle, that is, that *God
seeth all the thoughts and actions of men.*   I question
whether I could propose any truth, which would be so
readily granted, and so little understood.   Who doubts
whether God knoweth his thoughts and actions ?   Nobody.   Who understands the knowledge of God to be in
constant harmony with all his other perfections ?   Very
few.   Let me aspire at the honour of increasing the
number this evening by teaching you to think justly on
this subject.   Should I inform you that somebody had
seen a man stab your brother, you would understand nothing but a bare seeing the crime committed : but should
I tell you that the man who saw the murder done was
your father, you would understand something more than
seeing, and you would know, without being told, that it
was impossible for him to see this bloody action without
disapprobation and horror ; and you would suppose his
horror, rising out of a sense of the injustice of the action, would incline him to follow the law, and bring the
guilty wretch to public punishment.   Sanctify this
thought by applying as much of it to our Father in heaven, as agrees with the eminence of his perfections.
He beholds all the children of men, their " down-sit-
ting, their up-rising, their thoughts afar off."   " He compasseth their path all day, and their bed at night, and
is acquainted with all their ways.   He besets them behind and before, and there is not a word in their tongues,
but, lo, he knoweth it altogether : he sees if there be
any wicked way in them."   God doth see the actions of
men, and he knows what he sees ; he never mistakes a

sin for a virtue, and he knows what degree of guilt is in
every action : hence it is said, " The Lord is a God of
knowledge, and by him actions are weighed. Thou,
most upright, dost weigh the path of the just." God
not only knows justice and injustice when he sees them :
but as he himself is a just and holy being, he cannot behold both with indifference to either : " The righteous
Lord loveth righteousness, but him that loveth violence
his soul hateth." There is not in God any horror at
sin like what we feel, for pain is not necessary to his
love of justice : but there is in him a perfect approbation of what is right, and an extreme irreconcileable-
ness to what is wrong. The God who sees, and knows,
and judges, and approves or disapproves of the actions
of men, is able to reward the right, and to punish the
wrong : and his almighty power is at perfect agreement
with his love of holiness, he must protect right and punish wrong. Every man in the world would agree to
all this, had he not some wicked self-interest in not having impartial justice done.

Our next principle is, that *the present life is not a
state of rewards and punishments.* Some have said,
that God punishes a few wicked men here with remarkable judgments, lest we should forget he governs the
world ; and he punishes only a few criminals here, lest
we should forget a future state of punishments. Perhaps this may be true : but I dare never go out of
Scripture on this principle. Such instances as Judas,
and Belshazzar, and Pharoah, we allow on the testimony
of the inspired historians ; but we should be liable to
rash judgments, and cruel mistakes, were we to walk in
this dark path without an inspired guide. What we affirm is, that this is not the general condition of mankind .
here. Our Lord fully settles this doctrine by saying,
" Suppose ye that the Galileans, whose blood Pilate
mingled with their sacrifices," or that the " eighteen
upon whom the tower in Siloam fell, and slew them,
were sinners above all men that dwelt in Jerusalem, or
above all Galileans ? I tell you, nay : I tell you, nay."
These Galileans sacrificing imperfectly to the true God,
were not more superstitious than others of their neigh--

bours, nor so superstitious as the heathens, who sacrificed to an idol; much less were they so wicked as some others, who worshipped no God at all. Probably those eighteen unfortunate debtors, upon whom the walls of their prison fell, were not more in debt than others in Jerusalem, nor so guilty as some whose extravagance had brought them into debt, and whose arts had enabled them to escape justice. This life is a state of trial, and the next is the state of rewards and punishments. This is the doctrine of Jesus Christ, and on this principle he grounds some excellent rules of practice; as, to avoid rash judging, to submit patiently to afflictions, and so on. " Judge not, that ye be not judged. Judge not according to the appearance." The apostle thoroughly understood this, when he said, " What have I to do to judge them that are without? With me it is a very small thing, that I should be judged of you, or of man's judgment: yea, I judge not mine own self, for I know nothing by myself: but he that judgeth me is the Lord. Therefore judge nothing before the time, until the Lord come, who both will bring to light the hidden things of darkness, and will make manifest the counsels of the hearts."

Here we are come to a difficulty. There is no difficulty in regard to the wicked, for as soon as they die they go to a prison; at the resurrection of the dead they will be brought out to take their trial; and after that they will be punished, each according as his iniquities deserve. Then will be " tribulation and anguish upon every soul of man that hath done evil." " As many as have sinned without a written law, shall perish without a written law: and as many as have sinned against a written law, shall be judged by that law: for the judgment of God is according to truth, and he will render to every man according to his own deeds." Here is no difficulty; all is fair, clear, open, and just. The difficulty is in the case of others, who, though they were once " idolaters, adulterers, thieves, covetous, drunkards, revilers, or extortioners, yet inherit the kingdom of God." Merciful God! on what principles are these, as deep in guilt as others, admitted to ever-

13

lasting communion with thee? Art thou partial, and hast thou one law for one thief, and another law for another? That be far from thee! Is thine abhorrence of sin suspended in behalf of these people? That be far from thee! Thou art " in one mind, and who can turn thee?" Did these people repent and reform, and didst thou pity and pardon them? Pity for the wretched is glorious in thee who art so able to help them: but is thy pity insensible to thy justice? These people did many unjust things, they have never been in a state of rewards and punishments, and therefore they have not received the just reward of their actions.

In regard to the wicked their punishments are abated in proportion to the good mixed with the evil: but these people escape all punishment, and have entered on a happiness as eternal as that of the purest angel in glory. Almighty parent! " Righteous art thou when I plead with thee; yet let me talk with thee of thy judgments. Behold now, I have taken upon me to speak unto the Lord, who am but dust and ashes! Oh! let not the Lord be angry, and I will speak yet but this once." Where, in regard to these people, are " the ordinances of justice," rigid, impartial, inflexible justice?

No doubt, my brethren, many of you can solve this difficulty: but how? Will you say high things of the goodness of God? Do so; it is impossible you should say too much on that delightful subject: yet after all, there is no justice done in this case, no punishments inflicted, no rewarding according to works. Will you say, These people felt much sorrow, and did, after their repentance, much good: Alas! their sorrow was not half enough; it undid nothing that had been done; they should have had innocence, not repentance; and all the good they did, and more than they could do, was due to God, and ought to have been done had they never offended him. Do you say, These people gave their gold and their silver, their cattle, yea; themselves to God? Alas! are you so ill-informed as to call these things theirs? I hear another voice, saying, " Silver is mine, gold is mine, every beast of the forest is mine, the cattle upon a thousand hills are mine, the fowls of the mountains are mine, all souls are mine, the soul of the father is mine, the soul of the son is mine, the world is mine, and the fulness thereof." Poor man! dost thou give thy silver, and thy family, and thyself to God? No, God is the Creator of thee, and of all thou hast. Thou livest upon gifts: but he is an independent being, and lives of himself.

Christians, suppose we should go with this difficult case to God, and humbly ask him on what principles he acts in the salvation of sinners? I said at first this was an article of pure revelation, and we thank God the answer is given in a thousand declarations of Scripture. The text says, " Without shedding of blood is no remission." The same chapter tells us, " The blood of Christ obtained eternal redemption for us;" and other passages inform us, that " God was in Christ reconciling the world unto himself, not imputing their trespasses to them;" that " He made him sin for us, who knew no sin, that we might be made the righteousness of God in him;" that " one died for all;" that " by the obedience of one, many were made righteous;" that " we were reconciled to God by the death of his son;" that " we are justified by his blood, and saved from wrath through him;" that " he his own self bare our sins in his own body on the tree:" that " Christ hath once suffered for sins, the just for the unjust;" that " the blood of Jesus Christ cleanseth us from all sin." Of all these passages, and a great number more to the same purpose, we make a religious principle, and add it to the former truths, as a ground of hope, laid by the love of God for hopeless man, whom reason, assisted by Scripture, leads from principle to principle, from truth to truth, till, but for this, he would fall into deep despair. Despair be banished now! He that hath ears to hear, let him hear. " God so loved the world, that he gave his only begotten Son, that whosoever believeth in him should not perish, but have everlasting life."

Collect all the truths we have laid down into one point. We said there was such a thing as natural justice, a sense of right and wrong ... that all mankind

have done wrong, and are in a state of injustice ...
that God sees and knows, abhors and must punish injustice ... that the present life is not a state of punishment, and that the wicked are punished in a future
state ... that some who have been guilty of many crimes
yet escape punishment, and are made happy in heaven
... and that this forgiveness is effected through the
great love of God, and through the death of Christ.
This is the substance of what we have been saying. If
some deny this truth, if others perplex it, and if others
abuse it, we are sorry for such things : but " let God be
true, but every man a liar."

This doctrine is described in Scripture in plain, proper, literal terms, which establish the matter of fact ;
and it is also described by similitudes, or fashions of
speaking among men, which are intended to explain the
subject, and to make us more sensibly affected with it.
I will give you an example of each.

The apostle Paul says twice expressly, " We have
redemption through the blood of Christ, even the forgiveness of sins." This is a plain declaration of a matter of fact, and informs us, that though the crucifixion
of Christ was a horrible murder committed under forms
of human justice against all the laws of real justice, yet
from this death we derive redemption, not merely from
the yoke of Jewish ceremonies, and heathen superstition, but a release from punishment due to us for sin :
" We have redemption through his blood," one principal
pal part of which is the " forgiveness of sins." There
is a multitude of passages of this sort, and your discernment will make proper inferences from them in the
course of your reading the Holy Scriptures.

To give an example of the other sort. The apostles
Peter and Paul both call the blood of Christ, the " blood
of sprinkling." The first says, " Peace be multiplied
unto you through the sprinkling of the blood of Jesus
Christ." The other says, " Ye are come unto the blood
of sprinkling, that speaketh better things than that of
Abel." This is a fashion of speaking taken from the
Old Testament, where blood was not only shed, but
taken into a bason, and sprinked on the altar, and on

the people, and the apostle explains himself by saying,
" If the blood of bulls, and the ashes of an heifer sprinkling the unclean, purified the flesh, how much more
shall the blood of Christ purify your conscience from
dead works to serve the living God ?"   The case was
this.   It was thought necessary for many prudent purposes to distinguish people, who touched the dead, and
to require them by some public token to avow the fact.
It was guarding the lives and properties of all the people.   Such an end is answered among us by tolling a
bell, which gives the whole parish notice that the state
hath lost a member, and any may inquire whether un-
fair practices were used to deprive him of life; that
house, or land, or something is fallen to an heir, who is
hereby summoned to make his appearance, and put in
his claim.   Among the Jews, a man having touched the
dead was obliged to separate himself from his family for
seven days, and during that time he was called unclean,
not fit for company, or to appear in public.   At the end
of this time the person was freed from uncleanness by being sprinkled with water mixed with the ashes of a heifer
that had been burnt.   It is to this ceremony that the
apostle alludes, and his reasoning is as much as to say,
if a Jew derived from his ceremonies of religion the
benefit of going boldly to worship God, and to exchange
solitude for good company, in which he might enjoy
himself, how much more should you, Christians, enjoy
yourselves, your friends, and your God, since your religion sets forth a Saviour, who died to procure all these
advantages for you.   If their general sacrifices were
applied to individuals, and brought home to personal
use, so are the great events, that constitute your religion, and particularly the death of Christ, from which
all Christians derive personal advantages.   In this general likeness you may accommodate all the similitudes
(I cannot think of a plainer word : but if there be any
word you do not fully understand, come into the house
to me after I have done, and I will try to explain my
self), I say, in this general manner explain to yourselves
the similitudes, and allusions of Scripture, which relate
to the benefits we derive from the death of Christ, but
13*

by no means attempt to spiritualize particulars, for it is childish, and will lead you into gross error.

Consider all the sacrifices of the Jews and Patriarchs, as the apostle Paul hath taught you, as figures, or patterns of heavenly things ; as for example : the high-priest was the chief person in the Jewish religion, and the whole worship of God was under his care ; Jesus Christ is the chief in the Christian church, and the Christian religion is under his care. The Jews worshipped God with bloody sacrifices ; Christians approach God through the death of Christ. The high-priest prayed to God in a part of the temple separated from the rest by a thick hanging of tapestry, called the Holy Place, into which he went once a year with blood ; Jesus Christ died covered with his own blood, and when he rose from the dead, he ascended to heaven, and according to his promise prayed the Father to send another Comforter, the Spirit of Truth, to abide with his church for ever. In this manner the apostle recommends the Christian religion to the Jews, and perhaps the Epistle to the Hebrews was written chiefly for the use of that people, when they shall in some future time, according to prophecy, look favourably upon him whom their forefathers pierced. The apostle strives to convince his readers of the excellence of the Christian religion above that of the Jews, and consequently above that of every other nation. The chief person of that religion was a man ; our chief is God : they had a succession ; our chief hath no successor : their religion was for a time ; ours is for ever : their worship was by repeated sacrifices ; our approach to God is a benefit flowing forever from that one event, the death of Christ : their religion stood in performing ceremonies ; ours in informing the mind, improving the heart, and amending the life : their religion was for themselves ; ours is for every body ; for " Christ, by the grace of God, tasted death for every man."

There are some similitudes of this subject taken in Scripture from history, and other occurrences of common life, as well as from the religion of the Jews. Jesus Christ calls his crucifixion, " giving his life a ransom "for many." A ransom is a price paid to the conqueror for the release of a prisoner of war. Jesus Christ likens the forgiveness of sin to a release from an obligation to pay a debt. These similitudes ought to be soberly explained, because some are intended to set forth some of the benefits of Christ's death, and others other benefits; for there is no one action in the world, or ever was, that can fully express all the benefits of that great event. Certainly our Divine Master intended we should always keep in memory this event, because he appointed bread and wine to be publicly eaten and drunk by his followers in their religious assemblies in remembrance of his death till his second coming.

Let us finish by examining some of the benefits, which we derive from the death of Christ. Here we study, and here we learn the true and real *character of God*, particularly his unyielding justice, and his unbounded love. God made the world a noble present, when he created wheat; a nobler still when he made the sun: but when he gave the world a Saviour, he unfolded his goodness in a manner beyond all our expectations. Man had abused his wheat, and his sun, his light, and his reason, and all his other gifts: but this gift shall express his justice, as fully as his love, to prevent abuse of goodness. Will Jesus Christ stoop to become the friend and instructer of man? Must he to this purpose be born and live among men? He must die too, and befriend man at the expense of his life. Jesus Christ had the highest reason to rejoice at the approach of death, yet he was in agony at the prospect of it, because the bitterness of death due to sinners was felt by him instead of sinners. We said, some time ago, that the punishment of sin was so necessary to a Holy God, that it could not be dispensed with: but remember, God is as great and good as he is just, and in virtue of either his prerogative as the first of beings, or his love as the best of beings, he might choose either to punish sin in the person of the sinner, or in the person of another, whom all parties would agree without any loss, and with great advantage, to put in the place of sinners. The death of Christ then, as it regards God, is to be considered as a free and bright display of the goodness, the justice, the greatness, the holiness, the condescension of God.

The death of Christ gives us the highest esteem for *his own* character. He appears eminently in this as " the image of the invisible God." What cool and wise knowledge of the whole case before him, the honour of God, the worth of himself, the necessities of men, the horror of losing souls, the pleasure of saving them, the stamping of the image of God deep, clear, and for ever, upon the souls of men! How prudent, patient, mild, and even, were all his steps through life up to the cross! How generous and disinterested, how far beyond all that we call largeness of heart was it to stoop to die, were it only to teach us how to die! How doth his love of justice shine ; others have been praised for executing justice upon offenders, and praiseworthy it is to administer justice to any : but to give up his own just right to live, in order to obtain a right for the unjust to live to repent and be happy, " behold, what manner of love is this !" If it be a benefit to know such a pattern of holiness as Christ, it is a benefit derived from his death. Love of Jonathan to David! Tears of Rachel weeping for her children! Esteem of Abraham for Isaac! Feelings of David for Absalom, crying, " O my son, my son, would to God I had died for thee !"—depart, you are only worth my attention in the absence of this " Lamb in the midst of the throne." " Herein is love, not that we loved God, but that he loved us, and sent his son to be the propitiation for our sins !"

In the death of Christ we see *the nature of sin,* how horrible, and passing all belief it is. It hath been said, if goodness should take a mortal shape, and live among mankind, all mankind would respect it. Alas! how little we know mankind! How little we think what one single seed of sin is capable of producing! The sinner " flattereth himself in his own eyes, until his iniquity be found to be hateful," which he doth not know till he has practised it some time, and then the consequences appear worse than he imagined. When Elisha looked steadfastly in the face of Hazael, then only an officer in the army of the king of Syria, he blushed and wept.

Hazael said, " Why weepeth my Lord?" The prophet answered, Because I know " thou will set the strong holds of my country on fire, slay young men with the sword, dash their children in pieces, and rip up their women with child." " What!" cried the captain, " is thy servant a dog that he should do this great thing!" To which the Prophet mildly replied, " The Lord hath shewed me that thou shalt be king over Syria." As if he had said, I see you are a proud man; your pride will make you an unjust man; your injustice will make you cruel for your own safety; and your cruelty will make you a monster. Accordingly, after he returned, his first word was deceit, and his first action quickening the death of a dying man: but on he went from crime to crime, till, in defiance of all the modesty of a murderer, he ript up women with child. Before the coming of Christ we knew, man could do a long list of crimes: but who would have thought man could have gone so far as to affront, and wound, and kill an express image of Almighty God? Goodness, justice, power to give goodness and justice effect, wisdom, and every excellence, have taken a mortal shape, and appeared in the " likeness of sinful flesh:" but what is the history of this beauty? It was crucified between two thieves without the gates of that city, where only God was known, and where, if in any part of the world, perfect innocence might have expected esteem. Draw near, sinner, who flatter yourself that it is not in your power to do this. Is not ignorance in your power? Is not envy, and pride, and the fear of man in your power? These were the sins that put the Son of God to death. One only loved money more than justice, and he sold him: others only loved the praise of men more than the praise of God, and they bought him: the officers only did as their masters bade them, and they took him, and bound him, and struck him: the soldiers only made themselves merry with a stranger, and they dressed him in an officer's coat, and mocked him, and crowned him with thorns, and called him king, and bent the knee, and spat in his face: Pilate only wished to be popular, and he adjudged him to die: the thieves only did as other peo-

ple did, and they reviled him. One of them repented
and found mercy. God grant, you all may repent, and
like him find mercy! Always when you feel pride, or
envy, or any sin stirring in your heart, you may know
what it would grow to, if it had time and room, and on
this account you should always hate the seed for the
sake of the fruit, and say, I know what you would be at,
you would poison me, and kill, if it were possible, the
God that made me.

.In the death of Christ the Christian reads the "*for-
givenesss of sins.* Sin is nothing to some men, but they
are ignorant men ; for to one who knows the nature of
it, it is a poison that drinks up the spirits, and the remembrance of it reduces a bold and cheerful man to a
low and trembling state. Every thing tends to increase
the wretchedness of such a man. If he thinks of a great
God, it is a great God against him : if he thinks of a
good God, it is a good Father, despised and insulted; if
he thinks of the law of right and wrong, he hates himself for having been an enemy to right, and a friend to
what all good men abhor ; if he thinks of heaven, it is
a happiness forbidden to him, and guarded like paradise, with a " flaming sword turning every way ;" if he
thinks of hell, it seems just, but intolerable ; if of his soul,
it is lost, and if of his body, it must return to the dust,
and rise at the last day to the " resurrection of damnation." This man doth not resemble the raven let out
of the ark by Noah ; she could alight and feed on the
floating carcases of the dead. He resembles the dove
that "found no rest for the sole of her foot." It is not
a general guess concerning unknown mercy, that can
satisfy this man ; it is not the glossy surface of his own
imperfect works, that can calm his conscience ; justice
sits there, and disdains every impure offering, saying
in the name of God, " If ye offer the lame and sick, is
it not evil ?" " Offer it now unto thy governor, will he
be pleased with thee, or accept thy person, saith the
Lord of Hosts ?" " Cursed be the deceiver, who hath
in his flock a male, and voweth and sacrificeth unto the
Lord a corrupt thing : for I am a great King, saith the
Lord of Hosts." " Cursed be the man that trusteth in

man, and maketh flesh his arm." Trembling soul, afraid and ashamed to look upon God, listen to the voice that saith, "If any man thirst, let him come unto me and drink. My blood is drink indeed. Except you drink the blood of the Son of Man, you have no life in you." "Whoso eateth my flesh, and drinketh my blood, hath eternal life, and I will raise him up at the last day." Do not say with the captious Jews, "How can this man give us his flesh to eat?" For he hath explained his meaning so that you cannot misunderstand him, by saying, "He that eateth me shall live by me, just as I live by the Father." God the Father is a pure Spirit; he hath no flesh and blood to be eaten and drunk: but Jesus Christ lived by believing in his wisdom, goodness, power, and so on. Exactly so in your case. There is no flesh and blood of Christ on earth for you to eat and drink, "Him the heaven hath received till the restitution of all things:" but "this is the will of him that sent the Son, that every one who believeth on him may have everlasting life." Live then the life of faith, and by believing what the Scriptures affirm of the Father, and of the Son of his love, live happy till faith is changed into sight in heaven. Then in "the general assembly of the first-born," behold "God the judge of all," and "Jesus the Mediator of the new covenant." Till then "see that you refuse not him that speaketh."

In the death of Christ let us learn how to live. What is there in this life which we can call our own, except religion? Have we character? In this world even innocence is not safe, for the glory of mankind was "numbered with transgressors." So many people have an interest, and what is more a pleasure in blasting the reputation of such as excel, that a good man should learn not to overprize even this jewel, for there are times, and places, and persons, where scandal is an honour, and where it is glorious to say, "If this be to be vile, I will yet be more vile." Is prosperity desirable? In this world the wicked prosper, and Herod is a king, Pilate a judge, and Caiaphas a priest, in a city where the wise and upright Judge of the world taught among the miserable,

and died among the wicked. The "man of sorrows
was oppressed and afflicted, and made his grave with
the wicked." Let us be thankful for prosperity: but
let us remember it is not always a companion of piety.
Is health and long life desirable? Christ was cut off in
the midst of his days. Health and long life are not the
chief good, and when it pleases God to deprive us of
them, we ought to be content. Is friendship desirable
to sweeten life? Remember what a friend Judas was
to Christ; remember too that when he most needed
his real friends, they slept while he was in agony, and
at his death all "forsook him and fled." Let us not set
our hearts too much on friendship. In this world it is
sometimes a dangerous, and at all times an uncertain
thing. Let us live with our friends as Christ did with
his; so that a Judas may avow our integrity. In a
word, let us, like Christ, consider life as a day, religion
the work of that day; and let us aspire at the glory of
saying in the evening of it, " I have finished the work
which thou gavest me to do; and now, Holy Father, I
am no more in the world, but I come to thee."

Above all, in the death of Christ, let us learn *to die*.
O lovely example of a departing soul! Would to God
" my last end may be like thine!" Jesus Christ died
calm and composed in the midst of a mob, in the full
exercise of piety to God, pity to the wretched, forgiveness to his enemies, tenderness to his family, with dignity in himself, and a lesson of instruction to all mankind. My soul! Perhaps thou wilt not struggle to
quit thy tabernacle of clay amidst a cursing, reviling,
gaming, laughing, insensible crowd, dead to all thy feelings, and alive to nothing but their own brutal passions;
but thou wilt, on some bed of thorns, be in agonies to
depart, thou wilt make the " keepers of the house tremble," thou wilt " darken the sun, the moon, and the
stars," thou wilt "loose the silver cord, break the gold-
en bowl, the pitcher at the fountain, the wheel at the
cistern, return the dust to the earth," and thyself " unto
God who gave thee!" Would to God thou couldst learn
of thy Saviour to do all this coolly and calmly! Why
shouldst thou flutter? " Whither thou goest thou know-

est, and the way thou knowest." Say after the great
Master to Mary, who stands weeping, "Woman, why
weepest thou? I ascend unto my Father, and your Father, and to my God, and your God." Jesus Christ died
in the exercise of piety. The severity of Providence
did not shock him; he, unshaken as the rock in the tempest, called him Father, and said, "Into thy hands I
commend my spirit." Let us die in an act of adoration,
and go bowing into the presence of the King of kings,
our Father and our God. Jesus died · in the exercise of
pity to the wretched thief, who repenting said, "Lord,
remember me when thou comest into thy kingdom :"
and he replied, "Verily I say unto thee, to-day shalt
thou be with me in Paradise." Let us remember the
wretched when we die, and if we can, let us leave a token that we bore their griefs, and carried their sorrows
in our hearts, even when prudence forbade us to administer much relief. Christ died forgiving his enemies,
and praying his Father to forgive them. Let us do
likewise, and lest death should take us unawares, let us
" agree with our adversary quickly." " If thou bring
thy gift to the altar, and there rememberest that," not
thine adversary, but " thy brother hath aught against
thee, leave there thy gift before the altar, and go thy
way; first be reconciled to thy brother, and then come
and offer thy gift." Jesus died full of tenderness for his
family. There stood by the cross his mother, his aunt,
Mary Magdalen, and that lovely youth, the apostle John.
In the hearing of these three Marys, he made his will,
and knowing that a " sword pierced through the soul" of
his mother, he provided for her after his death by saying to John, " Behold thy mother," and to his mother,
" Woman, behold thy son : turn thine afflicted eyes from
this bloody cross, and look for me in that generous young
man, who, when I am dead will work to support thee,
and will reverence thy hoary head for my sake. One
word was enough for such a man as John, and " from
that hour, he took her unto his own home." O how
dreadful are some of the kind offices of life ! To lead
such a mother home from the execution of such a son,
how it rends, yet how it heals the heart ! Let us, after

14

the example of our Divine Master, show kindness to our families and friends through life, and a profusion of it when we die. Are any of our families like to be turned out of doors when we die? perhaps God will provide a John to take them in. We must not take the liberty which the Lord of all took, but we may "leave our fatherless children to God, he will preserve them alive;" let us tell our "widows to trust in him." Let us learn by the command given to John, how we ought to behave to people left in their old age to a wide world to struggle at once against poverty and the infirmities of age. If we cannot take them home, yet let us never forget the voice that said, "Behold thy mother! Behold thy son!" Jesus died in perfect character, a dignity that never left him; no command about the vain show of a funeral, no trifles about the world, no dread and despondency about Providence, no reaching out entails, nothing little, nothing mean; but like himself, one constant, undiminished excellence of character. There was no need of attention to these little things. Every thing feels a good man's death, and all that knew him are his mourners: but heaven and earth felt and trembled at the death of Christ, and the whole world have celebrated his praise. Christ died an example of dying, and showed mankind how to meet their fate. Happy for us if we learn to imitate him, and if after we have shown the world the dignity of a Christian life, we are enabled to show them how Christians, whose hopes are full of immortality, ought to die. "If we be planted together in the likeness of his death, we shall be also in the likeness of his resurrection." "If we be dead with him, we shall also live with him." "If we suffer, we shall also reign with him." "Unto him that loved us, and washed us from our sins in his own blood, and hath made us kings and priests unto God and his Father, to him be glory and dominion for ever and ever." Amen.

DISCOURSE IX.

MATTHEW xxiii, 10.

One is your master, even Christ.

IT was a custom formerly, in some Christian church-es in the eastern part of the world, for people new-ly baptized to wear, seven days, white garments, and crowns on their heads. They intended to inform their neighbours, by their white clothes, that the Christian religion was innocent and holy, and by the crowns or garlands on their heads, that Christians were advanced to dignity. The custom was needless and superstitious; for the ordinances of religion, like the stars in the fir-mament, were formed in such perfection, that they are not capable of improvement; and, as one Christian hath as much right to alter religion as another, if it were al-lowable to alter any thing, it would be allowable to al-ter every thing, and to multiply fanciful improvements till the religion of Jesus would be entirely lost. It was owing to this false principle, that formerly our forefa-thers in this country worshipped the Virgin Mary and the saints, after they had worshipped Jesus Christ, and made offerings of money at altars built in the churches for the purpose: but in process of time, the altar of Christ went out of fashion; and when our king Harry the Eighth abolished these superstitions, the books of the cathedral church at Canterbury proved, that in one year the people had offered above nine hundred and fifty pounds to one saint Thomas, a little more than four pounds to the Virgin Mary, and to Jesus Christ nothing at all.

When we trace most errors and superstitions, we find they took their rise in some truth; and though in the present case it was superstitious to crown Christians newly baptized, yet it is true that the man, who embraces the Christian religion, does actually rise into dignity by doing so. The Scripture saith, " Jesus Christ makes his disciples kings unto God," that is, he advances men from a state of ignorance, to a state of wisdom; from vicious company to virtuous company; from slavery under sin to a dominion over their own passions; and in this advancement stands the true dignity and glory of a Christian.

It was with a view to raise the apostles to this honour, that our Lord admonished them in the chapter, out of which I have taken the text, to " beware of the Pharisees." In one part of his discourse he guards them against their cruelty; in another against their ignorance and hypocrisy; and in that part to which our text belongs, he inculcates humility and brotherly love, in opposition to that spirit of pride and dominion, which the Pharisees in every thing discovered. They pretended to know more of religion than others, and took the title of Rabbi, master or doctor, and along with that, dominion over the faith and practice of the common people. " But," says our Lord to his disciples, " be not ye called Rabbi, and call no man your Father upon the earth; for one is your Father, which is in heaven, and one is your master, even Christ." This is the doctrine which I am going to explain and enforce.

If you would understand this doctrine, you must take care to restrain it to that subject, to which only it belongs, that is, religion. We affirm, that Jesus Christ is the governor, and the only governor and director of all his disciples: but we mean the governor of the religion of his disciples. I will explain myself more at large.

We do not mean that Jesus Christ taught a body of

laws of *civil government*. When mankind agree to live together in society, it is necessary they should agree together on certain rules or laws by which they should conduct themselves to one another; and as all mankind, if they choose to make use of their reason, are able to judge what laws are most proper to answer the end of their associating together, which is self-preservation, so there is no need of a Divine interposition. Our Saviour never once spoke to his disciples on this subject. If the inhabitants of one kingdom choose to submit the absolute disposal of their lives, liberties, and properties to one person of one family; if the people of another country choose to resign themselves up to twenty families; and if the inhabitants of another part of the world choose to keep the disposal of these invaluable blessings in their own hands; in all these cases praise is due for the exercise of reason, or blame for the disuse of it. Christianity is no further concerned with civil government than as it teaches its disciples to make a virtuous use of their reason. If men reason virtuously, they will be led to accommodate the preservation of themselves to the safety and happiness of their fellow citizens; and though Christianity doth not teach a form of civil government, yet it doth teach all the virtues that are necessary to make men happy in society. When, therefore we say, Christ is the only governor of his disciples, we do not mean to disturb the civil order of making and executing human laws for the preservation of the lives, and liberties, and properties of mankind.

Nor do we mean to apply the text to *universities*, or other academies of literature. We consider learning as the embellishment, or, if you will, the clothing of a country, and it would be easy to show that our universities have informed and adorned all Europe. Too great praise cannot be given to these learned bodies, nor can too much respect be paid to the members of them; for it is owing to their unwearied studies and indefatigable pains, that you are enabled to read a Gospel in English, which was at first taught in Hebrew and Greek. To their learned labors in several arts and sciences, at a vast expense, and at the hazard of their

14*

lives, you are indebted for that inestimable annual present, an almanack; a book of more value than the ten
folio volumes of St. Augustin. Hence you derive physicians to administer healing in your sicknesses; and
hence, in a word, thousands of improvements in all the
useful labours of life. The religion taught us by Jesus
Christ includes no directions on this subject. It doth
not tell us whether to prefer a private academy, or a
public foundation; and much less doth it censure, as
some of the old Puritans thought, the conferring of degrees in arts and sciences. Religion affects literature
only as it affects governments, by teaching us a habit
of virtuous reasoning.

Further, we do not apply the doctrine of the text to
public charities, alms-houses, work-houses, or common
practices in life. It is not conceivable, that Jesus
Christ gave any laws for or against medical matters;
as, for example, inoculation, or that he wasted his time,
and the attention of his hearers about comparative trifles; for where reason is sufficient, revelation is unnecessary. In all manner of cases, except in that of the
direct and immediate worship of God, there is one, and
but one general law, which may not improperly be expressed in these words, " Whatsoever things are true,
whatsoever things are honest, whatsoever things are
pure, whatsoever things are lovely, whatsoever things
are of good report; if there be any virtue, if there be
any praise, think on these things."

It is to religion, and to religion alone, then, that we
apply the doctrine of the text, " One is your master,
even Christ." Jesus Christ taught us a perfect religion. It is perfect in its kind, because it is religion,
and it wants nothing that a religion ought to have: and
thus our master differs from all teachers in the heathen
world. It is perfect in degree, because it adapts itself
to all the conditions of mankind, and herein the Christian religion differs from that of the Jews. That of the
Jews was perfect in kind, for it was all founded on the
knowledge and fear of God; but it was not perfect in
degree, because it was incumbered with ceremonies,
and intended only for that nation; whereas Jesus taught

a religion fit " for every creature in all the world."
Our master believed and practised every part of the
religion he taught us. This religion is practicable by
us : every doctrine may be understood, and every duty
performed. Our guide commanded us to follow his example, and rested the proof of our love to him on our
obedience to his commandments.

To be more explicit. Let us divide Christianity into
four parts, the facts, the proofs, the duties, and the motives ; and let us examine each of these parts, in order
to explain what we mean when we call Jesus Christ the
only governor of the religion of his disciples.

Observe first, the *facts* reported in the New Testa
ment. That there is a God . . . that he takes notice of
the actions of men . . . that in love to mankind he sent
his son to instruct them . . . that this illustrious person
was born as the Prophets had foretold in the reign of
Herod, at the town of Bethlehem in the country of Judah, of a virgin of the family of David . . . that he taught
a state of future rewards and punishments, and that he
vehemently exhorted men to seek the first in a course
of virtue, and to avoid the last by laying aside the practice and the love of sin . . . that he himself exemplified
his doctrine in his own person . . . that he took a few
men under his immediate tuition, and left them to instruct mankind after his death, promising to give them
extraordinary assistance . . . that having finished his ministry he was crucified between two thieves ; his virtuous sufferings being highly acceptable to God, and exceedingly beneficial to all his followers . . . that three days
after his crucifixion he rose from the dead, and appeared to his disciples, and that having given them full instructions what to believe, and how to act, he forty
days after ascended to heaven, and entered on the enjoyment of that honor and happiness, which his merit
demanded, and which all good men approve. This is a
set of facts exhibited by our Divine Master in person to
his disciples, and by them in their writings to us. A
man, whose understanding is governed, as it ought to
be, by evidence, examines these facts, admits them to be
true, and so yields to what I call the sole government of

Jesus Christ, in regard to the true authentic history of
his life.

· To these facts several additions have been made by
curious Christians in these latter ages; but it is the belief of the genuine facts recorded in the New Testament, and not a crediting of fanciful additions, that constitutes a Christian submission to that pure revelation of
Jesus Christ, which he thought proper to make of himself.
That he was born, is a fact; but that he was born in
December, is an addition. If we be governed by Scripture evidence, we shall believe the first; but if we be
dissatisfied with the simplicity of revelation, we must
contend and come to some resolution about the last.
The Christian, who enters into the spirit of our doctrine, will content himself with the sufficiency of revelation; and will believe that if the day of his master's
birth had been necessary to any good purpose in religion, the New Testament would have marked it. We
will not pursue this thought any further, but we will
leave you to meditate on this subject of facts and additions, hoping and praying that you may hold yourselves
bound to believe nothing for religion but what is stamp-
ed with the authority of your Divine Teacher; for " One
is your master, even Christ."

Remark next the *proofs* of the truth of these facts.
There are four sorts of proofs, which we have very often mentioned, and which we wish to have you so familiarly acquainted with, that it would be unnecessary
to mention them any more. The first are taken from
Prophecy, or rather from a comparison of the events
which happen in the world, with what the prophets
foretold should come to pass. The dispersion of the
Jews is an event of this kind; the persecutions of Christians is another, and the corruption of Christianity is a
third. The second sort of proofs are miracles, which
Christ wrought, and which his bitterest enemies never
denied, though they were wicked enough to attribute
them to the devil. A third set of proofs is taken from
the lives of the writers of the Bible; and the last from
the goodness of the doctrine contained in it. The Christian who endeavours to support Christianity by tempo-

ral rewards and punishments, affects to be wiser than his master; but he, who dares rest his holy religion on its own rock, enters into the spirit of the doctrine in our text, "One is your master, even Christ."

Observe the *duties* of the Christian religion. The Gospel is considered both as a revelation of mercy, and an obligation to duty; and if it be the first, gratitude will allow it must be the last. The duties of a Christian are of two sorts. The first are, what are called *moral*, or the duties which we owe to God, to ourselves, and to one another, both as creatures and as Christians. The other are called *positive* duties (forgive this technical term, I cannot think of another just now), and by positive duties we mean Baptism and the Lord's supper, which Christ expressly commanded his disciples to observe. The Christian who performs both these kinds of duties, acts like a Christian, by obeying his Divine master; while he, who incorporates superstitious practices into the Christian life, discovers either the arrogance of a master, or the servility of a slave. Either he himself hath introduced a performance without the authority of his master, or he hath submitted to some other person who hath done so.

Consider the *motives* of the Christian religion. Our heavenly director did something more than laying down a plan; he gave it effect, by including in his scheme of happiness such powerful and forcible considerations as were sufficient to give actual enjoyment. Had God given man a scheme or plan of the heavens, or of the sea, or of the earth, or of a single flower, and uo more, man would have had a fine speculation; but he could neither have made a world nor a violet. Had Christ given us only a plan of virtue and happiness, we could never have obtained either; he did this, but he did more; he drew back the veil that hid futurity from our eyes, and brought forward to our sight the rising of the dead, the coming of the Judge, the happiness of heaven, the misery of inextinguishable fire; or rather, he showed us in these facts the true character of Almighty God, and so conveyed that force into his doctrine, which renders it irresistible and glorious. The man, who, unacquainted

with these great moving powers, endeavours to keep
Christianity alive by a few feeble, worldly maxims, doth
not enter into the spirit of our text: on the contrary,
the Christian, filled with these motives, resembles Mary, who enjoyed all the power of religion, by only " sitting at the master's feet."

Sum up these articles, and they amount to this.
Christ, the founder of our holy religion, hath ordered
as much of his history to be recorded, as it is necessary
for us to know ; and he hath established the truth of
the facts on such proofs as he thought most likely to
support it; he hath commanded and exemplified all the
duties necessary to be performed by us; and he hath given
us such weighty reasons for performing them, as in his
judgment were equal to the establishment of knowledge,
virtue, and happiness. To enter into his views, is to
receive him for master ; and to refuse every other director in matters of religion and conscience, to require
no more to make a Christian than he required, is to admit the meaning of this declaration, " One is your master, even Christ."

My fellow-citizens ! I cannot sufficiently express the
feelings of my heart on this occasion. When I survey
this great company, assembled in this sequestered mead-
ow, the sun smiling, the air fanning, the blossoms and
the flowers perfuming, the river running gurgling by,
and all of us come with perfect ease, a part to be baptized on their own profession of faith, and the rest to
attend to the reasons of the practice ; when I behold
the decent inquisitiveness of many, and know the principles of most, I cannot help congratulating you in the
borrowed language of the wise man, " Many daughters
have done virtuously ; but thou excellest them all."
Allow me to explain myself.

The Catholic church at Rome " did virtuously," when
she shook off the authority of heathen emperors in matters of religion. Before the coming of our Lord Jesus
Christ, the heathens united the character of high-priest
with that of king ; so that the religion of heathen countries was not directed by the reason of the inhabitants,
but by the arbitrary orders of an unjust and cruel ty-

rant. The Roman emperors were in possession of this prerogative, when Christ was born ; and when the Gospel was first preached in the provinces of the empire, it was supposed to be an invasion of the imperial authority. The Gospel, however, was taught at Rome, and all over the empire, which is called in Scripture, "the whole world." The Apostles taught the heathens to think and act for themselves, and strongly inculcated this in their writings. The people did so, and renouncing the prejudices of their education and the superstitions of their country, became Christians on their own conviction of the truth and excellence of Christianity. Individuals thus converted, formed themselves into little societies, called churches. There was one at Philippi, another at Corinth, and another at Rome, to all which the Apostle wrote letters of instruction, not by authority of the Emperor, but by virtue of a commission received from Jesus Christ. The Christian church at Rome made no formal declaration of rights, but they practically claimed the liberty of renouncing the Emperor for a master in religion, and receiving Jesus Christ. In the reign of mild Emperors, they were permitted to live in quiet; and when cruel Emperors persecuted them, they wrote modest apologies, persevered in their profession, and sealed their profession with their blood. Would you think, my brethren, that a people, who had the virtuous courage to resist the first of mortals, a Roman Emperor, should have the meanness to resign their liberty to one of their own teachers, a creature of their own election, who was, only because they chose him to be ? So it was, and for ages past, to this day, the whole church of Rome, consisting of many kingdoms, do not even pretend to think for themselves in religion, but, on the contrary, avow the infallibility of one single man. The clergyman at Rome, called Pope, that is, papa or father, is to them, instead of conviction, instead of conscience, instead of reason, instead of Scripture, instead of Christ himself; and this exchange is called the Holy Catholic and Apostolic religion of Jesus Christ.

The church of England " did virtuously" to shake off

the authority of the Bishop of Rome, in matters of religion.   The history of our country is hardly worth attention till the reign of Henry the Seventh ; and then it
seems not to be the country which we now inhabit; so
gross was the ignorance, and so very abject was the
slavery of our ancestors.   It was a glorious day, when
the reformation took place, and when the title of the
Bishop of Rome to dominion, over conscience was fully
and fairly examined.   This was done under many dis-
advantages, with many imperfections, and at the expense of much treasure, and much human blood; but it
was done, and it was well and thoroughly done; and
Christians once more heard the joyful sound of the text,
" Call no man your Father upon earth ; for one is your
Father, which is in heaven, and one is your master,
even Christ."   To read the first writings of the refor-
mers, you would suppose they were going directly into
the spirit and practice of Christian liberty ; but, certain
it is, they fell short, and vindicated that liberty against
a foreign Bishop, only to place it in the hands of civil
governors ; so that, though the Scriptures were restored
to the people, yet the sense was retained by the crown,
and expressed in certain articles of faith ; and though
Christ was reinstated in name, yet he was to be adored
only as a printed ritual allowed.   We grant, this' revo-
lution was a noble amendment; for the government of
this country being partly in the hands of the people,
partakes of popular freedom ; and the prerogative of establishing religion is so justly softened with toleration
in the letter of the law, and with liberality of sentiment
in the spirit of government, that nobody has any thing
to fear at present on a religious account in this country.
You may, if you please, adopt the established faith, and
you may, if you think proper, renounce it.

   The Protestant dissenters in this country have " done
virtuously" in not accepting the emoluments which are
affixed to the established religion, and in following their
own convictions, without fee or reward.   There is nothing so unmanageable as a man's own understanding.
He opens his ears to religious instruction, and before
he is aware, truth seats itself in his mind, and will reign

there in spite of him. It is not in his power to unlearn
what he understands ; nor can he choose to believe that
false, which he knows to be true. If he refuses to act
according to his convictions, conscience arraigns him,
and he seems 'to be tried for his life. He becomes unhappy as a condemned criminal, and his conscience will
admit of no calm, till his conduct corresponds with his
convictions. What can he do ? The answer is easy. Let
him act uprightly, and be happy : " One is his master,
even Christ." When men thus follow their own convictions into a Christian church, there they ought to be
at peace : but even they cannot be at peace, if any one
man presumes to require others to think and act as he
does; for this would be to exclude Christian liberty, and
in effect to say, One is your master, even the imposer of
a creed. They " do virtuously," who claim Christian
liberty for themselves ; but they, who along with that
claim, allow it in its full exercise to all their brethren,
in their community as well as out of it, they " excel them
all."

A doctrine so free from venom, so placid in itself, so
conducive to the virtue and happiness of mankind, so
full of " mercy and good fruits," so much like the sun
that " riseth on the evil and the good ;" can such a doctrine come from him, who " was a murderer from the
beginning ?" Shall we say of a teacher of this doctrine,
" How sayest thou, ye shall be made free ?" " Say we
not well, that thou art a Samaritan, and hast a devil?"
My God ! what charms do thy children find in bondage ?
Whence this unnatural shuddering at the sound of freedom ? Can it be difficult to inspire the souls of mankind
with a love of liberty ; their own liberty, the liberty of
loving and adoring thee according to the dictates of
their own conscience, conscience, that vice-God upon
earth ! Well, let us try, let us examine whether the
sole government of every man's conscience by Jesus
Christ, in the manner we have been explaining it, hath
any reasons to support it.

First then, we affirm, there is *no need* of any other
dominion over conscience, than what Jesus Christ exercises, the dominion of argument to support the fact of

15

his mission. If the Gospel were a hard and difficult science, it might be beyond the capacities of some of our fellow-creatures; but it is not so. We contend, that there is nothing in the Gospel, written by the Evangelists, necessary to be known in order to salvation, which is too hard for any plain man to understand. Let any man take the Gospel according to any head of a party, for example, according to St. Augustin, which is contained in ten great folio volumes, and which is expounded by a set of learned men in the church of Rome, and let him give every man his own opinion, till there remain only the pure texts quoted by them, and written by the Evangelists, and he would find himself just where I would place him; that is, in possession of the pure Gospel, with as much right, and as much ability to judge of its meaning, as all these gentlemen expositors had. Should it be said, these scholars inform us that the name Jesus comes from the word Joshua; and Joshua from another word; and should they inform us of a thousand such things; we should reply, all these are true, but the knowledge of these is not necessary to salvation, and therefore is not that Gospel, without the belief of which we cannot be saved. In a word, we consider every order to believe what other men affirm to be true, exactly like an act of Parliament, requiring all the inhabitants of Great Britain to wear spectacles, though the far greater part of them have good eyes, and no need of glasses. When the apostle Peter lay "sleeping between two soldiers, bound with two chains, the angel of the Lord smote him on the side, and his chains fell off." The angel accompanied him through the wards, and caused the iron gate to open without Peter's moving a finger; but the same angel ordered him to "gird himself," to "bind on his sandals," and to "cast his garment about him." It would have been needless for the angel to have required Peter to open the gate, and to knock off his chains, for he had not power to do so: and it would have been needless for the angel to buckle his girdle, or to bind on his sandals, because he had power to dress himself. Thus we affirm concerning the Gospel. If any parts of it be beyond our capacities; it is needless to require us to believe them, for we can never believe what we cannot understand. If other parts of the Gospel be within our reach, it is needless to require others to do that for us, which we are able to do for ourselves. The Gospel of some Christians is very hard; it is not fair to require us to believe it; they say they do not understand it themselves; but the Gospel, according to the four evangelists is not of this kind. Christian, know the Gospel of your master, and the dignity of yourself, and say to every pretender to dominion over you, "No doubt but ye are the people, and wisdom shall die with you. But I have understanding as well as you; I am not inferior to you: yea, who knoweth not such things as these? And be it indeed that I have erred, mine error remaineth with myself."

Consider in the next place, that the exercise of this Christian liberty cannot possibly be an injury to other Christians. Which of the ten commandments does a man break, by following his own convictions in religion? Suppose the worst, that he is in an error; yet "his error remaineth with himself." Is any one of us less wise, less just, or less safe, because another does that for himself, which we every day do for ourselves? Our safety is not endangered by his taking the liberty to think for himself: it is we who endanger his safety by taking the liberty to think for him. In such a case we should be less wise and less just than we ought to be; as he would be, if he allowed us to run our liberty into such licentiousness. How is it that men, Christian men too, can see one another's sicknesses, and hear of one another's misfortunes, without any emotions of anger, and with all the feelings of humanity and pity that Christians ought to have for one another; and that they cannot bear to hear a conscientious man avow sentiments different from their own, without a red resentment, that like a hot thunderbolt hisses, and wounds, and kills where it falls? No, it is not justice, it is not prudence, it is not humanity, it is not benevolence, it is not zeal for these dispositions: it seems as if it were the explosion of an infected heart, where the milk of human kindness never flowed. If such emotions can proceed from Christians,

we must suppose, what we are loath to think, that is,
that some Christians are in some unhappy moments di-
vested of all the principles of their holy religion, and
actuated by the dispositions of the most ignorant and
cruel of mankind. But, say they, though we receive
no injury, yet God is dishonoured. Ah! is God dishonoured? Imitate his conduct then. Does he thunder,
does he lighten, does he afflict this poor man? Behold
his sun enlightens his habitation, his rain refreshes his
fields, his gentle breeze fans and animates him every
day; his revelation lies always open before him; his
throne of mercy is ever accessible to him; and will
you, rash Christian, will you mark him out for vengeance? I repeat it again, imitate your heavenly Father, and at least suspend your anger till that day, when
" the Lord will make manifest the counsels of men's
hearts; and then shall every man have praise of God."
Then will you perfectly understand the justice, as well
as the kindness of these interrogations. " Who maketh
thee to differ from another? and what hast thou that
thou didst not receive? Now if thou didst receive it,
why dost thou glory as if thou hadst not received it?"
As therefore dominion over conscience is needless, so
the utmost exercise of Christian liberty is innocent, and
there is no restraining it without incurring guilt.

Remark, further, that free inquiry in religion is *essential to the virtue* of a character. The virtue of man
consists in his making use of all his own faculties; not
in believing that other men have made a virtuous use
of theirs. Now it is possible, a man may make use
of all his faculties, and yet not be able to perceive the
evidence of some opinions, which are called articles of
faith; and consequently he may doubt the truth of those
articles, yea, it is necessary to the virtue of his character that he should doubt them; for it is not in his power to believe without proof, and it would be unjust to profess to believe what he does not believe. Let us not be
so weak as to imagine, that a man cannot think justly
unless he thinks as we do. Let us allow that his justice
consists in thinking, and reasoning, and acting as well
as he can; and that he is accountable for all this, only

to " one master, even Christ." As freedom of thought is the parent and guardian of all virtue, so the want of it is the nurse of vice, and particularly of that general disposition to all sin; I mean servility. A low, servile soul, habituated not to think for itself, but to be led by a guide, is prepared for the commission of any crime, or the belief of any absurdity, that a mercenary guide may find convenient to enjoin. No men teach the depravity, the extreme and excessive depravity of human nature, with a better grace than these men. Were I disposed to sink a soul into the lowest degree of wretchedness, either as a citizen of the world, or as a member of a church, I would inculcate, with all my might, a spirit of servility, and that would answer my end better than any other method in the world. I would not shock a man with the sounds of perjury and blasphemy, impiety to God and injustice to men; but I would gently inform him, that he was a poor, depraved, foolish creature, not able to judge between good and evil, truth and error, and that he would discover great arrogance if he thought otherwise: but that I was a wise and sacred man, wishing well to his soul, and that by believing what I said to be true, and by doing what I directed to be done, he would be pious, and safe, and happy. There is therefore no virtue, but a great fund of iniquity in implicit faith.

Observe further, that a Christian, who takes Christ for his only and sufficient governor in religion, is *supported by the examples* of all genuine Christians, from the days of Christ to this moment. The apostles had no master but Jesus Christ. The primitive Christians had no other master than he; for the apostles exercised no " dominion over their faith," though they were " helpers of their joy." The church of Rome, when they shook off the imperial yoke, acted under the same authority. All other churches, when they cast off the dominion of the Bishop of Rome, went on the same principles, and were justified in doing so. If you imitate these examples, you incorporate into your conduct what was excellent in theirs; and if you allow others the same freedom, which you yourselves enjoy, you excel

15*

latter Christians, and copy the lives of the first and
purest professors of the Christian religion.

It would be endless to enumerate reasons in support
of this doctrine; and I am happy to observe, that you
are in full possession of one practical argument, which
triumphs over all suspicion. You have made an *experiment* of this doctrine. You are free yourselves, and
your brethren are free along with you. Hence that
freedom of speech in your teachers; for nobody is so
weak as to imagine that all our hearers should adopt
all the principles we lay down. We propose a subject,
you think of it, you do not see evidence of it. What
then? Nothing at all.

Hence that spirit of free inquiry, which is cherished
among you. You habituate yourselves to read the
Scriptures, to make use of your own understandings, to
inquire of one another how it is written, and of whom
speaketh the prophet. Hence that investigation of a
subject, which you pursue, and those interesting, eager,
and friendly debates, which you conduct with so much
edification to one another, and with so much honour to
the soundness of your understandings, and to the sweetness of your tempers. You have learned the happy art
of hearing without any unkind emotions your own sentiments contradicted, sifted, and tried; and it never enters into your minds to injure, to grieve, or even to suspect the good and honest soul, who thinks for himself,
but who does not think with you.

Hence comes that mild and gentle discipline, which
sets open the Lord's table to all who profess faith in
Christ and repentance towards God. I have spoken improperly. You have not set the Lord's table abroad;
it was he himself who did so: but you have avoided the
folly of inclosing it, of obliging all to approach it by a
strait, dark passage, kept by a surly animal, in shape a
man, in temper a mastiff. Hence that honest proposal
of believers' baptism as a primitive institute of Jesus
Christ, and that just liberty given to every brother to
judge of the nature and necessity of what you propose.
If he believes, he is baptized; if he thinks infant baptism a divine institute, exemplified by Christ, and en-

joined on the children of his disciples, he procures a neighbouring teacher to baptize them; and though this hath been the practice of this society for more than a hundred and fifty years, yet there is no instance in your recollection or in your *records*, of the least degree of bitterness or incivility on that account.

Hence that generous regard, which you manifest to all good men of every denomination. You hear their instructions with mildness; you examine them with integrity, you adopt them with gratitude, or you refuse them with civility, accompanying your unbelief with a thousand kind offices, far better to the good men than your orthodoxy. Hence that just distinction, which you make in regard to all the duties you owe your fellow-creatures. You observe that you are bound by the law of nature, and by the express revelation of Scripture, to love your neighbour as yourself; your *neighbour* in general, not your *sound* neighbour in particular.

Hence comes the inexpressible joy of your hopes. You see at no great distance, death. You consider dying as a passage to immortal life. You consider immortal life as the inheritance of all good men; and there you hope benevolence, which, in its utmost exercise here, is only in the bud, will ripen into fruits of inconceivable extent, duration, and beauty. Much of the joy of such prospects arises from the exercise of benevolence. What interest have we in the destruction of our fellow-creatures? Is it impossible for us to be happy unless some of our fellow-creatures be miserable? How can a bigot be happy by believing, that the infinitely wise and good God will contract himself into the size, the narrow size of a school-boy's soul, will make his childish distinctions, enter into his silly schemes, and rule and judge a world of " ten thousand times ten thousand, and thousands of thousands," not by the perfections of his own nature, and the well known laws of his government, but will make all move to the drowsy musick of the tinkling bells of a pedant. A happiness founded on benevolence, rests on the pillars that support the universe: it may be shaken; it never can be subverted. On this subject we have no reproofs, and but one exhortation to give you, and that is contained in one word, PERSEVERE. " As many as walk according to this rule, peace be on them, and mercy!" They are " the Israel of God." " Grace be with all them that love our Lord Jesus Christ in sincerity." Amen.

DISCOURSE X.

THE CHRISTIAN RELIGION SHOULD NOT BE CONFOUNDED
WITH HEATHENISM.

[*AT LITTLE SHELFORD.*]

COLOSSIANS ii. 8, 9.

*Beware lest any man spoil you through philosophy and
vain deceit, after the tradition of men, after the rudiments of the world, and not after Christ: for in him
dwelleth all the fulness of the Godhead bodily.*

" Beware lest any man spoil you" ... What ! is it
possible to spoil a Christian? Indeed it is. A Christian may spoil himself as a beautiful complexion or a
proper shape may be rendered disagreeable by circumstances of dress or uncleanliness ; he may be spoiled by
other people, just as a straight child may be made
crooked by the negligence of his nurse ; or exactly as a
sweet-tempered youth may be made surly or insolent
by a cruel master. " Beware lest any man spoil you."
Is it possible for whole societies of Christians to be
spoiled? Certainly it is. Nothing is easier. They
may spoil one another, as in a family, the temper of
one single person may spoil the peace of the whole ; or
as in a school, one trifling or turbulent master may spoil
the education, and so the usefulness, through life, of two
or three hundred pupils, successively committed to his

injudicious treatment. All human constitutions, even
the most excellent, have seeds of imperfections in them,
some mixtures of folly, which naturally tend to weaken
and destroy; and though this is not the case with the
Christian religion itself, which is the wisdom of God
without any mixture of human folly; yet even this pure
religion, like the pure juice of the grape, falling into
the hands of depraved men, may be perverted, and
whole societies may embrace Christianity thus perverted.

Beware lest any man spoil you through . . . what?
Idolatry, blasphemy, profligacy? No. Christians are
in very little danger from great crimes; but beware
lest any man spoil you through *philosophy*. What hath
philosophy done, that the apostle should thus guard
Christians against it? Did not he know that before his
time, while mimics were idly amusing one part of the
world, and heroes depopulating another, the peaceable
sons of philosophy disturbed nobody, but either improved mankind in their schools, or sat all calm and content
in their cells? Did he not observe that in his time
Christianity was reputed folly, because it was taught
and believed by unlettered people; and that if philosophers could be prevailed on to teach it, it would have instantly acquired a character of wisdom? Whether the
common people had understood it or not, they would
have reckoned it wise if philosophers had taught it.
The apostle knew all this, and, far from courting the
aid of learned men to secure credit to the Gospel, he
guards Christians in the text against the future temptation of doing so. Had this caution been given us by
any of the other apostles, who had not had the advantage of a learned education, we might have supposed,
they censured what they did not understand; but this
comes from the disciple of Gamaliel.

The wise apostle assigns two reasons for the caution.
" Beware lest any man spoil you through philosophy."
Why? Because philosophy doth not go on the same
ground as Christianity. Philosophy is a body of wisdom made up of the speculations, and conjectures, and
inferences of studious, learned men; but Christianity is

a body of information reported to us by the express command of Almighty God. This is the meaning of the expression, " After the tradition of men, after the rudiments of the world, and not after Christ," that is Christianity. The apostle observes, that there is a perfection in the information given us by Jesus Christ, for he taught us only *facts :* but philosophy, which is the science of investigating the *nature* of facts, is on this very account uncertain, vain, and deceitful, when applied to the Christian religion. Reduce the subject to two parts, and they amount to this; the wisdom of the heathen schools was vain and deceitful, because it was not true ; and the wisdom of modern schools, though true in itself, is deceitful when applied to Christianity. It is this last view of the subject, on which we mean to fix your attention ; and we shall only aim to explain and improve it. God Grant we may be edified !

I am sure it is not necessary in this assembly, to prove, that there is nothing in this text, or in any other text in the Bible meant to injure human learning. Jesus Christ did not honour the schools with his presence ; but Jesus Christ had the spirit of God without measure. The first apostles were illiterate men ; but Jesus took them under his tuition before he sent them to teach. There are thousands of good Christians now, who have no learning ; as there are thousands of generous hearts, who have no money. There are many edifying teachers, who can only just read their Bibles, and expound it by their own feelings ; and when they prudently teach such parts of religion as belong to experiment, who is not animated by their instructions ? There are many who affect to have learning, which they have not ; and there are some who have it and abuse it ; but none of these is sufficient to induce us to condemn the wisdom of the schools. The design of the apostle is not to destroy, but to direct philosophy. He knew, a learned man could no more teach the Gospel, without his literature, than other men could hear it without their konwledge of husbandry, gardening, building, and so on ; but as each of these branches of knowledge ought to be restrained to its own subjects, so ought philosophy. If, at any time, a young gentleman should, under pretence of teaching us the Gospel, set forth all his fine things, and waste the hour devoted to religion, in jingling his silver bells, let us consider him as we consider our sons, when they come from school, and talk Latin, or propose hard questions in arithmetic to their mothers. Both classes are good at heart, for they intend to give us pleasure. Both err from the same cause, the infancy of their understandings; and age and experience will complete their education.

To come to the point. Let us distinguish Christianity from the *philosophy* of it. By Christianity I mean the Christian religion. By the Christian religion I mean that set of facts, which Jesus Christ taught, and which are all recorded in the Gospel. Our notion is, that these facts are reported to us for the sake of the use to which we are able to apply them, and not laid down as philosophers lay down their speculations in the schools, for the sake of exercising the geniuses of young gentlemen to make improvements. This distinction between facts and their uses apart from the philosophy of them, is founded in nature: and it is the more credible, because it makes Christianity exactly like the world in which we live, and so gives it a character of divinity, showing that the maker of the world is the author of our holy religion.

I must not go down this evening from this frame, till I have some way or other conveyed this subject into the minds of all my hearers. The day's work is done, the cattle are all at rest, the evening is pleasant, the fragrance of the trees in blossom all around us, is highly refreshing; the grass on which many of you sit is an elegant carpet, and you seem all to be very attentive; can I ever choose a time more proper to treat a subject, which, though not hard when the apostle wrote, is become so now by what philosophers have done to it?

Consider me this evening as doing nothing with this subject except what you all do in saffron time. You gather the flowers early, with great care; and after you get home, you leisurely pick off the beautiful blue bell and throw it away, for the sake of the more valuable chive in the middle, which you save, and by the help of a kiln bring to the consistence of a dry, fibrous cake, which you call saffron, and sell to pay your rents, and to maintain your families. Now, who is there in this assembly that cannot distinguish between the fact, the use, and the philosophy of saffron?

Observe first the fact, and the use of knowing the fact. Every man in this parish knows the bulbs, which you call *heads*. Every child knows how to drop them, one by one, at equal distances, into the trenches after the spadesman. Every body knows that cattle must be kept off by fences, and that the ground must be clean hoed just before the saffron is expected to spring up. All the month before saffron-time the parish become prophets, and half the poor men spring up in the morning, before it is well day, and run without their clothes out of doors to look after their old benefactors, the clouds. No rain, no saffron. Thus a fine shower makes all the children smile in hopes of a plentiful saffron-time, and consequently new clothes against winter. When the time comes, how cheerfully you rise by the moon or the stars, flock into the field, and pick the flowers before the sun is up! Presently the streets are all flowers, the tables and the kilns are covered with chives, and the end of all is, the whole is exchanged for money, money for clothes, a Bible and a hymn book, and these convey instruction to you and your families, to fear God and keep his commandments, which make you live soberly, and die peaceably, in hopes of a joyful resurrection.

Now here is a set of facts and uses, all which you perfectly understand, and your knowledge in this view is complete; but the philosophy of all these facts is a very different thing. Some have no knowledge at all of it, and they that know most of it are only as far above others as a man upon a mole-hill is above one of his own size, on the level ground. Were a man inclined to spoil your saffron trade, he could not take a more proper method than to require you to account for the size, and shape, and colour, and scent of saffron; and could you be prevailed on to waste the whole saffron-

16

time in disputing on questions of this kind, instead of practising what knowledge you have about facts and uses, you would be spoiled to all intents and purposes. This is not only the case with the knowledge of flowers; it is the same, with all other things in the world. We know the uses of things, but we do not know the nature of them. As it is with the saffron-grower in his rood of land, so it is with the mariner, who sails all round the globe ; and as it is with common observation, so it is almost with the deepest speculation ; a glass can carry the eye a little way ; and intense thought can carry reason a little way further ; but the discovery of vast and boundless tracks beyond, will always leave a studious man very modest, because it will always leave him very near his plain neighbours.

What we contend for is this ; that our holy religion exactly resembles the world in which we live ; and to make my meaning as clear as I can; I will lay a few truths before the two sorts of men in question ; the plain Christian who confines himself to facts and their uses, and the Christian full of philosophy. By the way, there are many Christians extremely ignorant of the wisdom of the schools, who yet will be always applying the science of other men to their own ideas of religion ; and what with learned words and vulgar ideas, polished phrases and gross notions, great sounds and little or no meaning ; they make the Christian religion the most abstruse of all hard things in the world. Do you wonder you do not understand them ? They do not understand themselves.

One fact reported in Scripture is, that " all have sinned and come short of the glory of God." The proof of this fact is made, by bringing out Divine law, and comparing it with our conduct. The plain Christian attends to this fact; he examines his life, traces his actions, and finds they take their rise in disordered passions in his own bosom. This was an action of pride, that was an exercise of revenge ; a third proceeded from anger, and a fourth from an immoderate love of the world. He carries back his reflection, and finds that his passions have been in disorder ever since he could remem-

ber. He soon finds out the use of the knowledge of
this fact; for if it would give him pain to discover that he
had lost his children, or his property, or his health, it
must needs fill him with sorrow, to find that he has lost
his innocence, and with that all right to be happy.   Full
of this just grief, he checks sin, and avoids temptations
to commit it.   Give this sad truth to a philosopher, and
he will perplex it with hard questions, and answers yet
more hard than the questions themselves, and will go
into abundance of labyrinths, some before the creation
of the world, and others after the consummation of it.
There will come up in this man's religion, a great army of infants and angels; there will be Adam and Eve,
and our immediate parents, and a world of people from
all corners of the globe, and every one will bring a new
question, and all together will lead us off from the great
use of the knowledge of the fact, which is sorrow for
our own sin, and not that of Adam and infants, and angels and heathens.   When the good man of the house
hath caught cold, and the good dame puts a little saffron into his drink, does she, doth he, doth any one in
the family attend to any thing more than the effects
which they know by experience will be produced?

It is reported in the Holy Scriptures, that there is a
God, the first cause of all things, the Creator, the Preserver, the Benefactor, and Friend of mankind; that
he sent word to us by prophets and apostles; and above
all by his Son Jesus Christ, our Lord: that though he
blamed our conduct, yet he pitied our condition, and
would freely forgive all our offences, of every kind,
through the mediation of Jesus Christ. The plain
Christian hears this information, and examines it.   He
is not surprised that God should esteem man his creature, for he knows love is natural to him.   He is not
shocked that God should blame sin, for he himself is
obliged to condemn it, though by so doing he passes
sentence on himself.   He knows it must be in the power of God to make the wretched happy; and he at once
perceives it will be highly to the honour of his wisdom
and goodness to do so.   He observes, that if any despise
what it is so much to the honour of God to propose, he

is exceedingly to blame, and ought to suffer the consequences. He is not offended that God should choose
to dispense all this goodness by the hands of Jesus
Christ; for he sees that there is but one first cause, and
that God communicates his goodness to us by means, in
every case. He soon finds the use of this information;
it resembles the fragrance of a flower, or the warmth of
the sun ; it draws, and we walk after it, admiring, adoring, enjoying, and imitating God. Give a philosopher
this truth, and he will perplex every part of it, by inquiring how this God subsists, what is the precise nature
of Jesus Christ, and so on, till, having dissected the subject into a thousand parts, given each an Egyptian, or
a Hebrew, or a Greek name, and garnished the whole
with scholastical ghosts, summoned by a kind of magic
from all schools, ancient and modern, he will render
this glorious truth hardly credible, or glaringly false.
Allow me to make one reflection, while I think of it.
You have heard some of your ministers speak of a dangerous set of men, whom they call, if I recollect the
word rightly, *deists*, or some such name. I humbly beseech you not to be rash in censuring people for being
enemies to the Gospel. There may be, for any thing I
know, such men in the world; but I shall never believe
that sincere men are such, till they are distinguished as
the Jews are in Rome, by wearing a red hat. I do declare, and I am acquainted with several, and so are you,
that some are reputed enemies to the Gospel, only because they are enemies to that abuse of the Gospel, of
which we are speaking. It is not the Gospel according
to the Evangelists that they find fault with, it is the
Gospel according to Wittemberg, where Luther taught;
or to Geneva, where Dr. John Calvin lived: great men,
but they would have been much greater if they had not
applied their philosophy to religion.

The Scripture requires us, if we believe Christianity,
to profess it by being baptized, and to keep the death
of the author of it always in memory, by eating bread
and drinking wine in our religious assemblies. Nothing
can be plainer in the world than these two ordinances;
nothing was better understood, before learned men per-

plexed them ; and, what is very wonderful, though the
schools have rejected the old philosophy, on finding it
false, yet they have retained it in these two ordinances.
There were formerly in the schools, what they called
occult qualities. Do not set your eyes on me as if I
could explain them ; nobody ever understood them, and
the words were only used for a cloak to conceal the ignorance of learned men. By supposing two such qualities in these two ordinances ; they have both been rendered ridiculous in the eyes of sensible men. In regard to baptism, you must not object that an infant cannot answer, and therefore ought not to be questioned ;
or cannot believe, and therefore ought not to be baptized into a profession, which he doth not understand
and approve. A Catholic philosopher will tell you, that
he believes with the faith of the church, and that the
godfather represents the church on this occasion. One
reformed philosopher will tell you, that the child was
born in sin, and that the water washes it away ; and
another will inform you that the water conveys grace,
and that the child receives faith, and hope, and so on.
You do not see the child commit any sin; you cannot name
the sin that he is capable of committing ; you do not see
him practise any virtue ; you cannot conceive a virtue
that he is capable of practising ; and you cannot think
it just either to burn him for his vice, or to reward him
for his virtue ; no matter for all your objections, there
are *occult,* or hidden qualities. The same in regard to
the Lord's supper. We see nothing but bread in the
Catholic church in the administration ; we smell nothing, we taste nothing but bread : no matter, it is the
flesh, and blood, and bones of a man, and there is no
bread there. We see nothing but bread and wine in
the Lutheran church, yet they say, the flesh and blood
of Christ are there, just as fire is in a red hot iron. It
is very likely that Jesus Christ should order his disciples to practise baptism and the Lord's supper in the
manner mentioned in Scripture ; but it is not at all likely that he should propose them to us in the manner last
mentioned. They talk a deal of the danger of the Gospel in the hands of the poor and illiterate ; but have
16*

the unlearned ever done any thing like this? " Beware lest any man spoil you through philosophy and
vain deceit."

Our religion teaches us some great motives to engage
us to be good; such as the immortality of the soul, the
resurrection of the dead, the eternal happiness of heaven, and the endless misery of hell.   These plain truths
are facts of prophecy, which we are taught to believe
will come to pass.   The proof that they will be accomplished lies in the person of the prophet, who foretold
them.   All animals die, and man as well as the rest.
There is no instance of any animal coming to life after its
death, except man.   The man Jesus, who taught us that
we should live in a future state, condescended, in his
own person, to die in the open road, in the presence of
a multitude of beholders, pierced to the heart with a
spear, so that his death could not be doubted.   Three
days after, he came to life again, and showed himself
to his family, and afterwards to great numbers, to five
hundred at one time.   As to the fact, that it was the
same person with whom they had been acquainted before, they were fully assured of it by conversing with
him, and handling him.   As to the use of the fact, that
they ought to infer that the doctrine of such a person
was true, they perfectly understood that too : and both
these are as easy to us, if not easier than they were to
them.   They did not know, nor was it necessary to the
truth of the fact, that they should know, how all this
was effected.   A plain Christian imitates the apostles,
obtains proof of the fact, that Christ rose from the
dead, and then applies his knowledge to the use of hoping that he shall live in a future state, as Jesus hath
foretold.   When a philosopher goes to work upon this
doctrine of immortality, he takes man all to pieces, and
divides him into many parts, and says, This is earth, earth
is not immortal; this is fire, fire is not immortal; this
is thought, thoughts are successional ; which of them is
immortal?   My brethren, leave the worthy man to his
learned meditations; by and by they will hang round
him like icicles, and, when he begins to freeze, his own
pain will make him cry, " Where is God, my Maker?"

Should he come up against you, and attack your faith in a blessed immortality; do not be afraid of his points, but take up this weapon and defend yourselves. Say, I do not trouble myself to study whether I be naturally mortal or immortal; but, be that as it may, if God declares man shall live in a future state, undoubtedly he who keeps him alive forty years, can make him live forty millions, if he pleases. He hath not required me to determine which atom is perishable, and which is not; but he hath taught me that man shall live in a future state, and he hath shown me in the resurrection of Jesus Christ from the dead, the rising again of all mankind.

It is not only the doctrine of Christianity that is hurt by philosophy; the spirit of it is exceedingly injured. The temper and spirit of Jesus was modest, mild, peaceable, full of mercy and good fruits. The Gospel is of the same disposition, and where it is considered as a train of events to be applied to use, it never fails to produce the same just and gentle dispositions. When it becomes a science, it becomes disputatious, haughty, sour, and full of mischief. Whence came persecution, with all its infernal train? It was from this spirit. The disputes, which have affected the peace of the whole Christian world, have not been about the Lord's prayer, the Ten commandments, and the Sermon upon the mount; but about curious and knotty questions, which have something plausible on both sides, and are therefore like to make work for contentious men to the end of the world. Whence is it, that we do not know whether we ought to love a fellow-creature, much less whether we are bound to respect him as a Christian, till we know how he understands some old stale questions of the schools, which ought to have been buried with the first inventors of them? The questions are harmless enough in themselves; for in general it does not signify much to practice, which side we take. They are harmless enough in some people, whose good sense, and sweet temper, and great piety, correct all their actions, and make every thing they say, and do, agreeable and edifying; but they play the mischief in unskilful or designing hands.

We have run through a brief explication, and now we will subjoin two cautions, and so conclude with the use of the doctrine. Let no one imagine, in the first place, that there is any thing in Christianity, which will not bear the strictest scrutiny. We say that of every part of the Christian religion, which we affirm of every flower in the universe. There is not one, that doth not contain a whole volume of information : but we contend, that in regard to you, in this parish, neither the rose, nor the water lily, nor any other flower in the world, is the subject of your chief attention ; it is saffron, and saffron alone, that you are called by Providence to study. Thus we say, The business of your poor people in this parish is with the Bible, and as your time and circumstances will allow you to read but one book, the Bible is the book in the world the best fitted for you. As we said concerning the one flower, which makes the business and the wealth of some of you ; so we say of the Bible : You should attend to the facts, and know the uses, and let questions about natures alone. I call this a perfect religion for you ; and I verily believe you cannot mistake the uses of the various parts of the Bible. What is the use of a book ? I ask the little girls. Were I to put one into your hands, you would directly open and read it ; that is, you would apply it to the use for which I gave it you. Should you find a prayer in it, composed by Jesus Christ, beginning " Our Father, who art in heaven," you would know that this was intended to be spoken upon the knees to Almighty God. Should you find a passage where God calls himself a " shepherd," and men " the sheep of his pasture," you would directly know the use of this, that it was intended to engage you cheerfully to trust yourself, and your children, the lambs of the flock, to the conduct of his wise Providence : and so of the rest. In the next life, where we shall not be interrupted by wants, or bounded by time, or blinded by sin, we shall see to the bottom of every thing, and feast our souls with the sight : there you will become philosophers without any danger of error : but here, where time is short, " beware lest any man spoil you through philosophy and vain deceit."

Let us use another precaution to guard the practice of religion, as we have endeavoured to guard the doctrine of it. "Let us beware lest any man spoil us." There are two ways of spoiling Christians, the one is very long and expensive, the other short and cheap. The long way is by taking a little boy before he be able to reason and judge for himself, by prejudicing him against the Gospel, by learning him to shake his head over it as a deep, dark, difficult book, which cannot be understood, without a vast stock of human learning : by expending all you are worth in the world, or by burdening some public charity with a boy, neither lame nor blind, to be brought up to understand the Gospel : by getting him taught the follies and the trifles of old heathen writers ; by giving him to understand as he grows up, that he is a youth of extraordinary wisdom, and of a higher order than the rest of mankind ; by learning him to dress fine, to become expensive, and to find a thousand things necessary to his rank, of which none of his family ever heard the names before ; by teaching him to take learning in lieu of piety ; and the dignity of a priest to give force to religion, instead of reason, modesty, and a holy example ; by habituating him to consider Christianity as under a sentence of death, unless such as he condescended to maintain its reputation in the world. Do not say, " He speaks parables." Indeed I do not. I tell you a true history. Did you never see a farmer's son made a minister of the Gospel without any religion ?

There is a short way of spoiling men : perhaps you may think I could not prevail with you to believe or to say, that when you are so kind as to pay me a friendly visit, you were at London at the same time. This, however, I affirm, is nothing to what I could do without any expense or trouble, provided you would agree to one thing. Only lay it down for a rule, that, though you are to make use of your senses and reason, your eyes and your judgment, in all other cases, yet when I speak to you, you are to make use of none of them ; but to believe what I say without examining ; or, which will answer the same end, to say you do. Grant this, and I

will bring you, if not to believe, yet to affirm, and kill
and slay in proof of it, that you drink me in a tea-spoon
full of wine ; that a hundred people beside, do the same,
and that ten thousand people in different parts of the
world do so too, at the same time ; and yet I, the man
thus distributed shall continue standing and preaching
in this place all the while.   Thus the doctrines, the ordinances, and the disciples of Jesus Christ may be spoiled of all their truth and beauty, till they, the glory of
the world, are thrown aside as the rubbish of it.

Happy would it be for a teacher of Christianity, if he
could always close here, well assured that nobody would
pervert his doctrine.   Happy, if all hearers of Christian sermons had a habit of dexterously applying each
part to its proper use.   This is, through our inattention,
sometimes difficult.   Lest any such mistake should affect you, let us, before we part, apply the subject to the
worst condition that can be supposed among you, the
condition of a man actually spoiled.   I will not irritate
your grief by asking, Who " gave you for a spoil ?"
Where were you going when you " fell among thieves,"
who stripped you of your raiment, wounded you, and
left you half dead ?   Let us, for the present, omit such
mortifying questions, and let us address ourselves to
your relief.   " Peace be to thee, peace be to thine
house, and peace be unto all that thou hast !"

See, the spoilers have not robbed thee of the *Scriptures.*   Here are all the Prophecies, and all the accomplishments of them in plain, true history.   Here are the
" words of eternal life," spoken to Peter and others, and
written for your use.   Here are all the promises, like
all the flowers that adorn the earth in spring, fresh and
fragrant, as if they had never administered pleasure to
the scent of man.   Here is the book of the Acts of the
Apostles, shewing us how they understood their Divine
Master.   Here are all the Epistles, comments upon the
Gospel.   Here are numbers of such as yourself in both
Testaments saying, " Come see a man, who told us all
things that ever we did ; is not this the Christ ?   Behold the Lamb of God that taketh away the sin of the
world."   " Blind Bartimeus !   Be of good comfort, rise

Jesus calleth thee." Here are even "Psalms and
Hymns, and spiritual Songs," ready composed for you
to sing the praise of your deliverer. Here are prayers
fitted to the weakest understandings, and the shortest
memories, "words to take with you" and say, "Take
away all iniquity and receive us graciously; in thee the
fatherless findeth mercy." Thanks be to God, whoever the spoilers were, the profligate or the formal, the
learned or the ignorant, they have not been suffered to
rob you of this inestimable treasure. This was not owing to your care, negligent man, but to that watchful
friend who "loved you with an everlasting love," and
who, all the while you lived in sin, said, "There shall
be a day, that the watchman shall cry" to that forlorn
man, "Arise, and go up to Zion, unto the Lord your
God."

See, again, the spoilers have not robbed you of your
sense and reason. I am sorry to say they are damaged;
but, let us be thankful, they are not irrecoverably lost.
You have eyes to read, and ears to hear; and the best
use you can make of them, and the only way to recover
them to their first strength, is to say, "I will go even
to the seat of God. I will order my cause before him,
and fill my mouth with arguments. I will know the
words which he will answer me, and understand what
he will say unto me. Will he plead against me with
his great power?" What a question, what a dangerous
question is this for you, great sinner, to agitate? How
will you procure an answer? Shall any ascend up into
heaven to fetch it down? Open your eyes and read;
or your ears and hear: the answer is here in my hand.
"Will he plead against you with his great power? No,
but he will put strength in you, suffer you to dispute
with him, and deliver you forever from your judge."
You have not lost your reason. "Stand still then, that
I may reason with you before the Lord, of all the righteous acts," the fit and proper acts, "of the Lord, which
he did" to such as you. When the Jews cried, he "sent
Moses and Aaron to bring them out of the land of Egypt.
When they forgot God, he sold them into the hands of
the Philistines. When they cried and said, We have

sinned, but now deliver us, and we will serve thee; the Lord sent judges to deliver them." This hath been his manner from the beginning, and to you, as well as to the Jews, he saith, " Come now, and let us reason together; cease to do evil, learn to do well; though your sins be as scarlet, they shall be white as snow; though they be red like crimson, they shall be as wool."

See, further, the enemy hath not spoiled you of your *friends*. Christians come round a returning prodigal, and say, " We have heard a voice of trembling, of fear, and not of peace. Alas! It is the time of Jacob's trouble, but he shall be saved out of it." He shall not be " called an outcast, saying, This is Zion, whom no man seeketh after." Penitent, what a multitude of tender hearts and generous hands will " pity, and bemoan thee, and go aside to ask how thou doest!" Teachers will instruct thee, elders will pray for thee, and show thee, by example, how Christians address God; the courageous will go first and embolden thee, the lively will quicken thee, all, like Job's friends, will comfort thee; " every man will give thee," if not " a piece of money, and an ear-ring of gold," yet, what is beyond all riches, wisdom and virtue and friendship. All their knowledge will be thine; for this is a sort of treasure which no Christian saith is " his own, but they have all things common." " All things are yours, whether Paul, or Apollos, or Cephas, or the world, or life, or death, or things present, or things to come, all are yours, if you are Christ's."

What ought to give full relief to a man in the condition I have supposed, is, that the spoilers have not robbed him of his *Saviour* and his *God*. Jesus Christ hath directed his beloved apostle to say, " If any man sin, we have an advocate with the Father, Jesus Christ the righteous; and he is the propitiation for our sins, and not for ours only, but also for the sins of the whole world. I write this," said the apostle, " unto you, my little children, that ye sin not." You have sinned; but it is possible you may sin more, and add to the list of your crimes the sins of obstinacy and despair: it is to prevent these that I set before you an advocate with

the Father, and " if you know him, you will keep his
commandments." He that saith, " I know him, and
keepeth not his commandments, is a liar, and the truth
is not in him." Jesus Christ is the good shepherd, who
came into this wilderness in search of his lost sheep;
and far from grudging relief, when he finds it, he " lay-
eth it on his shoulders rejoicing, calleth together his
friends," and saith unto them, " Rejoice with me, for I
have found my sheep which was lost. There is," saith
he, " more joy in heaven over one sinner that repenteth, than over ninety and nine just persons, who need
no repentance."

God every where expresses his tender love, and cordial regard to a returning sinner; hence these just and
beautiful descriptions : " Behold I will bring the blind
and the lame, and a great company together. They
shall come with weeping, and with supplications will I
lead them ; I will cause them to walk by the rivers of
waters, in a straight way wherein they shall not stumble : for I am a father to Israel, and Ephraim is my first-
born. Hear ye the word of the Lord, O ye nations, and
declare it in the isles afar off, and say, He that scattered
Israel will gather him, and keep him as a shepherd doth
his flock."

I lay aside a multitude of rich and delightful passages of Scripture, full of instruction on this subject, the
mercy of God to a sinner, Jew or Gentile, returning
from the error of his way ; but allow me to mention
one, which always strikes me as full of beauty. You
know the Jews. They were, like you, " planted a noble
vine, wholly a right seed :" and their misconduct occasioned the planter to say, " How then art thou turned
into the degenerate plant of a strange vine unto me."
Their crimes were so provoking that the Lord said,
none of their future services could ever efface their
guilt. " Though thou wash thee with nitre, and take
thee much soap, yet thine iniquity is marked before me,
saith the Lord God."

. The sin of this people lay in what we have been
complaining of among ourselves, the incorporating of
heathen principles and heathen tempers into a religion

17

revealed from heaven. Nothing could stop their career. The prophets said, "Withhold thy throat from thirst;" and they replied, No, we "have loved strangers, and after them we will go." For a long season the Lord had patience with them, and loaded them with benefits; to all which they were insensible: "but he being full of compassion, forgave their iniquity; yea, many a time turned he his anger away, for he remembered that they were but flesh." At length, it became necessary to bring them to their senses by afflictions; and the heathens, who had been their betrayers, became their tyrants and scourges. It was not enough for the compassion of a God to forgive the wretched Jews: he did more, he declared by the prophets he would forgive the tyrants and spoilers of his people, the Egyptians, the Assyrians, the Ethiopians, and number them with the people of God, saying, "Blessed be Egypt my people, and Assyria, the work of my hands, and Israel, mine inheritance." The description of this is the beautiful expression I mean; "In that time shall the present be brought unto the Lord of Hosts of a people scattered and peeled, a people terrible from their beginning hitherto, a nation meted out and trodden under foot, whose land the rivers have spoiled, to the place of the name of the Lord of Hosts." It was a law with the Jews, given by Moses, to divide the prey taken in war into two parts, one half to the soldiers and the other half to the people. Out of the half belonging to the soldiers, "one soul of five hundred," and out of the people's half, "one of fifty," both of men and beasts were dedicated to the Lord, and this was called "the Lord's tribute." In allusion to this the prophet saith, "A present of a people scattered and peeled, a present of a terrible people shall be brought unto the Lord of Hosts." Methinks I see the inhabitants of Jerusalem assembled, the solemn procession of the army through the city, the spoils taken in war carried in triumph, the numbers of the slain published by the heralds, the trembling captives in chains going with aching hearts, full of remorse, contrition, and repentance, up towards the temple, dreading and adoring the God, whom, till now, they had never known, and who, by this terrible calamity, brought them to the knowledge and fear of himself. Go forward, ye once terrible people! You are the Lord's tribute, a present to the Lord of Hosts; ascend the mouutain, enter the palace of the King of kings, his incense is smoking, his sacrifices are bleeding, his priests are in waiting, his Levites singing his praises, and his high priest, the chief officer in his service, hath an express order to disappoint your fears, to exceed your hopes, and say to you, "Blessed be Egypt, my people. Behold, Philistia, and Tyre, with Ethiopia; Ethiopia shall stretch out her hands unto God." All these figures will be realized at the last day, when "ten thousand times ten thousand, and thousands of thousands out of every tongue, and people, and kindred, and nation, the ransomed of the Lord, shall return and come to Zion with songs, and everlasting joy upon their heads, and sorrow and sighing shall flee away." Among that happy company may you all be; and in order to that, "beware lest any man spoil you through philosophy and vain deceit, after the tradition of men, after the rudiments of the world, and not after Christ." God grant you this grace. To him be honour and glory forever. Amen.

DISCOURSE XI.

THE CHRISTIAN RELIGION SHOULD NOT BE MIXED WITH
THAT OF THE JEWS.

[AT FENSTANTON.]

---

1 TIMOTHY vi. 20, 21.

O Timothy, keep that which is committed to thy trust, avoiding profane and vain babblings, and oppositions of science, falsely so called : which some professing have erred concerning the faith.   Grace be with thee.

BRETHREN,

You have heard of a court of priests in some foreign countries, called the Inquisition, a cruel court in which men are tried (not by the laws of Christ, you may be sure), cast, and condemned to die for not believing as they are ordered. I have heard of a blunt prisoner, who, after the judge had passed a terrible sentence of being burnt to death on him, which he finished with praying the Lord to have mercy on his soul, cried, " My Lord, I am sensible of the favour your lordship intends me, but cannot I go to heaven without all this ?" A shrewd question, and not foreign to the purpose ; for if the same ends may be obtained by easy and gentle measures which are proposed to be obtained by difficult means, prudence requires us to choose the former. This exercise of discretion, as it appears in a wise man in the management of all his worldly affairs, will certainly appear in religion; and when he hath the whole of religion, all the ends to be obtained, and all the means proper to obtain them, he will be perfectly satisfied, and count every addition an incumbrance. Such were the sentiments of the apostle Paul in regard to the Christian religion, with this caution, that the Christian religion was not framed by man, and put together by the discretion of a frail mortal; but it was the prudence of God, that is to say, the wisdom of God applied to the practice of the duties of life. On this account he considers religion as a deposit, a religion committed to the care and trust of the apostles of Christ, and to be laid up in their writings without any alteration, for the use of Christians to the end of the world. "The glorious Gospel of the blessed God was committed to my trust." In the same just and beautiful light he exhorts Timothy to consider himself, and in him all other Christians, as put in trust, and holding what they held of the Christian religion, much or little, as trustees, who would be called to give an account. "O Timothy, keep that which is committed to thy trust."

The virtue of a trustee is fidelity, a doctrine fully taught by our Saviour to his apostles. "He that is faithful in that which is least, is faithful also in much; and he that is unjust in the least, is unjust also in much. If therefore ye have not been faithful in the unrighteous mammon, who will commit to your trust the true riches? And if ye have not been faithful in that which is another man's, who shall give you that which is your own?" This reasoning is very fair, and perfectly applicable to our subject. The Christian religion is not ours; the wisdom that designed it, the goodness that is displayed in it, the power which effects it, all belong to God. The Scriptures are not ours, the prophecies are his, the history is his, the promises, the commands, the ordinances, the threatenings, are all his, and we have nothing but the use of them. If we lose this just notion, and dispose of one part, the same principle will justify our disposal of another part: if we be " unjust in the least," we may be " unjust in the greatest" article, and so might dispose of the greatest and most

17*

essential part of this divine religion, and get rid of the
Mediator himself. Our apostle thought the primitive
church " a glorious church, not having spot, or wrin-
kle, or any such thing, but holy and without blemish ;"
and so it is in its constitution. Its doctrines are perfect,
its practice complete, its power sufficient; and on this
principle he exhorted Timothy to " keep the good confession," which " Jesus Christ witnessed before Pontius
Pilate, without spot, and unrebukable," until the ap-
pearing of our Lord. When Pilate was trying Christ
for his life, he asked him, " Art thou a king ?" To
which Jesus replied, " My kingdom is not of this world."
This is the good confession, which Paul exhorted Timothy to " keep without spot," and he calls this confession
a commandment ; for it included, as he expressed it a
little before, " righteousness, godliness, faith, love, patience, meekness," and all the other virtues of a Christian profession.

The Christian religion stands distinguished from the
Jewish dispensation in this respect. Religion among
the Jews was performed with a great many ceremonies;
and if a man would have shown his reverence of God
in that country, he must have purchased beasts, and other offerings, and sacrificed them in the temple devoted
to that purpose ; if he would have dedicated his children to piety, he must have caused them to be circumcised, and so of the rest : but religion as Jesus Christ
taught it, is freed from all these ceremonies, and delivered from a vast expense, a world of trouble, and a
thousand occasions of sin. With a view, therefore, to
preserve the Christian religion in this purity, Paul often attacks, in his writings, a sort of Jews, who in the
main approved of Christianity, but who thought it would
appear less liable to censure, and to more advantage in
the eyes of their countrymen, if it were administered
as the religion of the Jews had been, for which too,
they had the examples of Moses, and many other eminent men, whose names were honourably recorded in
their genealogies. The apostle vehemently opposes
this kind of men, and speaks even with contempt of the
subject, which they wanted to incorporate with the in-

stitutions of Christ; for they had added the traditions of the elders to the writings of Moses. Saith he, " Give no heed to fables, and endless genealogies; refuse profane and old wives' fables; avoid doting about questions, and strifes of words: shun profane and vain babblings, and foolish and unlearned questions; rebuke Jewish fables and commandments of men, and avoid contentions, and strivings about the law, for they are unprofitable and vain." Agreeably to all which he speaks in the text, " O Timothy, keep that which is committed to thy trust, avoiding profane and vain babblings, and oppositions of science, falsely so called; which some professing, have erred concerning the faith. Grace be with thee."

It is not worth while to trouble you with what are said to be the " vain questions" of these men, nor with the " vain janglings," which were occasioned by them: but I shall address myself to the subject, as it concerns you; and lest you should " err concerning the faith," I shall endeavour to convince you that the Christian religion should not be mixed with that of the Jews. It will be necessary to explain this subject, for the Jewish religion is a compound of religion itself, and the modes in which it was practised among the Jews: the first is Christianity, the last is Judaism. It will be further necessary to enforce our doctrine, and to show you the reasons why we say the Jewish religion ought not to be mixed with the Christian. God grant, we may " remember the words spoken by the apostles of our Lord Jesus Christ, and be built up in our most holy faith."

I divide the religion of the Jews into four parts, and by distinguishing these parts I explain our apostle, who expressly saith, Christians are " under the law," and Christians are " not under the law;" understanding by the law the whole Jewish œconomy, or disposition of things among that people before the coming of Jesus Christ.

Observe, first, the Jews had a body of *doctrine* containing truths, first principles, or grounds on which the whole of their worship was built. These are the same doctrines as we have; and our doctrine only differs from theirs as broad day light differs from twilight, or

as a man differs from himself when he was a boy. Jesus Christ placed all these doctrines in a light more
clear, and more striking, than that in which the prophets had set them ; and for this reason " the appear-
ing of our Saviour" is said to " make the purpose of
God manifest," to " abolish death, and to bring life and
immortality to light through the Gospel."

The Jews believed one living and true God, a wise,
a just, a kind, a powerful, an independent, an everlasting Being, who created the world, and all things therein, and " before whom all nations were less than nothing
and vanity." This is a first principle of the Christian
religion, " for though there be that are called gods,
whether in heaven or in earth, as there be gods many,
and lords many, yet to us" Christians " there is but one
God, the Father, of whom are all things, and we in
him."

The Jews believed the doctrine of Providence, the
care of God to forecast, to direct, and to provide for all
his creatures. In their history every thing is ascribed
to God, and generally to God immediately, without taking any notice of second causes, and means, by which he
governed events. Thus Job saith, " The Lord hath
taken away," though it was lightning that burnt his
sheep, the Sabeans who stole his oxen, and a great wind
which overset the house that killed his children by its
fall. Thus an act ascribed in one place to God, is in
another place attributed to Satan : one saith, The Lord
moved David to number Israel : another saith, Satan
provoked David to number Israel. In the same manner we are to expound the Lord's hardening the heart
of Pharaoh, and many such places, agreeably to the
true and real doctrine of Providence, as it lies in the
Jewish Scriptures, in which God is made the first cause :
" I have given you want of bread, I caused it to rain
upon one city, and caused it not to rain upon another
city. I have smitten you with blasting and mildew ; I
have taken away your horses, the worm hath devoured
your vineyards." How did I cause all this drought, insects, famine, and death? By " forming the mountains
and creating the wind," and at the creation, disposing

the powers of nature so that they should produce these effects at an exact time, in an exact proportion ; and all which I foresaw, as you foresee, when you construct a machine, what it will do, and where, and when. This doctrine of Providence is a first principle in the Christian religion ; from the ravens and sparrows, lilies and grass, Jesus Christ hath taught us, that we, as well as Israel, have a keeper, who will " neither slumber nor sleep, a shade to preserve us from all evil.".

The Jews had in their religion, in their prophecies, the doctrine, and in their ceremonies a pattern of the Mediator : hence they " died in faith, having seen the promises," and being persuaded of the truth of them so as to " embrace them, and confess that they were strangers and pilgrims on the earth." Hence the sufferings of Moses were esteemed by him afflictions for Christ. He knew God had promised, that " the seed of the woman should bruise the serpent's head," and that this extraordinary person should be of the tribe of Judah ; and he considered it necessary for him to submit to all the difficulties of bringing a people out of slavery, settling them in a land of their own, and giving them a religion to serve till the appearance of this person, the " prophet like unto himself," as introductory to this most desirable event. This Mediator is come, and to us is the good news sent. " Behold," said the angel to the shepherds, " unto you is born a Saviour ; good tidings of great joy to all people."

The Jews had also the same kind of law, or rule of action, as we have ; for they had a written revelation of the mind and will of God ; and by this they were obliged to act in all cases of religion, and it was never safe, however good the intention, to act without it. David, full of riches, honour, and piety, observed that his own house was of cedar, while God was worshipped in a tent. He proposed to a prophet to build a temple for Divine worship ; and the good prophet thought the Lord was with him, and bade him go, and do all that was in his heart. The principle was good ; and even God said to him, " Thou didst well that it was in thine heart ;" but God would not suffer him to build the temple, for two reasons, the one because " he had been a man of war, and had shed blood;" and the other because he acted without express order; and so his well-meant action would have subverted the great principle of all actions in a revealed religion, which is conducted by a set of servants under the direction, in writing, of one master, from whose precepts it is a crime to depart. " In all the places wherein I have walked with all the children of Israel, spake I a word to any of the judges of Israel, whom I commanded to feed my people, saying, Why build ye not me an house of cedar? I have not dwelt in a house unto this day, but I have gone from tent to tent, and from one tabernacle to another. Go tell David, my servant," said the Lord to Nathan; go and unsay what you have said; you have been too complaisant; go tell David, " Thou shalt not build me an house." This is the great rule of faith and practice in the Christian church. The Lord Jesus, came by commission from the Father; the apostles acted by commission from him; and they had from him no warrant to teach men to observe any thing except what he commanded them, and to teach " all things whatsoever he had commanded." They accounted themselves only stewards, and required other men so to account of them, and with fidelity, which they declared was the chief virtue of a man in trust; they " kept back nothing, but declared all the counsel of God." On this principle goes our text, which is the language of an apostle to a private Christian; so I call Timothy, to distinguish him from those public characters, the apostles, who were inspired to write the Gospel for the use of Timothy, Titus, Philemon, Theophilus, and other uninspired Christians. Our doctrines, then, were those of the Jews; but with this difference, we have the same truths in a higher state of improvement.

A second part of the Jewish religion was *morality*; that is, the doctrine of the duties of life. We have often observed to you, that all religious duties, the performance of which is called morality, are contained in these words of the apostle Paul, " Live soberly yourselves, live righteously with your neighbours, live godly towards your Maker." These are the three branches into which the duties of life divide; and these were so necessary to the Jews, that their prophets not only dissuaded them from idolatry, because idolatry was, so to speak, a wicked religion, or rather wickedness under the name of religion; but they reprobated the ceremonies of their own religion, when the performance of them was not accompanied with pure morality: " he that killeth an ox is as if he slew a man; he that burneth incense as if he blessed an idol." Why? What makes idolatry and Divine ordinances, murder and sacrifice, alike? Because the worshippers " do evil before mine eyes, and choose that in which I delight not, saith the Lord." Morality is the glory of the Christian religion; and though that of the Jews is incorporated, every branch of it, into our religion, and makes a principal part of it, yet it is in a state far more refined than it was among the Jews. I need not enlarge on this article, because each may fully inform himself, by reading the Sermon of our Lord upon the Mount, in which he saith, " I am not come to destroy the law, but to fulfil;" that is, to explain and enforce it. " Ye have heard, that it was said by them of old time, Thou shalt not kill; but I say unto you, Thou shalt not be angry. Ye have heard that it was said by them of old time, Thou shalt not forswear thyself; but I say unto you, Swear not all. Ye have heard that it hath been said, Thou shalt love thy neighbour; but I say unto you, Love your enemies." The morality of the Jewish religion was the same with ours, only not in such a high degree of improvement. The Old Testament resembles a goodly tree in full blossom in the spring; the New Testament, the same tree loaded with all its mellow fruits in autumn.

The third part of the Jewish religion is *experience*, and this also is incorporated into Christianity, and improved by it. By experience I mean those effects which the truths of religion produce in the heart. It must be granted there were many truths and many events in the Jewish religion adapted to give pleasure and pain, and the pious Jews had great experiments tried among them to make a discovery, to themselves and to others, of the good or bad state of their hearts. Had we nothing but the book of Psalms, we might trace all the affections and passions, desires and aversions, joys and sorrows, hopes and fears, anger, shame, and sense of honour, with all their various objects, and with all their keen emotions, which Christians feel; but the book of Psalms is exactly framed as the rest of the Old Testament is; and there lies the human heart open to public view, in an extreme of joy, as in the Song of Moses, and in an extreme of sorrow, as in the Lamentations of Jeremiah. "Behold and see, if there be any sorrow like to my sorrow!" Yes, there is a sorrow in the New Testament like your sorrow, and as far beyond it as love to the whole world is beyond your love to your country; and there is a joy as far beyond the joy of Moses, as the salvation of a world from everlasting misery is beyond the salvation of one nation from the cruelty of Pharaoh: there is an union between the joys and sorrows of the two Testaments, for they were both just, and all the saints unite to sing " the song of Moses," and " the song of the Lamb," the one " the servant of God," and the other " the King of saints."

Observe the *truths* taught in both the churches, as the being of a God, the care of Providence, the salvation of sinners from punishment through a mediator, the influences of the Holy Spirit on the dreams, visions, minds, and hearts of inspired men, a future state of rewards and punishments, a judgment to come, and a restitution of all things; and you will at once see, that information of this kind cannot but affect, and very much affect the hearts of men, and the hearts of those most, who have the happiness to live under the clearest instruction. Observe the *events*, which took place under both the dispensations, the calling of Abraham from idolatry to the worship of the true God, the calling of the Gentiles to imitate his example, the various fortunes of the family of the Patriarch, and the various prosperous and adverse events of the apostles, and all the succeeding Christians; sometimes "strangers in a strange land," and at other times " preparing cities of their own for habitation." Observe the appearance, and miracles, and death of Moses, and other great men ; and the birth and life, the miracles and death, the resurrection and ascension of Jesus Christ. "Consider the " backsliding" of the Jews, and the " falling away" of Christians; the cruelty of Nebuchadnezzar, the generosity of Cyrus, the captivity of the Jews, the rigour of some tyrants of the Christian church, the clemency of some princes towards it, the severity of God, and the distresses of his people ; the restoration of the Jews, and the reformation of Christians, with the many, many thousands of events, which are always taking place in the religious world by the conversion of some, and the glorification of others. Observe how all these events interweave themselves with the best and dearest interests of mankind ; I say, sum up all the truths of religion, and all the events produced by it, and then tell me, whether religion can be in the world without producing the most lively feelings in the hearts of mankind ? How is it possible, that this declaration, " God so loved the world that he gave his only begotten Son, that whosoever believeth in him, should not perish, but have everlasting life ;" how is it possible this truth should lie in the world as cold as this other, Two and two make four ? The Jewish religion had a share of pleasure and pain in proportion to the truths and events of their times ; Christians know what happened to them, and a thousand truths and events, of which they never heard ; and consequently their pains are more acute, and their pleasures more delicious. A sober, decent man feels pain and pleasure at the sight of gross wickedness, and eminent virtue ; but how his pains and pleasures magnify and multiply when he becomes a Christian !

The fourth part of the Jewish religion is its *form of government*, and this is the great difference between their religion and ours, and the difference is amazingly to our advantage. Nothing can be so necessary to enable a Christian to read the Old Testament to edification, as a clear notion of this part of our subject ; for it is remarkable that, amidst a great number of quotations from the Old Testament by the writers of the New, there is

18

not a single passage quoted as a rule of church government. Should a Christian think it right to introduce any thing into the worship of God because the Old Testament told him the Jews did so and so, we should think him, perhaps, a well-meaning man, but not well instructed in his own religion; we should think him wanting in this great branch of religious knowledge; the difference, and the reasons of the difference, between a Christian and a Jew.

The Jewish church was national, and all the females were members of it by birth, and all the males were admitted members at eight days old by circumcision; but the Christian church consists of only believers; and no person can be properly admitted a member of it but by a profession of faith and repentance; and every person making such a profession hath a right from the Lord of the church to all the benefits of his community.

The Jewish church was confined to the little country of Judea; but the Christian church is of all countries, and in Jesus Christ, " whether we be Jews or Gentiles, bond or free, we are all baptized by one spirit into one body."

The men who officiated in the Jewish worship were a distinct order, of one family, and on account of their attendance on the worship of God, were supported by a tax on the people; their persons were held sacred, and their presence necessary to every act of public worship; but the worship of Christians consists only of prayer and praise; and any Christian who is able, may be a mouth for the rest; and as to public instruction, any person who can, may give it, provided he have the consent of his brethren; for they who officiate in the Christian church are not a separate family, or what is the same, a distinct order, multiplying and continuing themselves by acts of adoption; nor are they sacred persons under any of the solemnities of unction; but Christians may elect whom they please to preside in their assemblies, to instruct, and to administer ordinances, and all under the great law, " Freely ye have received, freely give. Provide no gold, for the workman is worthy of his meat."

The religion of the Jews was splendid and costly : but the worship of Christians is neat, clean, and plain; nothing but prayer is necessary to prayer, and " where two or three are gathered together in the name of Christ, there is he in the midst of them."

The spirit and temper of the Jews, like the economy under which they lived, was stern, sour, and tending to servility; and if we compare the good done in the world, and the temper in doing it, of our one apostle Paul, with those of the most famous of their kings, even Solomon himself, the comparison will be greatly in favour of the apostle. The most glorious day of Solomon's life was that on which he dedicated the temple, and offered up, amidst a vast multitude of people, and more sacrifices than the altar could contain, that fine prayer recorded in Scripture ; but glorious as this was, it was the prayer of a Jew, and Israel, Israel in their various conditions of prosperity and adversity, Israel is all he thinks of. Our apostle, who had " the love of God shed abroad in his heart by the Holy Ghost given unto him," had a soul that contained the whole world, and after he had done good enough to content a common man, laid out more and more noble plans to be executed for the benefit of mankind ; all his writings and history are full of this. He sails into Syria, arrives at Ephesus, proceeds to Cæsarea, goes down to Antioch, all over the country of Galatia and Phrygia, purposes in spirit to pass through Macedonia, and Achaia, goes to Jerusalem, saying, " After I have been there, I must see Rome also." Paul was thirty-four years a Christian, two and twenty years of which time we have little or no account of, and almost all the great works done by him, and recorded in Acts, are the services of only ten or twelve years : but it is not imaginable, that such a man spent two and twenty years in idleness ; but if they were spent like the other twelve, " in journeying often, in perils of waters, in perils of robbers, in perils by his own countrymen, in perils by the heathen, in perils in the city, in perils in the wilderness, in perils among false brethren, in stripes, in prisons, in deaths oft, in hunger and thirst, and cold and nakedness, with the care of all the churches," and with a heart full of zeal and humanity, saying, "Who is weak and I am not weak? Who is offended and I burn not?"—I say, if Paul did all this in a spirit of benevolence to mankind, and if I must needs glory in a man, it is not Solomon, but Paul; for, in my eye, Solomon in all his glory was not such an ornament to the world as this one apostle.

Thus let us understand the religion of the two Testaments, which, strictly speaking, is but one religion, though differently administered; and let us learn how to read and apply the Holy Scriptures, so as to avoid what the apostle calls "profane and vain babblings" about the law, and "oppositions" of pretended "science" to obstruct the free course of that perfection of beauty, the Christian dispensation.

There are many ways of doing this. Should we apply the Jewish "science" of admitting members into the Christian church, we should "oppose" the design of Jesus Christ, which was to form his church of wise and good men, not of infants and profligates; for it was written in the Prophets, concerning the Christian church, "They shall all be taught of God, every man therefore, that hath heard, and hath learned of the Father," and no other man, "cometh unto Christ." Our Saviour will not lose his dignity by stooping to take infants at surprise; nor will he make his church "the hold of every foul spirit," and "a cage of every unclean and hateful bird."

Should the Jewish "science" of office be applied to the Christian religion, it would "oppose" the holy purpose of Jesus Christ, which was not to create offices of dignity, emolument, ease, and dominion, to fire the ambition, and stir up the worldly passions of his followers; but so to arrange his institutions as not to tempt men to the exercise of such unworthy dispositions. He meant to make them a family of love, and intended to show the world that love could do more kind offices, than wealth and honour, fondness for ease, or love of power. When his disciples so far forgot his instructions as to ask him, "Who is the greatest in the kingdom of heaven; he called a little child unto him, and set him in the midst of them." What a lesson, a great lesson for the twelve most wise and able men in all the kingdom! One evangelist says, he "took him in his arms;" another says, he set him "by him." Probably he did both these while he discoursed on the subject; for he said, "Except ye become as little children, ye shall not enter into the kingdom of heaven;" and "whosoever shall humble himself as this little child, the same is greatest in the kingdom heaven." The church of the Jews was a "kingdom of priests," and therefore in some ages a kingdom of pride; but the kingdom of Christ was intended to be a kingdom of virtue; and in such a kingdom, modesty and humility are the ground work of the whole.

Should any apply the Jewish "science" of ceremonies to the Christian religion, and pretend to set off the service, and attract the eyes of fine folks in the world, they would "oppose" the wise design of Jesus Christ, which was to supply the wants of the poor with the goods of the church. When he had probably only a little, he had a purse for the poor. Though his disciples admired "the goodly stones and gifts" which "adorned the temple," he said, "As for these things," they will soon be destroyed; but here is one thing far more worthy your attention, here is a poor widow casting two mites into the treasury, she hath cast in more than all the rich men. When he comes to judgment, he will take notice of that money, which shall have been employed in ministering to the necessities of the wretched; but as to music and paintings, and habits, and fine things, they ill assort with the religion of a poor man, who had not where to lay his head, who was crucified on a cross, and whose sincere followers have generally been an "afflicted and poor people," to use the language of a prophet, "a flock of slaughter, whose possessors slay them, and hold themselves not guilty, sell them, and say, Blessed be the Lord, for I am rich." Into two extremes, both contrary to the spirit of Christianity, this "science" leads people. They who can afford it, "oppose" the humility of Christ by a profusion of grandeur, all inconsistent with "the simplicity of Christ." They who cannot, "oppose" the dignity of Christ by applying in his

18*

worship a kind of dirty, cast-off finery; thus a Greek Bishop, who pretended he could not perform public worship without a crucifix, and not being able to procure one, contrived to make one on the spot with two bits of broken lath, as if the God he adored had been a finical being of small understanding and great ostentation.

Should any apply the "science" of the spirit of the Jewish religion to that of Jesus Christ, it would "oppose" the chief excellence of Christianity, benevolence, and universal love : it would gather up all the Prophecies, the four Gospels, and all the wonderful gifts bestowed upon men, into a little machine made to serve the sordid views of ten or twenty men, to the loss and ruin of ten times so many millions. If the Jews in their confined dispensation were taxed with the sin of "limiting the Holy One of Israel," how much guilt must lie upon Christians, if they presume to inclose, within the narrow lines of their own parties, mercy of evangelical magnitude!

Such in general are the reasons why we should not confound Christianity with Judaism, the New Testament with the Old, the teachers of the Christian religion with Aaron and the Levites, Baptism and the Lord's supper with circumcision and the passover, the laws of a state with the rules of an assembly gathered together only for the purpose of worshipping God : but as these reasons are only general, we will give you a few particulars.

The *folly* of mixing these religions will appear by four considerations. One is, that it implies two great errors; the imperfections of that Christianity, which Christ and his apostles taught and practised; and the right of Christians to alter religion, and accommodate it to their worldly convenience. If there be a truth clear and self-evident, it is that Jesus Christ was perfect, and that his introducing a more perfect religion than that of the Jews had been foretold by the prophets, and that his perfection was manifest in all he said and did. Neither his understanding nor his memory ever failed him; he forgot no orders, and did nothing by halves. Every thing he said was so proper, that nothing could be added, and the whole of his ministry may be likened to any one of his miracles, to which the skill and power of man could add nothing. He made the blind see, he caused the dead to live; the universe could do no more, the universe could not do so much. Far be it from us to consider Jesus Christ in the light of a teacher of letters, who indeed teaches the first principles of reading, but who is at an amazing distance from a complete scholar. Beside, the same arguments that maintain the right of one man to alter religion, will convey a right to all men ; and thus we should have all masters, and no servants in the Christian church. The miser would accommodate religion to his love of money ; the proud man to his love of shew ; the angry man to his love of vengeance ; and thus the holy one of God would be " the minister of sin," an office he never intended to execute, and the thought of which made an apostle cry, " God forbid !" It was this scandalous perversion of religion that made God complain of the Jews, " Thou hast made me to serve with thy sins. Behold I am pressed under you, as a cart is pressed that is full of sheaves." How foolish to practise any thing that implies such odious errors ; any thing that casts such unjust imputations upon the character of a Saviour, who deserves other treatment at our hands !

How void of understanding must we be, to put ourselves to so much trouble and charge to do that in religion, which would be as well, and better done without it ! Let me propose a plain question to you. It is commonly observed, that when gentlemen of rank take their farms into their own hands, they get less than their tenants can afford to pay to occupy them. Why ? You know. It is because they do every thing like gentlemen at a greater expense than husbandry will pay ; and their true prudence would be either not to take the character of a husbandman, or to submit to the plainness of it. What would you say to a silver-hafted sickle, a scythe with a mahogany handle, a gilt shock fork, a rope of silk, and an ivory flail ? There is a propriety in every thing ; and religion is as proper in its means as it is in its end ; and when the means answer the end, all additions are waste and folly. It is said, there was a gentleman, who would never presume to say his prayers before he was full dressed in his best clothes. Do you think God attended more to what he said on that account? If a man can be as wise and good without the incumbrance of Jewish ceremonies as with them, I think every prudent man would prefer the plain before the pompous, the doing of a little well and thoroughly, and as it ought to be done, before the undertaking of a large concern, which, peradventure he might never get through. The Jews " laboured and were heavy laden," and Jesus Christ said to them, " Come unto me, take my yoke upon you, my yoke is easy, and I will give you rest."

The folly of this mixture appears by the best reason given for it, that is, that Judaism strikes the senses and the passions, and so makes way for religion to the heart. Alas! Did you never hear how the Jews lost, in the purest ages of ceremony, the very doctrine of one God, and went into the worship of idols? Did you never hear that traditions " made the word of God of none effect?" Did you never hear to what this mixture hath brought the once famous church of Rome, to suffer " a man of sin, the son of perdition to exalt himself above all that is called God, so that he, as God sitteth in the temple of God?" This was not brought about by avoiding Jewish " science;" but by " forbidding to marry, commanding to abstain from meats," by incorporating Jewish customs with the Christian religion. There was a profligate gamester, whose converson was attempted by some honest monks, and they in order to break his heart for sin, put into his hands a fine picture of the crucifixion of Christ; but when they inquired what he was studying so intently in the picture, hoping his conversion was going forward, he replied, I was examining whether the dice, with which the soldiers are casting lots for the garment, be like ours. This man too well resembles bad men in the ceremonies of religion, and their hearts guide their eyes to what nourish their vices, not to what would destroy them.

Finally, the folly of this mixture will appear by making *persecution* necessary. The Jews with Herod for a

king, and Caiaphas for a priest, with Pilate in courts of
law, and Sadducees " akin to the High Priest" in the army and in the temple, could maintain traditions by force,
which could never have stood in the world one day by
argument: but you, an unarmed man, what can you do
in a church broke loose from tyranny, and chartered in
freedom by Jesus Christ! If you were an emperor in
an age of ignorance, you might kill and slay; but in
your condition you can do only a little of that kind of
work, which brought Jesus Christ to the cross. Like
the poor Jews you may show your ill-will by envy, by
" putting forth the finger," by " wagging the head," by
saying, " Aha, so would I have it," by crying, " The
man of God is an hairy man, and girt with a girdle of
leather about his loins," by turning good men into ridicule, and by " slanderously reporting, They say, Let us
do evil that good may come." Persecution, you see, is
a Jewish practice, and shedding of blood was a " science"
in which that people was too well instructed; to kill
" a lion in a pit in the time of snow," to " slay two lion-
like men of Moab," to deprive " a goodly Egyptian" of
his life " with his own spear," was to obtain among the
Jews an honourable name, though to destroy " eight
hundred at a time was more honourable" still. It is not
only the poor Jews, and the officers of their armies, but
their pious kings, and even Moses himself, who are not
to assume the honour of guiding Christians, either in
religion, that peaceable profession, or in war that sometimes necessary occupation. Should Moses enter this
door, inform us that some people were worshipping a
calf, and say to you, " Put every man his sword by his
side, and go slay every man his brother, and every man
his companion, and every man his neighbour;" say unto
your father and mother, " I have not seen you; do not
acknowledge your brethren, nor know your own children;" dare you do what the Levites did, and kill your
family and friends to the number of " three thousand?"
The only apology that can be made for these men, is,
they acted by commission from God, the sovereign dis-
poser of all events; but this brings us back to the point,
and turns the balance in favour of Moses and David.

The Jews acted punctually according to the orders they received from heaven: "go," you Christians, " and do likewise," "keep that which is committed to your trust," and avoid the practice of a "science" which you have not been taught.

Let us finish by observing the *sin* of mixing two dispensations so opposite. The Jews, though they had a commission from heaven, sometimes discovered a reluctance to comply with it. How many objections did Moses make against understanding the service, to which God appointed him? " Who am I that I should go unto Pharaoh?" . . . Behold when I come unto the children of Israel, they will say to me, What is God's name? What shall I say unto them? . . . Behold they will not believe me, for they will say, The Lord hath not appeared unto thee . . . O my Lord, I am not eloquent . . . O my Lord, send, I pray thee, by the hand of him whom thou wilt send." He foresaw the difficulties, and trembled at the work, he was going about. He could not be brought to circumcise his own son, till the Lord threatened " to kill him :" but we uncalled, rush into that at which a Moses shuddered. Probably he examined his own heart, and was afraid to undertake the services of religion without the purest principles; but we from principles the most base, not only undertake to perform religious duties, but to prescribe them. Moses required in himself refined principles to undertake an imperfect religion; but we with depravity in an extreme, rush into a perfect dispensation to pollute it. " We leave the paths of uprightness, to walk in the ways of darkness." To such principles our apostle ascribes the profane babblings in the text.

" Give no heed to Jewish fables," for " some desiring to be teachers of the law, understand not what they say nor whereof they affirm." Ignorance is a misfortune, wilful ignorance is a crime, and this crime is exceedingly aggravated by a pretence of teaching what we do not understand. It is not enough that we understand the world and religion as well as our neighbours; a man, who presumes to make religion of that, which Jesus Christ and his apostles never recommended, ought to understand it better than they did.   If any thing can aggravate the guilt of such a man more, it is his own creed.   Who are you?   I am a sinful, frail man, "of yesterday, and know nothing."   No, you are not a sinful, frail man, knowing nothing; you are another "Solomon, wiser than all men!   Behold thou art wiser than Daniel; there is no secret hidden from thee!   Thou hast been in Eden, the garden of God!   Thou art the anointed cherub!   Thou sealest up the sum full of wisdom, and art perfect in beauty!   Thou hast set thine heart as the heart of God!"   If you are not such a person, how dare you undertake what made Moses shiver!   Ignorance dare do what inspiration trembles at!

If a man "dote about" Jewish questions, "he is proud."   What sin less becomes a fallen man than pride?   On what can he ground his inordinate esteem of himself?   Above all, what an absurd sin is pride in regard to religion, especially to the Christian religion, which was never intended to feed the vanity of man?   To be "lifted up with pride," in the apostle's account, is to "fall into the condemnation of the devil."   Survey the whole Christian religion, and wonder what there is in it to nourish the pride of man.   A Saviour, born in a stable, brought up by plain parents, in a homely occupation, a companion of fishermen, tried like a criminal for his life, crucified like a slave, followed like one of his ancestors, by one in distress, another in debt, a third discontented, a people "hated of all nations for his name's sake;" is there any thing in all this to gratify pride?   Examine the doctrines of Christianity, which all unite to say, "No flesh shall glory in the presence of God."   Observe the duties of Christians, "to follow Christ, to deny themselves, to take up crosses, to lose life, to give the whole world in exchange for the soul."   All mortifying; all attacks upon pride.   Hear the devotions of Christians, all expressive of their own meanness and depravity; all Christians at prayer are in the condition of criminals throwing themseves upon the clemency of their judge.   Examine Christians in their intercourse with the world.   Their conversation is plain and direct, yea yea, nay nay; they cannot swear; they dare not

slander, they must not speak falsely, they are bound by
their religion to be "blameless and harmless in the
midst of a perverse nation," that is to say, they are
doomed, among all classes of bad men, to be "defamed
as the filth of the world and the off-scouring of all
things." What can a proud man do with all this? He
hath not the virtue and wisdom to resign his pride for
the sake of religion, and therefore he must accommodate his religion to his vanity; and the most plausible
way is to call in the aid of Jewish "science," and clothe
Jesus the son of Joseph in the glorious habits of Aaron.
If the plain Virgin Mary can be converted into a blessed lady, if the apostles can be canonized, and Peter the
fisherman, and Paul of Tarsus, called in to settle a point
in philosophy; if the doctrines of Christ can be accommodated to the dispositions of bad men; if the whole
Christian religion be converted into a secular policy fit
for armies, and navies, and all sorts of men to make
their fortune by; then will the offence of the cross
cease, and pride will condescend to walk in procession
with the people of God. Cruelty will become an advocate for God, and will "make a decree, that every
people, who speak any thing amiss against him, shall be
cut in pieces, and their houses made a dunghill, because
there is no other God that can do after this sort . . ."
signed, " Nebuchadnezzar the king."

What we have said of ignorance and pride, we might
repeat again of envy, love of money, youthful lusts, and
several other vicious dispositions, to which our apostle
attributes the teaching of Jewish fables. Let us endeavour to apply that general remedy to all those ills,
which the apostle suggests. Let us so live as not to
render "filthy lucre," or gain unjustly gotten, necessary
to our living, and less still to our religion. Let us be
ambitious to recommend it by a holy life, which is an
argument that goes home to an honest heart, and not by
the fine habits of the ancient Jews, which often served
only to cover the most dangerous and destructive dispositions. In this manner the mouths of unruly talkers
must be stopped. In one word, he who lives by no rule
is a heathen; he who lives by the Old Testament is a

Jew ; and he only is a Christian who makes the New Testament the rule of his faith and practice, the promises the ground of his hope, and the precepts the rule of his action. God grant us this grace ! To him be honour and glory forever. Amen.

19

DISCOURSE XII.

[AT FULBOURNE.]

MARK ii, 1.

And it was noised that he was in the house.

WHEN our Saviour described a holy life under the similitude of a road leading to heaven, he called it a *narrow way*, because a holy life is made up of a set of just
and proper actions exactly performed between two extremes. This is the case of all virtue in general; but
there are some duties more difficult than others through
the strength of temptations to extremes. The case before us is of this kind. " Jesus entered into Caperna-
um" to avoid the multitude; " but it was noised that he
was in the house." On the one hand, Jesus Christ was
a person so necessary to the city, that the citizens
might have thought themselves obliged to any person,
in any way to give notice of his coming; and as the
crowing of a cock was a signal to Peter to repent, and a
little necessary link in the chain of events, which composed the life of that great man, so sometimes little,
and seemingly ridiculous, causes are connected with, and
bring about great events. On the other hand, Jesus
Christ had so much right to retirement, that he ought

not have been interrupted, when he desired to be alone, and he was a person of so much dignity and propriety of conduct, and in general his true character so little known, even by his own neighbours, that it should seem dangerous to spread reports about him.   Shall we censure the citizens for "noising it that he was in the house?"   But the rumour collected the multitude, and produced an instructive sermon and a miracle.   Shall we commend all the rumours that were spread about? But they produced great inconveniences, and rendered the access of the most distressed impossible without " uncovering the roof, and letting the sick of the palsy down through the tiling with his couch into the midst before Jesus," while some unworthy " Scribes, and doctors of the law," who had " come out of every town of Galilee and Judea and Jerusalem," perhaps on a party of pleasure, were sitting by at their ease, though they thought the speaker uttering blasphemy.   Let us neither approve all, nor censure all ; but let us try to make a just separation, and on the whole adore that God, who, though he denounceth a " wo unto them that call evil good, and good evil ; that put darkness for light, and light for darkness," yet knows how to " command light to shine out of darkness," and " to give the light of the glorious Gospel of Christ" to a world blinded by unbelief and prejudice.

Jesus had a little before cleansed a leper, and had commanded him to "show himself to the priest, and offer the gift for his cleansing, which Moses commanded," and " he charged him to tell no other man."   Nothing could be more proper than this conduct ; for the leper could ascertain the fact of his cleansing to the priest : but probably he was not sufficiently instructed to describe the character of his benefactor.   The man did not enter into these views ; but " out he went, and began to publish it much, and to blaze abroad the matter," and perhaps thought he did much good ; but the event was, " Jesus could no more openly enter into the city, but withdrew himself into the wilderness and prayed."   So Moses, after the people had made and worshipped a calf, said unto them, " Ye have sinned a great sin ; and now I will go up unto the Lord, peradventure I shall make an atonement for your sin." He went, and said, " Oh, Lord, this people have sinned a great sin, yet now forgive their sin, and if not, blot me, I pray thee, out of thy book !"

" After some days," when the hubbub was over, Jesus returned home, "and it was noised that he was in the house," and the consequences were, as we have already observed, very beneficial to some, and very inconvenient to others: but I am going to apply the subject to ourselves, in order to determine the conduct of some good men in regard to the imprudences of other good men. There are yet confused accounts of Jesus Christ, and as we ought not to give up our understandings so as not to know truth from error, so neither ought we to lose the command of our tempers, and to defend the cause of Christianity with " the instruments of a foolish shepherd." May that God, who hath given us an exact standard of truth, and a perfect rule of action in the Holy Scriptures, grant us " wisdom to discern between good and evil," and preserve his church from that confusion, which renders it difficult to " discern the noise of the shout of joy, from the noise of the weeping of the people !"

I will not attempt to conceal my design, but will avail myself of the liberty you always allow me of using great plainness of speech. I hope I shall never so far forget the respect due to you as to abuse such an indulgence. When in teaching I interfere with any thing beside religion, reprove me, and I will be silent; but when religion is concerned, allow me to " know no man after the flesh." I am going to show you . . . that many sincere persons spread false reports about Jesus Christ . . . that though they often do a great deal of harm, yet sometimes they do good . . . and that in this state of things, which we cannot alter, our wisdom lies in bearing with the evil, and promoting the good.

You will readily allow, that all we know of Christ is by report of those, who were " eye-witnesses of his majesty." Their whole report is contained in the New Testament, and the world hath no more intelligence of him since the canon of Scripture was closed, signed with the hands, sealed with the blood of the reporters, and " confirmed every where" by its effects, or, as an Evangelist expresseth it, " with signs following." We know nothing of this report but by reading it, comparing one part of it with another, and so forming a just judgment of the whole. Sincerity is a necessary qualification, no doubt; but unless an honest intention be accompanied with a sound understanding, we may suppose we understand the whole report, when indeed we understand only a part. To understand only a part is a qualification to make a true report of that part; but an attempt to report the whole of what we know only in part, is like pretending to draw an exact picture of a man, of whom we had seen no part except one of his fingers. Should I cut out of the Bible two or three leaves of the life of Moses, or David, or Christ, and give them to a stranger for the whole life of the person, I should act exactly like the people, whose conduct we are reproving. What can a man know of Scripture by a few single detached passages; or what can that man know of the whole of Jesus Christ, who never considers him except in the moment of his crucifixion? So far as we understand, so far we may report; but all the rest is conjecture, it may be, and it may not be, and in our depraved condition it is most likely our conjectures about such a person as Jesus Christ should not be true. To partiality therefore, and not to malice; to a sincere desire to favour the cause, mixed with inattention, prejudice of education, and such things, we attribute the giving of confused accounts of Jesus.

How sadly have some confused the Scriptural account of the *nature and government of God!* His *nature* hath been (pardon the word, I cannot think just now of a better), *anatomized,* and laid open by curious dissections into distinct parts called persons, and many rash things have been said on the subject.

The *government* of God, too, hath been all laid out in the same confused manner, and is daily so stated by teachers, most of whose divinity lies before the first chapter in Genesis, and who, as if there were music in
19*

the words, begin and end, and ring perpetual changes on, " From everlasting to everlasting." The Father in council was angry, the Son was mild; the Father proposed a plan, the Son agreed to submit to it, and the Holy Ghost acceded, and became a party, and so a covenant of grace was formed for the salvation of man; as if it were possible for Almighty God to have a pause, a difficulty, a second thought, or to need an assistant; as if such similitudes as were taken from contracts among men, to let down a great subject into the little mind of children of men, could possibly be applied literally and properly to him, who is necessarily " exalted above all blessing and praise." God hath been supposed to govern the far greater part of this world, and at some times the whole of it, by the ministry of an innumerable multitude of devils, to whom fancy hath given form, shape, and colour, and whom custom hath so habituated us to consider under the idea of black, that we have no suspicion of danger from white and red, or from pride and envy. This convenient being serves all sorts of purposes, and hath found his way even into our laws; for an indictment must run, that such an one " not having the fear of God before his eyes, but being moved and seduced by the instigation of the devil," did so and so. The dexterity of some Christians in the use of this doctrine is wonderful. Do they sin? It was not they, the devil tempted them. Do they fear the effects of sin after having committed it, and doubt their own piety? It is not the natural effect of their conduct, but an extraordinary and unexpected suggestion of the devil. Let us entertain more sober notions, and more agreeable to the real doctrine of that very figurative book, the Bible, which personates every thing; gives thunder a voice, hands to floods and trees; and ascribes discourse, that " shakes the bones," and makes " the hair of the flesh stand up," to a spirit in a standing posture, though " the form thereof could not be discerned," and in this manner describes a dream. The man who begins his creed with, " I believe in God," should pity but not persecute the " brother of low degree," who begins his with, " I believe in the devil." God hath been supposed to govern the world by arbitrary decrees, so absolute as to render the miseries of life, and the punishment of hell utterly unavoidable by some of his creatures doomed before the beginning of the world to reprobation. Others have supposed he left the world to a loose sort of management called luck, chance, or fortune; and so careless have some been on this article, that what the Bible reads, " We bless you in the name of the Lord," hath been rendered, and is daily read in public worship, " We wish you good luck in the name of the Lord." At this rate, not only the most serious and solemn events of life, but the whole worship of God is a game at hazard. Some have reported the present life to be, not a state of trial, regularly conducted by a necessary chain of causes and effects, but by extraordinary interpositions of Providence; so that every affliction is a judgment; and to such a degree had this confusion of ideas risen among our ancestors, that they taught us to pray, " From the crafts of the devil, and all other deadly sin, from lightning, and from sudden death, good Lord deliver us;" for sudden death was then reckoned a judgment, and a mark of reprobation. I call all these, confused reports of the nature and government of God. The Scriptures give us no account of the nature of a spirit; and the government of God, the first and wisest spirit must agree with the eminence of his perfections; and there is not one of these reports, which doth so agree with him. Some affect his unity, others his independence, some his wisdom, others his goodness, others his power, and all are contrary to his express declaration, " My thoughts are not your thoughts, neither are your ways my ways, saith the Lord. For as the heavens are higher than the earth, so are my ways higher than your ways, and my thoughts than your thoughts. To whom then will ye liken God?"

The same kind of confusion is gone forth in the rumours about Jesus Christ, and they affect the Scriptural report concerning his person, and the three principal offices, which he was so kind as to execute in our favour. The Scripture gives us no more information concerning the nature of Christ, than it doth concerning the

nature of other beings mentioned by incident, nor was
it necessary; for truth of fact according to appearance,
and not description of properties, which perhaps we
could not comprehend, is the only important article to
us in the present state.   Three men inquiring the nature of Jesus Christ, agreed to be set down by the apostle John.   The first took his Gospel and read, " The
word that was made flesh was God; that is, said he, by
office."   The second took the book and read, " The
word that was made flesh was God; that is, said he,
by nature."   The third took the book, read the same
words, and said, " I do not know what the nature of God
is, so that I fear to say, Jesus Christ is God by nature :
I do not know fully what the nature of God is not, and
therefore I dare not say, Jesus Christ is so God by office that he cannot be God by nature.   In this difficulty
I apply to the inspired apostle, and he says nothing.   I
respect his silence, perhaps he knew no more : perhaps
God who inspired him ordered him to add no more.
Like him therefore I will call Jesus Christ what he
calls him, pay him all the homage he pays him, and be
silent on a subject, which I do not fully understand."
    In regard to the *offices* of Christ, his prophetic office
hath been most surprisingly injured by false rumours
about it.   His work as a prophet was to teach religion,
not husbandry, government, or any other kind of science.   As he was a prophet completely qualified for
his office, we have a right to expect a body of religion
perfect in all its parts, founded on perfect principles,
directed by perfect rules, and productive of the full and
perfect ends, which it was given to answer.   Such is
our Prophet, and such is the religion he taught us : but
if this be a just notion, what have dreams, visions, impulses, and new revelations been but mere " noises that
he was in the house !"   By dreams it pleased God formerly to instruct the Prophets, and what time so proper for men to receive impressions of new and religious
subjects as that, which silence, absence of company, and
all objects of sense contributed to render respectable
and fit ?   By dreams, sometimes religion, as well as other businesses of life, impresses itself upon the heart;

and fancy, sanctified by understanding and memory, takes occasion sometimes to refresh, and at other times to terrify and fatigue the mind. Thus a good man may have thoughts while he is asleep, which he may remember after he is awake, and continue to recollect as long as he lives, and such recollections may influence his actions. A vision is a seeing of something either real or imaginary; thus Peter, and James, and John saw Moses and Elias along with Jesus on the mountain, and Paul saw at Troas in the night, a " man of Macedonia," that is, he dreamt he saw such a man, and heard him say, " Come over into Macedonia and help us;" the first was a true literal sight with the eyes; the last was a perception of the mind. No doubt, people may have visions in the latter sense, and may dream they see, and converse with both the living and the dead. Impulses are impressions or influences on the mind, and we understand, in general, by impulses, such impressions of sorrow, fear, pleasure, and so on, as we cannot account for. Now all these no further affect the prophetical office of Christ, than as they are supposed to do the work of Scripture without the use of Scripture; I mean, to reveal the mind and will of God in regard to religion; and in this view they are erroneous; for we affirm, there hath not been one new idea of religion communicated immediately by God to mankind since the day inspiration ceased, and the canon of Scripture was closed. We say more; we believe there hath not been one thought in the world, except the first thoughts of inspired men, which might not be accounted for, were we properly skilled in what is called association of ideas, the connexion, union, joining, linking (where shall I find a word plain enough?) the connexion of one thought with another thought. This chain of thoughts is a law of nature; it may be beclouded; but it never can be destroyed. It is excellent advice given us by one of the prophets in the name of the Lord: " The prophet that hath a dream, let him tell a dream," let him tell it for a dream, and welcome, and no more; and " he that hath my word, let him speak my word faithfully," let him speak my word as it is, without any additions and

mixtures of his own. " What is the chaff to the wheat ?
saith the Lord.   Behold I am against the prophets, that
smooth their tongues and say, HE saith."

As the prophetical, so the priestly office of Christ
hath been reported with much confusion.   The priestly
office of Christ hath generally been distinguished into the
two parts of atonement and intercession.   Not to trouble
you now with the Jewish meaning of the word *atonement*, we have a remnant of old English in Scripture,
which gives the meaning of it.   Moses saw two Hebrews strive together, and endeavoured to set them *at
one* again.   Had he succeeded, he would have produced
a *onement*, he would have made them *at onement*, in
plain English, he would have made them friends again.
This was effected between a justly offended God, and
sinful man, by the death of Jesus Christ ; and thus " God
was in Christ," not reconciling himself to the world,
but " reconciling the world unto himself, not imputing
their trespasses unto them."   This great event was pre-
figured to the Jews by their sacrifices, the blood of
which was shed at the altar, and sprinkled on the uten-
sils ; but when people incorporate these gross ideas of
washing in blood, and sprinkling Christians with blood,
and apply them to the blood of Christ, they do indeed
" make a noise" about an event " in the house :" but
they do not distinguish figures from facts, and to use the
language of an apostle, " except while they give sound,
they give a distinction in the sounds, how shall it be
known what is spoken?   He that speaketh shall be a
barbarian unto me."

Intercession is fervent and repeated pleading, inter-
posed by a friend to two parties at difference : thus, when
the prophet Jeremiah carried a prophecy to his king,
and the king threatened to throw it into the fire, three
of his courtiers " made intercession" to him, " that he
would not burn the roll," nor punish the prophet and
his scribe.   Jesus Christ often, very often prayed to his
heavenly Father for sinners, and the seventeenth chapter of John is an intercession in behalf of his apostles,
and not of " them alone, but of them also which shall
believe on him through their word."   An apostle saith,

" He ever liveth to make intercession for them;" but as he adds, " He needeth not daily to offer up sacrifice," though he " hath an unchangeable priesthood," and is a " priest forever," so, I think, we may safely say, He needeth not daily to exercise this other branch of his office, and make perpetual intercession, though he ever liveth to convey the benefit of it to all that come unto God by him. The apostle means to distinguish the benefits of Christ's mediation, which are eternal, from those of the Jewish intercessions, which were momentary. God is not inflexible, he loves the disciples " as he loved" the Master, and him he " loved before the foundation of the world." If therefore it is reported that God is hard to be moved to pardon sinners; that Jesus hath been pleading with him for many ages to do so; that he is in waiting to receive and carry in our petitions; that other intercessors are necessary to be joined with him; and that if we can ingratiate ourselves with Christ, he will recommend us to the notice of the Father; we do " noise it about that he is in the house;" but perhaps we may say, as was said in another case, " It is not the voice of them that shout for mastery, neither is it the voice of them that cry for being overcome:" we do not know what it is, " there is a noise of war in the camp." How different is the language of Jesus Christ! Just before he died he said, " It is finished;" and after his resurrection, his constant language was, " Peace be with you." " I had rather speak in the church" these seven words " with my understanding, that by my voice I might teach others also, than ten thousand words in an unknown tongue."

What abundance of confused things have been said concerning the *kingly* office of Christ. He was not a king literally; but he was, and continues to be the chief governor, the sole governor of all his followers. He gave us every thing necessary to the being and continuance of peace and good order; but since his ascension to heaven, we have had new masters, new laws, and new reasons for obeying them. The laws of Jesus Christ are of two kinds, called moral and positive; the first is the law of nature, the obligations of men to God,

to themselves, and to one another, which he both exemplified in his own conduct, and gave us a solemn
charge to make the rules of our actions : the last are
baptism and the Lord's supper, both which he positive-.
ly commanded his disciples to do, and teach to be done
till his second coming.   Instead of these Christian in-
stitutes, we have had an endless number of laws of religion, rules how to act through life, and at death ; and
there is hardly a head of any party, who doth not publish law, as if the law of nature, the life of Christ, and
the New Testament were not a complete body of Christian morality.   Hence councils, creeds, synods, church--
sessions, fathers, and rubricks from age to age, " noising"
that law is " in the house."   We have had new reasons
for obeying these laws, motives different from the love
of God, the fear of punishment, the pleasure of a good
conscience, the misery of depravity, gratitude to Christ,
the good of mankind, a joyful resurrection, a serene day
of judgment, a blessed immortality ; and taken from the
world and the maxims of it.

We build error upon error, and say to a youth, You
ought to profess yourself a Christian, because your parents, when you was an infant, without your knowledge
or consent, engaged that you should do so. Should the
young man ask, By what authority did you dispose of
me without my consent in a case which requires consent, and without which the transaction is null and void?
What could we reply?   We might " noise it" abroad,
" that reason was in the house," and Christ to be obeyed; and perhaps that might do.   Jesus expressly says,
" One is your master, even Christ;" and to him alone
all mankind are accountable for every exercise of religion and conscience.   Whoever or whatever presumes
to exercise dominion over reason and conscience ; whoever requires more to give right to all the benefits of
Christianity than Scripture requires; whoever injures
the civil rights of men under pretence of religion, does
that, which Christ never did, and becomes an invader
of a right granted by God, claimed by Christ, allowed
by his disciples, and confirmed by the reason and fitness
of things.   Yes, law is in the church, but it is the law

of Christ: motives are in the church, but they are the reasons of Christ: dominion is in the church, but it is the dominion of truth and virtue in the hand of a sovereign, whose "dominion is an everlasting dominion which shall not pass away, and his kingdom that which shall not be destroyed." Christians, shut your ears against groundless rumours, and say with a prophet; "All people will walk every one in the name of his God, and we will walk in the name of the Lord our God forever and ever." He "will assemble her that halteth," and will " gather her that is driven out, and her that is afflicted, and reign over them from henceforth, even forever."

The next article, I ought to mention, is that of the *Holy Spirit*, whose nature in himself, and whose influence in religion, have been both reported with a great confusion of ideas, true and false ; the false inconsistent, and the true disconcerted and out of order : but this is a subject of such great consequence, that it deserves a particular examination, and I shall endeavour to examine it fully, when I shall have the pleasure of meeting you here next month. Mean time turn your attention to the subject; I shall treat of it from the fourteenth verse of the eighth chapter of Romans ; " As many as are led by the spirit of God, they are the sons of God ;" and shall endeavour to convince you that the Holy Spirit guides all good men. It was a custom in some primitive churches for the teacher to give notice at the end of one sermon what part of Scripture he intended to expound at the next meeting ; mean time the people read and thought of the subject, and went prepared to understand it. An excellent method in some circumstances.

How painful it is to hear an unmeaning noise about the Holy Spirit! Have we a passage of Scripture in recollection? It is the Holy Spirit. Are we depressed through weakness of nerves? The Spirit of God hath deserted us. Are we animated by the rapidity of our animal spirits? It is the Holy Ghost living and acting in us. Do we pray? It is that he would reveal to us our interest in Christ. Do we teach so that you are edified? We teach with the " Holy Ghost sent down from heaven." Do the truths taught go pointed and sharp home to the conscience and conduct, and excite pain and displeasure? It is not owing to the prudence or imprudence of the teacher, or to the careless and disordered frames of the hearers: but write " Ichabod" on the pulpit, " the glory is departed from Israel," and alas! this. is the case every where; " I hate" the teacher, " for he doth not prophesy good concerning me, but evil!" surely " a lying spirit is gone forth in the mouth of all the prophets! Feed these fellows with bread of affliction, and with water of affliction, until I," who, though I walk at large, ought always to be comforted, and filled with " joy- unspeakable and full of glory," persecute them " until I come again in peace" . . . Before you go away, angry with truth and virtue for one of their most excellent properties, pressing pain into the service of religion, receive and retain this; false religion is a " kingdom full of darkness," where men " blaspheme the God of heaven, because of their pains and their sores, and repent not of their deeds." The Holy Spirit is in the church; but he is there as he is in heaven, in perfect truth and purity, and all the rest is only a confused " noise that he is in the house."

We are to observe next, that though false rumours about religion always do harm, yet sometimes they are accompanied with good. In our law the formal part, or method of proceeding, is unalterable, for justice would be perverted, if the course of law were arbitrary: however, great indulgence is always shown to a well meaning justice, making any undesigned slip in his practice; yea, there are many statutes to protect him, which provide, that he shall not be sued without notice before hand, and all suits begun shall be stopped on tender made of sufficient amends. The law distinguishes between malice and infirmity. Let us imitate this equity in religion. That false doctrine doth harm cannot be doubted. It hath hurt the bodies, the understandings, the consciences, and the tempers of mankind. It hath injured the reputation, the property, the peace, the lives, and liberties of thousands. It hath cramped trade, suppressed genius, perverted government. What evil hath it not done? It poisons one half of the church, and persecutes the other to death. The subject would fill volumes, and I can only give you a hint of one small article, that is, the dangerous consequences of impulses; especially when clothed in the language of Scripture, and reported by people of good character.

About one hundred and ten years ago there lived at Graystock, in Cumberland (I know the spot), a farmer named Henry Winder. This man in the spring of the year had buried one of his children, to the inexpressible grief of himself and his wife. In harvest time two women pretended to have a word from the Lord in prayer, went to Winder, and told him that the Lord had revealed to them as they were at prayer, that he and his wife had murdered their son, and that the Lord had sent them to say to him, "Yet forty days, yet forty days," are given thee to repent. The man and his wife were thunderstruck: but, knowing themselves perfectly innocent, they recovered their spirits, and thought the women distracted, till they understood that the scandal was made public, and that many of the congregation, to which the women belonged, knowing them to be devout persons of good character, supposed them inspired to discover sin, and to establish justice in the case. The matter at length became so serious as to interest the whole country, and the justices took it up. Winder denied, the women persevered, and delivered their testimony in prayers and tears, for they were very sincere, and the persecution of the farmer and his family lasted three years, and ended in an action for defamation, tried at the assizes at Carlisle, and the imprisonment and ruin of the two infatuated women and their families. Nothing could cure them; they knew no one fact to criminate the man; they had no feelings for the anguish of an innocent family taxed with murdering their own son; but the Lord had spoken, and in the faith of this they went to jail, named twins, of which one of them was delivered in prison, the one Innocent Prisoner, the other Harmless Sufferer, and protested "O Lord, thou hast deceived us, and we were deceived: every one mocked us since we cried violence and spoil; but thy word is in our hearts as a burning fire shut up in our bones; we are weary with forbearing, and cannot stay; everlasting confusion shall prevail against our persecutors." This one instance is enough to make every one afraid of impulses; for who can tell whither they may carry him? This is sufficient to make each of us pray, " Remove from me the way of lying, and graciously grant me thy law!"

Several of you knew a good old man, who departed this life twenty years ago, and who often exhorted you to live by the Ten Commandments, and not by impulses. He used to tell, you know, how he got free from that delusion fifty years before. Then he was pious and poor, and thought (he was only a lad), that all suggestions in Scripture style came from heaven. Walking in the field in want of firing by the side of a neighbour's hedge, he wished for some of it to burn, and the word came, " In all this Job sinned not," and in the faith of this he began to make free with his neighbour's wood; but presently he discovered his error, tried his impulse by the eighth commandment, " Thou shalt not steal," and so got rid of an error, which might have led him out of the church into the jail. Let us profit by the mistakes of others, and let us examine whither what we take for religion directs its course; if to piety and virtue, it is the spirit of Christianity; if to injustice and improper actions, it is nothing but turbulence and noise. The greater eagerness, with which we make such a noise, the greater the crime of doing so.

It would be endless to enumerate the mischiefs done by this confusion of tongues in religion. It turns prayer into " vain repetition," charity into the sound of a boaster's trumpet, fasting into a " disfigured face," teaching into " profane and vain babbling," Christian conversation into frivolous jangling, and even extraordinary gifts of learning and eloquence into " sounding brass or a tinkling cymbal;" it subverts all order and decency, it " makes the hearts of the righteous sad, whom God hath not made sad, and strengthens the hands of the wicked by promising him life;" it saith to the " man with a gold ring, Sit thou here in a good place;" and it teacheth him to say to the poor in plain raiment, " Stand thou here under my footstool :" in one word, a noisy tongue not governed by pure religion " is a world of iniquity," it " defileth the whole body, setteth on fire the course of nature," and consumeth all the ordinances of religion " in pleasurable sins."

. Yet, after all, it sometimes happens, that, though " the tongue is an unruly evil full of deadly poison, out of the same month proceedeth blessing and cursing." It " ought not" to be ; but it is so ; and justice requires us to respect the blessing, while we abhor the curse. We have observed at the beginning, that the *noise* mentioned in the text produced some good. A paralytic man was miraculously healed, his sins were forgiven, the word was preached, and the doctrine of forgiveness explained, numbers were pleased, and the " power of the Lord was present to heal" many. In like manner now, even confused reports produce good, and it is a great glory to the Gospel that it never changes its nature, but produces effects, which the most cruel and unnatural mixtures cannot prevent.

Report produces attention, and this is one benefit. When the apostles first received the gift of tongues, it " was noised abroad," and brought the " multitude together," and though some mocked, yet in the end " about three thousand souls gladly received the word." The men, who mocked the apostles then, had been scoffers of religion before ; they were no worse for the rumour, and three thousand were much better. It will be said, this noise carried men to hear truth from the mouth of an inspired apostle himself. True : this is what I say, if noise about religion conduct men to read the writings of the inspired apostles, as it often does, then it does good. Indeed, if men stop in the crowd, and take the report at second, or at fiftieth hand, the good is defeated : somebody hath made a proselyte, and that is all. In some countries the crowd that got nearest the apostles set an army to keep off those at a distance, and a man, who at this late hour of the world hears a noise about " one Jesus who was dead, whom Paul affirmed to be alive," must take his ideas from people appointed by the soldiers to give them; he must not read, or what is the same, he must not judge for himself. It is not so with you: you may read, and think, and act, and do any thing but disturb society. In this view I call even a confused account of Christ a comparative benefit, because any thing is better than being " dead in trespasses and sins," and every thing that sets men a thinking on religion does good, at least may do good.

Confused rumours sometimes stir men up to action, and invitations to do wrong sometimes rouse men to do right. When David was in the decline of life, the infirmities of age took up so much of his thought, that he neglected or forgot to settle the affairs of his own family and the kingdom. He had a favourite son to whom he had never said, " Why hast thou done so ?" who availed himself of the opportunity, and prepared to make himself king. A confused rumour of this excited Bathsheba, Nathan, and David to crown Solomon, and to crush a conspiracy that would have drenched a whole kingdom in blood. Thus in the present case, if zeal for error and superstition, excites emulation for truth and virtue, the noise made in favour of the former may strengthen and confirm the latter. I allow it is a low motive to duty; but any is better than none, and Scripture gives us many arguments of this kind. There was a people among the ancient Jews called Rechabites from Rechab, one of their ancestors. These people, in compliance with the advice of one of their Fathers, abstained from wine, and dwelt in tents without any fixed property. The prophet Jeremiah, to engage his countrymen to serve God their Father, invited some of the heads of these people into a chamber of the temple, and set before them " pots and cups full of wine," and intreated them to drink. No, said they, " we will drink no' wine," for " our Father commanded us and our sons to drink no wine forever, and we have done all that our Father commanded us." With this lesson, by the command of God, the prophet goes to the inhabitants of Jerusalem, and says, " Will ye not receive instruction ?" The Rechabites " perform the words of their Father unto this day; but I the Lord, have spoken unto you early," and "I have also sent unto you prophets; but you have not hearkened unto me." There are many arguments in Scripture of this kind.

Among all the clouds and darkness of error, which involve us poor mortals, there may be a ray of saving truth; at least God often makes, I perceive, merciful distinctions, where man would least think of them. The Jewish hermits just now mentioned, were blessed by him, though they exposed themselves to more severity than the laws of temperance required. Abimelech was forgiven for violating the laws of hospitality, and God allowed half his excuse, that "in the integrity of his heart," though not in the "innocency of his hands," he had done it; he approved the first and forgave the last. God girded Cyrus, though Cyrus "knew him not." He pitied the Ninevites, and "turned away from his fierce anger," though it was not repentance but superstition that starved the innocent cattle, and "covered beasts with sackcloth," the people exciting sorrow in themselves by the lowing of oxen, and braying of asses for want of meat. Naaman was pardoned, though his office at court obliged him to "bow in the house of Rimmon;" for God distinguished between waiting on a master and worshipping an idol, and knew, "he offered neither burnt-offering nor sacrifice unto any other God but unto the Lord." When God showed Nebuchadnezzar himself, his family, and his kingdom, under the similitude of a "high, strong, spreading, fruitful tree," and gave command, "Hew down the tree, cut off his branches, shake off his leaves, scatter his fruit, and let the beasts and the fowls get away," he added, "Nevertheless, leave the stump of his roots in the earth," and secure it "with a band of iron and brass, till seven years pass over him," to show that haughty monarch, that his kingdom should be "sure unto him, after he should come to know that the heavens do rule," and that "those who walk in pride, God is able to abase." God only is equal to distinctions of all kinds and in all cases; but while charity inclines us to hope the best, we should use all possible means to avoid the worst.

We conclude, then, that in a state of things, which we cannot alter, we should take pains to act properly. What can frail man do? Every thing hath been tried, but nothing hath succeeded except a wise and moderate course of action. Riches have been tried; but they corrupt religion; or, to speak more properly, bribe mercenary men to corrupt it. Honours have been tried; but they only give bad men credit to do mischief, and turn the church into a worldly sanctuary, where cabal and intrigue take place of religion and the fear of God. Amusements have been employed; but they turn the church into a play-house, and banish truth, gravity, and sobriety of manners, to make room for levity and pastimes. Power hath been used, and cruelties have been exercised; but reason, to say nothing of religion, hath blushed at the sight. When our King Harry the Eighth attempted to make himself head of the church of England, which he could not do without the consent of the house of convocation, a sort of Parliament of clergy, he sent some noblemen to state the business, and to take their answer. The bishop of Rochester objected to make the king head of the church, and asked, What if the king should alter religion, where is our remedy? What if he should oppress us, must we sue to the king against himself? What if a woman or an infant should succeed to the crown, can they be heads of the church? This would be to make the church no church, the Scripture no Scripture, and at last Jesus no Christ. The clergy felt this, and sent the king word, that they would agree to his being head of the church " as far as was agreeable to the word of God." When the noblemen returned with this answer to his Majesty, and told him, the clergy would agree to his demand as far as was consistent with Scripture, the king fell into a violent passion, and said with an oath to the noblemen, " Go back again, and let me have the business done without any *as fars* and *so fars*. I will have no *as fars* nor no *so fars* in the business; but let it be done." Doth not reason blush at such an unbounded power over religion and conscience in the hands of such a man? Let the persecuted answer. Such a remedy for enthusiasm is worse than the disease itself.

The proper method is a wise moderation. I will explain myself. By a wise moderation I mean a calmness of mind, that doth not proceed from ignorance or indifference, but from a cool and judicious consideration of the whole of the matter. It would be a sad misfortune to a man in trade not to know a guinea from a shilling, or a light guinea from one that was full weight; but it would be a much worse not to know truth from error, virtue from vice, religion from superstition, the voice of the shepherd from the noise of strangers. It would be a melancholy thing to be cold and indifferent to truth and error; to behold food and poison, my Father and my murderer, the God of truth and the father of lies, with equal feelings. Remember the saying of the apostle John, " No lie is of the truth." On the other hand, it would be very unpleasant to lose evenness of temper, for we never do so without pain, and seldom without guilt. A conduct made up of a wise discernment of truth from error, with a firm profession of the one and a hearty hatred of the other, together with a calm and gentle temper, is what we think deserves to be called à course of wise moderation. The advice of our Lord, when he sent forth his disciples as sheep in the midst of wolves, was, " Be ye wise as serpents and harmless as doves." The wisdom of the serpent alone is a dangerous subtlety, and the innocence of the dove alone is a pliableness to folly; but the union of the two in equal proportions makes a perfect Christian.

Our conduct should be *prudent* as well as wise and moderate. By prudence, I mean wisdom applied to practice. It is not enough that we can distinguish truth from error, we must endeavour to diminish error and vice, and to promote truth and virtue. Ills, which cannot be entirely removed, may however be abated by a prudent application of proper means, and circumstances must determine what means are proper. A ruler of the Jews besought Jesus to restore his daughter to life; when Jesus came into the house, and " saw the minstrels and the people making a noise," he only said, " Give place, why make ye this ado, and weep? The damsel is not dead but sleepeth :" but when they " laugh-

ed him to scorn, he put them all out, except Peter, and
James, and John, and the father and the mother of the
maiden." The crowd were not in a temper to profit by
the sight of a miracle, which they had the arrogance to
condemn without examination. Prudence requires us to
give an example of affection for truth in distinction
from error. It requires us to encourage and embolden
all the friends of truth in opposition to error. It requires us to use all proper means to inform the ignorant. It requires us not to conceal our hearty approbation of the one, and utter dislike of the other. It requires us to conciliate the esteem of the wandering in
order to allure them into the right way. In a word,
prudence requires us, while we " bear all things, hope
all things," and " endure all things," " to do nothing
against the truth but for the truth."

Lastly, our conduct should be *patient*, and we should
bear with the evil for the sake of the good. Let me
expound this case by another. Our Lord commands us
to " love our enemies." Most men complain of the difficulty of this duty, and think it harder than all the Ten
Commandments: but would not a little attention to the
meaning make this hard thing easy? When a neighbour becomes an enemy, we forget every thing of him
except his enmity: that day, that one fatal day, that action, that unjust, that unkind action, that word, that cruel word, occupies the whole of our attention: that we
hate, and it deserves hatred, and the Lord doth not require us to love enmity, injustice, and ingratitude, those
black and dismal crimes. Now could we find temper
to consider the whole of the man, we should find something lovely in him; and that lovely action we ought to
esteem, even in the person of an enemy. What! Is
virtue nothing, because the man who doth it does not
happen to be my friend? Perhaps I love virtue only
for the sake of the benefits I derive from it, and perhaps I should find in my heart to dislike an angel, who
should pass my door and visit my neighbour who is an
enemy to me. The man is not all enmity, he loves his
wife and family, and many people; he loves his country, and perhaps his God too, though he doth not hap-

pen to like me : but who am I, that I should make love
of me a test of excellence ? Am I perfect, and always
in every moment an object of esteem ? People will not
enter into these just and mild sentiments, and therefore
they see nothing to love in their enemies ; but, if they
once dislike, go on, like the Philistines and Edomites
towards Israel, till hatred is transmitted from father to
son, and becomes, as a prophet expresseth it, an " old
and perpetual hatred." Apply this to the case in hand.
If it be possible to find a little truth in a great mass of
error; that little truth deserves esteem, and we should
consider it as the Lord considered Lot, whom " he sent
out of the midst of the overthrow, when he overthrew
the cities in which he dwelt."

Having said so much against turning the church into
a Babel by confounding the pure language of God in
Scripture with the jargon of the world, it should seem
but fair to say one word before we part, in favour of
those, whose " axes and tools are heard in the house:"
for false rumours about Christ are not only abroad in
the world, but are actually in the church, and many a
cleansed " leper is making a noise," about what he doth
but half understand.

You are " Apollos, an eloquent man," and " mighty in
the Scriptures." You are " instructed in the way of
the Lord, and being fervent in spirit," you " speak and
teach diligently the things of the Lord." I respect you,
and admire in you your talent for speaking in public,
your great love of the Scriptures, and the zeal that animates your conduct : but you " know only the baptism
of John." Do not disgrace your fine abilities with
pride. Submit to be informed of " the way of God more
perfectly." There are tent-makers who have had the
honour of a long acquaintance with the writings of Paul,
and, having profited by his instructions, they can teach
you in private to understand what you may hereafter
teach publicly better than they.

The world blame you for making a noise about religion, and your brethren blame you for pretending to
teach what you do but imperfectly understand. Tell
the world, you have at all adventures the advantage of

them : there is something in religion substantial, and the little you know is worth contending for ; but they, who make far more noise than you, make it about nothing. Observe the prophet Jeremiah, how he describes the glory of Egypt. " Who is this that cometh up as a flood ?" It is " Egypt, who saith, I will go up and will cover the earth. Come up, ye horses, and rage, ye chariots, and let the mighty men come forth, the Ethiopians that handle the shield, and the Lydians that bend the bow." What saith the prophet to all this ? O mortifying truth ! the king of Babylon shall " sweep away" all this fine army, and Pharaoh's own soldiers shall say, " Pharaoh, king of Egypt, is but a noise." What but a noise about nothing, is honour, splendour, grandeur, majesty, when under all these great sounds you find nothing but a discontented, dying man !

Do the world reproach you with making a noise about religion ? Tell the world, that though you do not understand the whole of Christianity, yet you know enough of it to convince you, that many contentions of bad men, which make a great sound in the world, are for the obtaining of some wicked end ; and that you have no such ends to obtain. The prophets, who gave us many pictures of real life, will furnish you with many. Who are they, who " drink, and make a noise through wine ?" A company of sots gone raving mad in their cups. Who are they, that make the " noise of a cry from the fish-gate, a howling" from the dock, " and a great crashing from the hills ?" They are " merchant people," who bear " silver, leap on the threshold, fill their masters' houses with violence and deceit, saying in their heart, The Lord will not do good, neither will he do evil." Who are they, that make a city ring with " the noise of a whip, and the noise of the rattling of wheels, of prancing horses, and jumping chariots justling one against another, with flaming torches running like lightnings in the streets ?" They are " mighty men in scarlet, full of lies and robbery, lions tearing in pieces enough for their whelps, strangling for their lionesses, filling their holes with prey, and their dens with rapine." Who are they, that " lay waste cities, and make a full land desolate by the noise of their roaring ?" They are the slaves of a tyrant, " taxing land," and " exacting the silver and the gold of the people of the land, of every one according to his taxation, to give it unto Pharaoh." Who are they, whose every battle " is with confused noise, and garments rolled in blood :" who are they, that " make a noise like a dog, and go" snarling " round about the city ?" They are men " wandering up and down for meat, and grudging if they be not satisfied." Is it for such men, who disturb society, and set the world in a flame for the sake of obtaining a little money to spend upon their unruly passions, is it for them to reproach you ? " Lift up your voice like a trumpet. Smite your hands together. Stamp with your foot. Shake off the dust of your feet : verily I say unto you, it shall be more tolerable in the day of judgment for the land of Sodom and Gomorrah," than for such as reject even your faithful warnings, though they were all taken from the doctrine and spirit of John the baptist. Imitate your master ; say to the " publicans, Exact no more than that which is appointed you." Bid the " soldiers do violence to no man, neither accuse any falsely, and be content with their wages." Tell the common " people who have two coats, to impart to them that have none." Tell them all, " The axe is laid unto the root of the trees, and every tree which bringeth not forth good fruit shall be hewn down, and cast into the fire." Do more than all this : send your disciples to Christ, to say unto him, " Art thou he that should come, or do we look for another ?" Teach them to think and judge for themselves, and so do honour to your own understanding, and justice to the rights of mankind.

Let us all lament the wounds given to our Saviour " in the house of his friends." His is a great character : it should never be treated of with malice, levity, or carelessness. Let each of us undo, if it be possible, whatever we have done to defame his bright reputation. Let us live up to the light we have, and humbly look forward to that day, when even true prophecies,

21

and apostolical " tongues shall fail, and love, universal
love, shall abide the duty, the felicity, and the glory of
every upright soul; where the " feeble shall be as David, and David as an angel of God." May God crown
our homely endeavours with success.

DISCOURSE XIII.

THE SPIRIT OF GOD GUIDES ALL GOOD MEN.

[*AT FULBOURNE.*]

ROMANS viii. 14.

*As many as are led by the Spirit of God, they are the
Sons of God.*

CHRISTIANS,

You knew my text and my subject a month ago,
and I dare say you have been reading, and reasoning,
and conversing about it. For my part, I have observed
a powerful motive in the text to engage us all to do so:
they are " the sons of God," who are led by his Spirit.
This is the highest of all titles, and opens a prospect to
the highest of all happiness. Hear our apostle : " If
children, then heirs ; heirs of God and joint heirs with
Christ ;" first to " suffer," then to be " glorified with him,
with a glory to be revealed in. us," with which " the
sufferings of this present time are not worthy to be compared." He elsewhere calls it " a far more exceeding
and eternal weight of glory :" and this for men, in whose
" flesh there dwelleth no good thing." If such noble
objects be sufficient to fire and inflame our hopes, certainly the path that leads to the enjoyment of. them is
sufficient to inspire us with caution and fear.

No man, it seems, walks in this path to glory but he
who is " led by the spirit of God ;" he only, is a son of

God. What if I should miss the path! What if, when at the end of my days I think myself at the door of heaven, I should find myself at the gate of hell! O cold and cruel thought! Why should I indulge it? There can be only two just reasons for dread; and if these be not well grounded, there are no more. One is in the subject itself. If the leading of the Spirit be impossible to be known; if there be no certain rule to distinguish the work of the Spirit from every other work; then indeed I am liable to a fatal mistake, and become an object of the greatest pity, the greater for being invited by a respectable book to search after what the wisest in the world can never find. The other is, although the subject may be understood, yet if I have no heart to search, it would be madness to expect to understand. Peace be with all your consciences! The first I am sure, is a groundless fear; for God is so different from every other being, and the religion he hath taught us so distinct from every other exercise in the world, that there is no more danger of a man's not finding this part of the Christian religion, if he looks for it, than there is of his not finding the sun. If you be sincerely seeking to be directed by the Holy Scriptures, I can inform you for your comfort, that you will succeed; for we know who said, " Seek and ye shall find; every one that asketh receiveth, and he that seeketh findeth. Do you think, the Scripture speaketh in vain?"

The first thing that struck me in thinking of being " led by the Spirit," was, What am I thinking about? Who or what is the Spirit of God? I turned the subject on every side, began below to try to climb upward, and said, " Who knoweth the spirit of a beast that goeth downward?" Not I. " Who knoweth the spirit of a man that goeth upward?" Not I. Who hath " heard the voice, or seen the shape" of God? " No man at any time:" for the " bodily shape like a dove," called " the Holy Ghost," and said to " descend upon Jesus," and " light upon him," was neither the Holy Ghost in person, nor a real dove, nor a form like either the Holy Ghost or a dove; but it was a bright light hovering over Jesus, and at length settling upon his head, just as

a dove hovers and lights upon the ground.   How then
can any one know the Holy Spirit of God?   There is
only one way, and that Jesus Christ teacheth in these
words, "No man hath seen God at any time; the only
begotten Son, which is in the bosom of the Father, he
hath declared him."   It is to Jesus Christ then, and not
to scholars and philosophers, nor to our own conjectures,
that we are to go for information on this subject.   Our
Lord very often spoke of it, and what he hath declared
is all we know, or can know of the matter.   Now, as
we have often observed to you, should we make a list
of all the subjects, which Jesus Christ taught, and of
those which he mentioned only incidentally and by the
way, and ask, What hath the "only begotten of the Father declared" on these subjects, the proper answer
would be, He hath declared their USES but not their NA-
TURES, their influences upon us, but not the materials of
which they are made, and the manner in which they
subsist.

   To give you an infallible example of this manner of
expounding Scripture, I quote to you a passage in the
first Epistle of John.   The apostle repeats the same
expression, "No man hath seen God at any time," once
in his Gospel without an exposition, and only saying Jesus declared him, and once in his Epistle with an exposition how he declared him.   "No man hath seen God
at any time:" but if "we love one another, God dwelleth in us.   We dwell in him, and he in us, because he
hath given us of his Spirit . . . God is love, and he that
dwelleth in love dwelleth in God, and God in him."   In
this manner the Scriptures expound themselves, and on
this account I said just now it was as . easy to find the
truth as to discover the sun: but, alas! people are not
looking for what Jesus declared, but for something of
somebody's else declaring, for which indeed they have
a name, but of which they have no idea.   Should I set
one of you, not skilled in astronomy, any day to look for
the sun, you would soon find it; but should I say, brother, be so kind as look upward, east, west, north, and
south, and find Andromeda, you might very well never
find, when you did not know what you was looking for.

I wish, with all my soul, I could be so happy as to convey this idea so that it could not possibly be misunderstood; and admit the goodness of my intention as an excuse for a homely way of speaking. Suppose I were to take two samples of corn to market for two farmers at a distance, whom no man had seen or could see. Suppose yourselves to buy two loads of corn by these two samples. Suppose, when they were delivered, one should be as good as the sample, and fair Winchester measure, and the other worse than the sample, and short measure. Would not you instantly know these two unknown men? Yes, say you, we should know, and we should not know; we should not know whether they were tall or low, fat or lean, fair or brown, old or young; but we should know that one was wise and honest, and the other weak or wicked; and by looking into the Holy Scriptures we should know what the unseen and unknown God thought of them, for he saith, "Ye shall do no unrighteousness in measure. Just weights and a just bushel shall ye have," for "divers weights, and divers measures, both of them are alike abomination to the Lord. A just weight is his delight. Shall I count him pure with the bag of deceitful weights, and the scant measure that is abominable?" These are not the practices of good men, whom "the Lord requireth to do justly;" these are "treasures of wickedness in the house of the wicked." May God pardon us for speaking of him below his dignity! What can we, poor mortals, crawling out of darkness into daylight, do! though we first "see men like trees walking," yet after the great master "puts his hands again upon our eyes," we shall "look up, and see every man clearly."

It is then from the Holy Scriptures that we are to derive our notions of the Holy Spirit; and our first work shall be to examine the history of the Holy Spirit as these oracles of God report it . . . Having done this we will examine how the Holy Spirit leads or guides all good men . . . and these two articles will fully explain the text, "As many as are led by the Spirit of God, they are the sons of God," remembering all along, that we are not in search of an imaginary being set up before-hand

in our own fancies, but we are inquiring what conclusion we ought to come to under the direction of those
infallible guides, inspired men.   I think also, I need not
inform you, that we are not to determine any thing concerning the nature of the Holy Ghost by the similitudes
used in Scripture to describe his influence in the world.
The Spirit of God is not fire, he is not breath or air, he
doth not come or go, or proceed from one to another, he
is not capable of being grieved; the Spirit of God is
God, and none of these things agree with the eminence
of his perfections.   He "moved upon the face of the
waters . . . He garnished the heavens, and his hand
formed the crooked serpent . . . He filled Bezaleel and
Aholiab with wisdom to teach the engraver, the embroiderer, and the weaver, how to work all manner of
work for the service of the sanctuary . . . He is in man,
giving him life and understanding . . . He is one Spirit,
the Father of all, who is above all, and through all, and
in you all;" all the universe is a body, of which he is
the soul, and "in him we live, and move, and have our
being."   It is not the Spirit of God in any of these senses that we are searching for.   It is not God in the
mere exercise of his power as the Creator and Governor of the world; but it is God in the exercise of his holiness as the author and maintainer of religion, after
which we are inquiring; and it is to fix our attention on
this, that the New Testament calls God, exercising his
holiness in the church, near a hundred times the "Holy
Ghost," or the "Holy Spirit;" for the old English word
ghost signifies Spirit.   Indeed our forefathers were such
children in understanding, as to think that the souls of
departed men might return to this world, and walk
about, and be seen, especially in the dark, and such a
walking Spirit they called a ghost; and hence came the
word *ghastly,* that is dismal, horrible, melancholy in
the countenance; but nothing of all this belongs to God,
whom, as we have before observed, "no man hath
seen at any time," and of whom we know nothing except what is declared in Scripture, and the Scriptures
declare nothing of God in religion, except that all his
influences are to be known by their holiness.

The first appearance of God in religion, the ground of all the rest, was in revealing, or making known future events, "signifying before hand the sufferings of Christ, and the glory that should follow." In this, the first view, God proposeth himself to our consideration as a "spirit of prophecy," the first of which is, "The seed of the woman shall bruise the serpent's head, and the serpent shall bruise his heel." This information was given by God himself to our first parents. In after times, during four thousand years, it pleased God to communicate more of this subject to many men, sometimes in dreams, sometimes by visions, and at other times by suggesting new and extraordinary thoughts, and along with them an irresistible impulse to impart their knowledge to others. About two thousand years after the first prophecy, it pleased God to give his church by Moses a clear law to determine all cases of prophecy; for as prophesying gained credit in the world, a temptation rose to induce bad men to feign themselves prophets. Foolish and wicked men, who could do nothing else to procure the benefits of this life, could easily make a lie, and if that lie could gain credit, it answered all the end of ability and industry. The law of Moses is quite clear on this subject. It describes the case and determines the punishment. If the prophecy "came to pass," and if the prophet led men to holiness, then he was thought to be sent of God; but if either the prophecy did not come pass, or if it did, and the prophet added, "Let us serve other gods," then, saith the law, "That prophet shall die." The Jewish prophets not only foretold an event that was to come to pass long after their death, as the birth of Christ; but they foretold other events, which came to pass in their own times. When they spoke of very distant events, they were to be judged of by their moral character; and when they spoke of very near events, the accomplishment was to determine. Two passages of Scripture confirm this. Jeremiah says to a false prophet, "Hear thou this word, which I speak in thine ears, and in the ears of all the people. The prophets that have been before me, and before thee of old, prophesied both against many countries, and against great kingdoms, of war, and of evil, and of pestilence. When the word of the prophet shall come to pass, then shall the prophet be known, that the Lord hath truly sent him". True, saith Moses, " if the thing follow not, the Lord hath not spoken, but the prophet hath spoken it presumptuously, thou shalt not be afraid of him ; but if there arise a prophet, and the sign do come to pass," yet if he say, " Let us serve other gods, you shall surely kill him ; thou shalt not consent unto him, nor hearken unto him, neither shall thine eye pity him, neither shalt thou spare, neither shalt thou conceal him, but thou shalt stone him with stones that he die, because he hath sought to thrust thee away from thy God." This law was not always executed; but from the time of Moses to that of Christ, it was death by the law to utter a false prophecy, which no good man durst presume to do; and provision was made that the ingenious conjectures of bad men should not pass for prophecies to lead people off from their holy religion, which stood pure in the first and chief doctrine of one living and true God, the object of all religious adoration and praise.

Various as the prophecies of these holy men were, there was one event, which they all agreed to foretell ; that was the appearance of a prophet greater than themselves, and having the Spirit of God in a variety and fulness unknown to them. Moses saith in the name of God, " I will raise them up a prophet from among their brethren like unto thee." David said, " The Lord said unto my Lord, Sit thou at my right hand, rule thou in the midst of thine enemies, judge among the heathen, drink of the brook in the way, lift up the head, thou art a priest forever. God hath anointed thee with the oil of gladness above thy fellows." Isaiah saith, " Behold mine elect in whom my soul delighteth, I have put my spirit upon him to proclaim liberty to captives, to preach good tidings unto the meek. I will pour my spirit, as water upon him that is thirsty, and floods upon the dry ground, and an offspring shall spring up as willows by the water courses." Joel and others say, " I will pour out my spirit upon all flesh . . . I give thee

for a light to the Gentiles, that thou mayest be my salvation to the ends of the earth . . . In thee shall all
the families of the earth be blessed." All these prophecies were fulfilled in Jesus Christ, of whom the last
prophet of the Jews said, He is the Christ, " he cometh from above, and is above all; the Father hath given
all things into his hand, for God giveth not the spirit by
measure unto him."

The old prophets then had a spirit of prophecy, and
a spirit of holiness; that is, they had the Spirit of God;
they knew a little of those future events, which God
perfectly understood, and which little he imparted to
them; and they possessed a little degree of such justice
and goodness as God possesses in infinite perfection. Jesus Christ is a new character, having the Spirit of God
without measure, possessing wisdom, justice, goodness,
and every excellence in unlimited variety, and in absolute perfection. What did Jesus Christ with this fulness
of the Spirit of God? He communicated it to his disciples, " and so sent them even as his Father sent him,"
saying "Receive ye the Holy Ghost." Christ did not
communicate to them, for they were not capable of receiving it, all the Spirit of God that dwelt in him; but
he communicated it in part, therefore they " knew in
part, and prophesied in part." When they were children they thought and spoke as children; but when they
became men they " put away childish things." The
question is, What did Jesus communicate to his apostles
for the Holy Ghost? This question is properly answered by distinguishing extraordinary powers, peculiar to
themselves, and necessary to obtain a hearing of their
doctrine in the world, from ordinary communications
common to them and to all other good men to the end
of the world. When Christ came into the world, and
condescended to ask a distracted race of men to give
him a hearing, what glorious reasons did he stoop to bestow! He healed the sick, he raised the dead, he fed
the multitude, he empowered his apostles to speak with
divers tongues, and to perform many miracles, all for
the good of society, all to " convince the world of sin,
of righteousness, and of judgment." During the life of

Christ he communicated to his apostles his own ideas of things, what notion he had of God, what of Scripture, what of a future state, and his wisdom made them wise. He imparted to them his own just and gentle tempers; through his goodness they became good. He communicated to them proper actions, and by seeing how he conducted himself, they learnt how to behave themselves. These communications, ordinary and extraordinary, are what one of them calls, a " receiving out of his fulness grace for grace."

Before Jesus Christ left the world, he promised the apostles to supply his absence, after he should have left them, by " another Comforter, even the Spirit of truth," which, saith he, " ye know, for he dwelleth with you, and shall be in you;" that is, the truths you know now shall be increased and multiplied, and you shall know them better, and more to your comfort after my death than you have done before. After his resurrection, as he had promised, he " saw them again," and while he was eating with them, he commanded them that they should not go out of town, but wait at " Jerusalem for the promise of the Father, which, said he, ye have heard of me, for ye shall be baptized with the Holy Ghost not many days hence." Accordingly about forty days after his death, and a few days after his ascension, they received the Holy Ghost in a rich abundance both of ordinary and extraordinary powers, the first in a very high degree of excellence, and the last in a manner peculiar to themselves. The apostles had these powers in trust to communicate to others, and they executed the trust faithfully by imparting their extraordinary knowledge how to heal the sick, and how to speak with tongues to some others, and this knowledge ceased when these extraordinary men died; but such ideas as were necessary for the salvation of ordinary Christians to the end of the world they left in writing, and so bequeathed, as it were, to posterity that Holy Spirit, which they had received of their Divine Master for the use of all mankind.

Thus the history of the Holy Ghost stands in Scripture divided into three periods; the first, from Adam to Christ, was a Holy Spirit of prophecy; the second, in the life of Christ, was a Holy Spirit of prophecy, information, and promise, accompanied with wisdom to know how to work miracles, and power to give it effect; the third, from Pentecost to the moment in which the apostle John wrote the last line of his Gospel, was a holy dispensation of wisdom, goodness, and power, partly proper to that age and ceasing with it, and partly containing intelligence to inform and direct religion to the end of time.   We have had a fourth part of the history of the Holy Ghost published to the world; but it is a spurious one.   Who can believe that the Holy Ghost dwells infallibly in a fallible man at Rome, or that he is of a particular order of monks, or that he is the author of laws and tempers directly destructive of the laws and tempers of Christ ?   Who can imagine that the same Holy Ghost bids one man say, " Search the Scriptures," and another man say, " Search not the Scriptures;" commands one to say, " Love thy neighbour as thyself," and another to say, Injure thy neighbour when it suits thy convenience ; orders one to say, " The Holy Scriptures are able to make thee wise unto savation," and to another to say, Scripture is not able to make thee wise unto salvation.   This would be to sink the dignity of religion, to make a God in contradiction with himself, and to put all mankind into a state worse with a Holy Ghost, than the heathens were in without it.   They had reason ; we give up reason for religion, and receive a religion unreasonable itself.   Is it likely God would thus expose us poor children to such a perilous condition ; Is it likely he would give us a perfect religion, by the ministry of his Son, and then leave us in a state as imperfect and uncertain as before ?   Let us conclude then, that we have in the Scriptures a perfect religion, consisting of just and true ideas, which " came not at any time by the will of man ; but which holy men of God spake as they were moved by the Holy Ghost."   When they were " in the Spirit," they " heard a voice saying, I am the first and the last," and what you see " write in a book, and send unto the churches."   They are " the things which are, and the things which shall be hereafter."

Having thus seen the rise and the accomplishment of the promise of an universal religion under the administration of Jesus Christ, and having got possession of the book that contains the whole of that religion, let us proceed to examine the book, and particularly with a view to the Holy Spirit, and his influence in religion, for " as many as are led by the Spirit of God, they are the sons of God." To give you at once my notion of the subject, I think our apostle took his idea of the Christian church being " led" by the Spirit, from that favourite part of the history of his country so often mentioned in the writings of the Prophets, and so faithfully recorded by their first historian, Moses; I mean God's " leading" the Israelites through the wilderness into the land of promise. Sometimes it is said simply, " God led them" through the wilderness. Sometimes it is said, the Holy Spirit led them " by the right hand of Moses." Sometimes they are said to be led " with a cloud, and with a light of fire;" and in this manner the wise men of the east were led by a star to Jesus Christ. God in all these cases made use of means, and the work was no less his for using means to effect his purpose. In this manner I suppose the Holy Spirit by the Scriptures guides all good men. The cloud was not in the Israelites, nor was the star in the wise men; but there was in them a knowledge of the use and intent of these appearances, and a conformity of action to their own ideas.

Here then two things rise to view in our subject; a guide without us, and a disposition within us; and the last seems to me to be an effect of the first, and both the work of one and the same spirit. Suppose a world without a Bible, and you have no idea of any Spirit of God as a spirit of religion in the inhabitants of it. Suppose on the other hand a Bible in a world without an inhabitant, and you have no notion of influence: the " Spirit of God" is there, but nothing knows or worships him, " the earth is without form and void, and darkness is upon the face of the deep." If God calls for light, it will come; if for land and water, they will appear; if for sun, and moon, and stars, they will be; if for fish, and fowl, and beasts, they will appear; but there will be no religion till man comes, nor then any revealed religion till the book and the man meet; and then the child of God will be " led by the Spirit of God." My supposition is a fact. The Bible lies about in many parts of the world without readers, and there lies all our holy religion like Jesus dead in the sepulchre. There are on the contrary many places where the Bible is read; but it is not among men but mere animals, who eat and drink, and marry and give in marriage, and buy and sell, and build and plant, and are so full of these ideas, that they never attend to religious truth, before death comes and destroys them all. " So it was in the days of Noah, so it was also in the days of the Son of Man," and so it will be to the end of the world. In a word, there is no magic in the Bible to operate without reason and conscience ; and there is no religion in man without revelation. If we lay aside the Scriptures we have no standard to judge by ; and if we have no judgment the standard is of no use.

Let us apply these general observations to particular cases, in order to understand how the Spirit of God " leads" all good men. We have determined, that it is by means of Scripture truths, and that it implies the exercise of some dispositions in us. I am aware of the questions you will ask, and I only defer stating the question till it comes properly before us, as it will presently by supposing a case, which is not a mere supposition, because it comes to pass every day. Suppose a a man, who had never thought of religion, to lose by death the first of all earthly pleasures, the agreeable partner of his life, or, as a prophet calls his wife, " the desire of his eyes." O dreadful calamity, sound fit to raise the dead ! " Son of man, behold, I take away from thee the desire of thine eyes with a stroke ! I spake unto the people in the morning, and at even my wife died." Awhile the man thunderstruck can hardly believe it true, and hopes against hope, till time, cruel time, kills his hope, and drives him to despair. The more he thinks, the more occasion he sees for grief. Every thing he sees pierces him to the heart, and in every place a lovely picture of her that was, and the ghastly features of her that is no more, meet his eyes, and melt down all his soul in woe. The sun does not shine, the stars do not sparkle, the flowers do not scent, the world does not look as it used to do; the world seems dead, his house is a tomb, and all his domestics dreary ghosts. Now he feels the vanity of the world, takes up his Bible, perhaps to look after the desire of his eyes, and try whether he can find any thing in her present state to assuage his pain. This man hath religion to seek, and it is indifferent which end of the Bible he begins at, either will " lead" him right. If with the Prophets, they will hand him on from one to another, till they conduct him downward to Christ; if with the Apostles, they will direct him upward to the same person, who is a " light to lighten the Gentiles, and the glory of the people of Israel." This man, thus led to Christ, will be instructed by reading his sermons, by observing his actions, and by examining how his apostles understood and explained his meaning, by applying it to several cases, both of individuals and collective bodies, which fell out after his death, and during their inspiration; and perceiving the truth and beauty of all this, and finding a satisfaction in it calming his mind and producing in him a pleasure never experienced before, he will become a convert to the Christian religion, and choose to make the truths of it the rules of his action, and the ground of his hope. This man is led step by step to a moment in life, in which he becomes a new man, rises, as it were, from the dead into " newness of life," and when he makes his appearance among Christians, the question will naturally be asked, " Who hath begotten me this man? Who hath brought up this man? Where hath he been? Christians, come round this man and inquire : " he is of age, ask him, he shall speak for himself." By whose direction did you come into this Christian assembly? His answer is; Jesus Christ informed me, that " where two or three are gathered together in his name, there" is he " in the midst of them;" and " that if two" of his disciples " shall agree on earth as touching any thing they shall ask, it shall be done for them of" his Father " which is in heaven." I come to join with you in worshipping God : and to be instructed by you, who have studied religion longer than I have, in the truths contained in the Holy Scriptures. Ask him again, How came you, an Englishman born near two thousand years after Christ, a Jew who lived and died in the Eastern part of the world,— how came you acquainted with Jesus Christ? His answer is, I have been lately reading his history, written by those who had " heard and seen what they declared," and who " wrote unto us that we also might have fellowship with them, and their fellowship was truly with the Father and with his Son Jesus Christ." Think it not presumption in me, a Gentile, to appropriate to myself all the benefits of a religion, which though preached first to the Jews, was, " according to the commandment of the everlasting God, made known unto all nations for the obedience of faith." This is " made manifest to me by the Scriptures of the Prophets," and in finding Christ, " I have found him of whom Moses in the law and the Prophets did write ;" and the whole seemed to me as clear as the daylight, and as free as the air. Ask further, How came you to believe the truth of all this? He replies, I could not withhold my assent any more than I can help being warmed by approaching a fire. The evidences of the truth of the Gospel stood before me ; I seemed to myself surrounded with prophets and apostles : nobody asked any favour of me, they all bore witness to the truth of one fact, and I could not help yielding to the force of evidence. Ask him once more : This fact subverts the whole order of your former course of living ; how came you to examine a religion so utterly destructive of all your former sinful enjoyments? He tells you : " I was stript of all the pleasure of living, by a death in my family, which, though I can never cease to lament, I am obliged to confess seems to me now necessary to rouse me out of that dead sleep of sin in which I lay. It seems a severe part of the government of God, but necessary to a man in my condition ; and I consider it now as the language of one, whose absolute right to dispose of me empowered him to say, when he struck the blow, " Awake thou that sleepest, arise from the dead, and Christ shall give thee light." Once more, inquire how an event, which some scarcely feel, made him so very unhappy? He will go out of religion into a thousand subjects, as the accomplishments of his partner, the tenderness of his own feelings, and other articles of a like kind, all which traced back, will at last appear to have God for their first cause. This man hath always been a child asleep in the bosom of his Father, and when he woke he found himself in his arms. Call in now all the means used to " lead" this man to the spot where he now is, and examine, which of them made this man a Christian. Was it any one of your prophets or apostles? We brought indeed " the message which we heard of God, and declared" unto him; but we were not acquainted with him till lately; he had, when we found him, eyes to read, ears to hear, and understanding to judge, a conscience to reprove, and he was in a condition neither melancholy nor mad, but disposed to make use of them. In a word, there is a chain of events, one of which brings on another, and of all which God is the first cause, and if you can suppose the life of the man just now mentioned to consist of a chain of five thousand events, and that three thousand and fifty came to pass before he touched the Holy Scriptures, and that his reading them was the three thousand and fifty-first event, I should call three thousand and fifty, acts of God as the God of nature; the three thousand and fifty-first an act of God as the God of grace; and though I should think him " led" all along before by the same God, yet I should from that moment date his being " led by the Spirit of God" as a Spirit of truth and holiness, revealing himself in Scripture as the Saviour of sinners, and in no other way.

When the Spirit of God " saves a soul from death," by " converting a sinner from the errour of his way," what doth he? Doth he create any new senses or faculties, new eyes in the body, or new powers in the soul? Certainly not; for as there is no want of any new powers, so if they were, they would not be what Christ came to redeem, nor would they need sanctifica-

22*

tion. The whole work of the Spirit seems to me to consist in two things : the one a proposing of the truths of religion, and this is done in the Holy Scriptures: the other a disposing of the mind to admit the truth, and this is done by means of various sorts, by prosperity, by adversity, by education, by conversation, by sickness, and by a thousand other methods, parts of a whole complicated government, of which God is the first cause. In order to explain the subject, or rather (it becomes me to say of such a subject) my notion of it ; I beg your attention to three reflections of reason, Scripture, and experience.

I call it *reasonable* to give God as much glory for bringing an event to pass by means, as without them ; yea, in some sense more. I will explain myself. It is the opinion of some Christians, that the Holy Ghost régenerates a soul immediately, that is, suddenly, and without any thing between himself and the soul, and they are zealous to support this idea of regeneration for the very laudable purpose of securing all the honour of this work to God. We praise the motive, for too much care cannot be taken to render to God a glory so justly his due : but we cannot see that the work is less his for his making use of means to effect it ; for whose are the means but his own ? The more means he thinks proper to use, the more he displays his glorious perfections. In all his other works he makes use of means. He warms us by means of fire, he feeds us by means of bread, he refreshes us in the day by air and in the night by sleep, he creates us and brings us into being by means of our parents, and he removes us by means of diseases. Name, if it be possible, a single event in the whole world brought to pass without means. If we go from the body to the mind, still the same wise order prevails. Our eyes distinguish colours, but colours are not God, but rays of light differently disposed. Our ears distinguish sounds, but sounds are only air. Our feelings find out hardness, softness, rough, smooth, and so on. There is not a single thought, in all the multitude we have in our minds, which hath not been brought thither by some means or other. What is more, every thought is connected with another thought, and that with another, and so on, till we are lost in the distance or the crowd. · Now, we ask, Is that which God doth by means less his doing than if it were performed without means? Is not the last effect as much his as the first? Who gave us this year a plentiful harvest? You say, God. You say right, because God formed six thousand years ago sun and earth, air and water, wheat and barley, and fixt all in such a state that they came to you last harvest exactly in such proportion as he at first appointed them. One great argument for the truth of the Christian religion is, that it exactly resembles the world of nature, and so proves itself to be the work of the same God; and if it were not so, if religion were not like other things, which we are sure God made, we should have no certain rules to know, when we received a religion, whether it were a body of truth coming from God to make us happy, or a set of errours contrived by wicked men to make us miserable. Did ever any man conceive that the sun, or the air, or the water, or the trees, or fish, fowl, and cattle, were the invention and production of man? Nobody ever thought so. Why? Because they have characters of size, shape, duration, and perfection, above all the skill and power of man to produce. Bring forth ten thousand things to view having the same characters of perfection in their kind, and we instantly know the maker; but produce something with different characters, and the author becomes doubtful, and it is no further probable that he created it than as it resembles his other works. Apply this to our subject. If God regenerates us by means, if he makes us wise by informing us of truth, and good by proposing good reasons to us for being so, then religion resembles his other works; but if we be wise without truth, and good without motive, then a new work appears without the characters of his other works, and consequently without any evidence to persuade us it is his. Thus, reason seems to plead for the truth of our notion of the work of the Holy Spirit.

The chief objection against this account seems to me a strong reason in favour of it. If this account be true, say some, the work of the Spirit may be explained and described as clearly as any other part of religion, and we shall know what the work of the Spirit is; whereas we have been taught to believe that the work is a mystery, which no man knoweth, no, not he that receiveth it, and this notion seems confirmed by this text, "The wind bloweth where it listeth, and thou hearest the sound thereof, but canst not tell whence it cometh, and whither it goeth: so is every one that is born of the Spirit." In answer to this, and every other objection taken from Scripture, we have proposed to make a second reflection on the language of Scripture concerning this subject, and we shall put the passages into two classes.

In the first we put such as speak of this work under figures or *similitudes;* as where the Spirit is said to be like *wind, fire, water.* All Scriptures of this kind are explained by one distinction between the nature and the effects of things. It is one thing to know the nature of fire, and air and water, and it is another to know the effects they produce. No man fully knows the first; but the last are as clear as daylight. Is there a man in this assembly, who doth not know what effect fire will produce in wood or water, and wind in mill work, and so on? When our Lord said, Every one that is born of the Spirit is so as you, Nicodemus, are in the wind, he knows the effects, and that knowledge is sufficient to direct his actions; my instructions are intended to make men good men, and not philosophers: observe, it was Nicodemus who said, *How* can these things be? And the reproof given him by Jesus Christ would have been improper, had the subject been a mystery; " Art thou a master of Israel and *knowest not* these things?" We speak that we do *know,* and testify that we have *seen.* The subject of their conversation was not the nature of the Spirit, but his influences in religion. Now, said our Lord, the religion I teach is spiritual; it doth not stand like yours in " meats and drinks, and divers washings, and carnal ordinances imposed until the time of reformation for the purifying of the flesh," but in effects upon the mind and heart : you see no temple, no priesthood, no sacrifices in my religion : let not this offend you; my religion resembles the wind, which no man ever saw, but the effects of which you and all other men perfectly understand. "The wind bloweth where it listeth, and thou hearest the sound thereof, but canst not tell whence it cometh, and whither it goeth: so is every one that is born of the Spirit." In this manner expound all the passages that speak of the Spirit's work under similitudes, and you will find no difficulty in them.

In a second class I put all such Scriptures as *describe* the work of the Spirit. The apostle Peter had seen a great deal of this work, and one day of his life, such a day as that in which "three thousand souls were added," produced more and better experiments than ordinary teachers have an opportunity of seeing in their whole life. He saw religion in every form, and examined single conversions, separately and alone, and his whole life was a course of experiments, a part of which are recorded in Acts; and we have reason to believe, though we have no account of the twenty-four last years of his life in Scripture, that he continued to old age in the exercise of instructing and converting mankind, or, as our Lord calls it, "feeding the lambs and the sheep" of Christ. The testimony of such a man is extremely respectable. It is a testimony of inspiration explained and confirmed by experiment. Now he says, that the "strangers scattered throughout Pontus," and other countries, who were "elect through sanctification of the Spirit," were "born again of incorruptible seed by the word of God, which word by the Gospel was preached unto them." This account of regeneration is partly literal, and partly figurative. The Gospel is the word of God . . . the Gospel was preached unto you . . . these are literally true; the Gospel containing the word of God which was preached unto you, is an "incorruptible seed," of which you were born again; these are figurative expressions, and must be expounded by the literal terms, and clearly mean a dependence of the three excellences that constitute a regenerate man on the three principal parts of religion, in which they had been instructed. The Gospel proposes a set of clear

truths : Christians examine and believe these truths.
The Gospel proposes a set of motives : Christians feel
these motives ; fear hell, desire heaven, love holiness,
and so on.   The Gospel proposes a set of rules to live
by : Christians reduce these rules to practice.   Christians thus are born into a new world, having the *new
powers* necessary to live in that world : they have new
objects and new ideas : they have new motives and new
feelings : they have new laws and a new life.   The
apostle not only saw all this in others, but he felt all
this exemplified in himself.   He was in the exercise of
his trade, " casting a net into the sea," when a person
walking on the beach called to him, and said, " Follow
me, and I will make you a fisher of men."   This word
of the Lord was like that at the creation, " Let there be
light ;" and the history of the rest of Peter's existence
may be contained in this word, " There was light."
When he afterwards fell into a swoon, and returned
again to sin and to fishing, he was " begotten again, unto a lively hope," not without means, but " by the resurrection of Jesus Christ from the dead."   Here is the
work, the whole ordinary work of the Holy Spirit, but
all wrought by means :- these strangers " purified their
souls in obeying the truth through the Spirit," that is
through the knowledge of things " reported unto them,
by them that preach the Gospel with the Holy Ghost
sent down from heaven," to enable the preachers to
speak the divers tongues of these strangers, and of all
others to whom they were sent, that so their faith might
stand on what they clearly understood.
     Strictly speaking, there are two kinds of passages in
the New Testament descriptive of this work : the first
are short, and are a sort of first principles, and these are
mostly in the Epistles ; as " If any man be in Christ he is
a new creature . . . my preaching was in demonstration of
the Spirit . . . your faith stands in the power of God . . .
God called you unto the fellowship of his Son . . . God
shined in our hearts . . . the power is not of us, but of
God."   This is the first sort of passages ; but there is a
second class, which show us these first principles in real
action, and this sort is in the Gospels, and in the Acts

of the apostles, and by these the former are expounded. What would you know of a tree by seeing it in its first principles? Could you know an oak by seeing an acorn, or a briar and a hawthorn by seeing hips and haws? An acorn is an oak in principle, and an oak is an acorn drawn out in practice. Explain the short principles in the Epistles to the Corinthians by the history of the conversion of the Corinthians in the Acts of the Apostles. Paul's preaching was in demonstration of the Spirit, that is, he was "pressed in Spirit" at Corinth, "and testified to Jews and Greeks that Jesus was Christ," and "he reasoned in the synagogue every Sabbath." The faith of the Corinthians stood in the "power of God," that is, the reasoning of Paul "persuaded the Jews and the Greeks," who "hearing, believed." If any Corinthian be in Christ, he, the man, is a new creature; that is, the Corinthians, who had been heathens and Jews, when they "believed on the Lord, were baptized into that new and holy religion, Christianity. God shined in our hearts, I planted, Apollos watered; that is, I "continued a year and six months teaching the word of God among you," and Apollos, after he had been instructed by Aquila and Priscilla, "helped them much which had believed through grace, for he mightily convinced the Jews, shewing by the Scriptures that Jesus was Christ." The apostle had a right to conclude, that though they were "labourers together with God," yet the Corinthians were "God's husbandry, God's building." God created Paul and Apollos; he converted the one in an extraordinary way, and the other by ordinary means of instruction; but Aquila and Priscilla were his, the Scripture was his; "neither is he that planteth any thing, neither he that watereth, but God that giveth the increase." In this manner expound Scriptures by themselves, and observe all along that it is granted on all hands, the conversion of a sinner is the work of the Holy Spirit, and all the honour of it due to him, and the only inquiry is, whether he doth this work with means or without them, and if without them, what is the use, the pure and proper use of means.

This brings us to our last reflection on Christian ex-

perience. If means have no place in the Christian religion till after the production of something in the soul
containing the whole new man, then the use of means
is only to nourish and cherish this new principle, that
is to say, they are to a Christian what air and earth and
moisture are to an acorn. All Christians seem to act as
if they thought the means appointed to produce the end,
and the fitness of the means is the support of Christian
action. On this principle we educate our children, because instruction seems to us a proper method of producing in them knowledge. On this principle we read
and expound the Scriptures in public; not that the
Scriptures want any expounding, to cool and attentive
minds, but because the minds of most men are not in
such a state, but blinded with prejudice, custom, and
passion, and because we know such a mind is not prepared to attend to reason. On this principle we address the Gospel not only to the righteous and well-dis-
posed, but also to men of a quite different character.
One great argument in defence of our holy religion is,
that it is fitted not only to saints, but also to sinners,
even to such as are in the last and most deplorable sta-
ges of vice. If you say, God works in the means; this
is what we plead for; if you affirm on the contrary that
he works immediately, then there is no more fitness in
instructing the ignorant, and reasoning with the wicked, and expecting knowledge and reformation to follow,
than there would be in planting and watering flints and
pebbles, and expecting them to grow into oaks. Go
further, go back to the regeneration of any one Christian in this assembly, and divide yourselves into two
parts. Some of you do not know the time of your conversion; that is as much as to say, the work of the Spirit was so connected with other events, that one thing
brought on another, till all together issued in your conversion, for you are a sincere convert to the faith of
Christ. Others of you resemble the man supposed some
time ago, and you know what events fell out when you
became Christians; but the connexion of an effect with
a cause destroys the notion of immediate influence. One
says, such a Providence set me a thinking; another

says, Such a discourse set me a repenting ; a third says,
Such a book gave me information that produced comfort. All of us believe, the means of religion are highly fitted to answer their end, and the certainty of obtaining the end in the use of means is the sun that rules
the day, and the moon that rules the night, of life.

We cannot conclude this subject without two reflections. First, we perceive a wonderful inclination in
Christians toward something in religion so sublime as
not to be understood; whereas the true sublimity of religion lies in its plainness, as the true excellence and
dignity of man consists in his becoming such a plain man
as Jesus Christ was. This inclination is a remnant of
the old education given this country by monks and
priests, whose majesty stood in the credulousness of
their followers. They made creeds, or articles to be
believed, and gave them to our forefathers to say over.
You do not understand them, said they, but we do ; and,
while they were doing that, the creed-makers ran away
with their houses and lands. Let us renouuce this disposition, and let us believe nothing but what we understand.

Lastly, we observe with great pleasure that all Christians allow the Spirit of God is a Holy Spirit; and even
they who think him hidden, think they have no right
to conclude he is where they suppose, till the fruits of
a holy life declare it. Should a man, who had lived
wickedly all his days, be intoxicated with liquor over
night, and regenerated at six next morning by an immediate work of the Spirit, no Christians would believe it
that day, and should he, like Saul, " assay to join himself
to the disciples, they" would be " all afraid of him, and
not believe that he was a disciple," till some Barnabas" should declare two things unto them ; one,
" how the Lord had spoken to him ;" and the other,
" how he had boldly preached at Damascus ;" till he
had given substantial proofs by his conduct that his pre-
tensions were true and real. If an extraordinary conversion was not credible without proof, how much less
are ordinary changes ? The proof of proofs is laid by
the Holy Spirit where it ought to be. " If ye be led
23

by the Spirit, ye are not under the law, for the fruit of the Spirit is love, joy, peace, long-suffering, gentleness, goodness, faith, meekness, temperance ; against such there is no law." Let not " a man think himself to be something when he is nothing : but let every man prove his own work, and then shall he have rejoicing in himself alone, and not in another man." God grant us this grace! To him be honour and glory forever. Amen.

DISCOURSE XIV.

[AT CHESTERFORD.]

GALATIANS V. 6.

Faith worketh by love.

Let not my first words alarm you. Do any of you know what an abstract word is? To speak more exactly, Had ever any one of you an abstract idea? Words are names of things; abstract words are names of abstract things; and abstract ideas are perceptions of the things so named. Have you any idea of whiteness, hardness, wisdom, love? You know what a white cloud, a white rose, a hard wood, a hard hand, a wise man, a loving child is; but you have no idea of any one of these things separate from the bodies, of which they are properties. Try now, whether you can conceive of whiteness or wisdom alone and apart from every thing except itself. Yet these are very convenient words, and express many real qualities; and there is no danger in the use of them, except when they are supposed to stand for something which is not to be found; and should that something be a part of religion, we should be perplexed and confused, " ever learning, and never able to come to the knowledge of the truth," the folly of which is " manifest unto all men."

Observe the text: " In Christ neither circumcision

availeth any thing, nor uncircumcision, but faith which
worketh by love." Circumcision, uncircumcision, faith,
love, these are names of things not to be found alone
and apart; but circumcision is put for the condition of
the Jews, uncircumcision for that of the Gentiles, who
had not submitted to that rite of the religion of Moses :
faith signifies belief of the truths of the Christian religion, and love, the instrument of faith, that friendly disposition, which a belief of the truths taught in the
Christian religion produceth toward all mankind.   It is
as if the apostle had said, If you Jews believe the Gospel, you will love the Gentiles; if you Gentiles believe
the Gospel, you will love the Jews; and if both of you
believe the Gospel you will love God, and all your fellow-creatures; for in the Gospel of Christ, what you
were by birth, education, and worldly distinctions avail
nothing; the great point is, Do you believe the truths
of the Christian religion?   You need not hesitate about
this; a belief of these truths never fails to produce the
kind offices of love.

I speak thus, because many Christians perplex themselves in that necessary duty prescribed by our apostle,
" Examine yourselves whether ye be in the faith."
They turn their attention inward, and look for faith, and
not being able to find any thing abstracted, apart and
alone, that answers to their general notion of faith, they
rashly conclude against themselves, that they are not
Christians, and so go willingly down into a dungeon of
doubts and fears, and lie there waiting for execution, as
if faith wrought by despair.   " Examine yourself whether you be in the faith," is equal to saying, Examine
yourself whether you be in "temper;" and as in the
latter case you would not inquire after calmness, or moderation, but whether you yourself were calm and moderate ; so in the former case you should not search for
faith as for something separate from yourself, but incorporating it with yourself, you should say, here on the
table lies the Gospel, Do I believe it? or, if this be too
much, say, Here in the Gospel, in the twenty-fifth chapter of Matthew, lies a description of the day of judgment; do I believe this to be true?

Simple and artless as this may appear, it was, however, the principal question, the constant declaration, and the perpetual description in primitive religion. Jesus Christ said to those who came to him for healing, " Believe ye that I am able to do this ? . . . Dost thou believe on the Son of God ? . . . If thou canst believe, all things are possible to him that believeth ;" for believing him to be the Messiah was the ordinary condition of his working a miracle. After his resurrection, people were admitted to profess Christianity only on a declaration of faith. " May I be baptized?" said the eunuch. " If thou believest, thou mayest," replied Philip : " and he answered and said, I believe that Jesus Christ is the Son of God." The declarations concerning Christians run all throughout the New Testament in the same style ; and in the same manner Christians are described, as, " Believers were added to the Lord, be thou an example of the believers, he that believeth on me hath everlasting life ;" and, to say all in one word, the commission, which Christ gave his apostles to preach the Gospel, divides the world into only two parts ; " He that believeth shall be saved, but he that believeth not shall be damned." This is the constant style of Scripture. You see, Christians are not described in general by their actions and affections, but by their faith. It is not said, they are the industrious, the frugal, the honest, the supporters of the poor, though all these are true ; but they are named believers, because this expresses the point in which they all agree, the distinguishing excellence of their character, and that disposition from which all other good dispositions proceed. We have therefore, reason to affirm that faith and holiness are inseparable ; and it is to the establishing of this truth that I shall this eveing address myself. May God crown our labour with success !

Faith is belief, and Christian faith is " belief of the truth" of Christianity. Some Christians believe a few of the truths of Christianity, and their " faith is weak," because though they believe some truths, yet they do not believe others, which perhaps they have overlooked, or against which it may be they are prejudiced : their lan-

23*

guage ought to be, "Lord, I believe, help thou mine
unbelief." Lord I believe thou wilt judge the world,
but forgive me for not believing that thou " wast lifted
up," that " whosoever believeth in thee should not
perish, but have eternal life," for I fear I was excepted.
Others believe all the truths of Christianity, and they
are " strong in the faith," and they say, " This is a
faithful saying, and worthy of all acceptation, that Jesus
Christ came into the world to save sinners; for this is
the record, that God hath given to us eternal life, and
this life is in his Son ;" and " these things are written
that we may know we have eternal life." The truths
of the Christian religion resemble the stones of a well-
constructed arch thrown over an impassable gulf, to
serve for a bridge for travellers, and each truth supports and is supported by another truth, and all together
make an assemblage of convenience, strength, and beauty. Let us not consider faith as the key-stone, that binds
the two sweeps together ; but let us consider it as a
greater or less degree of knowledge of building an arch
in the travellers who pass over it. The builder will
have no fear, and travellers who understand his principles, or believe his report will have no fear ; but they,
who neither understand the principles of the builder,
nor give him much credit for his report, may, yea, must
go over with fear and trembling.

Let us come to particulars. There are some *trushs
which you need not believe*, I mean, the belief of them
is not necessary to salvation. A great scholar, and an
excellent Christian in one of the Protestant churches
abroad, printed a book, in which he said, Jesus Christ
was born at *Jerusalem*. A friend asked him, whether he was not mistaken ? He replied, No, certainly.
However he was soon convinced, that Jesus Christ was
not born at the city of Jerusalem, but at a village called
Bethlehem. He must have known this ; but he had
forgot it ; yet he never forgot Christ, but believed his
Gospel, and imitated his example. Suppose a man
should not know a hundred such truths concerning the
year, and the day, and the place of the birth of Christ,
the form of his person, the name of the mountain on

which he was crucified, the years of his ministry, the order in which the Gospels and Epistles were written, What then? Nothing. No such truths are proposed to us as grounds of our hope, and rules of our practice. By believing the Gospel, then, we do not mean a belief of all the incidents that fell in occasionally, and beside the main design; so that you may easily account for the conduct of your teachers, when they affirm that the knowledge and belief of these circumstances is not the faith spoken of by the apostle in our text.. This kind of knowledge, far from " working by love," often works by levity, intemperance, superstition, and cruelty. When Jesus Christ said, " If ye believe not that I am he, ye shall die in your sins ;" how hard would our lot have been, if he meant to say, If ye believe not that I was born at Bethlehem in the tribe of Judah, in the days of king Herod, in the reign of Augustus Cæsar, and when Cyrenius was governour of Syria, " ye shall die in your sins !" Set your hearts at ease on all these subjects, and when you examine whether you be in the faith, leave out that great mass of information, which comes under the description of incidents. If you have time and opportunity, examine every circumstance, the pleasure will amply repay the labour, for all knowledge brings pleasure ; but you may know the true character of a benefactor without knowing any of the flowers that adorn his garden.

As there are truths, which you need not believe, so there are truths which you *cannot believe* because they are either not told, or not directed to you. It is true of some of you, that you Thomas, or you John such an one, are a good man, a believer in Christ, and will be saved; but who ever expected a Bible of this kind? If a man understands by believing the Gospel, believing something that is not in the book, and which, had it been there, would have marked it with folly, he may continue to read, and look. and search through life, he will never find, for this good reason, it is not there. Even a great number of articles, which are written, are not addressed to us. When Jesus Christ said, " I give thee the keys of the kingdom of heaven, and whatsoever thou shalt bind on earth shall be bound in heaven, and whatsoever thou shalt loose on earth shall be loosed in heaven," it would be intolerable not to observe, that this was addressed personally to Peter, and not to us. Under pretence that it was not addressed to us, but to Peter, the Bishop of Rome pretends it was addressed to him, as the successor of Peter, and on this presumption he makes laws, and dispenses with the breach of them, and his right to do so is allowed by many, merely because he hath sealed his instruments with swords and keys. The Bishop of Rome hath set us the example of thus abusing the Holy Scriptures, and we have been too faithful followers of this blind guide. Is one ashamed of the profession of the Gospel? He satisfies his conscience by saying, Jesus " charged his disciples that they should tell no man that he was Jesus the Christ." Is another indolent, and an enemy to free inquiry? He justifies his conduct by saying, " If any man shall say unto you, Lo, here is Christ, or there ; believe it not. If they shall say unto you, Behold, he is in the desert, go not forth : Behold he is in the secret chambers, believe it not. For there shall arise false Christs, and false prophets." If another lives carelessly, and expects inspiration without study, he says, it is written, " Take no thought how or what ye shall speak ; settle it in your hearts, not to meditate before, what ye shall answer, for it shall be given you in that same hour what ye shall speak, for it is not ye that speak, but the Spirit of your Father which speaketh in you." None of these people consider the circumstances of time, place, person, and so on, nor the meaning of such passages as this, " Verily I say unto, this generation shall not pass away till all be fulfilled." Should a man believe all the passages of Scripture of this sort, we should not therefore think him a believer of the Gospel, but an officious intermeddler, who was weak enough to thrust himself into business with which he had no concern, and which the master of the family appointed other servants to do. Faith of this sort doth not " work by love ;" but by idleness, timorousness, presumption, and fury. It is on this undistinguishing ground, that some Christians perplex themselves, and distress their friends, by puzzling the Gospel, and bewildering honest but unwary travellers; nor considering, that it is not enough for an article to be true, it must be revealed, and it must be addressed to me, before it can become a necessary article of my faith. When therefore we propose truths for the ground of your hope, and the rules of your lives, we do not mean inferences drawn from the Gospel, false or true; nor do we mean truths taught along with the Gospel, but not addressed to you.

This is the proper place for us to observe what the Scripture calls the faith of devils. The apostle James saith, "Thou believest there is one God: thou doest well: the devils also believe, and tremble." A Christian believes there is a holy God, and he trembles, because, being convinced of his own impurity, he is persuaded God is the patron and protector of holiness, and the punisher of sin. Hence he infers, that he is in no better state than that of devils; they " also believe, and tremble." The inference is not fair for three reasons. First, the trembling man is one to whom God addresseth the glad tidings of salvation, but these tidings were never addressed to devils, and if they believe the history of our salvation, it is only as we believe the history of their destruction, with this difference,—our obstinacy may make their history ours, but their utmost efforts can never make our history theirs. Secondly, the scope and design of the apostle was not to alarm Christians by showing them how much they were like fallen spirits, but by convincing them that faith in revealed truths could not possibly be unproductive of effects. For this purpose he introduces a supposed man among the " brethren:" not a believer; but a man saying he had faith, when he had it not; for, in the apostle's account, faith was that to a profession of Christianity, which the soul was to the human body, and he reasons, that as the body without life was judged a mere carcase, so a profession of religion, without the belief of religion, was a dead, unanimated thing. He inquires what, on his principles, the brethren could say to such a vain man ? " He may say he hath faith, and hath not works:" but any one of you may say, " Shew me thy faith without thy works," and as he cannot do this, you may inform him, that faith without works is dead, that his profession of faith resembles a carcase, it not only hath not such a life as devils have, but it hath no life at all, it is dead. The apostle therefore is not speaking of believers, and of their likeness to the fallen angels, but of unbelievers, who boasted of a faith which they had not. Hence, thirdly, appears the propriety of introducing the belief of devils. You, " vain man," you profess yourself a believer of the Gospel; but you boast of what you have not. You have not such a faith as we have, profitable to the " naked," and to those who are " destitute of daily food." You have not such a faith as Rahab had; she justified her belief of the message by respecting the messengers. You have not such a faith as Abraham had; he believed God, and respected him as a friend. You have not such a faith as the devils have; they believe the justice of God, and dread him as an enemy. You say you " do believe there is one God." Very well, and I say in return that you do not, for all belief produces effects. Had you been a fallen angel, you would have trembled : had you been an Abraham, you would have been a friend of God; had you been a Christian, you would have been a friend to the poor; but you are nothing but a vain man boasting of what you have not. What is there in all this to terrify Christians, seeing it is impossible their faith in the Gospel should resemble the faith of devils, to whom the glad tidings of salvation were never so much as proposed.

To return. As we cannot believe what is not reported, and as we ought not to appropriate what is not addressed to us, so neither can we believe truths which are directed to us, *unless we attend to them.* Is it imaginable that all such as repeat the belief, and say, " I believe in God the Father Almighty, and in Jesus Christ, who suffered under Pontius Pilate:" I say, Is it credible that all who repeat this creed believe any thing, or know any thing about Pontius Pilate ? Why then do they repeat it ? They take it for granted : but let us remember, a truth taken upon trust without examining, is no truth in regard to him who takes it, and it worketh in him exactly as he takes it, that is as a prejudice, and not as a truth. Should one man give another diamonds for pebbles, the latter taking them on trust, would value them as pebbles, and sell a bushel for eight pence, the price of pebbles. We wonder when we hear people, who profess to believe all the articles of the Christian faith, deny every article both in words and actions. Let us cease to wonder; the truths of religion are no truths to them, but mere prejudices of education, which they have taken as they found, without suspecting them to be false, or proving them to be true. When I speak of inattention to the truth of an article of faith, I do not mean inattention to the article, but inattention to the truth or the falsehood of it. Let me explain my meaning by a similitude. Should I ask you, how high you think the tenth elm timber on the right hand side of such. a row is, probably the true answer would be, We have seen the tree a thousand times, but never thought of the exact height of it. Thus we may have heard of truths all our days, and have talked of them, and yet never have thought of them in this point of light: we have supposed them true, or rather, we have thought nothing about them. If we may judge by the lives of most men, we must believe this to be the case. Had they examined religion, and found it false, they would scorn to be called Christians, for it would be equal to calling themselves hypocrites, and they would be above baptizing their children into a profession of falsehood. Had they, on the contrary, by examining Christianity, found it true, they could not live in the neglect of it. We must therefore conclude, for there is no other way of accounting for their conduct, that they have taken religion on trust, and value it as they value other prejudices. When Lydia heard the conversation of the apostle Paul, she "attended unto the things which were spoken," she fixed her mind on what he said, and this bent of the mind is well described by the wise man: "My son, attend to my words : incline thine ear unto my sayings. Let them not depart from thine eyes : keep them in the midst of thine heart. For they are life unto those that find them, and health to all their flesh." The attention which we pay to truth, ought to be proportioned to the importance of it; and it will always be proportioned to our opinion of the importance of it. What we think of consequence, we shall certainly pay great attention to, and what we think trifling we shall not much heed; it may be true, it may not be true, it does not much signify to us. Examine mankind on this article, and you will allow, if they spend six days in eager pursuit of the world, and on the Lord's day only a drowsy hour or two in a place of worship, they have neither attended to the vanity of the world, nor to the importance of religion. With them eating and drinking, buying and selling, and getting gain, are matters of the utmost importance, and whether there be a God, or a heaven, or a hell, or a a judgment to come, are matters that deserve little or no notice; they may be, they may not be, it does not much signify whether they be facts or fables. It is a shame to call the talk of such men a profession of faith, for what they call faith doth not " work by love" of any thing but sin. Certainly our apostle did not mean to say, " Faith worketh by love" of sensuality and sin; a persuasion that God is the chief good, worketh by love to sin as the chief good!

You cannot believe what you do attend to, *unless it appear to you to be true;* and the more closely you fix your attention on what appears to be false, and the more you try to believe it, the more fully will you feel yourself unable to believe, even though all your worldly interest should be at stake. Falsehood may conceal itself under appearances of truth, and truth may be disguised under appearances of error: but should these appearances be taken off, and religion and sin be placed before us in their true colours, it would not be in the power of the worst of us to hate God and love sin, to " believe a lie" and to disbelieve " those things in which" Christians " have been instructed." Observe an expression of the apostle Paul. He informs the Thessalonians, that there should " come a falling away" among Christians. He represents this under the figure of a

" man of sin, setting in the temple of God," not as a man of sin, but " as God" with " signs, and lying wonders, and with all deceivableness of unrighteousness ;" and he represents such as fall away from the " belief of the truth" to the " believing of a lie" as being under " strong delusion." This is the constant method of error ; it conceals itself under an appearance of truth, and by such means sits easy on a conscience that would otherwise be unhappy. Now, if we be able to prove that the Christian religion is true, and that it hath certain characters, marks, or tokens of its truth, so clearly impressed upon it that they cannot be denied, and that these recommendations of itself are so forcible that they cannot be resisted,—what must we say of that man, who constantly avoids them, and contrives to keep out of the way of this irresistible beauty? He must see the sun if he comes up above ground, and therefore he chooses the life of a mole, and spends his days in burrowing under ground, burying all his time and all his talents in employments of a momentary life.

There is in the Christian religion every character of truth : it resembles the God from whom it came. Attend to it for a moment in two or three points of light. Suppose the Gospel to be the direct contrary of what it is, and try how it would sit upon your minds. You know it must run thus : Thou shalt hate God with all thine heart, and with all thy strength, and thou shalt hate thy neighbour as thyself. Jesus Christ hated God and man, and God so hated the world as to give Jesus to embolden men to express their hatred of God and one another. Moses and Aaron were two " idle" men, who led their nation out of Egypt, settled religion and government among them, and wrote five books, called Scripture, only because they did not know what to do with their time. All the Jewish prophets were fools, and their " spiritual men" were " madmen." Jesus and his apostles were " pestilent fellows," and " movers of sedition" throughout the world. " All things come alike to all ; as is the good, so is the sinner, and he that sweareth, as he that feareth an oath." " A man hath no pre-eminence above a beast ; as the one dieth, so di-

24

eth the other." There is "nothing better for a man, than that he should eat. and drink, and delight his senses." Suppose the whole book of Scripture to consist of such principles, and to contain the histories and recommendation of such practices; I ask, Could you believe, and love, and practise this Gospel, and dare you read it to your children and recommend it to them? The Gospel then hath a character of "holiness," and it appears to you that holiness is a character of a true religion.

Examine the Gospel on the article of likeness to God, from whom it pretends to come. Observe with what unyielding dignity and *majesty* it prescribes to all mankind, consulting no man's passions and sinful interests, how distinguished soever his rank may be. Herod is a "fox," Cæsar is "a lion," the "princes" of this world know nothing, "priests" have no neighbours, scribes and Pharisees are "hypocrites," the masters of the world are "filled with all unrighteousness," the whole world "lieth in wickedness," and "the soul that sinneth it shall die; as I live, saith the Lord God, the soul that sinneth it shall die." The same majesty runs through every thing said to the righteous, and the whole book is the language of a master, who hath nobody above him, and who speaks every thing like one who had been accustomed to command and to be obeyed. Now, doth it not appear to you that a religion coming from God, ought to speak thus, and that if it spoke otherwise, and abounded in compliances and civilities, and accommodations, it would render itself contemptible and unworthy of credit? Here then is another character of a true religion; and it appears to you to be such a character as a religion from heaven must necessarily have.

Observe the character of *goodness.* The Christian religion professes to be built on the love, the everlasting love of God. It comes to us in a way, which evidently proves, that God consulted our peace more than his own splendour: the latter is in no danger; the first had been torn up by the roots. Had God formed the method of conveyance with a mere design to display his greatness, all the powers of nature would have been too

little to express it : thunderings the most terrible, lightnings the most dreadful, winds, and rains, and earth-
quakes, and hurricanes the most horrible, angels the
most magnificent; all would have been far beneath his
dignity, and all these could have been only messengers
crying each in its own alarming way, " Prepare to meet
thy God, for lo, he that formeth the mountains, and cre-
ateth the wind," will in person " declare unto man what
is his thought." God hath not done thus; but he hath
consulted our peace by addressing us by men like ourselves, all whose language is, " Come, my people, enter
thou into thy chambers, and shut thy doors about thee :
hide thyself as it were for a little moment, until the indignation be overpast. For, behold, the Lord cometh
out of his place to punish the inhabitants of the earth
for their iniquity; the earth also shall disclose her
blood, and no more cover her slain." This tender regard to the best interests of mankind; this pity to the
wretched, pardon to the guilty, relief to the oppressed,
patience with the wicked, and protection of the good,
this lenity flows through all the Christian religion like
the gentle river that watered the garden of Eden, and
not confined to paradise, parted itself, and ran dis-
tributing its benefits in ten thousand different streams
among all sorts of men.

In this manner let us consider the whole Christian religion as full of motives to credibility, or reasons to be
believed, and, let us not deceive ourselves, we are bound
to examine and admit the claim. Divide all religion
into the two parts of law and Gospel, duty and mercy.
If you attend to the law, it is a hill brought in by the
Lord against his tenant : can the tenant refuse to examine it? Consider the Gospel in the light of a generous
discharge : can the wretched bankrupt refuse to examine such a receipt? It is the excellence of the Gospel
that it preserves its features, say what it will; and each
part taken separately, as well as the whole taken together, is an irresistible claim of credit. For example,
take the character of Christ as a teacher sent from God,
or take his resurrection from the dead, which was one
only out of many of his works; examine either of these,

and you will find all the characters of religious truth, for each is plain, clear, kind, just, and full of majesty; and to deny these is to admit the opposite, which is full of all impiety and iniquity. The pretended religion of the world is a sepulchre " full of dead men's bones, and of all uncleanness :" the religion of Christianity is like the temple of God, " adorned with goodly stones and gifts, where the Lord commands the blessing, even life for evermore." One chief excellence of this religion is, that each part supports its truth in our understandings by proofs, which support the whole ; so that if a man admits either of the truths just now mentioned, he must for the same reasons admit the whole ; and for this reason we pronounce the weak believer, who admits only one truth, in a state as safe as that in which the strong believer is. Before a man can admit one truth, he must put off many prejudices, and love of truth must reign in his heart: now where love of truth prevails over prejudice, the mind is prepared to admit all truths on conviction that they are so. O that Christians would enter into these sentiments, so just to God, and so friendly to man ! O that they would " open the gates" of their churches, " that the righteous nation which keepeth the truth may enter in !" Instead of this, we make out human articles of faith, call him a strong believer who credits the whole, him a weak one who doubts the whole, and him an infidel who questions a part ; we possess ourselves of the door way, and, though the benches within are empty, and though the voice from above cries, " Compel the halt and the maimed to come in, for yet there is room," somehow or other in our hurry we mistake the voice, and set a brother, the most gigantic and grim we can find, to keep the door and compel them to keep out? Ye blind, and halt, and maimed, ye limping followers of the physician and friend of sinners ! do not take the character of your friend from that of these men. Indeed he was not like them ; he was quite another man ; he was not like better servants than they, he was far better than the best of his followers ; further above them than they are above the worst of mankind. " What manner of men" were the apostles ? " Each one

resembled the child of a king." What noble sentiments!
What a princely way of thinking in religion had they!
What innumerable exercises of "wisdom and understanding, and largeness of heart, exceeding much, even
as the sand that is on the sea shore!" But what was
all their generosity but as a "drop of a bucket" compared with the "rivers of pleasures," the "fulness of
joys," which flow, through the mediation of Jesus Christ,
"at God's right hand for evermore!"

A believer, then, is one, who is convinced in his own
mind, of the truth, the whole truth, or a part of the
truth of the Christian religion; and this conviction in
him is an effect produced by those characters of truth,
which distinguish all truth from falsehood, and particularly the truths of religion from the mistakes of sin.
Now let us apply this notion of faith to the text. Belief worketh: belief of any thing worketh: belief of a
part of Christianity worketh a partial conformity to
Christianity: and belief of the whole worketh universal obedience: belief of a painful truth worketh fear:
belief of a distant good worketh desire: and belief of
the great love of God to us worketh love to him, and to
all his creatures. If I had a mind to lull your souls into a fatal security, I would endeavour to persuade you
that you might have faith without feeling any effects,
or bringing forth any fruits for many years: but who
can imagine that a belief of truths such as those of the
Gospel can lie dead in the heart? To say nothing of
virtue, even our vicious passions would rouse such a
disagreeable stranger into action. To those who believe the testimony of Scripture, the proof is at hand,
for thus the oracle of God declares, "Faith, if it hath
not works, is dead;" and again, "Wilt thou know, O
vain man, that faith without works is dead;" and again,
"As the body without the spirit is dead, so faith without works is dead also." Were it possible for a man to
comply with the apostle's requisition, and "shew his
faith without his works," and some men can do this by
producing a creed in writing, what then should such a
man do? He would prove that he was a dead man. It
would be as if a dead carcase would come forth out of a

24*

grave, stand up, and próve by its putrefaction that it had been dead and buried forty years. No, you may be prejudiced in favour of religion, and take things as you find them : but it is impossible you should admit the proofs of a truth without feeling effects. " Faith is the substance of things hoped for ;" it substantiates " things not seen," brings distant objects near, and makes them stand true in the mind, just as the object we look at is in the eye, the form we love ever in the memory, where recollection clothes it, and fancy gives it a thousand charms. It is extremely difficult to assort faith and feelings, because we have been brought up in the midst of the truths of religion, and our belief, and pleasures, and pains, have interwoven themselves, one with another : but these effects of believing are not the less real, nor the less connected with exercises of believing, for our not making the distinction.

I will explain myself by a supposed case. Imagine our Lord preaching at Jerusalem, and one of the inhabitants coming into the assembly just as he was uttering the three parts of the twenty fifth chapter of Matthew. The first is the parable of the ten virgins, the second is that of the talents, and the third is an explanation of the other parts in a description of the day of judgment. Let us suppose our hearers to have lived till then in ignorance and sin, and now for the first time attending to the truth of one part of religion, the righteous judgment of the world at the last day. Let us suppose him convinced of the nature, necessity, and equity of a day of judgment. How would this man return home, think ve, and what would his condition be, while his instructer was gone out of town ? Would he not say to himself, " I am one of the foolish virgins ; I am that wicked and slothful servant, who hid his Lord's talent in the earth ; I have seen my fellow creatures hungry and thirsty, and naked and sick, and have not ministered unto them ; I deserve, in a state of just distribution of pleasure and pain, to be denied happiness, and plunged into misery : I fear this state, and I have reason to fear it; love of justice will oblige the judge to punish me ; yes, he must set the sheep, my good father, and my pious mother, and

all like them on his right hand, while I and my wicked
companions must stand confounded on the left: O I
think the day is come, and I hear the Judge saying,
Cast the unprofitable servant into outer darkness. O my
God! what shall I do?" "Whither shall I go from thy
Spirit? or whither shall I flee from thy presence? If
I ascend up into heaven, thou art there. If I make my
bed in the grave, behold thou art there. If I say, Surely the darkness shall cover me; even the night shall
be light about me. Yea, the darkness and the light are
both alike to thee. Hell and destruction are naked before the Lord; how much more then the hearts of the
children of men!" The faith of this man is a belief of
the day of judgment, and it works by fear of punishment, like that of Noah, who "being warned of God
of things not seen as yet," was "moved with fear," and
"prepared an ark to the saving of his house." What
was this patriarch afraid of? He was moved with the
fear of being drowned. Why moved with the fear of
being drowned, but because he believed the testimony
of God, who warned him of the flood before it came,
and of his danger on account of it? Suppose this man
to attend to a second discourse of Jesus Christ on the
subject of forgiveness, and to hear him utter the parables contained in the fifteenth of Luke, that of the lost
sheep, the lost silver, and the lost son, which he addressed to "publicans and sinners;" suppose him to believe the truth of forgiveness; is it not clear, that he
would return home full of this delightful subject, "Joy
shall be in heaven over one sinner that repenteth?"
Faith in the truth of the report of God's parental love,
expressed in finding and forgiving his lost children,
would work by love, gratitude, obedience, caution, and
perpetual hatred of sin.

Most of the truths of religion are of a mixed kind,
and therefore they produce various effects. One example shall serve: there were in the Corinthian church
several disorders, which the apostle Paul thought fit to
reprove sharply in his first Epistle. A man of his generous kind never uses reproof by choice, and the necessity that compels him to it, gives him pain. Good man

that he was ! His " flesh had no rest," he was " troubled on every side, without were fightings, within were
fears."   He even " repented," that he had " made them
sorry with a letter," for it was " in his heart to live and
die with them," well knowing that a Christian church,
with all its disorders, is a more desirable abode than a
" blaspheming" synagogue, or a magnificent temple filled with " craftsmen" trading in the glory of the great
goddess Diana.   In this condition Titus found him, and
informed him, that the Corinthians had been extremely
unhappy that they had given him occasion to censure
their conduct; but that they had been convinced of the
justice and friendship of the reproof, and entertained
the most fervent love for their kind reprover.   This
filled our apostle with great satisfaction : he wrote a
second Epistle, and gave a most beautiful description of
the fruits of godly sorrow.   " What a carefulness it
wrought in you ; yea, what clearing of yourselves, yea,
what indignation, yea, what fear, yea, what vehement
desire, yea, what zeal, yea, what revenge : in all things
ye have approved yourselves to be clear in this matter."
All truths made up of justice and mercy, the rights of
the law and the grace of the Gospel, because they are
mixed in themselves, will necessarily produce various
emotions in us.   Some will be painful, some will be
pleasant; but all together will constitute that body of
Christian virtues called the *new man*, which consists of
" kindness, humbleness of mind, meekness, longsuffering, forgiveness, charity," and " which after God is created in righteousness and true holiness."
    On these principles our apostle affirms in the text
" faith worketh," and, as the immediate work before
the Galatians, to which the apostle exhorted them, was
a work of love, it was highly proper to affirm, " faith
worketh by love."   Let us finish by observing, that
there is a close connexion between the Christian religion and faith, faith and love, love and good works ; and
let us apply this observation to the case of the church
at Galatia, and in that to our own.
    There is a close connexion between the Christian re-
ligion and faith ; that is to say, Christianity is fitted to

obtain belief, and does actually produce it, as an instrument in the hand of the great " master of assemblies," whose " words are wise, acceptable words, even words of truth," and therefore " as goads," and " as nails fastened in a sure place." Take the whole of our holy religion together, and it deserves to be called as it is, simply *love*. Often, very often, the whole is called love. What is God as he is described in this religion? " God is love." On what principle did he act when he designed the Christian religion? " God loved the world." What is Jesus Christ? " The gift of God, the unspeakable gift of God." What is the whole part of Jesus Christ in this religion, his doctrine, his death, his Spirit, his precepts? It is a " love that passeth knowledge." How doth the Gospel of Christ work upon the minds and hearts of men? It draws them with " cords of a man, with bands of love." It resembles the love of a parent to a little child, " teaching him to go, taking him by his arms," though he " knows not" the soft hand that supports him. What is the short history of revealed religion in the heart and life of man? The author tells us, " I have loved thee with an everlasting love, therefore with loving kindness have I drawn thee." What we affirm is, that this religion of unutterable love is very credible, more than likely to be true. Is it incredible that God should love? What can be more worthy of belief than this? Is it improbable that he should love man, the creature in the world made in his own image, when his tender mercies are over all his works? Let us reason on the subject of Divine love as the Psalmist reasoned on that of Divine knowledge : " He that planted the ear, shall he not hear? He that teacheth man knowledge, shall not he know?" In like manner we ask, he that formed the hearts of those good parents, Jacob and David, will he " forget to be gracious?" He that put irresistible eloquence into the tears of an outcast babe, in a flag basket, so that a stranger " had compassion on him, and" disinterestedly " said, Go call a nurse, his name shall be Moses, I drew him out of the water;" will he who compels us by our own feelings to be kind, " in anger shut up his own tender

mercies?" Hear how the God of the whole earth condescends to answer our questions : " Like as a father pitieth his children, so the Lord pitieth them that fear
him.   Can a woman forget her sucking child, that she
should not have compassion on the son of her womb?
Yea, they may forget, yet will I not forget thee." Such
speculations as these were all to be collected from the
world of nature before Christ came, but if to these we
add what the Scripture calls the " acts," the " mighty
acts" of the Lord, how many blind eyes he hath opened, how many hard hearts he hath softened, how many
crimes he hath forgiven, how many disconsolate and
wretched people he hath made happy by the life, death,
and resurrection of his Son, we shall conclude, that
" the Lord is gracious and full of compassion, slow to
anger, and of great mercy, great, and greatly to be
praised, and his greatness unsearchable."   No, great
God! we are not infidels.   We will not offend thy goodness by denying light at noonday. · Behold, the tears
that trickle down the cheeks of this assembly, say, " He
brought me up" also " out of a horrible pit, out of the
miry clay, and set my feet upon a rock, and established
my goings, and put a new song in my mouth, even
praise unto our God.   Many, O Lord, my God, are thy
wonderful works which thou hast done, and thy thoughts
which are to us ward : they cannot be reckoned up in
order unto thee : if I would speak of them they are
more than can be numbered.   Whom have I in heaven
but thee ; and there is none upon earth that I desire
beside thee !"

Thus " wisdom hath builded her house, furnished her
table," and " sent forth her maidens crying, Forsake the
foolish and live, and go in the way of understanding ;—I
will speak of excellent things, my mouth shall speak
truth, all plain to him that understandeth, and right to
him that findeth knowledge."   But wherein lies the
excellency of wisdom, and what gives it advantage over
folly?   It hath advantages in every respect : but one of
the chief is, that it necessarily produces happiness by
·means of holiness, so that you may safely conclude, as
religion is fitted to produce faith, so faith is fitted to

produce love, and love good works; for this is an end
worthy of the means, and does honour to God the first
cause. Is it conceivable that when such a religion as
this gets into the mind, it should skulk like a reptile,
and lurk beneath the shade of some poisonous weed, the
fruit of the curse? Doth it not rather enter like a judge
into a court to " sit chief," and dwell there like a " king
in an army ?" Who shall answer these questions ? Let
those who have best understood religion, and exercised
most faith on the truths of it. See, what a " great cloud
of witnesses compasseth you about, Christians! Read
at your leisure the eleventh chapter of Hebrews, and
observe the men and women, " of whom the world was
not worthy, who through faith subdued kingdoms,
wrought righteousness, obtained promises, stopped the
mouths of lions;" who " had trial of cruel mockings
and scourgings, yea, of bonds and imprisonment;" who
" wandered about in sheep skins and goat skins, being
destitute, afflicted, tormented;" and who preferred all
these before the " pleasures of sin," and esteemed even
" the reproach of Christ greater riches than the treasures of the world." Faith and obedience then are inseparable, and as these men cheerfully obeyed their orders, because they believed the facts, which made their
obedience necessary ; so Christians obey the orders in
the New Testament given them, because they believe
the facts, which the New Testament reports for true.
It would be easy to show you that faith in the Christian
religion is closely connnected with love, and necessarily produces it : but this I think not needful now, for
who doth not know that belief of such a God as Christianity describes, compels believers to love God and
adore him? And who doth not know that if a man say,
" I love God, and hateth his brother, he is a liar : for
he that loveth not his brother, whom he hath seen, how
can he love God whom he hath not seen ?" The apostle
doth not mean by " brother" one of our own party, nor
a believer of any other party : but one of our own class
of creatures, a brother man. In my opinion there is no
danger of heresy or sin in saying, If I love God, I shall
love my brother Christian, my brother Jew, my brother

negro. " Have we not all one Father? Hath not one God created us? Why do we deal treacherously every man against his brother?" What if Judah hath " profaned the holiness of the Lord, which he ought to have loved;" what if the miserable heathens have " married the daughter of a strange god," and " for this cause are given up unto vile affections;" is it for us to deal in thunder and lightning, to " deck ourselves with majesty, and cast abroad the rage of our wrath?" Let us know our religion better, and let us always remember, that " in Christ Jesus neither circumcision availeth any' thing, nor uncircumcision, but faith which worketh by love."

This notion of religion was highly proper to answer the end for which our apostle wrote it. You read in the fifteenth of Acts, that some Jews, who had become Christians, but had not well understood either their own religion or that of Jesus Christ, endeavoured rather to reform the Jewish religion than to abolish it wholly in favour of Christianity. They approved of the pious principles of Christians; but they were for retaining them under the forms of Jewish ceremonies. These men were a great trouble to the churches, so great that our apostle wished, for the good of society, they had been " cut off." They began by pressing the necessity of circumcision; but this was only to pave the way for all the other ceremonies of Moses, for the " weak and beggarly elements of days, and months, and times, and years." This Epistle was written directly against this class of men, who had been at Galatia, and had " bewitched the foolish Galatians." Good, simple souls, they had been heathens, and had received the Gospel in transports, so that " if it had been possible, they would have plucked out their own eyes, and have given them" to their teacher. Such converts are very apt to be prejudiced in favour of any thing that has the appearance of piety, for they are not aware of the spirit and tendency of such alterations. Our apostle destroys the four great arguments used by these Jewish teachers. The first is an argument of authority: Peter, and James, and the whole church at Jerusalem were cir-

cumcised. Very well, says our apostle, I am not a dep-
uty from them; I had an " immediate revelation" as
well as they, and when I told them, I was sent to the
Gentiles, " they gave to me and Barnabas the right
hands of fellowship, that we should go unto the heathen,
and they unto the circumcision."   But, they said, Paul
had changed his opinion, and had circumcised Timothy;
But, replies our apostle, Titus, a Greek, also was with
me, and he was " not compelled to be circumcised;"
and " I, brethren, if I yet preach circumcision, why do
I yet suffer persecution?"   They added, The promises
were made to Abraham and his seed : True, said the
apostle, but you have mistaken the word, " he saith
not, And to seeds as of many, but as of one, And to thy
seed, which is Christ;" the promises were made to Abraham, and to one of his posterity, not to all his descendants, and that son of Abraham is Christ; it is in him,
and not in your teachers of circumcision, that " all nations shall be blessed."   Their fourth argument was taken from the Prophecy of Isaiah, that children should
be born from among the heathen to Jerusalem : Another
mistake, says our apostle; the prophet doth not speak
of the Jewish Jerusalem, but of the ancient Jerusalem,
in the hands of the Jebusites, " Jerusalem, which is
above, is free, which is the mother of us all."   Weary
with these trifling arguments, destructive of the genius
and spirit of the Christian religion, the apostle observes
in the text, that in the religion of " Jesus Christ, neither circumcision availeth any thing, nor uncircumcision, but faith which worketh by love:" as if he had
said, I preach to you a revealed religion of truth and
love: do not tell me of authority, I respect Peter, but
Peter was blamed, and what authority is equal to that
of Christ, under which I act?   " When it pleased God
to reveal his Son in me, I conferred not with flesh and
blood."   Do not plead my example, and from an occasional action of mine, infer a general rule of conduct to
bind all people in different circumstances. You quote
Scripture : read it again, the text is right, but your exposition is wrong : you have not understood the Scriptures; it is impossible to pervert them so as to banish

25

love from religion, to make room for dry ceremonies, party zeal, and false teachers, who " constrain you to be circumcised, only lest they should suffer persecution for the cross of Christ," who sacrifice truth, virtue, and the happiness of a whole world to their own servile fear of man and worldly interest. Christians, apply these truths to yourselves, as far as circumstances require, and remember that no authority, no examples, no not those of inspired apostles, no texts of Scripture about Abraham and Jerusalem, ought to prevail for a moment to darken a religion of truth, and faith, and universal love. " Though we, or an angel from heaven, preach any other Gospel unto you, let him be accursed. In Christ Jesus neither circumcision availeth any thing, nor uncircumcision, but a new creature : and as many as-walk, according to this rule, peace be on them and mercy, and upon the Israel of God !"   God grant us this grace !   To him be honour and glory forever.   Amen.

DISCOURSE XV.

INCORRIGIBLE SINNERS WILL BE WITHOUT EXCUSE AT THE

LAST DAY.

[*AT FOXON.*]

MATTHEW xxii, 12.

And he was speechless.

UNDER the similitude of an entertainment given by a king to his subjects on the marriage of his son, our Lord sets forth the blessings of the Gospel, and, in the text, that degree of guilt beyond excuse, under which they who perish in Gospel times must lie. It is in this view that we are going to consider the text: but before we come immediately to the subject, we will make one remark on the context, and one on the manner of expounding parables.

In this and the foregoing chapter there are three parables, which contain the history of three periods of time. That of the "householder," who "let out a vineyard to husbandmen," is a true history of the Jews from the time of Moses to forty years after the death of Christ; all that time was employed either in cultivating and adorning the country, enjoying the produce of it, hearing and disobeying the prophets, crucifying Christ, or in suffering an entire destruction for that and for all other crimes. In the days of Joshua, David, Solomon, and such princes, they were "hedging in" the vineyard, "digging" wine-presses, "building" towers, and so on. When the prophets came, they were "killing" one, and "stoning" another. When Christ the Son came, they "slew" him. When the Jews were driven out of their country by the Romans, and the land left to other inhabitants, the Lord was "destroying these wicked men," and "letting out his vineyard to others." The second parable of the man who had "two sons," whom he ordered to go work in his vineyard, is a history of the time of John the baptist. The third parable of the marriage of the king's son, out of which we have taken the text, is a history of the times of the Gospel from its being first preached by Jesus Christ to the Jews, to the time of his second coming to judge the world. In this plain and comprehensive manner did Jesus Christ draw great events into a narrow point of view, omitting the fate of empires to lay before us the destiny of religion, in which we are more interested than in that of learning, or commerce, or any thing else in the world.

Our Lord usually taught by parables; that is, by continued similitudes or likenesses, and the best rule for interpreting a parable is not to interpret it too much, if I may speak so, but to take the *general* likeness, or one doctrine from the chief figures. A parable is a kind of history-painting, and should we see a picture of Abraham offering up Isaac, we should trifle, and receive no instruction, were we to fix our attention on the "thicket behind," the order of the wood, the knife, and so on, for the picture was not drawn for the sake of representing these things, so much as the principal object, which was, the patriarch in an exercise of the noblest confidence in God, in earnest to slay his son at the command of God, and "accounting that God was able to raise him up even from the dead," though there had never then been in the world an example of one rising from the dead. Thus in parables, if I could allow myself willingly to teach you to trifle with the Scriptures, and to think yourself wiser than others for knowing better than they how to play the fool, I would show you the conformities between God and a "king," "a certain" king, for we must not lose a word, Christ and a "son,"

conversion and a " wedding," preaching the Gospel and
" bidding" to a marriage. I might tell you the likeness
of " oxen and fatlings" to the doctrines of the Gospel;
of the " wedding garment" to the righteousness of
Christ; and thus we might go through all the parable,
and crumble it into as many doctrines as there are words
in the twelve verses. Having done this, I might compare the parable in Matthew with the same parable in
Luke, and reconcile seeming contradictions. I might
show you that if Matthew calls the feast a " dinner," it
was because the Gospel was preached in the middle age
of the world, and if Luke calls it a " supper," it is because the Gospel is preached in the last ages of the
world. This is what I meant just now by interpreting
too much; for by making every thing out of a parable,
we teach the parable to say nothing. It is evident, by
this parable our Lord chiefly intends to show the levity
with which the Jews treated the Gospel, and consequently the justice as well as the goodness of God in
sending it to the Gentiles. The first " would not come :"
the last furnished the table " with guests both bad and
good;" but, that we might thoroughly understand the
purity of Christianity, he informs us that bad Gentiles
as well as wicked Jews would be inexcusable, if they
" turned the grace of God into lasciviousness." This
is the sense of the text, " And he was speechless."

However bold men may be in denying, or however
ingenious they may be in deceiving themselves by
keeping the subject out of sight, certain it is the text
speaks of a very serious and sad event, which must
come to pass, and to which we are hastening as fast as
time can carry us. How rapid is life! How far are
some of you down a stream, which none of you can stop;
a little longer and you will be lost in the ocean, and
heard of no more till the sea shall " give up the dead.'
Then, should you be found " speechless," we should
forget all your pleasant days of prosperity in this life,
and one thing would strike us dumb with astonishment:
there he stands : stands before his judge : and stands exactly as the Gospel foretold: " speechless !" How
comes it to pass that a subject so true and so terrible is
25*

so little attended to? Is it ignorance? How is that possible? Are you not here present? Am I not standing here before you with the Gospel in my hand? Have I not read the parable distinctly? Is not this the clear meaning of our prophet and judge? Let us leave that excuse to the heathens; it is impossible for us to make it. What is the cause?... To whom am I speaking? Not one of us intends to be the man of the text. Each goes to-day to his "farm," to-morrow to his "merchandize," and each intends some future day to put on the "wedding garment." The king bath a wardrobe for the accommodation of his guests, and I shall be ready in an instant when I receive notice of his approach. Ah! this is the cause of your present unpreparedness to die; and if the man in the world who hates you most, and most heartily wishes for your destruction, were to give you advice, he could give you none so likely to glut his malice as this, which you both give and take yourself. Do you mean to say, " Let that which should have been for my welfare become a trap? Let my days be few, and let my prayer become sin!" This is the language of an enemy. Let us not be such enemies to ourselves. The voice of friendship says, " O come let us kneel before the Lord our maker! To-day if ye will hear his voice, harden not your hearts: lest he swear in his wrath, You shall not enter into my rest."

It may happen, that a man apprized of danger may not know how to escape it, and lest any of you should be through my negligence in such a state, I will endeavour to show you what is necessary to avoid the shame mentioned in the text. It may also happen, that a man, who is apprized of his danger, and hath a general notion of a method of escaping it, may loiter away his time, and trifle a day too long. In friendship for such, I shall endeavour to convince them that they are, and will forever be, inexcusable for doing so. Avail yourselves of these precious moments, and all the while I am speaking, remember a saying of Paul, " God limiteth a certain day, saying, To-day hear his voice. Are not your days like the days of an hireling?" Can you lengthen your day a single moment, and have you any

choice what year or what day to die, and have you any
security that this is not the day, and this the hour?
" God limiteth a certain day." " This is your day,
hear his voice."

Lest any one should be ignorant of the way of escaping the misery mentioned in the text, we must inquire,
what the way of escape is. I do not know what the
" wedding garment" is. I do know that princes and
great men kept wardrobes to accommodate their guests,
and I could name one Roman, who had five thousand
habits in keeping for that purpose ; but we are no nearer
to our Lord's meaning for knowing this ; for, you see, I
think parables are not understood by being taken to
pieces, but by being put together. The thing speaks
for itself; the " wedding garment" is that which is necessary to salvation, and whatever is necessary to salvation is the " wedding garment."

We need not waste time in proving, first, that a man
living and dying in the practice of sin is expressly excluded from the kingdom of God. " Know you not that
the unrighteous shall not inherit the kingdom of God?
Be not deceived : neither fornicators, nor idolaters, nor
adulterers, nor effeminate, nor abusers of themselves
with mankind, nor thieves, nor covetous, nor drunkards,
nor revilers, nor extortioners, shall inherit the kingdom
of God." It is not only on the testimony of Paul that
we affirm, such people cannot be saved; reason and the
nature of things lead us to the same conclusion. For
example, a drunkard wishes to avoid pain; the pain of
what? The pain of being sober, and the more intolerable pain of thinking and reflecting, which sobriety
would bring on. He wishes to be happy; but what is
his happiness? It is to gratify his senses, to drown his
reason, to sink himself into the condition of a brute.
Admit only that a future state is not a state of sensual
gratification; but that it is a condition of reflection and
thought, and it is easy to determine that the bare
living in such a state would be a cruel punishment to
this sort of men. Yes, if there was no " unquenchable
fire," no " great wine-press of the wrath of God," no
" outer darkness," no " devil and his angels," a bare ne-

cessity of thinking without a possibility of stupifying thought by subjecting the soul to the senses, that would be a great misery to such men. " The unrighteous shall not inherit the kingdom of God." A life of sin is therefore " the broad way that leadeth to destruction," and the direction of that way, like that of every other road, is not altered because " many go therein:" it will lead the whole, and it will lead each individual, to the very same spot. The observation of our Lord, that " many" go in this road, is a strong reason to dissuade us from going in it ; for what kind of men are they ? If any man could bring himself to live with such men as bloody Cain, cruel Pharaoh, intoxicated Nabal, covetous Judas, with liars and thieves, and blasphemers, could he also prevail with himself to call such monsters about him when he finds himself dying, and can he choose such for his companions in a future state, where, without any mixture of sober and decent men, all are the refuse of the world ; " reprobate silver shall men call them because the Lord hath rejected them ?" This class of men certainly have not on the " wedding garment."

There is a second class called by our Lord " unprofitable servants." These useless people, serving none of the purposes of religion, are, however, generally found, if not in the church, yet not in company with the profligate part of mankind. A thousand causes, none of them religious, produce the decency of this sort of people. Birth and education, constitution and connexion, necessity of character, and love of gain, smart for first trials and fear of future consequences, and many such things, are sufficient to produce a worldly decency of living. This class, therefore, are not so bad as the former, who have broke through all these considerations ; but as they do not act from principles of religion, they certainly have no right to the rewards of it. " There was a law in Rome, that those who in a storm forsook the ship should forfeit all property therein ; and the ship and lading should belong entirely to those who staid in it. In a dangerous tempest all the mariners forsook the ship, except only one sick passenger, who by reason of his disease was unable to get out and escape. So it happened the ship came safe to port. The sick man kept possession, and claimed the benefit of the law; but it was agreed that the sick man was not within the reason of the law, for the reason of making it, was to give encouragement to such as should venture their lives to save the vessel; but this was a merit, which he could never pretend to, who neither staid in the ship upon that account, nor contributed any thing to its preservation." "Unprofitable servants" are in the condition of this man, and they can claim nothing under Christianity as a law, because they never acted on the reasons of it. They stand on the same ground as heathens do, with this difference: heathens, like the sick man, were incapable of embracing the Gospel, through a necessity of condition; but these, living under the Gospel, wilfully put themselves into the condition of heathens, without any necessity, and against the most pressing remonstrances to act otherwise. Far from disgracing the "wedding garment" by pretending that such men wear it, the very pretence is an aggravation of their crimes; and when the Judge says of one of these, "Cast that slothful, unprofitable," and therefore "wicked servant, into outer darkness, he" will be "speechless."

If the "wedding garment" be that, without which a man cannot be saved, we must examine what that is, and the Scriptures will readily inform us. It is "holiness, without which no man shall see the Lord:" it is "faith, without which it is impossible to please God:" it is repentance, for "except ye repent, ye shall all perish:" it is perseverance, for he only "that endureth to the end shall be saved:" it is "feeding" the "hungry," and "clothing" the "naked," for to these "shall the King say, Come, ye blessed:" it is to be a true and real Christian. There are different degrees of Christianity, as there are different sizes and shapes among men; but all are alike in kind. "Little children" in religion "know the Father: young men are strong, the word of God abideth in them, and they have overcome the wicked one:" and "fathers have known God from the beginning." All these differ from one another in

degree; but they all differ in kind from other men, who
" are in darkness, walk in darkness," and " know not
whither they go, because" ignorance "hath blinded their
eyes." The " wedding garment" of a little child differs in excellence from that of a father; but it hath an
excellence in its kind. Let this guide our present inquiry, and let us fix not on any *degree* of religion, but on
the *sort* of religion, which distinguisheth a Christian
from all other men, and which at the same time pro-
vides for very great distinctions between Christians
themselves.

I can think of nothing more likely to direct us properly than this expression of our Lord, " Except a man
be born again, he cannot see the kingdom of God." Not
to detain you with a list of interpretations, but to come
directly to the point, I take the new birth to mean three
changes, or, to speak more properly, one change, which
it is most easy to consider under three different views:
a change of ideas: a change of tempers: and a change
of actions: the first is the Christian religion in the mind;
the second is the same religion in the heart; and the
third is still the same religion in the life and conversation. This is a real alteration, which the Christian religion makes in every true disciple of the Son of God,
and the alteration is so great that it may with the utmost propriety be likened to a being " born again."
Let us examine ourselves upon these articles.

By *ideas* I mean thoughts. By Christian ideas I mean
the thoughts of Jesus Christ on articles of religion, as
on God, and the worship of him; on man, and his condition; on sin, its cause and consequences; on a future
state of rewards and punishments; on himself, and his
office as mediator; and so on. You will readily allow,
that Jesus Christ perfectly understood these subjects,
and thought of them very differently from all bad men
of every description in the world. When I say the
thoughts of Jesus Christ must become ours, I suppose
him to have not carried back his secret thoughts to
heaven, but to have left his true and real sentiments in
the Holy Scriptures; some clearly expressed in words,
and others in actions. Now if a man takes his thoughts

of these subjects from the Scriptures, he is in possession of the ideas of Jesus Christ. Like him, he thinks
there is one God, who loved the world so as to give his
Son, and so on. This is one view of the Christian religion : it makes a body of sound thinking in the understanding of a good man; and he, not having thought of
these subjects in such a manner before, is said to be
" born again." Every thing in religion takes a new
form, and the Christian seems to see with new eyes.
Lay it down then for a certain rule, that knowledge of
the Christian religion, and a persuasion that it is true, is
necessary to entering into the kingdom of God.

By *temper*, I mean the frame of the heart, the condition of all those movements in us which are attended
with pleasure or pain, such as desire, fear, hope, anger,
and so on. You will readily allow that all these dispositions were in a state of the highest perfection in Jesus Christ; and you will as readily agree they are not
so in other men. Now if we learn of Jesus Christ to
be mild and lowly, and so on, we are altered from the
temper of bad men, and from the frame of our own
hearts, before we had the honour of admiring the character of Christ. These dispositions of the heart are under the government of our ideas or notions of things.
If we think the world man's chief good, we shall chiefly desire and pursue the world; if on the contrary, we
are convinced, by the instructions of Jesus Christ, that
the world is vanity, that sin is the greatest evil, and God
the chief good of man, we shall desire and love, hope
and fear, and act accordingly. These tempers are necessary to the practice of religion here, and to the enjoyment of God hereafter. Without these, therefore, a
man " cannot enter into the kingdom of God."

By Christian *actions*, I mean such a course of life as
Jesus Christ pursued, which was made up of single actions of piety, justice, and temperance, connected together, and following one another in constant succession. Such a life cannot be described better than it is
by the apostle Paul; " Whatsoever things are true,
whatsoever things are honest, whatsoever things are
just, whatsoever things are pure, whatsoever things are

lovely, whatsoever things are of good report; if there be any virtue, and if there be any praise, think on these things :" for " these things ye have both learned and received, and heard, and seen in me." A man, who knows, and loves, and lives the Gospel, will be saved; he is " born again," and hath on " the wedding garment :" but the man destitute of knowledge, love, and obedience is excluded both by the sentence of Jesus Christ, and by a necessity of condition ; for, were it possible to reverse the sentence, he is not in a condition capable of being made happy by the Gospel, he cannot " enter into the kingdom of God," he cannot " see the kingdom of God."

If any one in this assembly be found at last in such a condition, he will be " speechless." This is the express testimony of Jesus Christ in the text. The man in the parable was not awed into silence by the dreadful appearance of the king, but by reflecting on his own state, and by finding himself inexcusable. " When the King came in to see the guests, he saw there a man, which had not on a wedding garment ; and he said unto him, Friend, how camest thou in hither, not having on a wedding garment ?" You are not properly qualified to be here : whose fault is it ? I allow you liberty to account for your conduct : speak. Is it my fault : are there no habits in my wardrobe ? Is it the fault of my servants ? Have not they and the rest of the guests " wedding garments ?" Is it your fault : is the " wedding ready : are all things ready :" and are you who was bidden not worthy ? "How camest thou in hither ?" Speak. " And he was speechless :" he could make no reply to such reasonable questions. Here lies the agony of a man in trouble : and his anguish would abate, if he could satisfy himself that he was brought into his present condition, not through his own neglect, but by means of others. He would cease to be an object of blame, and would become an object of pity, and the least that his judge could do for him would be to put him out of his misery. How hard must a man be driven to find reasons for sin, when his only hope is, that his destruction will be attributed not to himself, but to God ! What a desperate venture : rather, what a raving madness ! Jesus Christ hath considered and determined the case, and he affirms the lost man will have nothing to say, but will be "speechless:" but the lost man saith, he also hath considered the case, and affirms, in contradiction to Jesus Christ, he shall not be speechless, but shall have to say, that God himself was the author of his destruction. In this case men do not act by conjecture without information; but by obstinacy in direct opposition to it. This is a strange part for a man to act: surely none of you intend to act this part! If you have flattered yourselves into a vain hope of succeeding, I conjure you to stop a few minutes, and examine this hopeless undertaking. Will you "provoke the Lord to jealousy?" Are you "stronger than he?" To a modest man, the declaration of Jesus Christ is sufficient: but, at present, we will lay that aside, and confirm what he says in the text by the determination of three infallible judges: by reason, which attends to the nature and fitness of things: by Scripture, which settles this point on principles of religion: and by experience, both that of others and that of yourselves. All these judges will say to thee, "Sit thou silent, and get thee into darkness; thy nakedness shall be uncovered, yea, thy shame shall be seen."

When man lives and dies in a state of rebellion against God, and when he makes his appearance before him as the judge of the world, will he be able to justify his conduct? This is the question, which we require *reason* to answer. Can such a man establish any facts, from which he can infer the blamelessness of his condition? The question is not, whether he be to blame for being in pain, but for committing sin; for the pain of remorse is nothing but a necessary effect of the commission of sin. The heathens have not the Gospel. Idiots are not to blame for not believing the Gospel, though they hear it; because they have not a natural capacity to understand what they hear. A man, who hath the Gospel, and capacity to understand it, cannot plead either of these facts in favour of his own unbelief, and consequently he can urge nothing to prove the reasonableness of it. On the contrary, if a man have faculties, the highest reason may be given why he should use

26

them: and if he have the Gospel, it is very fit and right that he should employ himself in those just and proper actions, which the Gospel directs. The Gospel requires us to love God supremely, and assigns for a reason, that God is the chief good. It is impossible to deny the fact, that God is the chief good, and therefore it is impossible to deny the inference, that we ought to love him supremely. The same may be said of all the *duties* of religion: they are nothing but inferences drawn from true facts, and if the facts be true, the inferences necessarily follow. It is on this principle that the Christian religion is called a " reasonable service ;" that Christians are required to give " a reason of the hope that is in them ;" and that the wicked are required, in order to their conversion to " come and reason" with the Lord. We conclude then, that reason condemns an impenitent sinner to silence, and that at the last day he will be " speechless ;" and the Scripture shows the inexcusableness of the impenitent on the two grounds just now mentioned; that they have the Gospel, and that they are capable of judging of it. Our Lord mentions the first in these words; " If I had not come, and spoken unto them, they had not had sin : but now they have no cloak for their sin." The apostle Paul mentions the second in these words, " Whosoever thou art that judgest, thou art inexcusable, O man ; for wherein thou judgest another thou condemnest thyself: for thou that judgest doest the same thing." The apostle proves that every man is capable of distinguishing right from wrong, and that every man doth actually make the distinction when he judges another man : and hence he infers, that he hath the same capacity to judge of his own actions, and is inexcusable for not doing so. For these reasons the text says, the unconverted man " was speechless."

Did not daily observation put it out of our power to deny the fact, we could hardly believe that impenitent sinners would presume to urge *Scripture* in their favour. There are, however, three observations to be made concerning Scripture, which condemn such men to silence. First, God expressly declares he is not the author of man's destruction. " Say unto them, as I live,

saith the Lord God, I have no pleasure in the death of
the wicked, but that the wicked turn from his way and
live. Judge, I pray you, betwixt me and my vineyard.
What could have been done more to my vineyard, that
I have not done in it?" In a thousand places the inspired writers speak this language in the name of God,
and, if punishment be the effect of sin, it is impossible
to charge God with our punishment, unless we first
charge him with our sin, which would be abominable.

Observe in the next place, God actually chargeth the
sinner with his own destruction: " Hast thou not procured this unto thyself? O, Israel, thou hast destroyed
thyself." In this manner all the writers of Scripture
express themselves, and all agree to charge home every
man's ruin upon his own conscience.

Observe, lastly, there is not a single article in the
whole Christian religion to countenance the pretence
of laying the blame on God: nothing in the doctrine of
decrees, nothing in the doctrine of man's depravity, nothing in the doctrine of Divine assistance, nothing in
any doctrine to countenance such a plea. Hence, "the
law" is said to speak so "that every mouth may be
stopped, and all the world become guilty before God :"
and hence the Gospel, far from being an apology for
people in this condition, is an aggravation of their crime,
and, by opening a door of hope to men under sentence
of death by the law, must render those inexcusable, who
do not avail themselves of such a provision of mercy.
If the author of the Bible be not very sincere, and very
much in earnest to instruct, convert, and save the souls
of men, he acts a part unworthy of himself, unworthy
of the pity of a friend, and much more so of the majesty
of a God; he irritates a grief, and insults a wretchedness, which he cannot relieve. The Scripture, so far
from excusing an impenitent man, renders all his excuses to the last degree contemptible. If the Bible
were a hard book, he might complain of difficulty; if
the benefits of religion were sold at a high price, he
might complain of poverty; if he had made trial and
could not succeed, he might complain of Providence ;
but if nothing of this can be said, there is no remedy,

and the impenitent, before his Judge, must be "speech-less."

Let us come to *experience*. Of all kinds of knowledge that which is gained by trial and practice is the most certain, and, it should seem, there lies no appeal from our own experiments. We will then examine our subject in the experience of three sorts of sinners. In the first instance we inquire of a true and real penitent. He once lived in sin, as some of you do now. He now lives in the daily exercise of faith and repentance, and he well remembers the whole history of his own life. Had you, good man, when you first discovered your condition, any thing to say in your own defence? In that day when a judgment-seat was erected in your own bosom, when your sin was "set in order before your eyes," when reason, and religion, and conscience would be heard, had you any excuse fit to be urged in your own behalf? On the contrary, wast thou not "confounded," and didst thou not determine "never to open thy mouth any more because of thy shame?" There was no thunder and lightning, no diseases and death, no "heaven and earth fleeing away," no "dead standing before God," no "great white throne," no "books opening," no "lake of fire;" there was nothing but the cool exercise of reason and conscience, and yet you "sat alone and kept silence," and "put your mouth in the dust, if so be there might be hope." And yet you was a young man, in perfect health, with a long life before you to be filled up with good actions: but if you were "speechless," if you could find neither a reason for continuing to sin, nor an apology for having dared to do so, how is it possible that impenitent men should have any thing to say in their own behalf at the day of judgment?

Examine a second class of sinners, who, to use the language of a Prophet, are taken, and are "ashamed as the thief is ashamed when he is found." Hear Pharaoh after all his vain boasting: "Moses, I have sinned. The Lord is righteous, and I and my people are wicked. Intreat him that there be no more thunder, and I will let you go." This a true picture of many a sinner in a storm. In a fine day, " Who is the Lord that I should serve him? I know not the Lord, neither will I obey his voice." In a tempest, when the " everlasting king bringeth forth lightnings, and rain, and wind out of his treasures, the heathen are dismayed at the signs of heaven," and then, " call Moses and Aaron; the Lord is righteous, and we are wicked." What? Is the Lord more righteous, more powerful in a tempest than in a fine day? Is not wickedness as reasonable in a storm as in a calm? Are not thunderings and lightnings guardians and protectors of reason? The sinner, in spite of his pretended ignorance knows they are, and trembles for himself, because he is in an unreasonable state. This is not being speechless: this is worse: this is pronouncing sentence on himself. Observe Belshazzar at a "great feast, drinking wine" with " a thousand of his lords, and his wives, and concubines," and singing profane songs in honour of idolatry and debauchery. A hand writes three words in unknown characters on the wall, and he becomes " speechless." " The king's countenance was changed, and his thoughts troubled him, so that the joints of his loins were loosed, and his knees smote one against another." Observe Judas. He " repented himself," carried back the price of his treachery, said, " I have sinned, in that I have betrayed innocent blood, and departed, and went and hanged himself." There are a few such cases recorded, and they may serve to direct us in regard to other cases not recorded, and whether the consciences of sinners be awakened in this world or not, they serve to convince us, that whenever conscience doth awake, it will perform the same just but dreadful office; so true is that saying, " The wicked shall be silent in darkness, for by strength shall no man prevail." Let us not deceive ourselves: we may escape in this life, but at the last day a voice more terrible than the thunder that roused Pharaoh, recollection more keen than that of Judas, a hand more powerful than that which wrote the sentence of Belshazzar, will publish to every impenitent sinner, " Thou," thou also " art weighed in the balances and art found wanting. Thou hast not humbled thine heart, though thou

.26*

knowest all this : the God in whose hand thy breath is, and whose are all thy ways, hast thou not glorified." If such men as Belshazzar aud Pharaoh be struck dumb, what can he say, who hath lived under the light of the Gospel? Certainly he will be " speechless."

Once more, consult your own experience, if indeed you have ever attended to what passes in your own bosoms. Even men who live in sin, have moments of reflection, and, we may venture to affirm, the language of all such reflections is, " O Lord, righteousness belongeth unto thee, but unto us confusion of face, because we have sinned against thee. Evil is come upon us, yet made we not our prayer before God, that we might turn from our iniquities and understand thy truth." Where is the man, who can stand up and justify a life of sin ? Who would be so rash as to aggravate his offences by attributing wicked actions to righteous principles ? On what dangerous ground must a man go, who endeavours to reason in favour of a judge, who should give the rewards of virtue to a wilful sinner : who should say to an ignorant and wicked wretch, in the last day, in the hearing of the whole world, " Well done," blind blasphemer; well done, " covetous, boasters, proud, fierce, despisers of those that are good ;" well done, " traitors, lovers of pleasure more than lovers of God ;" well done, " wicked and slothful servants," you have borne a noble testimony to truth ; I am " an hard man, I do reap where I sowed not," you " ought" not " to have put my money to the exchangers, enter" you " into the joy of your Lord !" Such a perversion of justice as this might open your mouths; but it would strike all heaven dumb, and every angel and every good man would be " speechless !" There was a proverb among the Jews of great meaning, and it was sometimes used by wicked people : " Had Zimri peace, who slew his master ?" So Jezebel said to Jehu, and Jehu might have properly retorted, Had Jezebel peace, who slew Naboth ? Had Ahab peace, who " did sell himself to work wickedness" as " Jezebel, his wife, stirred him up ?" Hath any man peace in the practice of sin ? Hear a decision once for all. " The wicked man travelleth with pain all his days,

There is no peace, saith my God, to the wicked. The wicked are like the troubled sea, when it cannot rest, whose waters cast up mire and dirt."

Let us not resist the kind intention of Jesus Christ in describing the hopeless condition of an incorrigible sinner at the last day; for he meant, by describing the horror of such a state, to excite us to avoid it. Such is the love of God to us, that he hath addressed the whole Scripture to our senses, and reason, and feelings, in order to engage self-love in the cause of truth and goodness. Let us profit by this dispensation of mercy, and to this purpose, let us simplify the present subject, by so stating it that it may be understood, and by so enforcing it that its motives may be felt now upon the spot without delay.

We affirm, incorrigible sinners will be without excuse at the last day. The last day seems a great way off, and excuses are doubtful; let us therefore fix the excuse, and prove that incorrigible sinners are inexcusable now. When the servants in the Parable said, " Come, for all things are now ready, they all with one consent began to make excuse." We said, such people were inexcusable. Why? What is required of them? Strictly speaking, you are not required to obtain the end, but only to make use of the means. God hath connected the means and the end: the first is our duty, the last comes of course. God requires us to examine the Gospel whether it be worthy of credit: if we examine the Gospel impartially, we believe it: if we believe, we obey: if we obey, obedience is pleasant, and we persevere: if we persevere, we " receive the end of our faith, even the salvation of our souls." The proper language therefore of excuse is, Excuse my not examining the Gospel; excuse my not so much as trying the truth or falsehood of it, and do not tax me with injustice or imprudence for my conduct. We do not think it is in the power of any man to examine fairly the Gospel of Christ, and coolly to affirm, that there is not even a likelihood of its being true. Now if the Gospel be only likely to be true, we are able to prove that we are bound by every tie of justice and prudence to make it the rule of our faith and practice. Yes, if we are not able to prove the truth and goodness of the Gospel beyond all possibility of suspicion and doubt, and if we could only prove that it was very likely to be true; even in this case all rules of prudence would join to render the negligent inexcusable. If it be likely, that I at the last day should be in the "speechless" condition of the man without the "wedding garment," I ought to do every thing in my power to avoid a condition so shameful. The man, who says, the Gospel is not at all probable, hath not examined it, and we defy him to show any tolerable reason why he censures what he hath not examined. We do not say, he will be inexcusable at the last day; we say he is inexcusable now. To convince you of this, let us hear him.

This is the language, " I pray thee have me excused: I have bought a piece of ground: I have bought five yoke of oxen: I have married a wife:" I am engaged in the necessary affairs of life, " and therefore I cannot come." There are two things remarkable in these excuses; the one is, that people of this sort pretend to act on principles, and assign reasons for their conduct: the other is, that the reasons assigned are true facts, but imply a falsehood, by supposing the duties of religion to be inconsistent with the duties of life. Doth religion refuse a liberty of marrying? No: " marriage is honourable in all." Doth religion refuse to allow time for attention to business? No: " Be thou diligent to know the state of thy flocks, and look well to thy herds, for riches are not forever." There are two sorts of employments in life, the first lawful, the last unlawful. There is nothing in religion inconsistent with lawful business; but on the contrary, religion is necessary to the dispatch of it. Surely an industrious, sober, frugal, just, and pious man is better prepared to discharge all the duties of life than a man of opposite character. Religion indeed is inconsistent with unlawful business: but so is reason, common sense, and the good of society. If a man says, " I pray thee have me excused, for I must needs go" and defraud a minor, rob a widow, remove a land-mark, intoxicate one neigh-

bour, slander another, and enrich myself with the spoils
of all; it is not religion that will complain of him; all
the oppressed will " clap their hands at him, hiss him
out of his place," and say, " God forbid that we should
justify you till we die." The most innocent of all employments in the world, husbandry I mean, may become
extremely wicked, and always does so, when it is pursu
ed to the neglect of religion. Husbandmen rise early:
they have therefore a fitter opportunity to pray. Husbandmen leave off business early: they have therefore
much cool evening leisure to devote to religion. Husbandmen have seasons in which they can do no business
in the fields: they have then great opportunities for religious improvement. Husbandmen have but few temptations to dissipation: they have therefore great liberty
to turn their attention to religion. Husbandmen watch
times and seasons, and are perpetually employed in
examining the powers and productions of the earth:
they therefore spend their days in a library of books
written with the finger of God himself; " Man goeth
forth to his work, and to his labour until the evening,"
and a very stupid man must he be, who doth not see
reason to exclaim, " O Lord, how manifold are thy
works! In wisdom hast thou made them all; the earth
is full of thy riches." Let no man say then, I have
" ground" and " oxen, and therefore I cannot come, I
pray thee have me excused:" but let him rather say, I
have " ground" and " oxen," and therefore I can come;
and tillage, and feeding cattle, and all my employments
will render me inexcusable, if I do not love and adore
that God, who saith, " The ox knoweth his owner, and
the ass his master's crib: but I have nourished and
brought up children, and they have rebelled against me."

The man in the text was not one of this sort; he did
enter into a profession of religion, and sat with the
" guests," when " the king came in to see" them; for,
my brethren, there are many unworthy professors of religion, who are not born again, and who therefore have
nothing of religion but the name. Let us examine these
men, and as we have proved that it is a fault, and a man's
own fault entirely, not to profess himself a disciple of

Jesus Christ, so it is entirely the fault of a professor of religion, if he be no more than a professor. Every excuse that can be urged why a disciple in name should not be a disciple in deed, is an aggravation of the offence, because the same reasons, which oblige a man to profess himself a Christian, oblige him to be one. The man in the text may well be "speechless," for what can he say to the question, Friend, for such you profess yourself to be, "how camest thou in hither" without the dispositions of a friend? Let any man in this assembly show a good substantial reason, why he is not a Christian in deed as well as in name. Can any reason be taken from religion itself, the employments of life, the condition of man, the perfections of God, or the state of the church, and the world?

We have said a thousand times, that the Christian *religion* is so easy to be understood, and all the duties of it so free from difficulty, that nothing but an excess of depravity can keep men destitute of it. Examine this question, " What doth the Lord require of thee?" Doth he require thee to suppress thy desire of knowing, forbid thee to examine, and order thee to sink into the ignorance of a beast? Doth he require thee to travel and study, and search to find out a religion proper to glorify him, and to satisfy you? Doth he require " thousands of rams, or ten thousands of rivers of oil," offerings beyond thine ability to procure? Doth he require you to sacrifice the dearest comforts of life, your " first-born for your transgression, the fruit of your body for the sin of your soul?" Nothing of all these. He doth not require thee to find out a religion : " he hath shewed thee" one. He doth not require thee to waste thy property : but to do good with it; " he hath shewed to thee, O man, what is good." He doth not require thee to crucify thine affections, but to gratify them; " What doth the Lord require of thee but to love mercy?" He doth not require thee to rack thine invention first to commit sin, and then to conceal the horror of it; but he requires thee to be useful and happy by " doing justly." He doth not expect thee to flame with the zeal of an angel. or to preach with the powers of an apostle ; " What doth the Lord require of thee but to walk humbly with thy God ?" He doth not expect thee to act without rule, or to believe without proof: but when he condescends to set before you proofs to produce conviction, and laws to regulate all your actions : when his condescension stoops to render those proofs and rules so " plain, that he may run that readeth them ;" what can be said of you, except what a Prophet declares, " Behold, his soul is not upright in him ?"

Would you think it, Christians ? this want of upright-ness, this depraved *condition* of man, becomes in the mouth of the person whom we are reproving, an excuse for his continuance in sin : and yet this very depravity is a strong reason to induce men to flee for succour to religion. What a perverse way of talking is this ! I am ignorant, and therefore I ought not to search the Scriptures to become wise. I am weak, and disinclined to my duty, and therefore I ought not to examine the motives of religion, lest they should compel me to per-form my duty. I am " in danger of hell fire" for living in anger and malice, and therefore, though Jesus Christ hath instructed men how to avoid the flames of future punishment, yet I ought not to follow his directions. I am in a state of guilt, God treats me as a parent would a froward child, and sets before me forgiveness and fa-vour, and therefore I ought to " despise the riches of his goodness," and affect "not to know that the good-ness of God leadeth to repentance." I must die, and if I " believe not" that Jesus is the Messiah, I shall " die in my sins : faith is the gift of God," and God hath said, " If any of you lack wisdom let him ask of God, that giv-eth to all men liberally, and upbraideth not ; and it shall be given him." I cannot ask with such fervour and spirituality as I ought, and therefore I determine not to ask at all. " Faith cometh by hearing :" I will hear, but I will not so hear as to determine me to believe : I ought to hear the sound of the Gospel, but I ought not to attend to the sense and meaning, lest I should receive a conviction that the truths taught are worthy of cred-it. In a word, I ought to profess Christianity as if it were true, and to live as if it were false : I ought (for I am a fallen, depraved creature) to act the part of Judas, saying, " Whomsoever I shall kiss, that same is guilty of death, hold him fast." This is the wayward language of the life of an unconverted professor of the Christian religion. His words are, " I cannot:" but Christ, who knows him better than he knows himself, says, " He will not." If a man had made the trial, but could not succeed, there would be some reason in an excuse taken from depravity : but with what face can a man, who never examines, complain that he cannot understand ?

Is there any thing in the *employments of life* to furnish an excuse for the neglect of religion ? To reduce the question to a narrow compass, suffer me to ask, Is there any employment on the Lord's day that can furnish such an excuse? That day is purposely set apart for religious exercises, and if that one day be properly spent, religion must be understood, and if it be understood on the first day of the week, it will be practised the other six days. I do not say, a man cannot employ himself on that day in exercises inconsistent with religion. Alas! how much business do our sinful passions engage us to do on that day! What idleness! What sauntering about! What insignificant visits! What senseless labours do some men employ themselves in on the Lord's day! Let us however remember, that both religion and law require us to spend the day in the service of God ; and of all men husbandmen are the least excusable if they profane the Lord's day. Custom overcomes law and religion in some towns and cities, and compels many a weary worldling to perpetual drudgery, not excepting even the Lord's day : but in the country, where there are no fairs, no markets, no labours of the field, nothing to interrupt ; how intolerable is the excuse of worldly employments! You may on the Lord's day hear the Gospel ; you may read it and hear it read ; you may converse with one another on the meaning ; you may pray yourselves, and you may join with your fellow Christians in social prayer: what may you not do of this kind without neglecting any one honest employment of life ? There are in the four Gospels only eighty-nine chapters, and were each family to read only two chapters each Lord's day, the whole would be examined in much less than one year, and consequently the excuse, which ignorance takes from business, is to the last degree contemptible. The man who would make this excuse must, in his own opinion, be " speechless."

I said, some men pretend to take excuses for their negligence from the *perfections of God*: but to speak more properly, they take them from the imperfections of God. They ascribe imperfections to him, which are impossible to his nature, and then they reason from these imaginary defects. Hear one of these wicked and slothful servants, who though he had hid his Lord's talent, yet presumed to describe God as if he had spent his life in improving it. " I knew thee, Lord, that thou art a hard man, reaping where thou hast not sowed, and gathered where thou hast not strawed:" that is, I have formed such a notion of God as good men form of the devil, and I have acted accordingly : " I was afraid, and went and hid thy talent in the earth." You see, such a faith, such a practice. Nothing is more common than for men to form gross notions of God, and as surely as they do form them, they act agreeably to their notions. " Thou thoughtest that I was altogether such an one as thyself." And what saith God to such vain thinkers ? " Unto the wicked God saith, What hast thou to do to declare my statutes, or that thou shouldst take my covenant in thy mouth, seeing thou hatest instruction, and casteth my words behind thee ?" Thou idle soul, thou, who didst never in thy life spend one single hour in studying the nature and government of God, dost thou pretend to describe him ? Be " speechless :" thou knowest nothing of this subject. No, there is nothing in any of the perfections of God to furnish an unconverted man with an excuse for his sin. Will he speak of the goodness of God ? But he insults that goodness. Will he speak of his power ? But the power of God is the guardian of a good man, not of a rebel from the demands of justice. Will he speak of the wisdom of God, and tell how able he is to inform the mind, and change the heart in a dying moment ? But what right

27

hath he, who neglects the ordinary means of instruction, to expect extraordinary and unpromised assistance? - What if God, provoked with your conduct,
should say to you, as he said to the obstinate Jews, "Behold, I am against thee!" All my perfections wait
to befriend thee: but all my perfections condemn thy
conduct, and all will be employed to punish thee at last,
if thou continuest incorrigible. Miserable sinner! say,
if thou hast the heart, I would serve God; but he is impatient, and difficult to be pleased. I would seek him;
but he is unjust and unkind, and will not forgive my defects, nor reward my labours. I would serve him: but
he lies in wait to deceive me, and sets his power to resist me. I would love him as my chief good; but his
nature is not enough to render me happy: either he
doth not know how to make the wretched happy, or he
will not give his knowledge effect. Miserable man! Is
it out of thy power to say thus? Art thou obliged to
avow the direct contrary? And how then wilt thou
look the Judge of the world in the face? Ah! thou
wilt be " speechless."

Some are so hard driven for excuses as to take them
from the state of the *church*, and from that of the *world*.
The church, say they, is thin, poor, persecuted, and
some of the members of it fall into sin "seven times,"
and even sin against one another " seventy times seven
times in a day." True, some good men of bad constitution and in strong temptation do trespass against their
brethren many times in a day; but they " turn again"
as many times, " saying, We repent;" from hence you
argue that you, who perpetually sin, but never repent,
ought to be forgiven! Is this fair? True, " the just
man falleth seven times," but he " riseth again," and
" seven times a day praiseth God because of his righteous judgments:" and hence you infer, that you who
lie perpetually in wickedness ought to be applauded for
doing so. How is it, that while you observe the failings of good men, you are blind to their excellencies,
and to the greater excellencies of others who have not
their failings? Is it the failings of these men that you
disapprove? I fear you rejoice in their faults, and dis-

like their virtues. What if the church be thin, and poor, and persecuted, is it the less respectable on these accounts? Is it not the more so? These are the faithful souls, who realize what Peter promised, and each saith to Jesus Christ, "Although all shall be offended, yet will not I. If I should die with thee, I will not deny thee in any wise." These Christians ought to strike thee dumb; they have put it out of thy power to say, religion is impracticable. On your principles Christ and only twelve apostles, and they all in an upper room persecuted, "as when one doth hunt a partridge in the mountains," would have furnished you with an excuse as much more plausible as twelve are less than twelve hundred thousand. Your eyes, I perceive, are in the world, and thence you fetch excuses; but, as there would be no end of following such vain pretences, so we venture to say once for all, that if the whole world were up in arms against God, you ought, like Noah, to attend to the just and merciful voice, that saith, "The end of all flesh is come, behold the earth is filled with violence, I will destroy them; but come thou, and all thy house, into the ark." Who but a madman would perish for the sake of company!

After all, what are excuses of this kind good for? What end do they answer except that of colouring a black and desperate cause, a cause of rebellion against God, and wickedness, and wretchedness, and high treason against ourselves? Is there any thing in stupidity and sin worth all this, and can any thing be supposed so horrible, as that man should rack his invention to sink himself into the condition of a brute? How flimsy will all these excuses appear when sickness and death come? True, such a man will not be troubled with our exhortations then: but his conscience, his own conscience will accuse him; "he shall flee from the iron weapon, but the bow of steel shall strike him through. The heavens shall reveal his iniquity, and the earth shall rise up against him." For my part, I have consulted my pity, and if it were possible for me to frame an excuse, and to affirm, that man ought to be allowed to live in sin, I would not conceal it. Why should we conceal any thing that is just and right? but if any thing be unjust, why should we not expose it? No, we can find no excuse, and we declare, in the face of heaven and earth, that as the salvation of the righteous is all of the Lord, so the destruction of the wicked is all of themselves; and an unconverted professor of religion is inexcusable now for living in sin, will be inexcusable when he dies for dying in sin, and when the Judge shall require an account of his conduct at the last day, will be inexcusable and "speechless."

I finish with two reflections. First, let our text be an apology, if any apology be necessary, for the ministry, which your teachers exercise among you. They believe Jesus Christ, see the day a coming, dread the consequence to you, and endeavour to save you, "with fear pulling you out of the fire." Happy, happy in the highest degree, should God succeed our labours! Let the text also reconcile Christians to all they meet with here. What are afflictions, what are persecutions, what are the most severe trials in comparison with the shame and disgrace foretold in the text? Now the Christian may be, on many fashionable subjects, "as a dumb man that openeth not his mouth," and in whose lips there is no swearing, no slander, no falsehood, "no guile:" but in that day he will not be "speechless," he will be without fault before the throne of God, and will "cry with a loud voice, Salvation to our God, and unto the Lamb forever and ever. Amen." God grant you all this grace. To him be honour and glory forever. Amen.

DISCOURSE XVI.

[*AT WICKHAM.*]

———

1 CORINTHIANS xiv. 31.

Ye may all prophesy one by one, that all may learn, and all be comforted.

MUCH as I admire the modest soul that uttered these words, and greatly as I think they contribute to public edification, I confess freely to you, I should have had no heart to speak on the subject to night, had I not recollected a passage of Scripture, which I shall mention presently: for what am I about? I am going to try to convince you, that any person, who understands the Christian religion, may teach it. I say, I should have had no heart to teach this, for what a difference is there between us and the church at Corinth, to whom the text is addressed! " Jesus Christ had enriched them in all knowledge, and in all utterance, so that they came behind in no gift." When they assembled for the worship of God, one had " a psalm," another " a doctrine," a third " a tongue," a fourth " a revelation," a fifth " an interpretation," so that an ignorant unbeliever, if he came into the assembly, would be informed, and convinced, and would be obliged to " report, that God was in them of a truth." This was not peculiar to the church at Corinth, for these gifts were not bestowed with a niggardly hand, but in rich abundance on all the churches, and the vain

27*

boast of the king of Assyria was a sober truth in the mouth of Jesus Christ, "Are not my princes altogether kings?" Happy for mankind, these eminent men were saints, and their mighty powers were not dangerous instruments of mischief, not causes of "confusion, but of peace in all the churches."

How different are Christian churches now! The primitive Christians understood religion in all its parts; but we have forgotten some, added others, and perplexed all. They understood each part in all its extent; but we seldom trace a truth backward to its spring, or forward to its outfall. They knew what to say, and where to stop; but we rashly decide what they durst not determine, and have nothing to say on their chief subjects. Far from bringing a psalm or a doctrine to increase the stock, we can hardly carry them home in our memories when they are given us. We go to Christian assemblies, not like bees to their own hives, each to contribute a little to the general store; but like bees burnt out of their own hives to carry away the labours of others. In this, too general a case, who can wonder we should be slow to teach the doctrine of the text?

However, we are emboldened to teach this branch of Christian doctrine, not only from a consideration of its general usefulness, but from a declaration of God himself to Moses : " I appeared unto Abraham, unto Isaac, and unto Jacob, by the name of God Almighty, but by my name Jehovah, was I not known to them." Hence I infer, that religious knowledge is in different degrees in different men, who yet are all excellent in their kind. Jehovah was a name, which God condescended to take (for all names are beneath his dignity), to convey to Moses proper ideas of such perfections as he was about to display to suit the circumstances of the poor enslaved Israelites; and this name conveyed more knowledge of God than the Patriarchs had been favoured with, as their circumstances had not required so much information. Jehovah was a great name; but Jesus Christ taught us God under a much greater, by directing us to call him Our Father, abating nothing of the majesty of Jehovah, while he united with it the mildness of a parent. In the absence of Christ, who would not give Moses a hearing? In the absence of Moses, who would not think himself honoured to sit at the feet of Abraham? " The least apostle is greater than John the Baptist," but in the absence of the least of the apostles, who would not, " for a season, rejoice" in that " burning and shining light," John the Baptist? The Corinthians, and their extraordinary gifts have failed: but " charity never faileth; charity that covereth a multitude" of faults, " charity abideth;" and as long as this excellent dispositiou, which " suffereth long, and is kind," which " envieth not, and vaunteth not itself," which " doth not behave itself unseemly," and " seeketh not its own," which " is not easily provoked," and " thinketh no evil," which " rejoiceth not in iniquity but in the truth," which " beareth all things, believeth all things, hopeth all things, endureth all things :" as long as this gentle and generous love abideth, so long may we say, " Ye may all prophesy," that is, teach, " one by one, that all may learn, and all may be comforted."

To assist you in this excellent work, I will endeavour to show you how to understand religion . . . and how to teach it to others . . . and we will close by proving your right to do both. When God, in a vision, said in the hearing of Isaiah, and in the presence of a circle of glorious seraphims, " Whom shall I send, and who will go for us ?" the Prophet, though he thought himself, as well he might in such company, " a man of unclean lips," could not suppress the feelings of his honest heart, but said, " Here am I, send me." Happy if Christians had such a modest zeal! Happy the heart that says, Let me have the honour of pulling at least one soul " out of the fire." Do you know what God saith to such a man? He ordered an apostle to " let him know, that he, who converteth any sinner from the error of his way, shall save his soul from death, and shall hide a multitude of sins."

Among a thousand reasons to enforce the doctrine of the text, there is one, which always strikes me very forcibly. We complain of the general ignorance of Christians; they do not understand their own religion.

Why? They do not think it a duty to understand any other parts than those which immediately concern themselves: the rest they leave to their teachers, and except it be here and there an elect soul, most Christians believe a whole, understand only a part, and satisfy themselves with a persuasion that their teachers understand the rest. Take a youth of this kind out of one of our families, inform him that he is to teach religion, and directly he applies himself to understand it wholly. The same effect would follow any man's persuasion, that it was his duty to teach; for he would be instantly persuaded that it was his duty first to understand it himself. This therefore is " a doctrine according to godliness," and one chief recommendation of it is, that it strengthens every man's obligation to knowledge and virtue. God forbid we should sacrifice the virtue of all the brethren to the consequence of one! •

I said, any person, who understands religion, may teach it: the first duty therefore is to understand it, and in order to this I shall give you four exhortations founded on four first principles of religion.

I exhort you first to *search the Scriptures;* on this ground, the Scriptures contain the whole of revealed religion. The Old Testament contains the religion of the Jews, a great part of which is incorporated into the New Testament, which contains the whole religion of Christians. Strictly speaking, the four Gospels contain the pure religion of Christians, and the Acts of the Apostles, and the Epistles are comments, or annotations on the Gospels: the Revelation is a prophecy, in which many moral sentences are mixed. Our Lord considers the Old Testament as introductory to the New in these words, " The Law and the Prophets were until John: since that time the kingdom of God is preached." That the Acts and the Epistles are comments on the Gospels, you may easily convince yourselves. To give you only one example. In the twenty-third of Matthew, the latter end of the twelfth of Mark, and the eleventh of Luke, our Lord exhorts his disciples to beware of Scribes, Pharisees, and the " grievous burdens" of Jewish ceremonies, with which they loaded down religion.;

and he charged them neither to become masters over
the consciences of men, nor to suffer other men to rule
theirs, for, saith he, you have " one Father in heaven,
and one Master, even Christ." The fifteenth of Acts is
a history of an attempt made " to put" the Jewish " yoke
upon the neck of the disciples ;" and the Epistle to the
Galatians is a comment on the doctrine, and finisheth
with these remarkable words; " From henceforth let
no man trouble me ; for I bear in my body the marks of
the Lord Jesus." It was a custom, both with Jews and
Gentiles, to mark their servants : " his master shall bore
his ear through with an awl, and he shall serve him
forever." I am a servant of Christ, as if the Apostle
had said, and enter thoroughly into his doctrine, as I advise you to do, and neither to be slaves to your forefathers, nor tyrants to your successors. " One is my
Master, even Christ." Lay it down therefore as a sol-
id ground of action, that the Scriptures contain the
whole of religion, and every thing necessary to the faith
and practice of a good man, and though each of you
would be justified in receiving the Scriptures so, if you
were singular, and no other person in the world received them so, yet you may be emboldened by recollecting, that the whole Protestant world join with you in
maintaining this truth. There was a man " greatly beloved," who was " shewn things noted in the Scripture
of truth," when there was " none that held with" the
teacher of " these things, but Michael their prince."
The example of " an archangel" was more than that of
the whole empire of Babylon, and the prophet Daniel
was justified in following such a guide. You are not in
this condition ; and should you say, " I, even I only am
left," the answer of God would be, I have reserved to
myself " seven thousand men, who have not bowed the
knee to Baal."

Our second word of advice is, *read* the Scriptures
as they were written, for they were not written as they
are now printed. The writers wrote " by inspiration
of God," as it was more necessary that they should be
inspired to write the Gospel than to preach it ; because
after preaching they were alive to explain themselves,

but there lies no appeal from their writings. The proper way of reading the Gospels is to take what all the
four Evangelists say on any one subject, and to put the
whole together. The four Evangelists stand before us
exactly in the light of four witnesses in a court. The
first comes in, and relates what he knows of the fact;
the second does the same, and so do the other two.
Now on summing up the evidence, two things will give
weight to the witnesses, and both will establish the truth
of the facts. The witnesses all agree in attesting the
same facts, and so confirm the truth of the facts. The
witnesses all differ in some circumstances of these facts,
in the times, places, and order of relating them; and
this difference which hath not the shadow of a contradiction, clearly proves that the witnesses had not consulted together to make up a false tale to impose on
mankind.

I said, the Scriptures are not printed as they were
written. In the times of the Apostles, what we call
stops were in use in the schools, and were made use of
by masters to teach young gentlemen, not the sense so
much as the sound of words; and the Scriptures, which
were not intended for school books, were not marked in
this manner, but were written right on, and the best and
only rule of determining the proper place of a stop, a
pause, or a division of any part of the Scriptures, is to
follow the direction of common sense, as you do in reading a letter, which you sit down to make out, and get
into the meaning of. Schoolmasters have carried this
art of easing hard things to their scholars so far, that
some parents complain that they have made learning too
easy, and the young gentlemen have acquired the sound
of every thing, and the sense of nothing. In like manner, gentlemen by dividing the Scriptures into chapters
and verses, and by stopping words in order to make the
book easy, have rendered attention seemingly so unnecessary, that the book is the most read, and the least
understood of any book. We love ease; but we should
remember the ease of ignorance is only an easy death.
When you read the Scriptures then, read right on, never look at stops; your sense will stop where the story

ends, and I hope you will not leave off in the middle of
what you desire thoroughly to understand. It is a high
honour that God doth us ; he placeth each of us in the
condition of a "judge betwixt him and his vineyard."
We pretend to hold court. In the presence of men and
angels he sends his " witnesses, a spectacle unto the
world, to angels, and to men." And what do we? do we
sit and hear the whole patiently, suspend our judgments, and at length make up our minds? Alas ! as
they " reason of righteousness, temperance, and judgment to come," we adjourn the court, " Go thy way for
this time, when I have a convenient season, I will call
for thee." So we " shew the Jews a pleasure ;" but
" leave Paul bound." After a life spent in such trifling,
we go into our places of worship, and say to every
teacher of Christianity, " How long dost thou make us
to doubt?" If Jesus " be the Christ, tell us plainly."

Turn down, now you are here, and examine when
you go home, these two or three passages. The last
verse of the nineteenth of Matthew belongs to the twen-
tieth chapter. The last verse of the twenty-first of
Acts belongs to the twenty-second chapter. The first
of the seventh chapter of the second Epistle to the Corinthians belongs to the chapter before. The same may
be said of a great number of chapters and verses. In
regard to stops, take two examples: the apostle Paul
says, " Being justified by faith we have peace with
God." Some put the stop at the word *faith*, and say,
men are forgiven their sins on believing the Gospel, for
the Scripture saith, we are "justified by faith." Others put the stop at the word *justified*, and say, we are
forgiven our sins on account of the righteousness of
Christ, and thus being justified, " by faith we have
peace with God." So again in this passage of Jesus
Christ to the thief on the cross. " I say unto thee to
day shalt thou be with me in paradise." One puts the
stop at *thee*, and says, the thief went with Christ that day
to heaven, for it is written, " To day shalt thou be in
paradise." Another says, the thief did not go to heaven that day, and Jesus Christ only told him, " I say
unto thee to-day, thou shalt be with me," that is,

some time hence thou shalt be with me " in paradise."
I think the former the true sense. You will say, all
this requires attention, thought, and a diligent exercise.
True, and for this reason I urge the practice. You may
indeed, by such means, entertain very different ideas of
the same Scriptures ; but as there is no state so dangerous as that of dead ignorance, and no heresy like that
of imposing unexamined senses of Scripture on the consciences of tame believers, so while you retain the charity that " hopeth all things," you may, and ought to examine the Scriptures for yourselves.

Our third word of advice is, as you read, *dare to think
for yourselves.* Read the Scriptures with a generous
love of truth, and always believe yourselves as free to
think and judge for yourselves, as any other creatures
in the world are. Suppose this assembly, having never
seen a New Testament, were assembled to day by the
express command of God, to receive every person one
from the hands of Jesus Christ himself; and suppose
him to come into the congregation, followed by the
Evangelists, and the Apostles, with the books to deliver; and suppose him to say to each of us when we accepted the present, " Search the Scriptures, for in them
you think you have eternal life, and they are they
which testify of me." Is it imaginable, that at the next
meeting, or at any future time, one of us would have a
right to say to another, You, countrymen, search the
Scriptures ! You ought not to think about the Scriptures ; at least you ought to think of them as I do ; or if
that be impossible, you ought to say you do ; or if you
refuse that, you ought to be silent and say nothing ; and
if you persist in pretending to have as much right to
search, and think, and speak, as I have, you ought to be
driven out of the assembly. I will not set fire to you,
for I hate persecution ; but I will render your situation
so unhappy that you shall be obliged to remove yourself. To remove out of a Christian church for peace !
For the sake of peace to quit the territories of the
" Prince of peace," inhabited by the " sons of peace ;"
what a project, what a mad project is this ! And where
are people to go in search of peace, when it is not to

be found in a Christian church? For your parts, my brethren, your folly and guilt must be great, if you do not enter thoroughly into this part of our subject, for you have not even the plea of a temptation to excuse your negligence ; and so far from having " many masters," you have not one " Diotrephes, who loveth to have pre-eminence among you." Should such a savage ever rise up among you, say of him, " This is a deceiver, and an antichrist." Keep thinking as free as breathing, and, if any church be a prison, filled with foul and infectious air, let self-preservation induce you to avoid it. Who can enough deplore the misery of such Christians as choose to live and die in shackles, rather than assert "the liberty wherewith Christ hath made them free !"

Our last word of advice is, *Reduce as much Christianity as you know to practice.* Remember the saying of Jesus Christ, " If any man will do his will, he shall know of the doctrine, whether it be of God, or whether I speak of myself." For example, you know it is the duty of a Christian to pray. Exercise yourselves in prayer then. It is the duty of a Christian parent to teach his children. Instruct your children then ; and so of the rest. As you practise religion, you will make an experiment of the ease and pleasure of religious practice ; and consequently you will grow more and more into a persuasion that the knowledge of God is the chief good of man. Practise the duties of religion freely and openly, and ever look an enemy in the face. I recollect an example in the Old Testament. In the time of the Judges, the Midianites and the Amalekites used to come at harvest-time, " as grasshoppers for multitude," and carry away cattle and corn, so that the Israelites had no sustenance left, and, not aware of their own strength, they hid themselves in dens and caves. Gideon raised an army of thirty-two thousand men to rid the country of these bold robbers. The Lord, to convince this people that he was a patron of freedom, and that they, acting properly, had nothing to fear, reduced the army to three hundred. These were furnished with trumpets, pitchers, and lamps, and with the clatter of breaking the pitchers, with holding up the lights, with blowing the trumpets, and shouting, " The sword of the Lord, and of Gideon," they frighted this innumerable multitude away like a flock of fowls. A great lesson ; for tyrants are not unfrequently cowards, and Israel must blush that they had not acquired a victory so cheap before. To them, and to all other men acting properly in the fear of God, it may be truly said, " One of you shall chase a thousand, for the Lord is he that fighteth for you." Let no Christian be ashamed of any part of his holy profession ; let him reduce every command of God to practice, both such as are in the good graces of the world, and such as are out of fashion, and therefore contemptible. To sum up this matter, we advise all Christians to read the Scriptures, to read them so as to understand them, to expound them to themselves by their own good sense, and by a diligent course of holy obedience.

On supposition you understand religion yourselves, we proceed to show you " how to teach it to others." We suppose first the welfare of your children to lie nearest your heart. In vain you provide the comforts of life, and a settlement in the world for them, without training them up in the principles of religion. It is like loading a boat with valuable commodities, and sending it down a stream into the ocean, without any animal except a jackdaw aboard. These principles ought to be imparted in a manner suited to their own dignity, to yours, and to that of your children. All truths have a worth : but the truths of religion are the first in value, and ought to be the first in rank. Such subjects as the Scripture calls " milk for babes" are not mean ; for there is nothing mean in religion, but of the same kind with others called " strong meat." The *skill* of a teacher is seen in the choice of such plain and easy parts of religion as are proper to inform tender minds, and they sit easy on such minds when they are admitted freely to place themselves in the understanding. Let not the understanding be degraded into the seat of a beggar, a mere bench by the road side to hold whatever is put upon it: but train it up to know its own dignity, to refuse to admit what doth not appear to be true, and to preserve its rank as a seat of truth, a throne of God. Preserve also your own dignity as a parent. The father of a family is not a keeper of a prison to subdue by blows and hard fare : but he is like himself when he resembles a wise and placid patriarch. The Jewish schools were formed on this plan, and Paul, who was brought up " at the feet of Gamaliel," was " taught according to the perfect manner of the law of the fathers." Our Lord, when a youth, was " sitting" in such a school " in the midst of the doctors, both hearing them and asking them questions." No sullen orders, no hard, stern commands, accompanied with threatnings, not to understand, but to get by heart what cannot be understood, and what therefore the pain of learning prepares the heart to abhor. Man is a noble creature, and a little man in arms is a little " image of God." Providence gives us, children, each with this charge, " Take this child and nurse it for me :" take care of its health, cherish its understanding, form its manners, prepare it to be a citizen of " the heavenly Jerusalem," a companion " of angels, and of the spirits of just men made perfect." Far be it from you to spend life in contending for mastery with them, in subduing a free-born soul into the servile temper of a slave, in applying the discipline of a mere animal to a creature endued with reason and sense, in bringing forward sorrow before the calamities of life oblige them to suffer and to mourn, in neglecting to cultivate a soil so very improveable : far from your habitations be all such methods of mismanaging children.

There are two general ways of teaching children the truths of religion. Some make use of catechisms, which children are made to get by heart. This is an exercise of the memory, but not of the understanding, and therefore nothing is more common than to find children, who can repeat a whole catechism, without knowing any thing more than how to repeat it. The hardest catechisms are certainly the worst ; but the most plain are nothing but an exercise of memory. The chief recommendation of them is, they save a parent a great deal of trouble : but does not the death of a child save you a

great deal more? Yet who would part with her child
on that ground? The other method is by hearing them
read some little histories of Scripture, and by asking
them questions to set them a thinking and judging for
themselves. This is an exercise of the understanding,
and when the understanding is taught its own use, it is
set a going true, and if it gets no future damage, it will
go true through life. In order to instruct our children,
we should inform ourselves; otherwise they may put us
to the blush, and on this principle Joshua enforced religious knowledge among the Jews, "that," saith he,
"when your children ask their fathers in time to come,
saying, What mean you by these stones? Then ye shall
answer them, The waters of Jordan were cut off," and
so on.

You should teach religion by *conversation*. There is
an holy art of conversing on the subjects of religion,
and the first in this, as well as in every other excellence,
was Jesus Christ. "Master," said one of his disciples
as he went out of the temple, "see what manner of
stones, and what buildings are here." Hence Jesus
took occasion to speak of the destruction of the temple,
the accomplishment of the prophecy of Daniel, the end
of the world, and the nature and necessity of watchful-
ness. When the tax-gatherers came to Peter, and said,
"Doth your master pay tribute?" Jesus replied, " Yes,"
and went into the house; and hence he took occasion to
show the injustice of the Romans for taxing strangers,
and sparing their own citizens: we are taxed, and they
are free; however, "lest we should offend them, go"
and exercise your own trade, and I will prosper your
industry, and "give unto them a piece of money for me
and thee." When some told him the news, that Pilate
had killed some Galileans, and "mingled their blood
with their sacrifices," he took occasion to dissuade them
from rash judging, and taught them the necessity of living in habits of repentance, and in a most familiar manner confirmed this by telling them a sad event that lately
fell out at the tower of Siloam. We call this the art of
conversing like a Christian, when without any force,
without any rudeness and impertinence, people take oc-

casion in a natural, easy manner, to give conversation an edifying turn. The lips of some men are "sweeter than honey and the honey-comb, pleasant to the soul, and health to the bones." We could sit all the live-long day to hear such conversation, and like the disciples, we. should say one to another, "Did not our heart burn within us while they talked with us, and while they opened to us the Scriptures?" A fund of religious knowledge is necessary to this method of teaching Christianity, for it is "the heart of the wise," that "teacheth his mouth, and addeth even learning to his lips. Understanding is a well-spring of life unto him that hath it : but the instruction of fools is nothing but folly." What a number of motives enforce this duty! If any Christian among you aspires to possess the. hearts of his fellow Christians, and to form an eternal friendship, cemented by a necessity of love, let him try to excel in this heavenly art. Behold the picture of such a man : "When I went through the city, and prepared my seat, the young and the aged arose and stood up, princes refrained talking, nobles held their peace. When the ear heard me, then it blessed me, and when the eye saw me, it gave witness to me : the blessing of him that was ready to perish came upon me, and I caused the widow's heart to sing for joy." To live thus amidst the convictions and affections of wise aad good people, is like living in an eastern spice grove : and what is the price, what the qualification for all this? "I was as eyes to the blind, and feet to the lame ; I was a father to the poor, and the cause which I knew not, I searched out ;" and therefore, "when my speech dropped upon them, they waited for me as for the rain ; I sat as the comforter of mourners." This is not merely a description of a wise and upright judge, but of every wise and good man, who administers information and relief to people about him.

A third way of teaching religion is by *conference*. We all have leisure time, and it is well spent when it is employed in set conferences on religion. There the doubting man may open all his suspicions, and confirmed Christians will strengthen his belief. There the

28*

fearful may learn to be " valiant for the truth." There
" the liberal" may learn to " devise liberal things."
There " the tongue of the stammerer" may learn to
" speak plainly." There Paul may " withstand Peter
to the face, because he deserves to be blamed."
There " the Gospel" may be " communicated severally
to them of reputation." There, in one word, " ye may
all prophesy one by one, that all may learn, and all
may be comforted." One hour in a week, spent thus,
will contribute much to your edification, provided you
abstain from the disorders, that have often disgraced,
and sometimes destroyed this excellent Christian practice. Time should be kept, order should be preserved,
no idle questions should be asked, freedom of inquiry
should be nourished, immoderate forwardness should be
restrained, practical, experimental, and substantial subjects should be examined, charity with all its gentle
train should be there; " she openeth her mouth with
wisdom, and her tongue is the law of kindness."

Finally, you have a right, if you have ability and opportunity to *teach publicly*. We shall speak of the
right presently: now let us observe ability and opportunity. It is needless to repeat what we have all along
been inculcating, the necessity of *understanding* the
Gospel, before we attempt to teach it: but when it is
understood, there wants only one qualification more, and
that is *courage* to utter what we understand. When a
Christian prays, he should be bold, because God is merciful: but he should be modest, because " God is in heaven," a high and holy being, and " he upon earth," a
sinful and imperfect man. In like manner, in addressing our fellow-creatures, we should be bold, because the
Gospel we teach is true; and we should be modest, because when truths are taught by fallible men, they are
always taught imperfectly. The ability we mean is at
an equal distance from arrogance and slavish fear: it is
what the apostle Paul calls " openness," or great " plainness of speech." This ability, made up of " knowledge
and utterance," hath a certain proportion adapted to
particular places; and that, which is equal to all the
purposes of instruction in a small and obscure congre-

gation, may be very unequal to the edification of a large and better instructed assembly: but as there are various assemblies of Christians in various circumstances, the part of a discreet man is to weigh circumstances and abilities together, and so to give them all their "portion of meat in due season." The apostles were "faithful and wise stewards," equal to all kinds of instruction, in all places, at all times, and therefore them their "Lord made rulers over" all "his household." By opportunity, I mean convenience of place, time, and circumstances; and when we affirm, whoever understands Christianity may teach it, we mean at fit times, in proper places, and in suitable circumstances; for all which there are no certain rules; but "wisdom is profitable to direct. All things are lawful, but all things are not expedient: all things are lawful for me, but I will not be brought under the power of any." All methods of teaching must be enforced by example, and without example all instruction is vain, if not wicked and dangerous.

Let us finish by confirming the *right* of such teachers, as we have been describing, to exercise their abilities to the edification of the church. By right, I mean justice, not power. There is nothing wrong, but it is just and right for Christians, who understand their own religion, to teach it to others; but all Christians are not in a condition to claim this right, and to give their claim validity and effect. This article must be first explained, and then confirmed.

I said a right. To what? To teach, not to domnineer, and play the lord and master with insolence, and without control. Teaching naturally gives a man influence; but the moment his influence becomes a snare to himself, it becomes a misfortune to his brethren, and they will be under the painful necessity of teaching him to make a distinction, which he formerly made, when he was a hearer, but which his vanity hath made him forget now he is teacher. Doth he teach? Very well. Do you disapprove of any thing he says? That is not the sin against the Holy Ghost; but in his eyes it is the unpardonable sin. It is not enough that you hear him, you must believe all he says, and must confound the modest " teacher of good things" with that haughty heathen, called a dictator. The glory of the Psalmist will be your shame, and wo will be to him that saith, " I have more understanding than my teacher." When a church chooses a master over conscience, the members act wickedly; but when they choose a poor master they act weakly; for they, who have been mean enough to set masters over their own consciences, have been, however, wise enough in their generation to choose a pay-master; but where nothing is gained, and every thing hazarded; what but folly in its last stage can tempt Christians to bear a lord over understanding and conscience? Can any thing be so wretched as to engage to think always through life as our teachers think; or, if we judge otherwise, to act against our own conviction for quiet sake? Hear our apostle : " Ye may all prophesy : but the spirits of the prophets are subject to the prophets. Let the prophets speak two or three, and let the other judge. Let the women keep silence in the churches : but let them ask their husbands at home." Let " him that occupieth the room of the unlearned," not " say, Amen," till " he understandeth what thou sayest;" for though " thou givest thanks well, yet he is not edified. What! came the word of God out from you," Corinthians? the Jews have a right to dictate before you. " Came the word of God unto you only ! If any man be ignorant," after al! these cautions, " let him be ignorant;" his ignorance is wilful and incurable.

We said a right. To what? To teach, not to make a fortune. " The workman is worthy of his meat," and it is a law of justice that " they who preach the Gospel, should live of the Gospel." It is easy to determine how the first teachers of Christianity " lived of the Gospel," by the virtues prescribed to them. They were men " not given to wine, not greedy of filthy lucre :" but they kept " house," were " husbands of one wife," had " children," and were " given to hospitality." The apostle Paul, referring to the passage just now mentioned, saith, " So hath the Lord ordained that they who preach the Gospel, should live of the Gospel;" and he urges the reasonableness of the appointment from the law, and the nature of the case, as well as from the express institution of Jesus Christ: "but," adds he, "I have used none of these things." This was one of the things, which he thought "lawful, but," in his circumstances, "not expedient." He was a "single" man, he lived a travelling life, was "in journeying often," and had "no certain dwelling-place;" he lived an abstemious life, "kept under his body," and therefore a little served him; and what was more than all, he had a great and generous soul, and thought himself richly rewarded by making "the Gospel of Christ without charge;" beside he loved liberty, and liberty loves independence. No doubt, he enjoyed himself at Corinth, where he lodged at the house of Aquila, a tent-maker, wrought with his host at the same craft, and "reasoned in the synagogue every Sabbath day." Teaching, therefore, gives a right to support; but circumstances determine the expediency of accepting it. If any man considers teaching as a trade to acquire wealth, he renders his virtue doubtful; and if he exercises this trade with this view in our poor churches, he does no more honour to his understanding than to his heart.

I said a right. To what? To teach, and not merely to talk. To fill up an hour, to kill time, to sound much and say nothing, to use vain repetitions, how easy are these to some men! To teach is to inform, and to impress. To inform the understanding by opening and explaining the Holy Scriptures, and by saying something worth hearing, is one chief branch of instruction. The other is to impress, and set home information upon the heart, that it may abide there, and bring forth the fruit of a holy life. Every emotion of the heart should be pressed into the service of religion; and there is in the Christian religion a great choice of subjects, and of methods of teaching them adapted to fancy and fear, to kindle a sacred, and to quench a profane flame in the heart.

I said a right. To what? To teach, and not to tattle. Teaching the Gospel gives a man no right to interfere in the secular affairs of his brethren. He has nothing to do, as a teacher, with their families, their businesses, and their several employments in life. There cannot be a more mischievous animal in a Christian society, than a retailer of news, and tales, and slander, and solemn saws about the damnable sin of heresy, and the wonderment of an " old wife's fable." Far be it from us to plead the cause of such a man : " Let Baal plead for himself." Were we inclined to establish a right to do such wrongs, we would not introduce such a character under the notion of a teacher of religion, but under that of " a false witness that speaketh lies,". a man " that soweth discord among brethren."

When we say, Whoever understands Christianity hath a right to teach it, we do not say he hath a right to be heard ; for as one man hath a right to teach, so another hath a right to hear, or not to hear, as he thinks proper ; and the first ought not to exercise his right over the last without his consent. Sum up these articles, and they amount to this. Any person, who understands Christianity, may teach it : but his teaching gives him no right to assume the character of a rule over the con- sciences, or property of his brethren, no right to trifle with their precious time, to interfere in their worldly affairs, to oblige any to hear without their consent, or un- der any pretence whatever to introduce disorder and inequality into a family, where " one is the master, even Christ, and all" the rest, without excepting one, all the rest " are brethren," and where the highest en- dowments can make them no more.

Let us not mistake this article ; teachers are not only brethren to one another, they are so to all the rest of the disciples of Christ. They have a right in common with other good men to be called the " salt of the earth," the " lights of the world," and so on : but they have no right to inclose such passages for their own use, and to forbid other Christians to enter ; for this would change the character of teacher into that of engrosser. Much less have they, or any other Christians, a right to deck themselves with titles given to the Apostles, call them- selves ambassadors for Christ, whose persons are to be held sacred, and who say, they " are set for the defence

of the Gospel," and whose decisions are of so much consequence, that "whatsoever they bind on earth shall
be bound in heaven," and "whatsoever they loose
on earth shall be loosed in heaven." Christians have
one Lord, whose "work is honourable and glorious,"
who "sent redemption unto his people," who "commanded his covenant forever; holy and reverend is his
name."

Having explained this right, it remains only that we
confirm it. Should a teacher of Christianity assume a
right to himself, to the exclusion of his brethren, and
should he pretend to teach you, and to justify his claim
by ever so many instruments of paper, parchment, or
steel, it would be a very sufficient, though a very short
answer for every Christian to assign;—you have not received such a right from me, and no other person in
the world could possibly give you such a right over me
but myself.

To be more explicit. The right of Patriarchs to
teach their families hath no place here, except within
the walls of a man's own house: for Christians are
" born not of blood, but of God." The church of Christ
is made up of " one of a city and two of a family: there
indeed " is Benjamin and Judah," but there also are
" Rahab and Babylon, Philistia and Tyre, Ethiopians,
Barbarians, Scythians, bond and free. There is" absolutely " no difference between the Jew and the Greek."
There men say, " How beautiful are the feet of" Jews
or Greeks, barbarians or Scythians, " that preach the
Gospel of peace, and bring glad tidings of good things."

The right of conquerors to dictate to slaves, of generals to harangue their armies, of Demetrius to make
speeches to his fellow-craftsmen, have no place in a
church, the members of which are not united by maxims
of war or trade, being " born not of the will of the flesh
but of God." Every society should be nourished and
cherished by the same maxims by which it was constituted; but the Christian Church was formed on pure
principles of their own conviction and consent.

The right of ruling in civil governments hath no
place in the Christian Church, for the Christian church

is a creature, " not of the will of man, but of God."
Civil states are creatures of reason, and men may form
what government they think proper: but the church of
Christ hath no such licence ; it is a creature of Revelation, and constituted under the express direction of Jesus Christ: it is " not of the will of man, but of God,"
and it is composed of men, to whom " he gave right,
power, and privilege to become the sons of God."

The right of inspired men hath no place here. What
am I saying ? All the powers of working miracles, fore-
telling future events, speaking with divers tongues, none
of all these powers gave their owners an exclusive
claim to teach, for he, who saith, " I thank my God, I
speak with more tongues than you all," yet adds, much
to his honour, " Brethren, be not children in understanding, ye may all prophesy one by one, that all," and I
among the rest, " may learn, and may be comforted."
All the instructions of these men run in the soft style of
beseeching and persuading, and Paul not only reasoned
with Felix, a man of rank, but he reasoned also with
his brethren, and where his reasoning did not succeed
with a plain Christian, he sat down content: " I greatly
desired Apollos to come unto you, but his will was not
at all to come at this time, but he will come when he
shall have convenient time." If men of such extraordinary endowments founded on them no claim to teach,
to the exclusion of their brethren, is it not abominable,
that an ordinary Christian should found such a claim on
the glorious pretence that he can read the history of
the Gospels in two languages, whereas you can read it
but in one ! Tell such a man, that the Gospel is a set
of facts, of which you are as able to judge, as you are
when you execute the office of jurymen in a court of
law, and a cause is tried in your hearing. Tell him,
evidence of the truth of the facts doth not depend on a
frivolous attention to single terms, but on a general
view of the whole put together, and it is indifferent in
what language information is conveyed, if it be conveyed at all. Tell him, a Christian life is nothing but an
effect of believing the great facts reported in the four
Gospels. Tell him, you consider a good teacher as

counsel on the side of truth, and a false teacher as the "orator Tertullus, who informed the governor against Paul;" with this difference, Tertullus accused Paul to his face when he was present to reply, but false teachers bring charges against him, now he is dead, which were never thought of during his life. Assure him, you respect learning, admire oratory, think him a very ingenious man, but, as you neither envy his habit, nor desire his fees, your attention is more taken up with truth than with an elegant and handsome way of telling it; and that this is a truth which meets your conviction and approbation, "You may all prophesy one by one, that all may learn, and all may be comforted."

We have all along taken the word *prophesy* in our text, for teach; and this seems so clear, both in the text and in the whole chapter, that it cannot be doubted. To prophesy in the sense of our apostle, is " to interpret Scripture." Ye may all prophesy, that all may learn: what, may all foretell future events, that all their hearers may learn to foretell future events? No such thing; but you may all interpret Scripture, that all may learn to interpret Scripture, and all be comforted by understanding it. The whole chapter is easy in this light, and it is quite plain that the scope and design of the apostle was to regulate the use of extraordinary gifts so as not to prevent the interpretation of Scripture; "Covet to interpret Scripture, and forbid not to speak with tongues. Let all things be done decently and in order."

The apostle founds the right of all Christians to teach, on three principles. The one is the authority of God: "The things that I write unto you are the commandments of the Lord." Nothing need be added to this: but as we have not always that reverence for the authority of the Lord, which we ought to have, the apostle urges the right of all Christians in our text, and in several other verses: a right to interpret Scripture themselves, and a right to judge of the interpretations of others. In the twelfth chapter (for this subject takes up three chapters of this Epistle), he likens the church to a human body, and shows the honour due to

29

the " less honourable and more feeble" parts ; " by one
spirit are we all baptized into one body, whether we be
Jews or Gentiles, whether we be bond or free, and have
all been made to drink into one spirit." The third reason is taken from the nature of interpreting Scripture,
and its use in the church. He makes a list of gifts bestowed by " one and the self-same spirit." He weighs
each in a just balance, estimates it by its usefulness, and
comes to the conclusion ; " Greater is he that prophesieth than he that speaketh with the tongues, except he
interpret, that the church may receive edifying." All
may interpret Scripture : but do all interpret ? No.
Why not ? It is because some of you are so vain of displaying your gifts of tongues for your own glory, that
you leave no room for others to exercise their ability
in interpreting Scripture for the public edification. One
of you " speaketh in an unknown tongue :" very well,
you " speak mysteries, not unto men, but unto God;"
you " edify yourself," but " no man understandeth you :"
but " he that prophesieth, speaketh unto men to edification, and exhortation, and comfort :" he edifieth the
church. For my part, " I had rather speak five words
to teach others, than ten thousand words in an unknown
tongue. Brethren, be not children in understanding :
howbeit, in malice, be ye children ; but in understanding
be men."

In one word, the primitive church met in public as
we meet in conference, and giving instruction was open
to all. How far it is prudent to revive this primitive
discipline, circumstances only can determine. This,
however, we venture to affirm, that any person, who
understands the whole of religion, may teach the whole,
and that he, who understands only a part, may teach
that part, by a right of original charter from the Lord,
by birthright as a Christian, and by right as a man to
contribute to the edification of the church and the good
of society : and I do think if Christians in general had
the spirit to claim this right, they would have the prudence to prepare for the exercise of it by a diligent
study of the Scriptures themselves; and they would not
consign as they now do the keeping of the whole Gos-

pel, both doctrine and ordinances, to one single man, " whose breath is in his nostrils," and all whose " thoughts perish in that very day" when " his breath goeth forth and he returneth to his earth." The fatal consequences of placing so much confidence in guides have been felt by a great number of Christian church- es. During their lives it is the sound sleep of free in- quiry, and at their deaths it is not unfrequently the dis- solution of a whole assembly. The Lord saith, "Cease from man whose breath is in his nostrils; for wherein is he to be accounted of?" But what do we say? When a teacher dies, we assemble the people, lament the loss, magnify the man, and, to comfort the church, preach from such a text as this, " Elisha died, and the Moabites invaded the land at the coming in of the year:" that is, while Elisha lived your doctrines and ordinances were safe, and if the enemy attacked you, he defended you: but now Elisha is dead, errors will invade the church, and none but a future Elisha can preserve you? What is this but to keep Christians in a perpetual state of infancy? How different is this from the spirit of him who said, " Would to God, that all the Lord's peo- ple were prophets!" How different from the language of one of the " friends of the bridegroom," who free from envy, said, " He must increase, but I must de- crease?" How unlike is this to the voice of him who said, " I bow my knees unto the Father of our Lord Je- sus Christ, that he would grant you to be filled with all the fulness of God!" How far from the spirit of the master of us all, who said, " Forbid not," in answer to John, who told him, " We forbad one," " Forbid not," forbid not one: " for he that is not against us, is for us."

My brethren, what objection can any good man have against seeing poor plain people assemble, and inter- pret Scripture to one another! A great blessing some- times attends it, for Christian knowledge soon shows it- self in practice, and the dress of the seedsman adds no- thing to the strength of the seed. The words of Christ are " spirit and life," and it is delightful to see how freely sometimes a little instruction grows. When our Lord had taught the woman of Samaria that he was the

" Messiah," away she went, leaving her pitcher, to inform the men of her city. They presently came, and
the Lord made this reflection to his disciples. Said he,
It is a usual saying, that there are " four months" between seed-time and harvest, and it is true; but see
what encouragement you have to scatter truth in the
world. I only just now told one woman that I was the
Christ; she hath told others, and many of the Samaritans have heard and believed. Here is seed-time and
harvest together. " Lift up your eyes, and look on the
fields;" see the Samaritans coming to hear me themselves, the fields " are white already to harvest; he
that soweth, and he that reapeth may rejoice together."
Thus is the prophecy fulfilled, " Behold, the days come,
saith the Lord, that the plowman shall overtake the
reaper, and the treader of grapes, him that soweth seed;
and the mountains shall drop sweet wine, and all the
hills shall melt." May God bless these instructions!
To him be honour and glory forever. Amen.

DISCOURSE XVII.

NO MAN MAY PUNISH CHRIST'S ENEMIES BUT HIMSELF.

[*AT LINTON.*]

———

ISAIAH lxiii. 1—6.

*Who is this that cometh from Edom with dyed garments
from Bozrah? this that is glorious in his apparel, travelling in the greatness of his strength? I that speak in
righteousness, mighty to save. Wherefore art thou red
in thine apparel, and thy garments like him that treadeth in the wine-fat? I have trodden the wine-press
alone, and of the people there was none with me: for I
will tread them in mine anger, and trample them in my
fury, and their blood shall be sprinkled upon my garments, and I will stain all my raiment. For the day of
vengeance is in mine heart, and the year of my redeemed
is come. And I looked, and there was none to help;
and I wondered that there was none to uphold: therefore mine own arm brought salvation unto me, and my
fury it upheld me. And I will tread down the people in
mine anger, and make them drunk in my fury, and I
will bring down their strength to the earth.*

ALL the time I have been reading the text, I have
felt the happiness of my situation. How delicious it is
to be a member of a Christian church that well understands the doctrine of religious liberty, where a man
may think what he pleases, and speak what he thinks;
where "the fear of man" that "bringeth a snare" is

29*

neither the law of the teacher, nor of the hearers; where " my liberty of conscience is not judged by another man's conscience." Such a situation renders life delightful, and seems to me preferable to a station of slavery in the court of a prince. There complaisance says to a prince, " Happy are these thy servants !" And in such a court as that of Solomon, civility speaks truth : but it is not in the courts of princes in general, it is in the church of Christ, that true happiness, the happiness of being perfectly free is enjoyed. Where conscience and conference are free, the place is indifferent, accomdations are indifferent, every thing else is indifferent, and the heart of each beholder exclaims, " How goodly are thy tents, O Jacob, and thy tabernacles, O Israel !" Thy " king shall be higher than Agag, and his kingdom shall be exalted. Blessed is he that blesseth thee, and cursed is he that curseth thee."

I speak thus, because I am going to interpret the text, not in the sense usually received, of Christ making atonement for sin ; but in what appears to me the true sense, Christ in the character of a JUDGE punishing the enemies of himself and his church.

That the person spoken of by the prophet is Christ, cannot be doubted, for the prophecy is quoted in the New Testament, and applied to him. " The word of God was clothed in a vesture dipped in blood, and he treadeth the wine-press of the fierceness and wrath of Almighty God." Long after the death of Christ the apostle John applied this prophecy to a future event, and expressly says, in this character " He doth judge." It is of the day of judgment therefore, that we are to understand this prophecy, and to this all the prophecy agrees ; the glorious person is a conqueror, not a sufferer. The blood on his apparel, " staining his raiment," is the blood of enemies, not his own. It is he that " smites the nations," and " tramples them in his fury :" it is not God smiting him. It is like the day of judgment, " the year of his redeemed :" but it differs from the time of his death, which, though it was a day of vengeance to the Jews, was not the day of vengeance to Edomites, and to " all men both free and bond, both

small and great," as this is said to be. He was " alone,
and" there was " none to help :" he will be so at the
day of judgment, for " the Father hath committed all
judgment to the Son." If Jesus Christ is said by the
prophet to " wonder" that " there was none to help"
him, it must be expounded by the circumstances of the
Jews, who, though they were commanded to punish
idolaters, yet often suffered them to escape, of which
we have many instances in Scripture. The prophet
then conveys reproof and instruction to his countrymen
in the prophecy, and did as much as to say, You have
been commanded to destroy idolatry, and to punish idolaters : but you resemble Saul, who for base reasons
spared Agag; you like Ahab let men go, " whom God
appointed to utter destruction ;" you make covenants
with these people, swear by their idols, and incorporate
their superstitions with the worship of a jealous God ;
it might have been expected you would have acted otherwise ; but do not flatter yourselves, neither they nor
you shall go unpunished, " mine own arm shall uphold
me." The apostle John, who wrote after this economy of things was dissolved, takes no notice of this part
of the prophecy : but on the contrary observes, that the
judge was followed by " armies in heaven upon white
horses, clothed in fine linen, white and clean," represented in this manner to denote their innocence ; they
had shed no human blood, they were " white and clean,"
and the judge was the only person whose " vesture
was dipt in blood."

Whatever you think of the text, you will allow the
doctrine which I am going to teach, that is, that no man
may punish Christ's enemies but himself. Confine what
I affirm to the subject of which I speak. By the enemies of Christ I mean mere enemies to Christianity,
who ought not to be persecuted for being so ; for the
" son of man came not to destroy men's lives, but to save
them :" but we do not mean to say that Christian magistrates ought not to punish such as are enemies to the
just civil laws of society. In this case rigour to a few
is mercy to a multitude : but if the consciences of Christians were accountable to the magistrate, the few would

be sacrificed to the ignorance and folly of the multitude, who having no conscience or religion, have no interest in the protection of either.

Let us then address ourselves to this subject, and examine ... who are Christ's enemies ... why we must not punish them ... and on the contrary what directions we have to perform all kind offices to them. " God of peace, our lawgiver, our king, and our judge ! Look upon the city of our solemnities:" let our " eyes see Jerusalem a quiet habitation :" let us " not see a fierce people, a people of deeper speech than we can understand:" let us experience " wisdom and knowledge to be the stability of our times :" grant our " bread to be given us," our " waters to be sure," and our "eyes to behold the king in his beauty !" Amen.

Who are the enemies of Jesus Christ? It is a general law of reason and justice, that great crimes require great proof, because reasons against committing them are so many, that it is supposed few men are capable of committing them. The bulk of mankind work but their own destruction by ordinary sins, rendered familiar by practice, and when men pass the usual bounds of sinning, even they who are no saints exclaim, " There was no such deed done nor seen from the day, that the children of Israel came up out of Egypt unto this day." Inattention, indolence, covetousness, and such like, are common : but enmity against Christ, as it is a great crime, so I am willing to hope it is a rare crime ; and the safest way is to suppose, no man can be so great a sinner, who doth not openly declare himself to be so. An enemy to Christ is an enemy to the pure religion of Christianity ; and though all other sins are inconsistent with the Christian religion, yet are they not direct oppositions against it, and men may be strangers to Christ, who are not, strictly speaking, enemies to him, though perhaps they would be so, did they know him. We do not, therefore, put in the first place the bulk of those, in this country who live in sin. Born in ignorance, misled by the example of their parents, never shown Christianity by their masters or tutors, mixed with a crowd in pursuit of honour, pleasure, or profit, seldom in a place of worship, nor even then hearing the pure religion of Jesus taught; they are " strangers and foreigners, without Christ, having no hope, and without God in the world." All these, to use an expression of an apostle, " are without," and " what have we to do to judge them ? Them that are without God judgeth." What a company, what a horrible company is this, Christians! " Without are dogs, and sorcerers, and whoremongers, and murderers, and idolaters, and whosoever loveth and maketh a lie."

Neither do we call those enemies of Christ, who are open and avowed enemies to some modes, in which Christianity hath been disguised. That the Christian religion hath fallen into the hands of mercenary men, who for worldly purposes have disguised it with error and superstition, every novice will allow. The religion of Jesus hath been debased by both heathen errors, and Jewish ceremonies, which in this case cease to be laudable, and become low superstitions, what an apostle calls " weak and beggarly elements," beneath, far beneath the dignity of such a religion as Jesus Christ taught. These habits of Aaron, and dreams of the heathen school, set forth under the name of Jesus Christ, have been called the Christian religion itself: but these are no more the Christian religion than the " linen," the " napkin" about his head, and the " sweet spices" at the grave of Christ, were Christ himself. Should any be so weak, or so wicked, as to give these to the disciples of Christ, for Christ, and instead of the Scriptures, every disciple would weep, and if asked, " Why weepest thou?" might justly say to an angel, " Because they have taken away my Lord, and I know not where they have laid him." No, such men are not enemies of Christ, they are his friends, our friends, and the friends of all mankind. " Happy shall he be! O daughter of Babylon, happy shall he be, that taketh and dasheth" thine idols " against the stones !""

Far be it from us, too, to call those the enemies of Christ, who doubt, dispute, and even deny what are usually called the great doctrines of Christianity. Did such men deny Christ to be the Messiah ; did they deny

him to be a teacher sent from God; did they deny the
Gospels the honour of being a true history; did they deny the Scriptures to be a perfect rule of faith and practice; did they deny the pure morality exemplified by
Jesus Christ; did they deny a future state of rewards
and punishments; we might exclaim, " This is a deceiver and an Antichrist. Look to yourselves. Bid
him not God speed." But do these men deny any of
these, and are not these the great pillars of the Christian religion? On the contrary, do they not call Christ
" Master and Lord," sacrifice every thing to conscience,
study the Holy Scriptures, and fall in with the train of
those who "follow" Jesus Christ " in the regeneration?" While the son of man saith, " When I sit in the
throne of my glory, you also shall sit upon thrones,"
do we presume to dispute his goodness, and to doom
such to persecution, or to hell? While he opens his
arms wide as the world, and saith, " Every one that
hath forsaken" worldly advantages " for my name's
sake, shall receive an hundred fold; and shall inherit
everlasting life!" do you, rash servant! " murmur
against the good man of the house, saying, Thou hast
made them equal unto us?" O hear his mild answer:
" Friend, I do thee no wrong. I will give unto this
last even as unto thee. Is it not lawful for me to do
what I will with mine own?" O most gentle and merciful Saviour! who can find in his heart to murmur
against thee for such goodness as this! What then, angry Christians! What is the crime of such servants of
your master as these? Do they judge for themselves?
So do you. Do they interpret the Scriptures differently
from you? And do not you interpret the Scriptures differently from them? And is not each of you in the exercise of a right of a man and a Christian, for which he
is accountable to none but his Lord? Discontented servant! Would you have your Saviour " dip his vesture
in the blood" of these men? Ah! Let us learn our
religion better. Let us not turn free inquiry, the glory
of a man into his shame. Rather let us say to every
such person, " Come in, thou blessed of the Lord; wherefore standest thou without?" Let us avoid the injustice

of those, who punish not for crimes in exercise, but in prospect, and which may never be committed, and ought not to be suspected without a cause. Let us despise the cruel policy of Pharaoh, who said, "Israel are mightier than we; come on, let us deal wisely with them: lest they multiply, and it come to pass, that when there falleth out any war, they join our enemies and fight against us:" as if injustice and cruelty made faithful friends.

Truth obliges us to make one distinction more between our enemies and the enemies of Jesus Christ. In this frail state "it must needs be that offences come." It may happen, alas! how often doth it happen that " brother goeth to law with brother, and that before unbelievers!" A case much to be lamented, and the more because such men have ideas of friendship so refined, that " a brother offended is harder to be won than a strong city: and their contentions are like the bars of a castle." A powerful reason why Christians should put up with a thousand slights and indignities, and even injuries, rather than begin an enmity that may never end. How easy to catch this fire, how hard to quench it. Sometimes it is not in the power of all a man's reason and religion; it is not in the power of all his friends; it is not in the power of all the excellencies of the brother he dislikes; it is not in the power of all the examples and commands of Scripture, to root out this horrid antipathy. A man should tremble when such a monster attempts to invade his soul, rack his invention, and destroy his peace: he should do this for his own sake; how much more should he do for the sake of example, and for the sake of his master in heaven? How such a case will be settled at the last day, it is not for me to determine: but the law saith, "If ye forgive not men their trespasses, neither will you Father forgive your trespasses." When the heart is poisoned with enmity, the eye of the mind is damaged, the understanding reasons partially, and the angry man thinks Christ reasons as he does, and expects fire to fall upon his enemy as if he were an enemy of Christ, and both these men think so of each other. Let us judge more soberly. Let us

believe, that men through a thousand unhappy causes
may be enemies to us, and yet not enemies to Jesus
Christ. Let us reason in this case as an apostle hath
taught us in another. " Is he the God of the Jews only? Is he not also of the Gentiles? Yes, of the Gentiles also." Is he the God of James only? Is he not
also of John? Yes, of John also. I repeat it again, Jesus Christ is such an honour to human nature, he deserves so well of mankind, he is so perfectly all we can
wish, he hath so many personal excellencies, and comes
to us with so many strong recommendations, that I am
loath to suspect my fellow-creatures of enmity against
him, and in this case I would never yield without undeniable proof. "·Brightness of the Father's glory! Express image of his person! First born of every creature! King of kings and Lord of lords!" What is
there in thee to disgust mankind! " Blessed is he whosoever shall not be offended in thee !"
    I call him an enemy of Christ, who openly or covert-
ly resists the great end of his coming into the world,
which was to set man free. A friend to slavery is an
enemy, not only to the knowledge and practice of religion, but to the noble principle on which all the
Christian religion is founded ; and to deny this is to
deny the ground of action. The Christian religion is
built on freedom : God " freely by his grace" formed
the plan ; Jesus Christ had power to " lay down his
life," or not to lay it down ; " no man took it from
him," but he laid it down of himself, and said, " Lo,
I come to do thy will, O God :" " he that is called" to be
a Christian " is the Lord's free man :" when Christ ordained the apostles to their office, he said, " Freely you
have received, freely give ;" and since he ascended to
heaven, he commanded all his churches to " say, Come,
and let him that is athirst, come, and whosoever will,
let him take the water of life freely." A foe to freedom therefore is an enemy to Christ, who, amidst a
thousand titles that adorn him, shines in heaven most
gloriously under that of a redeemer, " ten 'thousand
times ten thousand, and thousands of thousands," blessing him for " redeeming them to God by his blood."

Our Lord in his parable of the talents speaks of three sorts of men. The first improve their talents; they are good men and are rewarded. The second hide their talents; they are unprofitable men in the church, and are punished. The third are " citizens," who " hate him," and " send a message after him, saying, We will not have this man to reign over us." When the Lord hath reckoned with his servants, he gives a direction concerning these; " But those mine enemies which would not that I should reign over them, bring hither and slay them before me."

In this unworthy class we put all persecutors, Jews or Christians, who, knowing the Gospel to be a release of slaves, hate it on that account. The doctrine of Christ is calculated to unfetter the mind, the motives of the Gospel to loose the heart from shackles, and the duties of it to free the conduct both from gross sins, and human traditions. Persecutors, who aim at none of these advantages for themselves, refuse others the liberty of enjoying them, and to justify the procedure, send out many a message after the Gospel, the truth of which is, This man shall reign neither over us nor you. The errand of the messenger of a prince is a tale about sedition, that of a priest, concerning heresy; and he who can say nothing else cries, " Ye are idle, ye are idle, therefore ye say, Let us go, and do sacrifice to the Lord;" and every task master can say this. Such is the world in which we live, that numbers have an interest in keeping mankind in bondage. Without this what would become of absolute monarchs, blind guides, and all their wives, families, and dependents? " Dig they cannot, to beg they are ashamed :" too indolent for the first, too proud for the last; necessity obliges them to try to convince mankind that they are necessary to their happiness, and in some parts of the world their success is equal to their wishes. Amidst their glory and triumphs there is one object enough to fill them with remorse ; " the souls of them that were slain for the word of God, and for the testimony which they held;" and one appeal enough, if tyrants can tremble, to make the stoutest quake; these souls " cry with a loud voice,

30

How long, O Lord, holy and true, dost thou not avenge our blood on them that dwell on the earth ?"

In the same-black list we put bigots, men whose blind zeal turns the opinions of a part into a confederacy against the freedom of all, and so makes the Prince of peace the head of a faction. These differ from the former in that they claim the liberty of being Christians for themselves; but they agree with them in denying the same liberty to others. They agree with good men in that they hold religion firm and fast; but they differ from them in refusing others the same attachment to what they count religion. They differ from both persecutors and pious men, in that they resist Christ ignorantly; at least charity makes us hope so, though appearances are much against them. How can they read the New Testament, how can they justify Christ and his apostles, how can they account for their own conduct, how can they be deaf to the cries of the oppressed, how can they avoid hearing the just claims of such as require nothing but their birthright? They say, they cannot see equal and universal liberty to be a right either of reason, conscience, or religion. We give them credit: but " how can these things be ?" Each satisfies himself by saying, It is not I. It was the woman, said our first father. It was the serpent, said the woman. It was all of you, said the Judge. The ground is cursed for your sake.

To these two we add libertines, who are enemies to all the morality of Jesus Christ, and who, knowing the Christian religion to be a holy religion, hate it on that account. Against piety they oppose unbelief and contempt of God. Against universal love they declare a general war, now against the character, then against the property, and then against the peace and well being of society : enemies alike to every thing good; to day against the state, to-morrow against the church, the third day against an individual, and every day against some great law of nature, exemplified by Jesus Christ, and by him enforced on all his disciples. Instead of obeying the Christian laws of temperance, chastity, sobermindedness, and conscience, they live upon sin, drink poison every day, and wonder at fourscore that man must die. All these we have a right to call enemies to Jesus Christ. The guilt of some is greater than that of others; but the least degree of enmity against such a person, and such a religion, is a high degree of turpitude and guilt. The first hate the spirit and doctrine of Christ; the second detest his example; the third resist his laws; and all " abhor judgment, and pervert all equity," and say, " None evil can come upon us." Yes, evil will come upon you: not from us, from us you have nothing to fear: but "who is this that cometh from Edom? This that is glorious in his apparel, travelling in the greatness of his strength?" It is your mighty Judge, who says, " To me belongeth vengeance and recompense; your feet shall slide in due time."

Christians, the prospect of this day, so terrible, and yet so necessary, hath excited in you many fears and tears on your own account, and your charity will cause you to shed many a friendly tear for others, to whom the Prophet saith, "Give glory to the Lord your God, before he cause darkness, and before your feet stumble upon the dark mountains : but if ye will not hear, my soul shall weep in secret places for your pride." This is the disposition of a good man; and, though "the wicked gnasheth upon him with his teeth, yet he seeth that his day is coming," and weeps in secret places for his pride and all its fatal consequences. No, he doth not persecute : he doth not pretend with bigots to have the sole power or privilege of escaping the wrath to come; he doth not, like an abandoned profligate embolden men to sin by his own example; but he weeps in secret places, and when he hath opportunity asks a question, which the whole world can never answer, " Wherefore doth the wicked contemn God?"

Such conduct is founded on justice, and out of many reasons I will select a few to show you why the righteous must not punish the wicked for their enmity against Christ, and by these to confirm you in that peaceable deportment, which doth you so much honour.

First, we have no *authority*. Authority includes two

things, power and law; legal power, power founded on right: now Christians have no such authority; and that may be said to every one, which our Lord said to Pilate, "Thou couldest have no power at all against me, except it were given thee from above." There are only two possible sources of authority in matters of religion: our Lord mentions both in a case not unlike this before us. He was teaching in the temple. A committee of priests and elders waited on him to ask, "By what authority doest thou these things?" Jesus answered this question by another. He knew they had formerly waited on John the Baptist with the same question, and had received a clear, satisfactory answer, and yet persisted in opposing both John and himself. He therefore referred them to that transaction by asking them, "The baptism of John, whence was it, from heaven or of men?" These are the only two sources of authority. In the case before us, if you punish the enemies of Christ, and be asked, by what authority you do this? you cannot say, "Of men," because though persecutors have settled on themselves a right to oppress others, yet they have not given others a right to punish them. There is in fact no such right in being, for it would make an odd compound to give such an answer to an inquirer as this. He asks, The Christian religion, is it from heaven or of men? And persecutors answer, The doctrine is *from heaven*: but the power to enforce it is "of men." No: human authority hath no more to do with the support of Christianity than it had with the revelation of it. It remains then only to inquire whether a persecutor have his authority from heaven. "Call now," see "if there be any" inspired writer "that will answer thee," or "to which of the saints wilt thou turn?" So far from empowering thee, they all hold thee in abhorrence; their dignity, their duty, their inclinations, their examples, their writings all say, "The wrath of man worketh not the righteousness of God. If ye have bitter envying and strife in your hearts, glory not, and lie not against the truth. This wisdom descendeth not from above; but is earthly, sensual, devilish. For where envying and strife is, there is confusion, and every evil work."

As we have no direct authority to persecute, so we have no *prescription*, or rules authorized by custom. Read the Gospels, the Acts of the Apostles, the whole scripture history of preaching the Gospel, planting churches, and regulating the lives of men, and see whether you can find any rules to direct the practice of punishing the enemies of Christ. Had the Scripture said, A heretic of such a description you may laugh at; another of such a kind you may slander; a third of such a sort you may plunder; this order of persons you may banish, and that you may burn to death; these were the constant customs of Jesus Christ and his Apostles: but, on the contrary, should a Moses say, Ye shall " not commit these abominable customs," and should an Apostle say, " We have no such custom, neither the churches of God," as they may well be supposed to say, what could a persecutor reply? The justice of punishment depends on the quantity of it: too little is not enough to express the end of punishing, and too much is more than the crime deserves. How delicate and dangerous is it for frail mortals to pretend to administer justice without direction from above! When the prophet Elisha was dying, the king of Israel paid him a visit, wept over him, called him Father, and said, " The chariot of Israel and the horsemen thereof," flattering the Prophet, that he was the strength and defence of the country. The man of God, to convince the king that he had strength enough to do his duty, if he had a heart to make use of it, directed him to shoot an arrow, and smite upon the ground, in token of attacking the Syrians, who had wasted his country. The king " smote thrice and stayed." Oh, said the man of God, " thou shouldst have smitten five or six times," thou dost but half enter into the spirit of thy duty, thou dost but half love thy country: it is not me, but an entire love of our country, that is " the chariot of Israel and the horsemen thereof;" well, " thou shalt smite Syria but thrice," and some future prince shall have the honour of finishing what thou hast a spirit only to begin. While the Prophet " put his hands upon the king's hands," and said, " Open the window and shoot eastward," the king's heart was enlarged, and his views carried forward to the extent of his duty : but the moment the Prophet left him to himself, he fell short. Happy for us, when we act in all cases under the direction of our Divine Prophet! In the present case, presuming to act without direction, we shall give little punishment to whom much, and much to whom little is due.

Christians do not persecute, because they know persecution doth no good. To punish before the commission of sin is a perversion of all justice. To punish after it, is wise only when pain is likely to reclaim the offender, or to deter others when the offender himself is become incorrigible, and so bad as to be beyond all means of amendment. No enemy of Christ is in this last condition during the present life. As a king of Judah was in one part of his life an oppressor of his people, and imprisoned his reprovers in a rage : but Asa was recovered from his folly, destroyed idolatry, burnt the idol of his own mother, and reformed the worship of God; and therefore on the whole is said to be " perfect with the Lord all his days." Manasseh was a hardened cruel man, and " before he was humbled," committed many great crimes against God, and even " shed innocent blood very much :" yet " when he was in affliction, he besought the Lord his God, and the Lord heard his supplication." Afflictions from the hand of Providence humble men : but punishments from their fellow-creatures irritate and provoke them. " Behold, happy is the man whom God correcteth :" for if " he maketh sore he bindeth up ;" if " he woundeth, his hands make whole :" but when men oppress and punish one another, they are wicked, and " the tender mercies of the wicked are cruel." Well might David pray, " Let me not fall into the hands of man : let me fall into the hand of the Lord : for his mercies are very great !" As persecution can never proceed on supposition the persecuted are incorrigible, so neither can it be applied as a proper method of reformation. Can persecution inform the judgment; can it change the heart? Let us then dethrone reason, destroy Scripture, divest the Holy Spirit of his office, provide " weapons," not spiritual, but " carnal," and " bring every thought to the obedience of Christ !" If nothing of this can be done, let us renounce this " hidden thing of dishonesty," and let us leave all such practices to the workers of iniquity.

Christians cannot persecute, because they are taught to " love their enemies," to " bless such as curse them," to " do good to those that hate them," and to " pray for all who despitefully use and persecute them." Such is the love of a good man to his master, that he cannot help saying, O Lord, " I count them that hate thee mine enemies." And what saith the Lord in answer to your sincere and consistent love of him ? He saith, Do not hate thine enemies : " it hath been said, hate thine enemy; but I say unto you, love your enemies." Love them, because there is something lovely in the worst: love them, because your heavenly Father sets you an example: love them, because I command you : love them, because they may be won by your love to become friends : love them because I loved you, when you was an enemy to me. This, my brethren, is reason and religion; this is the " word behind thee, saying, This is the way, walk ye in it." Let not this word be the less respected by us because it is a " still small voice," and doth not come in wind, and earthquake, and fire, rending the mountains and slivering the rocks! It is man, great man, mighty man, who in the " glory of his high looks," speaks thus, or affects to speak thus as well as he can ; it is he, whose " stout heart saith, I am prudent, I have removed the bound of the people, and have robbed their treasures, and I have put down the inhabitants like a valiant man." It is " Lucifer, the son of the morning, who saith, I will sit upon the mount of the congregation, I will be like the most high." I felt no more plundering a nation, than at spoiling a bird's nest, for " there was none that moved the wing, or opened the mouth, or peeped." This is the language of a tyrant in religion: this is not the style of the just and gentle Jesus : he, the righteous judge, will indemnify the sufferers, and say to the tyrant, " A fire shall consume the glory of both soul and body. Who is this that cometh from Edom, with dyed garments from Bozrah ?"

Finally, the certainty of the day of judgment deters good men from persecuting. The wicked will not go unpunished. No class of bad men will escape. There, tyrants of every age, and of every description, must appear, and answer a question like this, " Whose ox, or whose ass hath he taken ?"   " Whom hath he defrauded ?"   " Whom hath he oppressed ?"   " Of whose hand hath he received any bribe to blind his eyes therewith ?"   Happy, infinitely happy the man, who can say, " The Lord is witness, and his anointed is witness, that you have not found aught in my hand !   I am pure from the blood of all men !"   There, bigots shall appear, and answer for their ignorance, injustice, and partiality.   There, they will be required to answer questions like these : " Why have ye stolen the king away ? Why did you despise us, that our advice should not be had in bringing back our king ?"   Why did you " hate and cast out your brethren" in the name of God, " saying, Let the Lord be glorified ?"   Why did you " forsake the right way, and follow the way of Balaam, who loved the wages of unrighteousness ?"   Why did you do worse than he, and curse whom the Lord hath blessed ?   There, the wicked of all sorts will be collected, and every individual will receive for the deeds done in the body.   The Christian foresees all this, restrains his passions, bears long and is kind, and saith, as David of Saul, when a rash friend said, " Let me smite him, even once, and I will not smite him a second time."   No, said David, " the Lord forbid !   The Lord shall smite him.   Either his day shall come to die, or he shall descend into battle and perish: but mine hand shall not be upon him."   He persecutes me, but " the Lord be judge between him and me."   Sentiments not of policy merely, but of humanity, justice, and religion.

It is not enough not to persecute the enemies of Christ; we are bound by every solemn tie to perform every duty, yea more, every kind office of friendship towards them.   This is not only expressly commanded, " If thine enemy hunger, feed him; if he thirst, give him drink: be not overcome of evil, but overcome evil with good:" I say these duties are not only commanded, and lie in our books to be read; but they live in the examples of all good men in some degree, and of some good men in a very high degree. Of all examples, that of our heavenly Father is the brightest, and ought to have most weight with us. It will be so, if we enter into the spirit of the Christian religion, or feel what the apostle Paul calls the " the love of God shed abroad in our hearts:" a love commended towards us by the very principle we are inculcating. The apostle considers mankind in three classes. In the first he puts *righteous* men, who just perform what the law requires, and asks, Who will die to obtain a right of living for such a man? *Scarcely one;* for the life of such a man is of little use to society. In a second class he puts *good* men, who not only discharge all duties to society, but moreover abound in all kind offices, to which they are not obliged, and which are the generous dictates of their own goodness. Peradventure (it is only peradventure), *some* may know the worth of this man so well, and love society so much, that they would " even dare to die," were it possible by dying in his stead to lengthen a life so valuable. But here is a third class, neither good nor righteous, but *sinners*, enemies. Who will die for them? Who indeed? " But God commendeth his love towards us, in that, while we were yet sinners; when we were enemies, Christ died for us." When the love that did this is " shed abroad in our hearts," we have learnt the doctrine of the text, the conduct of a good man towards the enemies of Christ, which is not only to suspend anger, but to be " full of mercy and good fruits."

Let us not abuse this doctrine by applying it to other things beside religion. The enemies of Christ, subtle enough in their generation, have sometimes gone beyond good men, and have been " wiser than the children of light." They have examined the peaceable principles of our holy religion, and ingeniously turned the doctrines of Christ to purposes of sin. Say they, You are forbidden to persecute, you must not resist us

when we persecute you. You are commanded to be
humble, your religion forbids you to exercise civil offices in a state. You are commanded to do all kind offices to us, and we expect them at your hands : your religion requires you to set your hearts on the world to
come, and the management of this world you should
leave to us. There is here and there an honest sim-
pleton, who admits all this, and calmly suffers himself
to be plundered of all his birthright. A wise Christian
makes a distinction between truth and the application
of it; and when the truths of religion are applied to
purposes of sin, cries *Treason, treason*, high treason
against the majesty of the King of kings, against the security of the Commonwealth, high treason to counter-
feit the great seal of heaven. Suppose a thief should
come in the night, break into your houses, steal your
money, and with the bag in one hand, and the Gospel
in the other, should awake you out of your sleep and
read, Jesus said, " Lay up for yourselves treasures in
heaven, for where your treasure is, there will your
heart be also;" would you calmly turn and compose
yourselves to sleep again, or would you rise and cry,
Stop thief? A very little discernment is sufficient to
convince us that mankind have natural and civil rights,
and that, though it is wrong to punish mere enmity
against the Christian religion, yet it is just to resist, and
proper to punish open acts disturbing society, and the
order of good government. The magistrates of Philippi whipped and imprisoned Paul and Silas for teaching.
Next day they sent to the jailer, saying, " Let those
men go," and he advised them to accept the favour
" and go in peace." No, said Paul, they have acted
illegally, and they shall " come themselves and fetch us
out." The same principles, that obliged us yesterday
to teach the Gospel, bind us to day to maintain the honour of the law, for " the law is made for the lawless
and disobedient." Human law is good or bad as it is
used ; bad if applied to religion and conscience, and
good if a man use it lawfully.

The Christian religion is so far from preparing men
to resign the benefits of society, that it is itself the best

preparation for the enjoyment of them. It inculcates all the virtues of good citizens, and teaches a man both how to rule and how to obey; " how to be full" as well as " how to be hungry ;" " how to abound" as well as " how to be abased; how to do all things through Christ who strengtheneth him." What is there in the offices of life, which religion disables a good man to do ? What is there that religion doth not enable him to do better ? A Christian judge cannot take a bribe. Is justice likely to be perverted on that account ? A Christian cannot perjure himself. Is it necessary to the good of society that an administrator of justice should forswear himself; and is he a proper man to administer oaths to others ? A Christian is not a blasphemer, a drunkard, or an unclean person. But are impurity, blasphemy, and drunkenness necessary to the offices of life ? A Christian is taught by his religion to " flee things which drown men in destruction and perdition, and to follow after righteousness and godliness ;" and therefore his religion doth not send to deprive him of his natural birthrights, but, on the contrary, prepares him to enjoy them all. If the administration of justice and order in the world be got into such channels, that a conscientious Christian cannot follow them, the more the pity. Our religion comes to our aid even in this case, and teaches us " therewith to be content." Mean while it calls us, and all within hearing, to fix our eyes on a future day, and inquire, " Who is this that cometh from" punishing " Edom ?" Is he come to punish, or to reward me ?

" Who is this that cometh to stain his garments with" human " blood ?" Is it any of you, tyrants of ancient history ? Is it Nimrod, Pharoah, Assyrian, " rod of God's anger," or you, Nebuchadnezzar, the " hammer of the whole earth," you proud " axes and saws," and sharp instruments of cruelty, that " magnified yourselves against him that shook you" over a guilty world, in mercy to provoke them to be virtuous and free ; scourges of mankind! Is it any of you ? No, your days had an end; the dead say of each of you, " Art thou also become weak as we ?" And the living say, " Is this the man that made the earth to tremble ? that made the world as a wilderness, and opened not the house of his prisoners?" Men of this kind have often been clothed in vestures dipt in the blood of their fellow-creatures; and for what mighty cause? For a few acres of other men's land: for a vain title: for the " offence of a single word:" for a nothing. What future times may produce, who can tell? To what degree of wretchedness vice may reduce mankind, who can say? No ancient shedder of human blood durst have carried his iniquity so far, had not luxury, debauchery, and poverty gone first to blind the understandings, and to tame mankind, who are naturally wild, savage, and not easily depressed and subdued. In this part of the world let us hope such a day far distant; but let us never forget, that like causes produce the same effects, and that people broke loose may be brought back to bondage by the same methods which brought slavery first into the world. Terrible as a tyrant is, he is not a self-created monster; slaves live first, and become the parents of all such. We should value the Christian religion, were it only considered in the light of a preservative from tyranny: and had we no more Christianity than what the Sermon on the Mount contains, that would be a sufficient preventive. " Do men gather grapes of thorns, or figs of thistles?"

" Who is this that cometh from Edom, with dyed garments from Bozrah, trampling" on men " in his fury," and " sprinkling their blood upon his garments," and saying, " The day of vengeance is in mine heart?" Is it " Jannes or Jambres," who " withstood Moses," hardened Pharaoh, and taught him to persecute the Hebrews for saying " Let us go and serve God?" Is it Zedekiah, who struck a Prophet on the cheek, because he did not say as he said, exclaiming, " Which way went the spirit of the Lord from me to speak unto thee;" he who flattered two kings, a whole court, and a fine army into swift destruction? Is it Caiaphas, who insulted a whole board of privy counsellors, for deliberating on the justice or injustice of an action, and not attending simply to the question of convenience? Is it one of the " grievous wolves" that " arose after the de-

parture" of the Apostles, not sparing the flock? Is it
" Diotrephes, who forbiddeth men to receive the Apostles, and casteth them out of the church?" Is it the
" mother of abominations" that " reigneth over the
kings of the earth, drunken with the blood of the saints,"
and with " the blood of the martyrs of Jesus?" Is it
any oppressor of religion and conscience of ancient or
modern times? All are unjust and cruel: but there
are degrees of injustice and cruelty, and the last are
the worst. They in Egypt sinned against nature and
reason. Those among the Jews sinned against an imperfect revelation: but among Christians oppression
of conscience is a crime of the deepest dye. This
crime came into the Christian church not by princes,
but by their own teachers, who, availing themselves of
the respect in which public instruction was held, step-
ped into the practice, called it an office of authority
and power, altered instruction so as to make God plead
for Baal, like death " put all things under their feet,"
and like death they will be the " last enemies that
shall be destroyed;" they in this world, death at the
resurrection. The love of Christians to their teachers
is just, their zeal for public instruction is right: but it
ceaseth to be " a zeal according to knowledge," when
it goeth so far as to put the judgments and consciences
of Christians into their hands. If such projectors should
" look to you for help, and wonder that there is none to
uphold" a single notion tending to give them the mastery; if on the contrary, they should wonder to see you
suspicious of teachers, and jealous of your liberty; if
they should be astonished that you turn your attention
to such little things; tell them, if you lose a single
doctrine while you are free, you may find it again, but
if you lose your freedom of inquiry, all is lost: tell
them, that if the primitive church had not slept over
these articles, no enemy, however willing, could have
sown tares: tell them you have profited by the mistakes of others: tell them there is no heresy like that
of dominion over conscience, which begins with anger
and ends in a " vesture dipt in human blood."

" Who is this that cometh from Edom, travelling in

31

the greatness of his strength, to tread down the people
in his anger?" This, this is "Alexander the copper-
smith," born in the church, a Christian by prejudice, a
trustee for the house, become rich by trade, and now·
Alexander would be "a lord over God's heritage!"
Poor man! And do you think that a people who have
had the courage to resist the most powerful and dreadful of mankind, who have "gotten the victory over the
beast, and over his image, and over his mark, and over
the number of his name," will ever have the meanness
to submit their consciences to you? Go, and enjoy
your prosperity in the world; but when you enter a
Christian church, a place where "gold," and "silver,"
and "brass" in the "purse," and "two coats," and a
pair of "shoes" are objects of nobody's consideration, at
least salute the house, and let the first word you say, be,
"Peace be to this house." If you say nothing else, at
least prepare to answer this reasonable question, "Comest thou peaceably?" and learn to reply, "Peaceably:
I am come to sacrifice unto the Lord, come with me to
the sacrifice."

God forbid, my brethren, any of us should set ourselves up for defenders of the cause of Christ, except
by reason, argument, and example! Every other method is sinful, contrary to the spirit of our holy religion,
conveying suspicion of its goodness, and offering an insult to its power. It resembles making pillars to hold
up the heavens, and if it does not always imply a depraved heart; it does actually imply a weak, disordered
head. Certainly it is just and right that sin should be
punished; but to do this is a work assigned to Christ,
as a part of his office as judge of the world. Let us
hear how the apostle John, and the whole Scripture
expound the Prophet Isaiah. "Who is he that cometh
from Edom?" It is "the word of God, called faithful
and true." His title is, "King of kings, and Lord of
lords." "Wherefore art thou red in thine apparel, and
thy garments like him that treadeth in the wine vat?"
It is because he is obliged as "judge in righteousness
to make war," and punish nations that rebel against Almighty God. Wherefore is "blood sprinkled upon

thy garments?" It is because the day of judgment will not, like other calamities, spend its force on herbage and cattle, and spare guilty man, but come home to his own person, " touch his bone and his flesh," and " hunt for the precious life." Wherefore is the " day of vengeance in thine heart?" It is because justice and virtue require it: because the wicked are past all amendment, and the righteous ought to be indemnified. " Wherefore art thou alone?" It is because I alone am equal to the task; I only have wisdom, integrity, and firmness enough to execute a work so great. Wherefore " of the people" are " there none with thee?" The people are not with me in office : but they are with me by their approbation of Divine justice, and " armies follow upon white horses." Wherefore is this day described by similitudes taken from worldly conquerors with fury in their hearts, and " blood upon their garments?" Because you are children in understanding, and have always accustomed yourselves to tremble at and avoid such calamities as these.

Methinks, Christians, I hear the Prophet say all this, and add in the language of another Prophet, " Thus will I do unto thee, and because I will do this unto thee, prepare to meet thy God." Yes, the day will come, the prophecy must be fulfilled, " heaven and earth shall pass away, but one jot or one tittle of the law and the prophets shall in no wise pass till all be fulfilled. Then every eye shall see him, and they also who pierced him, and all kindreds of the earth shall wail because of him." God grant you may all be prepared to " meet him in the air, and so be forever with the Lord!" To him be honour and glory forever. Amen.

MORNING EXERCISES.

31*

EXERCISE I.

PSALM V. 3.

My voice shalt thou hear in the morning, O Lord. In the morning will I direct my prayer unto thee, and will look up.

EARLY rising is a habit so easily acquired, so necessary to the despatch of country business, so advantageous to health, and so important to devotion, that, except in cases of necessity, it cannot be dispensed with by any prudent and diligent man.

Thanks to the goodness of God, and the fostering hands of our kind parents, this habit is so formed in some of us, that we should think it a cruel punishment to be confined to our beds after the usual early hour. Let us prize and preserve this profitable practice; and let us habituate all our children and servants to consider lying in bed after day-light as one of the ills of the aged and the sick, and not as an enjoyment to people in a state of perfect health.

If any of us have been so unfortunate as to have acquired the idle habit of lying late in bed, let us get rid of it. Nothing is easier. A habit is nothing but a repetition of single acts; and bad habits are to be broke as they were formed, that is, by degrees. An incomparable judge says, " Habit, like a complex mathemati-

cal scheme, flowed originally from a point, which in-
sensibly became a line, which unfortunately became a
curve; which finally became a difficulty not easily to be
unravelled." This difficulty, however, may be unravelled by application and prudence. Let a person accustomed to sleep till eight in the morning, rise the first
week in April at a quarter before eight, the second
week at half after seven, the third at a quarter after
seven, and the fourth at seven : let him continue this
method till the end of July, substracting one quarter of
an hour each week from sleep, and he will accomplish
the work, that at first sight appears so difficult. It is
not a stride, it is a succession of short steps, that conveys us from the foot to the top of a mountain. Early
rising is a great gain of time ; and should the learner
just now supposed, rise all the harvest month at four
instead of eight, he would make that month equal to
five weeks of his former indolent life.

Country business cannot be despatched without early
rising. In spring, summer, and autumn, the cool of the
morning is the time both for the pleasure and the rid-
dance of work ; and in the winter the stores of the year
are to be prepared for sale, and carried to market. The
crop of next year, too, is to be set, or prepared for.
Every business worth doing at all is worth doing well,
and as most businesses consist of a multiplicity of affairs,
it is impossible to disentangle each from another, to put
all in a regular train, and to arrange the whole so that
nothing may be neglected, without coolness and clearness of thinking, as well as indefatigable application.
The morning is necessary to all this, and the time and
the manner of setting out generally determine the success or the listlessness of the day. Beside, all businesses are subject to accidents, and to set forward early is
to provide for the repair, if not for the prevention of
them. The husbandman, of all men, is the most to be
blamed, if he wastes the precious moments of morning ;
for fallow-time, seed-time, weeding, water-furrowing,
hay-time, and harvest, must be caught at a moment, or
they will be lost for a year. It is a fine saying of Job,
"If my land cry against me, or the furrows thereof

complain, let thistles grow instead of wheat, and cockle instead of barley."

Early rising is beneficial to health. I am aware, that " to ask what is wholesome is like asking whether the wind be fair, without specifying to what port we are bound ;" for some animals live on poisons : however, it may safely be affirmed, that, in general, lying long and late in bed impairs the health, generates diseases, and in the end destroys the lives of multitudes. It is an intemperance of the most pernicious kind, having nothing to recommend it, nothing to set against its ten thousand mischievous consequences, for to be asleep is to be dead for the time. This tyrannical habit attacks life in its essential powers; it makes the blood forget its way, and creep lazily along the veins; it relaxes the fibres, unstrings the nerves, evaporates the animal spirits, saddens the soul, dulls the fancy, subdues and stupifies a man to such a degree, that he, the lord of the creation, hath no appetite for any thing in it, loathes labour, yawns for want of thought, trembles at the sight of a spider, and in the absence of that, at the creatures of his own gloomy imagination. In every view, therefore, it was wise in the Psalmist to say, " My voice shall be heard in the morning."

Our chief concern at present is with devotion, for which, we contend the morning is the proper time. The indolent man pretends, he lies in bed because he hath nothing to do : and yet he lives in the neglect of morning prayer. Let him arise, and do this, and he will find abundance of materials at hand to compose this good work ; the earlier he rises the more abundant his stores will be. To give a sort of order to this exercise, let us remark, that there are four funds of early devotion : reflection, observation, faith, and foresight. I will explain myself.

To reflect is to look back, and a *reflection* on six hours sleep affords abundant matter for devotion. The solemn stillness of the morning, just before break of day, is fit and friendly to the cool and undisturbed recollection of a man just risen from his bed fully refreshed, and in perfect health. Let him compare his condition

with that of half the world, and let him feel an indispo-
sition to admire and adore his Protector, if he can. How
many great events have come to pass in these six hours,
while I have been dead? I feel my insignificance.
The heavenly bodies have moved on, the great wheels
of nature have none of them stood still, vegetation is
advanced, the season is come forward, fleets have continued sailing, councils have been held, and, on the opposite side of the world, in broad noonday, business and
pleasure, amusements, battles, and revolutions have taken place without my concurrence, consent, or knowledge. Great God! what am I in the world? An in-
sect! A nothing! "In the morning, O Lord," thou
GREAT being, "unto thee will I look up."

How many of my fellow-creatures have spent the
last six hours in praying in vain for ten minutes sleep!
How many in racking pain, crying, "Would God it
were morning!" How many in prison! How many
in the commission of great crimes! How many have
been burnt out of house and home! How many have
been shipwrecked at sea, or lost in untrodden ways on
the land! How many have been robbed and murdered! How many have died unprepared, and are now
lifting up their eyes in torment! And here stand I, a
monument of mercy, "the living, the living to praise
God." "In the morning, O Lord," thou PATIENT and merciful being, "unto thee will I look up." I will bemoan
the vices, and sympathize with the distresses of my fellow-creatures. I will try this day to show my gratitude
to my Preserver by taking care not to offend him.

I admire the WISDOM of God in the formation of man.
By what means have I disburdened myself of that load
of weariness, with which I lay down oppressed! Whence
have I derived the vigour and the spirits, which I now
feel? A part of the night my rest was perfect, I felt
nothing. The other part, as I approached to waking,
my fancy treated me with many pleasing scenes. I
recollect them with I know not what satisfaction still . . .
In some such manner as this, will the early Christian
use his recollection in the morning, and will adore the
perfections of God. "In the morning, O Lord, will I
look up."

Let him avail himself next of *observation.* Let us look about us, and take notice, at least, of some of the beauties of nature in the morning, for " the heavens declare the glory of God, the firmament sheweth his handy work, and day uttereth speech." How incomparably fine is the dawning of the day, when the soft and stealthy light comes at first glimmering with the stars, and gradually eclipses them all! How beautifully fitted to excite our attention is the folding and the parting of the grey clouds, drawn back " like a curtain" to give us a sight of the most magnificent of all appearances, the rising of the sun! How rich the dew, decking every spire of grass with coloured spangles of endless variety, and inexpressible beauty! Larks mount and fill the air with a cheap and perfect music, and every bush and every tree, every steeple and every hovel emits a cooing or a twittering, a warbling or a chirping, a hailing of the return of day. Amidst so many voices, shall man be dumb? Surely, a good man must say, " My voice also shalt thou hear in the morning, O Lord."

It is in the morning, remarkably, that " the ox knoweth his owner," and " the ass his master's crib." Then, if ever, man feels himself the monarch, and to'him who rises first, all domestic animals pay their homage. One winds and purs about him, another frisks and capers, and doth all but speak. The stern mastiff and the plodding ox, the noble horse and the harmless sheep, the prating poultry and the dronish ass, all in their own way express their joy at the sight of their master; he is a god to them, for " the eyes of all wait on him, and he giveth them their meat in their season." It is to these animals, that the Prophet sends us for instruction, and from their behaviour to us he would have us learn our duty to God. Let us observe how much these creatures contribute to our ease and comfort through life; let us remark that we owe them all they look to us for; let us acknowledge the debt, and our inability to discharge it without the supplies of Providence; let un address our prayers and praises to that good Master ly heaven, whose stewards we have the honour to be; lτη

us lay up for this great family, who have "neither
storehouse nor barn;" let us supply them with a liberal
hand; and for wisdom and prudence to perform all these
duties, let us resolve with the Psalmist, "My voice
shalt thou hear in the morning, O Lord. In the morning will I direct my prayer unto thee, and will look up."

When man walks abroad in a morning, every sense
is feasted, and the finest emotions of an honest and benevolent heart are excited. It is next to impossible to
be sour or dull. Above, the spacious canopy, "the tabernacle," or tent "for the sun," in a thousand clouds of
variegated forms, glowing with colours in every conceivable mixture, skirted and shaded with sulky mists,
affords a boundless track of pleasure to the eye.
Around, the fragrant air, perfumed by a variety of flowers, refreshes his smell. He snuffs the odour, and tastes,
as it were, in delicate mixtures the sours and the
sweets. The village pours forth its healthful sons,
each with his cattle parting off to his work, with innocence in his employment, a ruddy health in his countenance, and spirits and cheerfulness in his address, that
make him an object of envy to a king. Here the sly
shepherd's boy surveys and plots for his flock, and there
the old herdman tales and talks to his cattle, and loves,
patting their flanks, to chant over the history of every
heifer under his care. And have I only nothing to do
in this busy scene : have I nothing to say among so many voices? Am I a man, and have I no pleasure in seeing the peace and plenty, the health and happiness of
my fellow-creatures! Have I no good wishes for them?
"O Lord, in the morning will I direct my prayer unto
thee, and will look up."

Should we make our observations on a different season of the year, on the morning after a tempestuous
night, in which the howling winds had torn up our tim-
bers by the roots, overset our tottering chimnies, and
carried half the thatch of our cottages away; or in
which our sheep lay buried in drifts of snow, and the
other cattle were deprived of 'all their green winter
meat: or in which our rivers had swelled into floods,
blown up the banks, laid all our meadows under water,

covered the very ridges of our corn, threatened the
lives of all our flocks, and " destroyed the hope of
man ;" in all these, and in all other such cases, the perfections of God are displayed, the emotions of men and
Christians excited, and the language of the text enforced, " My voice shalt thou hear in the morning, O Lord.
In the morning will I direct my prayer unto thee, and
will look up."

· · Having in some such way as this made our observations, let us proceed to extract devotion in the morning from the storehouse of *faith*. For this purpose let
us divide Scripture into the two general parts of history of the past, and prophecy of the future ; the first is
credible, we believe it hath been, the last is credible,
and we believe it will be. We suppose a good man's
memory to be well furnished with Scripture, and for
this purpose we have often advised young people to get
by heart every night, the last thing they do before they
go to rest, one verse, to think of it till they drop asleep,
and in the morning when they wake that verse will
probably be the first thought. This will always afford
a subject for a morning meditation, and the practice
continued for seven years will fill and enrich the mind
with the word of God. A great advantage through life,
and doubled when, along with old age, dimness of sight
or blindness comes, so that, however desirous, we cannot
then read the Holy Book.

In the historical parts of Scripture we may observe
in general that industry and early rising are inculcated
as a doctrine ; as, " Thou shalt diligently keep the
commandments . . . Give diligence to make your call-
-ing and election sure." They are exemplified as a
practice, as, " Awake, I myself will awake early . . .
Abraham gat up early in the morning . . . Jacob rose
up early in the morning . . . Moses rose early in the
morning . . . Joshua rose early . . . Samuel rose early . . .
Job rose early in the morning . . . King Darius rose very
early in the morning . . . Jesus came early in the morning into the temple, and all the people came early in
the morning to hear him." All these were probably
early risers by habit, and it is certain most of them

were. Moreover, the practice is encouraged by express promise, as, "I love them that love me, and those
that seek me early shall find me."

Beside this general view of Scripture history, there
is a particular and not unedifying view of some remarkable mornings, of which I will just give you a sketch to
direct your meditations. That was a morning long to
be remembered, in which the angel hastened Lot, and
led him and his family out of Sodom. The sun rose before he entered Zoar, and when "Abraham gat up early, and looked towards Sodom, he beheld, and, lo, the
smoke of the country went up as the smoke of a fur-
nace." It was an happy morning in the life of Isaac,
when peace and plenty were secured to him and his
family by a contract, confirmed by oath, between himself and a neighbouring king, to perform which "they
rose betimes in the morning." It was a morning sacred
to memory with Jacob and his posterity, when after his
dream of a frame with steps, opening a passage from
earth to the temple of the King of kings, graced with
heavenly officers going up and coming down, to teach
him the doctrine of Providence, he "rose up early, set
up a pillar," and dedicated both the place and himself
to God. Nor could time ever raze out of his memory
that other morning, when "a man wrestled with him
until the breaking of the day. Let me go," said one,
"for the day breaketh; I will not let thee go," replied
the other, "except thou bless me." What memorable
mornings were those, in which Moses "rose up early,"
stood before Pharaoh, and in the name of Almighty God
demanded liberty for his nation! What a night was
that, in which the Israelites passed through the sea, and
what a morning succeeded, when Moses stretched out
his hand, and the tide rolled back with the dawning of
the day, and floated the carcasses of the Egyptians to
the feet of the people of God on the shore! Early
every morning for forty years the cloud was taken up,
and the manna fell. What a busy morning was that, in
which Gideon suppressed idolatry at the hazard of his
life! What an honourable morning was that to Daniel,
when a great king visited him in the lion's den! And,

to mention no more, that was "a morning" sacred to memory throughout all generations, in which Jesus "the king of Israel was cut off." A belief of these true histories furnishes matter for early meditation, prayer, and praise.

There are two future mornings foretold in the Holy Scripture, both figurative, but each descriptive of a real event. Ignorance is called darkness, and it was foretold that after the death of the Apostles the Christian world would be beclouded and benighted with error: but it was foretold by the same men, that truth should contend against error, and at last obtain the victory. This notion, which is generally received among Protestants, is the ground of many popular phrases, as the " darkness" of popery . . . the "light" of Revelation... the " dawn" of the Reformation appeared in the time of Wickliffe . . . learning threw "light" on the Scriptures . . . the reformation was a "morning with clouds"... light hath gradually increased ever since . . . future times will be "broad noon-day." We have not time now to justify these popular notions by Scripture prophecies; let it suffice in general to say, they are very reasonable, strictly scriptural, full of motives to virtue, and abounding with consolation to all good men. Let "cities be filthy and polluted," let princes be roaring lions, judges evening wolves, prophets light and treacherous persons, priests violators of law:" no matter, we do not despair; "the just Lord is in the midst thereof, he will not do iniquity, every morning doth he bring his judgment to light, he faileth not," though "the unjust know no shame."

The other morning is that of the resurrection of the dead, the beginning of the day of judgment. Then "the dead shall hear the voice of the Son of man, and all that are in the graves shall come forth: they that have done good unto the resurrection of life; and they that have done evil unto the resurrection of damnation." This event will bring us to understand thoroughly the perfections of God, the wisdom and goodness of Providence, the true character of Christ, the dignity of man, the horror of sin, the excellence of virtue, the joy of

heaven, and the misery of unquenchable fire.   On these
accounts the judging of the world is called a "day, a
day of wrath, and a day of revelation."   Is it possible
to believe these events, and not feel emotions of piety?
Have we no fear of the Judge, no prayer to address to
him?   What time so natural, as that, in which we rise
from bed as from a grave, from sleep, that image of
death!   "In the morning, O Lord, will I direct my
prayer unto thee."

I hasten to a close by remarking another source of
devotion, which I called *foresight.*   An ill-chosen term,
say you, for we know not what a day shall bring forth.
True.   Let your ignorance of the events of the day,
then, engage you every morning to commit yourself,
and all your affairs by acts of humble adoration to God.
Profess your confidence in his good Providence.   Confess and bemoan your imperfection and sin.   Pray him
to give you grace to help in time of need.   Fill your
heart brim full of just sentiments, and so prepare for
whatever may come to pass in the day.

Amidst all our ignorance of the next hour, there are
some things which we foresee conditionally, and others
absolutely.   It is absolutely certain, that some day we
must die.   Perhaps this may be the day.   Let us then
this morning behave as if this were the day.   It is absolutely certain that some day we must be judged.   Perhaps this may be the day.   Let us examine this morning, then, whether our accounts be ready to put into the
hand of the Lord, whose stewards only we are?   On
condition we live through the day, we shall live, as we
have done, supported by God for ends of his glory.
Shall we not say in the morning, "Our Father, who art
in heaven.   Hallowed be thy name.   Thy kingdom
come.   Thy will be done on earth as it is in heaven?"
If we live, we shall live as we have lived, preserved
alive by eating, drinking, clothing, and so on.   Shall
we not, then, say to the Preserver of men, "Give us
this day our daily bread?"   If we live we shall offend
God, and others will offend us.   Let us pray in the
morning, then, "Forgive us our trespasses, as we forgive them that trespass against us."   If we live, we

shall live depraved creatures in a depraved world, full
of temptations to induce us to do wrong. Let us foresee
this, and say to our Heavenly Father, "Lead us not into temptation, but deliver us from evil." Let us rejoice, that there is such a being as God; and let us say
to him, "Thine is the kingdom" of nature, providence,
grace, and glory: "thine is the power" of upholding
and regulating each: and to thee be "the glory" and
the honour of the whole "forever and ever, Amen."

In this manner let us begin each day, ever remembering that the morning gives the day its turn either to
devotion or sin. Now let us depart, in peace with
God, with our own consciences, and with all mankind.
Let us go in the name of the Lord, one to his farm, another to his merchandise, and all to some labour useful
to society. "Grace be with you all." Amen.

EXERCISE II.

CAUTION.

[AT GREAT EVERSDEN.]

JOB xxiv, 5.

*Behold, as wild asses in the desert go they forth to their
work, rising betimes for a prey: the wilderness yieldeth
food for them and for their children.*

IT is not enough that we rise early, and pray in a
morning: we rise to live one more day, and we ought
to get up with all our senses about us, that we may con-
trive how to live like men and Christians in a world
not every where favourable to liberty, property, and
morality.

The book of Job was written to free us from the folly of imagining that the present life is a state of rewards
and punishments, and to inform us that it is a state of
trial and exercise, to prepare us for a future life. The

32*

precise intention of Job, in this chapter, is to convince us that the wicked often prosper, and the righteous suffer here : but that there is nothing in all this inconsistent with the perfections of God : on the contrary he bringeth good out of evil, and works virtue in the righteous by the vices of the wicked. Do the wicked " remove the landmark ?" The act will provoke the equity of a good man to replace it. Do they rob the widow of her ox, and the fatherless of his ass ? The oppression of these poor sufferers will excite feelings of sympathy, and flowings of generosity. " Why" says Job, " seeing times are not hidden from the Almighty, do they that know him not see his days ?"

Agreeably to this general sense of the chapter, I am going to remark to you the vices and dangers that surround you, and to exhort you to exercise that caution, which such a situation requires. May the God of the morning bless our meditation to virtuous and holy purposes !

To begin with the chapter. Let us take care of our *understandings.* We live surrounded with ignorant people, but saith Job, " Why do they not see the days of the Almighty ?" Why do they not perceive there is a God, who governs the world, who is a guardian of virtue, and a punisher of sin ? It is because they make no religious use of their senses, and therefore as they make no observations they have no understandings. There was an ignorant nurse in a certain family, to whom the care of an infant was committed : she, under some idle pretence of convenience to herself, made a practice every morning, when she dressed the child, of pinning down its little arms to its sides with a ribband. The consequence was, when the child could feel its feet, it had very little use of its arms. Had not this been discovered, and discontinued, two enfeebled arms would have fallen to the lot of the unhappy victim. Any limb, any sense may be lost for want of use. It is exactly thus with the mind, and an understanding not used is so near to none, that there is very little difference in knowledge between some huge-sized men, and infants and idiots.

There are two sorts of people who ought to attend to this case. The first are benumbed with popular errors, one of which is, that common people should not pretend to think, and debate, and determine on religion, but leave that to their guides. Take care of this error, and trust nobody : your guides may be right, but you must be wrong. At least, exercise your understandings to distinguish a wise from a foolish guide, a fallible from an infallible leader. The other sort continue in ignorance through false notions of religion. They think, personal religion is to come down like a shower of rain, and, not distinguishing themselves from plants and trees, are weak enough to imagine they shall grow good as a parched heath grows green. Will our gardens and fields produce a crop without cultivation? Will our lives and healths be preserved without food and exercise? Can we understand any thing without thinking about it? Can we please God without diligence, or enjoy him without virtue? Let us take care, then, to exercise our own understandings on the works of nature, which are along with us all the day; on the ways of Providence, which are constantly offering themselves to our view; and on the Holy Scriptures, which lie open before us, and call us to run the race of a holy life, and obtain the prize of immortal happiness.

Let us take care of our *property.* The context tells us, " Some remove the landmark ; they violently take away flocks, and feed thereof." They first drive away the cattle, next remove the landmark, and lastly claim and possess themselves of the herbage and the soil. Let us be cautious how we act, and to this purpose let us guard against three usual sources of injustice in ourselves, and the three sorts of people who would practise it upon us.

One cause of injustice is *idleness.* An idle man, like all other men, is subject to hunger, and thirst, and cold, and sickness ; and these necessities must be relieved : but as he does nothing toward his own relief, he is tempted to supply his wants with the earnings of the industrious ; and as thieving is less laborious than working, he yields to the temptation. Flee from idleness

and avoid the company of idle men, for their talk is pernicious; their maxims, like their actions, all go on the
great principle of saving trouble. When I see a poor
idle man, I always suspect he is a thief.

Wastefulness is another source of injustice. To consume, any thing unnecessarily argues an absence of mind
ungraceful in any man; but in a poor man waste is an
abomination, for which we have no name. When prudent rich people observe this in the poor, it shuts up
their generous hands, for it is not an alms, it is not day-
labour, it is not trade, it is not the fortune of a peer
that can fill this gulf, which ever yawns, and says, Give,
and never says, It is enough. A man, whom waste hath
brought to want, is strongly pressed by his necessities
to be unjust. The wise man informs us, " The slothful
in his work is brother to him that is a great waster."
Let such brethren keep company with each other; but
let good men avoid them both.

A third source of injustice is *an ignorant confidence in
wealth.* He, that " saith, to fine gold, Thou art my confidence," at once betrays the ignorance of an uninform-
ed mind, and the depravity of a wicked heart. His depravity lies in his placing such confidence in a creature,
as ought to be placed only in God. His gross ignorance
appears in his choice of gold; for what can gold purchase for him? Can he exchange it for innocence?
Will it buy repentance? Can it purchase immortality?
Alas! It cannot bribe old age, or sickness, remove a
single pain, or check one unhallowed passion. On the
contrary, unjust gain is both a crime that cries for vengeance, and a load that sinks a sordid cripple down to
care, to vice, to death, to hell. A youth, who would
acquire property, (and why should you not all acquire
it?) should be honest and industrious, frugal and religious. If he would marry, he should choose a partner
of the same virtuous kind. Hath he a family? He
should train them up in just notions of property. Hath
he companions? He should choose such as would not
endanger his morals, and his happiness, by their vices.
Hath he business in the world? Let him watch the
world, and let him beware of the idle, the wasteful, the

immoderate lovers of money, for somebody must bear their expenses, and sorrow will be to him on whom the unwelcome burden falls. The unwary is most likely to be the man.

Let us take care of our *lives*. Job saith, " They drive away the ass of the fatherless, and take the widow's ox for a pledge." Widows and orphans, whatever advantages they may have, are objects of pity ; for what can women and children do in the business of life ; especially, what can they do with oxen and asses, the tending of cattle, and the tillage of the field? In summer excessive heat, in winter extreme cold, in journeying difficult and dangerous roads, in the field hard labor, in fairs and markets tumult and fraud: how can women and children encounter all these? How can a man, who hath the least degree of esteem for his wife and family, bear the thought of laying violent hands on himself, and so of reducing these poor innocents to this forlorn state? If, in any gloomy day, pressed with difficulties, and afraid of consequences, we be tempted to destroy ourselves, let us repel the temptation by recalling to our minds the fatal consequences of the rash action to our widows and children. Let us picture to ourselves the unutterable agony of the family we love at the sight of such a horrid corpse. If, in any of our straits, we be tempted to steal, and to kill, let the supposed widow and children of a man hung in chains deter us. If, on any festival, we be tempted to excessive drinking, let us flee, lest one act of drunkenness should bring on another, and that a third, and so a habit of excessive drinking should shorten our lives, and expose an honest woman, and her innocent children to ills, which prudence might have prevented. Let us habituate ourselves to civility, and avoid a disposition to boast and quarrel, lest in some unguarded moment a word should produce a blow, lest that blow should be fatal, and leave a widow and a fatherless family to mourn over a deed that can never be undone. The last step of a worthless idle man in a parish is to go for a soldier, that is, to sell his own life for nought, and to leave a widow and fatherless children to lament their relation to such an un-

natural man. We ought to know the nature and the
worth of liberty; we ought to learn the use of arms;
we ought to be able and willing to protect our country
on principles of wisdom and virtue : but we ought not
to rush into the army merely to get free from labor, or
to gratify the evil passions of our hearts. If husbands
and parents do so, their taste costs their family dear.
   We live in a world, where many such widows and
orphans are. Let us never reproach them with the folly and vice of their heads. Let us pity their condition.
Let us wipe away their tears by kind offices. Let us
hold their property sacred. Let us lift the children, into life, and smooth the path of the widow to the grave.
And that we may enjoy this luxury of living, the pleasure of doing good, let us avail ourselves of every wise
precaution to enable us to obtain an healthy firm old
age. Let us be temperate in our diet, cleanly in our
habitations, cool in our pursuits, moderate in our enjoyments, calm in our tempers : in a word, let us live as
well, that we may live as long as we can.
   Let us take care of our *time*. The text says, The
wicked "rise betimes for a prey." There are many
classes of wicked men, who perform all their works of
darkness in the night, and to whom " the morning is as
the shadow of death :" but there are other classes, who
practise their vices by the light of the day. Not that
there is any difference in the nature of these crimes :
the difference is only in the degree. Sin in a small degree conceals itself under specious pretences, and seems
tolerable ; but when it hath grown to ripeness, and
thrown off its covering, its appearance is so very horrible, that they who have been always familiar with it,
shudder at the sight. A little anger, a small degree of
hatred, a single taking of the name of God in vain : is
darkness necessary to any of these ? No : it is murder,
which is a great act of anger or hatred; it is blasphemy; it is any, and every sin broke loose from restraint, and in the exercise of its utmost vigour, that
shuns the light, and is practicable only in the dark : the
criminal himself durst not see himself commit the crime.
   What a number of people are there in the world,

who rise betimes to make a prey of their fellow-creatures; who industriously live upon the vices and follies
of mankind; who 'have formed their own vices into a
trade, and profess to support it by arguments extremely
plausible, because it would be unfashionable to find
fault with what all the world applaud. Let us, however
be allowed to leave these early rising "wild asses" to
their own pursuits, and let us know the worth of our
time too well to waste it in such pursuits as theirs. If
a thief, who makes a prey of our property; if a slanderer, who devours our reputation; if a libertine, or a
dupe who buys us to sell our liberties; if an enthusi-
ast, who deprives men of reason and Scripture to make
himself necessary; if all these would condescend to
teach us their sciences, I hope we should not vouchsafe
to find time to learn. Let us be cautious how we dispose of a treasure so precious on pursuits so vile. The
command is short, but very plain : " Six days shalt thou
labour : the seventh is the sabbath of the Lord thy
God." We should allow no time to sin with the world,
none to superstition with Pharisees and bigots : for in
the latter case we should fall a prey to the folly of others; and in the former we should, like wild beasts, learn
to catch prey ourselves. Recollect, also, that people of
no religion have one day in seven more than you have,
a day in which you " do no manner of work ;" but a
day in which they spend in going over their grounds,
in seeing their distant stock, in paying their men, in settling their accounts, sometimes in buying and selling
cattle, and making bargains, and always in talking over
their worldly affairs, and consequently in improving
their knowledge on these subjects. A religious man
gives up all these advantages for conscience sake; but,
if he be a prudent as well as a pious man, he will gain
more than he looses by temperance, frugality, industry,
early rising in the morning, and dexterity in business
all the day.

Let us take care of our *children*. The text says,
" The wilderness yieldeth food for them, and for their
children." They live an idle, wandering life, and they
train up their children to be vagrants like themselves.

Children are great blessings ; " Happy is the man that hath his quiver," that is, his house, " full of them." Under the direction of a prudent parent, they are " as arrows in the hand of a mighty man," and will fly here and there to execute his orders. These children have every thing to learn, and they will learn every thing of those who are the nearest to them. To them example is better than all the books in the world, and indeed it is the only book they study. Let us not cheat ourselves into a neglect of them by groaning about Old Adam, nor by chanting over what nobody denies, that God only can make a Christian, which is equal to saying, God only can make a cucumber. God made the first fruit immediately by his own power ; but he hath made fruit ever since by means, and the most industrious will always have the best garden. Let us use our children early to do with little sleep. To put them to bed very early, to give them sleeping doses, and such other customs, are generally the practices of idle or impatient nurses. Let us never under pretence of fondness give them strong liquors. The water-bucket is the best supply of a poor child. Let us not lacquer their appetites, and learn them to be dainty, or voracious. It is a great misfortune to the poor to have remarkably great appetites. Such habits poison and kill. Let us accustom them to cleanliness and industry, to civility in their manners, and to reverence for their God. Let us never think of the savage custom of beating them, nor ever spoil them by the contrary folly of cockering and fondling. Above all, let us teach them to think and reason about religion, and to interpret Scripture for themselves. Let us take care to inform them that religion is justice, and nothing else. What is the religion of a poor woman's little girl, but to spin a groat a day ; for it is just and right, that she should contribute what little she can toward the maintenance of the family ? And what is the religion of a poor under boy on a farm in a cold winter day, but to rise early, to milk the cows clean, to breakfast the sties, to tend the cattle constantly and kindly, and so on ; for it is just and right that he should do so for the benefit of his master, who supplies

all his wants. Justice makes a good shepherd, a good
herdman, a good tasker, a good man in every work and
business of life. We should inculcate this principle in
these little folks early in life by every thing we do, and
this will settle them in services, and preserve them
from idleness, which leads to vagrancy, as that does to
pilfering and public punishment.

Let us now turn this subject into prayer, and for five
minutes address God, in whose hand is life, and breath,
and all things, that he would vouchsafe to prosper the
works of our hands while we are well, to grant us relief when we are sick, and to crown all when we die
with a blessed immortality, saying to each of us, " Well
done, good and faithful servant, thou hast been faithful
in a few things, enter thou into the joy of thy Lord."

EXERCISE III.

FRUGALITY.

[AT HAUXTON.]

JOHN vi, 12.

Gather up the fragments, that nothing be lost.

THE end of all instruction is to enable people to instruct themselves. With this view allow me to inform
you how to edify yourselves by interpreting Scripture,
which you read, by the world in which you live, and
which you every day see. It would mean nothing here,
to say the Gospel is best proved true by analogy; I
might as well say nothing, for such hard words have
not yet found their way into this village. Let us try to
do without them. Mark what I am going to say.

All the comfort we derive from the Gospel is on supposition the Gospel is true : but we are not to suppose
the Gospel is true without examining whether it be so.
Now what are we to examine it by? Suppose I should

33

give you a letter, and require you to determine whose
hand-writing it was, what would you say? We cannot
tell, say you, by this single paper; we must compare it
with other papers. Suppose by comparing it with some
of your landlord's receipts, I should observe, that every
word, and every letter, and every mark and flourish
were alike in both, what would you say then? You
would allow, for you know your landlord's hand, that he
wrote the letter, and especially as all the contents agree
with his known character.

Now apply this. I bring you a history of the glad
tidings of an exemplary Saviour written by a Jew, named John, who says, God employed him to write it; and
who adds, that the Saviour was like God, and we must
be like him. Am I to believe him? Yes, certainly, if
I find that his book agrees with the works, and the
character of God, as I have remarked it in a world,
which I am sure he created: but not else.

Let us try. Jesus fed a multitude. This is like God,
who hath filled the world with mouths, and who daily
fills the mouths of all with meat, and we should feed our
families as he fed his. Jesus taught frugality, and bade
his servants, " Gather up the fragments, that nothing be
lost." Another character of God, who, amidst all the
profusions of his bounty, hath so constituted the world,
that there should be no waste, and there is none. A
Prophet says, The Creator " weighed" the dust, and
" measured" the water, when he made the world. He
calculated to a nicety, and so much fire, so much water,
so much air, and so on, went to make up such a world
as this. The first quantity is here still, and though man
can gather and scatter, move, mix and unmix, yet he
can destroy nothing, the putrefaction of one thing is a
preparation for the being, and the bloom, and the beauty of another. Thus a tree gathers nourishment from
its own fallen leaves, when they decay. Something
" gathers up all fragments," and " nothing is lost."

Observe what passes in your own yards. The tasker
in the barn takes down a floor of wheat sheaves, and
threshes. The head-corn he throws and dresses, and
puts up for market. The tail he screens, and fans, and

ries, or rids of its dust and rubbish, to grind for the use of the family. The chaff he carries to the horses, the straw he turns out for litter for the cattle, and manure for another crop. Mark how the small stock turn the straw over and over, beat out every grain that escaped the flail, and spread abroad all the rubbish, one class picking up the wheat, another the wild oats, a third the seeds of darnel and other weeds, and all " gathering up the fragments that nothing be lost." Hence we say, these animals live upon nothing, and there is no waste in a well-stocked farm yard. We mean, Almighty God hath created for the honour of his goodness, and for the comfort of our lives, a set of animals on purpose to put every particle to use, and to turn, as it were, the whole mass of dead matter into animal life. One of old said, " Go to the ant, thou sluggard ;" we say, Go to the fowls, thou unthrift; or rather, Go to the Creator of fowls and ants, and learn that the voice that made the world spoke the text, " Gather up the fragments, that nothing be lost."

We are, then, to consider *frugality* as an imitation of Christ, and of God. To be frugal is to resemble both. I shall not detain you long : but as frugality lies all along-side of covetousness, we must guard the path, lest we should step over the line : and as we are apt to loiter even in a right road, we must try to animate ourselves. ‑ We will therefore observe *what* frugality is, and *why* we should practise it.

Let us be frugal in our *dress*. Clothes are for the safety, or ornament of the body. Becoming ornaments may be allowed to youth : but ornaments become none except the handsome. To all others ornaments only attract people's eyes to behold infirmity and ugliness. Adorn your persons with natural flowers, they are cheap and perfect : or adorn yourselves with good, not gaudy needlework of your own. Neat work, on a ground of cleanliness, set off with the natural charms of innocence and virtue, are a character to a young woman, which all her neighbours can read. Most of us need only study the safety of our health in our dress. We should adapt this to our circumstances ; we should buy them,

and wear them, and repair them without waste, and
without a passion for fashion and finery. To be neat
and clean, and dressed in habits fit for our employments,
is the true decency of a plain countryman.

Let us be frugal in our *diet*. The end of taking food
is the preservation of health. If food doth any thing
more than keep us well, it does too much. In the long
hot days of harvest, we require much nourishment, because we expend much strength: but the plenty that
abounds then should not tempt us to intemperance.
Enough of a plain, cheap, wholesome diet to keep us in
perfect health, and equal to our work, is all that is re-
quisite : nor should we waste food or drink, for winter
follows on the heels of harvest. Let us be frugal in our
furniture, and not gratify a passion, excited in a market
town, of filling our houses with expensive and useless
lumber. There is a fitness between the house and its
furniture. Strong, useful things, plain, whole and
cheap, become the situation and the circumstances of
inhabitants of villages.

Let us be thrifty of our *money*. There is a certain
skill, which our forefathers used to call a knack, an art
of doing things, and it is remarkably seen in many poor
women's laying out the earnings of their husbands. Call
it what we will, it is one of the highest qualifications of
a poor man's wife, and nothing contributes more to the
ease of his living than this female accomplishment.
How she reckons I cannot tell: but she keeps out of
debt, lives in cleanliness and plenty, and can always
spare half a dozen turves to warm a cold sick neighbour's cordial. She says, My husband's harvest wages
clothe himself and the children, my gleaning pays the
shoemaker, the orchard pays my rent, the garden does
this, the flail procures that, the children's spinning
wheels yield so and so ; and, good heart! she crowns all
by saying, " Bless the Lord, O my soul, and forget not
all his benefits. He forgiveth all thine iniquities, and
healeth all thy diseases. He redeemeth thy life from
destruction, and crowneth thee with lovingkindness
and tender mercies. He satisfieth thy mouth with good
things, so that thy youth is renewed like the eagle's.

Bless the Lord in all places of his dominion. Bless the Lord, O my soul!"

Let us be frugal of our *time*, and not spare one hour in the year for idleness or vice. Let us husband our *strength*, and not waste it in violent, imprudent, and unnecessary exertions. Let us be economists with our *reason* and *passions*. Let us leave others to wrangle about trifles, and let us save all our strength for the manly subjects of a Briton and a Christian. Let us habituate ourselves to understand and to defend this great truth, the foundation of government and good order, " Righteousness exalteth a nation ; but sin is a reproach to any people." Let us know how to reason for religion, " the mighty acts of the Lord." Let us not waste our passions upon improper objects. Let us reserve fear for God, love for justice, despair for happiness in sin, and hope for a blessed immortality.

I do think, I may leave off. You all know, or may know of one another *why* you should be frugal. One can say, If you be not frugal, you will be naked, and cold, and poor, and hungry, and without a friend to pity you : another will say, If you be wasteful, you will excite the indignation of all your neighbours for your barbarous treatment of your wife and children. The overseers will justly reproach you, when you ask for relief, and the rest of the poor will think your supply pilfered from their scanty tables. Others will tell you, your wastefulness deprives you of all the joy of doing good, and all the honour of giving the parish an example of virtue. · We all say you are not like Jesus Christ, and you are a scandal to his name. But what will the Judge say at the last day ? . . . The clock strikes . . . Depart . . . Peace be with you . — The first quarter of an hour you can spare, bid one of your children read to you the sixteenth of Luke ; it begins thus, " And he said also unto his disciples, There was a certain rich man, which had a steward ; and the same was accused unto him, that he had wasted his goods" . . . Let us say the Lord's prayer, and depart.

33*

EXERCISE IV.

COVETOUSNESS.

[*AT HAUXTON.*]

JOSHUA vii, 21.

When I saw among the spoils a goodly Babylonish garment, and two hundred shekels of silver, and a wedge of gold of fifty shekels weight, then I coveted them, and took them ; and, behold, they are hid in the earth in the midst of my tent, and the silver under it.

LAST month we spoke of frugality ; now let us turn our attention to covetousness ; for, as we have often said, there is only a thin partition between the last step of virtue and the first of vice. Justice carried too far becomes cruelty ; and excessive frugality is parsimony, or covetousness.

The man in the text, in one view, it should seem at first sight, was an object of pity ; for gold and silver and fine clothes, to be had for carriage, formed a great temptation. Hence arises a question, Why doth Providence put in our way such agreeable objects, and yet forbid us to touch them ? Let us give glory to God by acknowledging, that by such means we are exercised, first as creatures to discover the natural grandeur of our own passions, the incompetence of the world to make us happy, and, if reason be not asleep, the all-sufficiency of God. Next, these exercises try us as servants, and by the emotions of depraved passions we become acquainted with the natural rebellion of an evil heart, that disputes dominion with God. By these we learn to " abhor ourselves, and repent in dust and ashes." By these we discover the wisdom of him, who taught us to pray, " Our Father, lead us not into temptation." By an habitual deadness to these, because God commands it, we discover the true religion of a renewed mind, and enter on the enjoyment of conscious rectitude, a preference of virtue, the felicity of heaven.

Why then do we blame Achan? Because he was not a boy, for none but men above twenty bore arms, and he was old enough to know that he ought not to have disobeyed his general, or his God. Because he was a Jew, and of the tribe of Judah, and had been brought up in the nurture and admonition of the Lord. Because he must have heard what mischief the golden calf, the iniquity of Peor, and the murmuring at Kadesh had brought upon his countrymen. Because he knew God had expressly forbidden plunder. Had he exercised his understanding, some or all these reasons would have cooled his passions for perquisites. In like manner we say of ourselves. We have temptations and passions; but we have reason, too, to resist them. We have passions; but we have had a Christian education, and have been apprized of the danger of gratifying them. We have passions; but we have eyes and ears, and live among people, who daily die for gratifying the same passions which we feel. We covet; but God says, " Thou shalt not covet any thing that is thy neighbour's."

To covet is to desire beyond due bounds. God hath set these due bounds. He hath bounded passion by reason, and reason by religion and the nature of things. If a man of twenty years of age, to whom Providence hath given both reason and passions, should lay aside his reason, and make use of only his passions, he would act as preposterously as if, having both legs and arms, he should resolve to walk with his legs but never to make the least use of his arms. May I say? Yes, let me say, reason is intended to poise the passions, and to prevent a fall. Perhaps all this is too general; let us in a short detail show the unreasonableness of covetousness.

Covetousness is *unjust*. Let the prince enjoy the privilege of his birth; let the man, who hath hazarded his life for wealth, possess it in peace; let the industrious enjoy the fruit of his labour; to transfer their property to myself without their consent, and without put-

'ting something as good in the place, would be an act of injustice.   Only to covet is to wish to be unjust.

Covetousness is *cruel.*   A man of this disposition is obliged to harden his heart against a thousand plaintive voices: voices of poor, fatherless, sick, aged, and bereaved people in distress; voices that set many an eye a trickling, but which make no impression on a covetous man.

Covetousness is *ungrateful.* - A covetous old man was once a child; has he no feelings of gratitude for his nurses; or, if they be dead, has he none for other poor women now employed in nursing such as he was, and whose tenderness and care will never be half paid for? He was once. in business; hath he no feelings of gratitude for the old servants, who assisted him to get his wealth; or, if they be dead, are none of their children or grand-children left in want?   Shall the whole world labour for this old miser, one to feed him, another to guard him, and all to make him happy, and shall he resemble the barren earth, that returns nothing to him that dresseth it?   This is a black ingratitude.

Covetousness is a *foolish* vice; it destroys a man's reputation, makes every body suspect him for a thief and watch him; it breaks his rest, fills him with care and anxiety, excites the avarice of a robber, and the indignation of a house-breaker; it endangers his life, and, depart how he will, he dies unblest and unpitied.

Covetousness is *unprecedented* in all our examples of virtue.   The Scripture shows us many sorts of good men, and honestly acknowledges their faults.   One spoke unadvisedly with his lips, another cursed and swore, a third was in a passion, and a fourth committed adultery: but which of the saints ever lived in a habit of covetousness!   It is Judas, who hanged himself, and not such as Peter, whom covetous men imitate.

Covetousness is *idolatry.*   It is the idolatry of the heart, where, as in a temple a miserable wretch excludes God, sets up gold instead of him, and places that confidence in it, which belongs to the great Supreme alone.   The fears and the hopes, the sorrows and the joys of a miser hover about his idol, as the spirits of the just wait round the throne of God. In effect, the blasphemy of such a criminal addresses that to gold, which good men say to God, "Whom have I in heaven but thee? and there is nothing upon earth that I desire besides thee."

After all this we affect to wonder, that God should choose to give us one example of the punishment of such a sinner. We are not shocked at Providence, when we see a miser starve himself to death: but should the Judge of the world prevent his killing himself, and choose to make him edify the world by his death, after he had scandalized it by his life, why should we be astonished? This man in the text was doomed to be burnt, but not alive; he was therefore first stoned to death, then consumed by fire along with his accomplices and his plunder, and the place was called, as the place of every miser deserves to be called, "The valley of trouble" to this day.

Achan, and all such as he, cause a great deal of trouble, and, to pass every thing else, let us only observe what covetous men do with their wealth. "Behold it is hid in the earth in the midst of my tent."

Observe a miser with his bag. With what an arch and jealous leer the wily fox creeps stealthily about and about to earth his prey! He hath not a friend in the world, and judging of others by himself, he thinks there is not an honest man upon earth, no, not one that can be trusted. Doth it not vex an ingenuous soul to see such an image of a beast in the shape of a man? Disgustful triumph: "Behold it is hid in the earth in the midst of my tent."

Remark his caution. He turns his back on his idol, trudges far away, looks lean, and hangs all about his own skeleton ensigns of poverty, never avoiding people in real distress, but always comforting himself with the hope, that nobody knows of his treasure, and that therefore nobody expects any assistance from him. How vexatious to any upright soul to see a wretch feeding on falsehood, and revolving in his memory by way of pleasure, "Behold, it is hid in the earth in the midst of my tent."

Take notice of the just contempt, in which mankind hold this hoary mass of meanness. He thinks his wealth is hid : but it is not hid; his own anxious side looks betray the secret. People reckon for him, talk over all his profits, omit his expenses and losses, declare his wealth to be double what it is, and judge of his duty according to their own notions of his fortune. One lays out this good work for him, another rates him at so much towards such a charity, and all execrate him for not doing what is not in his power. Prudent men cannot justify him, and even they are obliged to allow that half the popular contempt is just. How painful to a benevolent man to see a hoary head despised! How much is his pain increased by knowing that the scorn is just, for "Behold," be his wealth little or much, it is not used, "it is hid in the earth in the midst of his tent !"

Mark his hypocrisy. He weeps over the profligacy of the poor, and says, it is a sad thing, that they are brought up without being educated in the fear of God. He laments, every time the bell tolls, the miserable condition of widows and orphans. He celebrates the praise of learning, and wishes public speakers had all the powers of a learned criticism, and all the graces of elocution. He prays for the down-pouring of the Spirit, and the out-goings of God in his sanctuary, and then, how his soul would be refreshed! What a comfortable Christian would he be then ! Tell this son of the morning, that there are schoolmasters waiting to educate the poor, tutors longing to instruct youth, and young men burning with a vehement passion for learning and oratory; tell him that the gratitude of widows, the hymns of orphans, and the blessings of numbers ready to perish, are the presence of God in his church. Tell him all these wait to pour themselves like a tide into his congregation, and wait only for a little of his money to pay for cutting a canal. See, how thunder-struck he is ! His solemn face becomes lank and black, he suspects he has been too liberal already, his generosity has been often abused, why should he be taxed and others spared, the Lord will save his own elect, God is never at a loss

for means, no exertions will do without the Divine presence and blessing, and beside, his property is all locked
up, " Behold, it is hid in the earth in the midst of my
tent !"

, Let us respect truth even in the mouth of a miser.
This ignoble soul tells you, that he would not give a
wedge of gold to save you all from eternal ruin : but he
says, God is not like him, God loves you, and will save
you freely. This is strictly and literally true. There
have been thousands of poor people besides you, who
have been instructed and animated, converted and saved, without having paid one penny for the whole : but
this, instead of freezing, should melt the hearts of all
who are able, and set them a running into acts of generosity. I conclude with the words of an ancient teacher in Italy, one Ambrose, more remarkable for his wit
than for the accuracy of his judgment. " Joshua," said
he, " could stop the course of the sun : but all his power could not stop the course of avarice. - The sun stood
still, but avarice went on. Joshua obtained a victory
when the sun stood still : but when avarice was at work,
Joshua was defeated." Grace be with you all. Amen.

———◆———

EXERCISE V.

SELF-PRESERVATION.

[AT FULBORNE.]

———

JOB ii, 4.

*Skin for skin, yea all that a man hath will he give
for his life.*

BEFORE the invention of money, trade used to be carried on by barter, that is, by exchanging one commodity for another. The man, who had been hunting in the
woods for wild beasts, would carry their skins to market, and exchange them with the armourer for so many

bows and arrows.   As these·traffickers were liable to
be robbed, they sometimes agreed to give a party of
men a share for defending them, and skins were a very
ancient tribute.   With them they redeemed their own
shares of property, and their lives.   It is to one, or
both of these customs that the text alludes as a proverb.

Imagine one of these primitive fairs.   A multitude
of people, from all parts of different tribes and languages, in a broad field, all overspread with various
commodities to be exchanged.   Imagine this fair to be
held after a good hunting-season, and a bad harvest.
The skinners are numerous, and clothing cheap.   Wheat,
the *staff* of life, is scarce, and the whole fair dread a
famine.   How many skins this year will a man give for
this necessary article, without which he and his family
must inevitably die?   Why, each would add to the
heap, and put " skin upon skin," for " all the skins that
a man hath will he give for his life."   Imagine the
wheat-growers, of which Job was one, carrying home
the skins, which they had taken for wheat.   Imagine the
party engaged to protect them raising the tribute, and
threatening if it were not paid to put them to death.
What proportion of skins would these merchants give,
in this case of/necessity?   " Skin upon skin, all the
skins that they have will they give for their lives."
The proverb then means, that we should save our lives
at any price.   Let us apply it to ourselves.

Life may be destroyed by *violence.*   How many
wretched people have fled for refuge to a river, a rope,
or a razor? Thy are always objects of pity, for a man
must suffer a deal before he can work himself up to
this cruel attack upon himself.   We generally hope such
a person was insane.   This is a charitable error: but
really in some cases we are forced to hope against hope.
What would it have cost some of these unhappy creatures to have saved their lives.   Nothing but a little
courage to have told their trouble to a friend, and to
have taken advice.   Nothing but a little patience to
have borne the calamities of poverty, disappointment, or
fear.   In such sad moments let us exert ourselves.   All
that a man can do, he should do to preserve his precious life.

The intemperance of the senses destroys life. Meat and drink of improper kinds, or in improper quantities, are slow poisons, which effectually kill people of inordinate appetites. Intemperance heaps disease upon disease, and persecutes life through every pore, till life is a burden, and death the only relief. Study your feelings, they are your best physicians, and, remember, it is health that gives life its glee. To be well, what a luxury! To be in health, and alive in every fibre, what a cheap acquisition, when only moderation is the price!

Life is destroyed by *excessive passions*. The body is a nice machine, wisely adjusted for the purpose of even and constant use. When passion, like a mad-man in a mill, sets all the powers a going without their proper balance, the machine takes fire, and the fool himself is consumed. Anger fires, envy gnaws, discontent frets, pride strains, avarice dries up, every passion racks the body somewhere, and all together rend it into shivers, and toss it by in the grave. Whence comes this whirlwind of destruction? What are we angry about? Whom do we envy? What advantage are we proud of? What is it that we are hoarding up? What! Will I not agree to live in my cottage because the squire occupies the great house! Will I not taste my cabbage because my neighbour has a larger! What! Am I so proud of my three skeps of bees, that I must spend three times the worth of them at the alehouse to talk over the courage, and the prudence, and the amazing accomplishments of a bee-master! Wretched people that we are! Is it thus we squander life away?

Life is destroyed by *carelessness*. Aged people and children should not be left alone : they are not equal to the task of taking care of themselves. Pious old people pay for being waited on by their edifying conversation, and the little folks will reward us by and by, if we use them properly. Let us not neglect their lives. Let us, too, take care of our own. We have often observed labouring men, early in the morning at mowing time, strip to work, and throw their clothes on the grass full of dew. At breakfast time, heated with mowing, we

34

have seen them take up and put on their clothes, not
considering that rheumatic pains, and agues, and consumptions, and a thousand diseases enter that way. A
little cold is a little death, a little more chills us to clay,
and fits us for the grave. It is not only life in general
that should be the object of our care, the life of every
part is inestimable. What would some people give for
one eye, or one ear, or one of the healthful pains of
hunger? If we have these blessings, and if care will
preserve them, we shall be inexcusable not to exercise it.

False religion will destroy life. When a man takes it
in his head that the knowledge of some subtle points of
the schools, or that the practice of some austere morti-
fications, is necessary to salvation, he hath embraced
an error; and when love to his fellow-creatures makes
him undertake our conversion, his error is mixed with
religion. Religion and falsehood thus united drive a
man mad, and impel him to harbour base passions, to
spend himself in unnatural and unnecessary exertions,
and to plot and persecute all for the glory of God and
for the good of mankind. We have in history a multitude of martyrs. Perhaps some few have died martyrs
to their own folly. What is necessary to preserve life
from this specious attack? A little common sense and
good temper. Recollect, I am not censuring any good
man, be his errors what they may, except he holds
them in a spirit of bitterness and persecution. No man
shall ever persuade me that such a spirit is friendly to
health and life.

Whatever such a religion may be to its owners, it
holds the lives of others cheap; and it seems to me to be
a remnant of that murderous part of religion, persecution. God forbid, we should preserve ourselves by destroying others. Is it not possible for us all to live and
be happy? Give me leave to read you a bit of a
letter, which a great and good man in the north of Europe, more than two hundred years ago, wrote to that
pious Protestant persecutor, Theodore Beza, minister
at Geneva.

" You contend, that Scripture is a perfect rule of

faith and practice. But you are all divided about the
sense of Scripture, and you have not settled who shall
be judge. You say one thing. My teacher says another. You quote Scripture, he quotes Scripture. You
reason, he reasons. You require me to believe you.
I respect you : but why should I trust you rather than
my own minister? You say, he is a heretic : but the
catholics say you are both heretics. Shall I believe
them? They quote histories and fathers. So do you.
To whom do you all address yourselves? Where is the
judge? You say, the spirits of the prophets are subject
to the prophets : but you say, I am no prophet, and I
say you are not one. Who is to judge? You have
broken off your yoke, allow me to break mine. Having freed yourselves from the tyranny of popish pre-
lates, why do you turn ecclesiastical tyrants yourselves,
and treat others with barbarity and cruelty for only doing what you set them an example to do? You say,
your lay-hearers, the magistrates, and not you, ministers, are to be blamed, for it is they who banish and
burn for heresy, and not you. I know you make this
excuse : but, tell me, have not you instilled such principles into their ears, or have they done any thing more
than practise the doctrine you taught them? Have
you not told them how glorious it is to defend the faith?
Have you not been the constant admirers and flatterers
of such princes as have depopulated whole districts for
heresy? Do you not daily teach, that they who appeal from your confessions to Scripture ought to be
punished by the secular power? It is impossible for
you to deny this. You have published books to justify
the banishing of one old teacher, and the execution of
another, and you seem to wish we would follow your
example, and kill men for not believing as we do. God
forbid. When you talk of your Lutheran confession,
and your Calvinistical creed, and your unanimity, and
your fundamental truth, I keep thinking of the sixth
Commandment, ' Thou shalt not kill.' Farewell, most
learned and respected Beza. Take what I have said
in good part, and continue your friendship to me."
I see by your looks you relish this letter. It does

you honour. It was written by a great master in the
school of religion and good manners. I well tell you
more about him some leisure day. Mean time, I will
lend you this letter, and see, here is one of the petti-
est bound hymn-books that ever I saw ; I will put the
letter into it, and the little boy, who brings me the fair-
est written copy of it this day month, shall have this
hymn-book. He that says it by heart, stands upright,
looks pleasantly, and pronounces it with a soft, but full-
mouthed gracefulness to me, as the writer would have
done to Mr. Beza, he shall have another like it : and
he that best explains some of the hard words to me,
such as *heresy, minister, magistrate, secular power,
prelate, Lutheran creed,* and so on, he shall have a
third. Do not be afraid. Ask your father, or the
school-master, or somebody, and come and tell me when
I come again. We shall make it out among us, I dare
say, and understand it as well as the writer did. Come,
let us finish by singing two verses of this incomparable
hymn-book.

> Our life contains a thousand springs,
>   And dies if one be gone :
> Strange ! that a harp of thousand strings
>   Should keep in tune so long.
>
> But 'tis our God supports our frame,
>   The God that built us first.
> Salvation to the Almighty name,
>   That reared us from the dust.

EXERCISE VI.

[*AT WICKHAM BROOK.*]

———

HOSEA iii, 5.

Afterward shall the children of Israel fear the Lord and his goodness in the latter days.

ALWAYS when I see a Jew, I recollect a saying of the Lord by the Prophet Isaiah, "Thou art the seed of Abraham my friend," and I find a thousand thoughts in my mind, impelling me to my duty. I am going this morning just to give you a sketch of a subject, that would fill volumes, and a subject of which we ought not to be ignorant.

First, let us inform ourselves of the general *history* of this people. The father of the family was Abraham. He was born in the east, of an idolatrous family, and, at the command of God, he became the first dissenter in the world. He quitted his country, and went, and set up the worship of one God in his own family, and *taught* them to practise it. From this man proceeded a family, which increased into tribes, and formed a people as the stars in the heaven, or the sand on the seashore for multitude. Idolatry and immorality sometimes infect·· ed a few: but the bulk preserved the belief of one God, and the imitation of his perfections inviolably for ages. They were shepherds, and lived, inbosomed in forests and fastnesses, a plain, frugal, laborious life, unacquainted with the world, and unpractised in the arts and luxuries of polished nations. They assembled to worship God by prayers and sacrifice at every new moon, where the old-heads of families taught morality, and inculcated the hope excited by the promise of God, that in one of their family all the families of the earth should be blessed with the knowledge of their God, and their morality. Thus read the book of Genesis, and

34*

other Scripture histories of the same times, and without forming any romantic ideas of imitation impossible except in their circumstances, admire the history, approve the prophecy, and copy the inoffensive purity of their lives.

When these people were in slavery in Egypt, they were at a school in which Providence taught them, by their own feelings, the nature and the worth of liberty, both civil and religious. What noble efforts they made to obtain it, and how God crowned their honest endeavours with success under the direction of Moses, Joshua, and the Judges, you will read in the four books of Moses, Joshua, Judges, and Ruth. When they changed their government into an absolute monarchy, they enslaved themselves, and overwhelmed their country with idolatry, immorality, and calamities of every kind. Read the Prophecies with the light of history of times, persons, and places, which is contained in Samuel, Kings, Chronicles, Ezra, Nehemiah, and Esther, and you will easily discover what religion had to object against a tyrannical government, an idolatrous worship, and dissolute manners; and what it had to do in bearing affliction, reforming worship, and cherishing hope of better times under the direction of the expected prince of the house of David.

When he came, and addressed himself to the blessing of all nations with an universal religion, some of his countrymen put him to death; but others espoused his cause, wrote his history, and reasoned to establish it, not in the form of a secular kingdom, but in the convictions and consciences of reasonable men. There it hath stood ever since, and, though the bulk of the Jews have been scattered and punished for crucifying Christ, yet, by being kept a separate people, they serve to prove the truth of the Gospel; and the text, with many others like it, promises that " they shall reverence the Lord in the latter days." The Epistle to the Hebrews lies ready for their use at that day. I think nothing can be easier than to apply this historical knowledge to its proper use; and yet some Christians have got such an unwise and wayward knack of reasoning as to quote whatever was among the Jews in proof of what ought to be now : as if the economy that crucified Christ was to restore him his character and dignity !

Remark next the *customs* of this people. They serve, as their history does, to interpret Scripture. Our text is connected with one. A part of this prophecy is a drama. The young gentlemen in the right hand corner know what I mean, and I will try to make you all understand me. A drama, in our present view, is a subject both related and represented. Divines call it preaching by signs. These signs were proper to represent to the eye the subject spoken of to the ear. Thus Jeremiah explained slavery with a yoke upon his neck ; and Jesus simplicity, by setting a " little child" before his disciples. The Prophet Hosea was ordered to open to the Jews their prostitution to wickedness and misery, the patience and goodness of God, and the effect, which in time his goodness would have upon their descendants. Full of these subjects, the Prophet comes into a public assembly of the nation, and brings along with him a prostitute with three children, one of which, it should seem, she had conceived and borne by her own father. He gives his children names suited to his views, and utters the prophecy contained in the two first chapters. In the third chapter he is described as coming again, and bringing with him, not a prostitute in single life, but an adulteress, perhaps in liquor, or acting as if she were, to represent a people remarkable for " loving flaggons of wine." This woman had been hired to act this part for several days, at a price agreed on between herself and the prophet. Imagine a great national assembly at a public festival. Conceive the public attention caught by the entrance of the prophet, and his scandalous companions. Suppose him to ascend an eminence, and to place these miserable objects near him in full view of every body. Imagine him to harangue on the nature and necessity of virtue, especially to the people under contract, as a wife to her husband, or a nation to their God. Suppose him to reason on the iniquity of violated faith in every form. Suppose him to expatiate in tears, " smiting with the hand, and stamping with the foot," on the poverty, contempt, guilt, and misery of such injustice. Imagine him to unfold the conduct of God, and the effects, which such goodness ought to produce in man. Suppose the wretched prostitutes and their children, on the last day, to be brought to public contrition, asking pardon of God and man, received again into favour, clothed anew in bridal ornaments, and sent away with a thousand emotions of gratitude and religion in themselves, and a profusion of benefits and blessings from the people. Doth it not seem to you, that the prophet might be very eloquent on these subjects, bring many to faith and repentance, and convert a custom indifferent in itself into a very powerful mode of information?

Further, let us allow the *merit* of the Jews. They deserve all the reputation, which the inspired writers give them. They exhibit single characters of consummate virtue, as Abraham for faith, Moses for meekness, Nehemiah for love of his country, and so on. As a nation they excelled in some periods in arms, in others in industry, commerce, splendour, and wealth; and in all, in good writers; for what historians are equal to Moses and the Evangelists, or what ancient poetry breathes such pure and sublime sentiments as that of the Jews? As a church they preserved the oracles of God, and at their fall their remnants became the "riches of the world." The apostle of us Gentiles was a Jew, and to say all in one word, the Saviour and the judge of mankind was a Jew. Let us respect the ancient Jews in the persons of their children, and for their sakes let us be friends to universal toleration.

Let us recollect the *sins* and the *calamities* of these people. Their sins were many and enormous; but it was the *killing* of Jesus Christ, that completed their ruin. Let us examine what sins brought Jesus to the cross, and let us avoid the practice of them. Nor let us forget their calamities. They have been under all the punishments foretold four thousand years ago by Moses, and seem doomed to travel over the world to recommend a Gospel which they reject and despise. Their prophets, we find, did not slander them; they are the people described, and their punishments prove the divine mission of their prophets. Thus God is glorified, whether man be lost or saved. In some future time he will be glorified in us, either his mercy if we embrace it, or his justice if we reject it, for to reject the Gospel is to reject both the mercy and the justice of God.

Let us finish by observing the *recall* of the Jews. The prophets foretell it, and a course of events renders it probable. They are preserved a distinct people, though the nations that conquered them are lost. They are more numerous now than they were when a nation. The Gospel is truth and virtue struggling against error and vice: it is natural to hope that the stronger must in time subdue the weaker. Error and vice are supported by man: but truth and virtue by God. Let us not despair. The Jews came out of Egypt under the conduct of a shepherd with only a rod in his hand to point out the way. Providence is at no loss for means to effect its purposes; " he worketh all things after the counsel of his own will."

There are four things implied in the text, which the Jews will reverence in the latter days. First, That divine *patience*, which bore with their provocations : *after* they have rejected Moses and the prophets, after they have committed crimes of every sort, after they have crucified Christ, persecuted his apostles, and persevered for ages in approving the crime ; *afterwards* shall the children of Israel reverence the Lord for his patience, which out-lasted all their perverseness.

Next, they will reverence his *providence*, which, when they were persecuted in one country, always provided them an asylum in another. Providence hath given them skill, and made them useful to many nations. It hath prospered their industry, and crowned it with plenty, so that their riches are almost as proverbial as their infidelity. When Jews from all countries, in the latter days, shall compile their own history of their dispersion, it must needs display a bright scene of Providence, which they themselves will reverence in those days.

Will they not also reverence the *grace* of God? The Lord will both forgive their offences, and restore them to favour. To this we add, the *glory* of God, as another object of reverence. Great and marvellous displays of Divine power have been made in favour of this people formerly, and, it should seem by the Prophecies, more such displays will be made in favour of them at their "return to their first husband." May God hasten it in his time.

What remains? Only this at present. Let us avoid putting stumblingblocks in the way of the Jews. Let us propose Christianity to them as Jesus proposed it to them. Instead of the modern magic of scholastical divinity, let us lay before them their own Prophecies. Let us show them their accomplishment in Jesus. Let us applaud their hatred of idolatry. Let us show them the morality of Jesus in our lives and tempers. Let us never abridge their civil liberty, nor ever try to force their consciences. Let us remind them, that as Jews they are bound to make the law of Moses the rule of their actions. Let us try to inspire them with suspicion of rabbinical and received traditions, and a generous love of investigating religious truth for themselves. Let us avoid all rash judging, and leave their future state to God. Read at your leisure the sixty-third chapter of Isaiah, in the beginning of which Jesus Christ is described as the *Judge* of the world, and the passage is explained in that sense in the revelation of John. It is the Judge alone, whose habit is stained with blood; the saints, white and clean, only follow him to behold and applaud his justice. Grace and peace be with you! Amen.

THE END.

Lightning Source UK Ltd.
Milton Keynes UK
UKHW020518070119
334942UK00008B/1207/P

9 780266 176114